Economic Force[illegible]
Selected Works by Armen A. Alchian

Economists treat their heroes well. All our great men have had their works collected in volumes which are treasured and studied. It was therefore to be expected that the economics profession would want to see Armen Alchian's major papers gathered together and published as a book. Such a collection makes it much more convenient for those who wish to study his thought (as many do, and will), but even more important, it exhibits in a way no single article can the essential character of his approach.

In 1950, Alchian published his paper on "Uncertainty, Evolution and Economic Theory" (reprinted in this volume), a paper of striking originality, whose importance was immediately perceived and which gained him international recognition. It was clear that economics had a new master.

Armen Alchian has made important contributions to the economic analysis of inflation and unemployment, and to the theory of costs and of the firm. He has played the leading role in the development of a theory of property rights. His writing is distinguished by his ability to disentangle the essential from the trivial, and above all by his skill in showing how the same basic economic forces are at work in a wide variety of apparently completely different social settings.

Alfred Marshall considered that it was an essential task of an economist to demonstrate "the Many in the One, the One in the Many." No modern economist has been more successful in accomplishing this than Armen Alchian.

—From the Introduction

ARMEN A. ALCHIAN is Professor of Economics at the University of California, Los Angeles. He has contributed to numerous professional and scholarly journals, and is coauthor with William R. Allen of the textbook *University Economics*.

RONALD H. COASE, who writes the Introduction, is Clifton R. Musser Professor of Economics at the University of Chicago Law School, and coeditor of *The Journal of Law & Economics*.

Economic Forces at Work

Armen A. Alchian

With an Introduction by
Ronald H. Coase

LibertyPress
Indianapolis

Armen A. Alchian, "Uncertainty, Evolution and Economic Theory," is reprinted from *The Journal of Political Economy* 58, no. 3 (June 1950): 211–21, by permission of The University of Chicago Press.

Armen A. Alchian, "Information Costs, Pricing and Resource Unemployment," is reprinted with permission from *Economic Inquiry, Journal of the Western Economic Association* 7, no. 2 (June 1969): 109–28.

Armen A. Alchian and Harold Demsetz, "Production, Information Costs and Economic Organization," is reprinted with permission from *The American Economic Review* 62, no. 5 (December 1972): 777–95.

Reprinted by permission. Armen A. Alchian, "Why Money?" *Journal of Money, Credit, and Banking* 9, no. 1 (Part 2, February 1977): 133–40. Copyright © 1977 by the Ohio State University Press.

Armen A. Alchian, "Some Economics of Property Rights," is reprinted with permission from *Il Politico* 30, no. 4 (1965): 816–29.

Armen A. Alchian and Reuben A. Kessel, "Competition, Monopoly and the Pursuit of Money," is reprinted from *Aspects of Labor Economics* (Princeton, N.J.: Princeton University Press, 1962), pp. 157–75. Copyright © 1962 by the National Bureau of Economic Research, and reprinted with its permission.

Armen A. Alchian, "Private Property and the Relative Cost of Tenure," is reprinted with permission from *The Public Stake in Union Power*, ed. by Philip D. Bradley (Charlottesville, Va.: The University Press of Virginia, 1958), pp. 350–71.

Armen A. Alchian, "The Economic and Social Impact of Free Tuition," is reprinted with permission from *New Individualist Review* 5, no. 1 (Winter 1968): 42–52.

Armen A. Alchian, "Corporate Management and Property Rights," is reprinted with permission from *Economic Policy and the Regulation of Corporate Securities*, ed. by Henry Manne (Washington: American Enterprise Institute, 1969). Copyright © 1969 American Enterprise Institute for Public Policy Research.

Armen Alchian, "Costs and Outputs," is reprinted from *The Allocation of Economic Resources*, by Moses Abramovitz and others, with the permission of the publishers, Stanford University Press. Copyright © 1959 by the Board of Trustees of the Leland Stanford Junior University.

Armen A. Alchian, "Cost," is reprinted with permission from the *International Encyclopedia of the Social Sciences* 3 (1968): 404–15. Copyright © 1968 by Crowell Collier and Macmillan, Inc.

Armen Alchian, "Reliability of Progress Curves in Airframe Production," is reprinted with permission from *Econometrica* 31, no. 4 (October 1963): 679–93.

Reuben A. Kessel and Armen A. Alchian, "Effects of Inflation," is reprinted from *The Journal of Political Economy* 70, no. 6 (December 1962): 521–37, by permission of The University of Chicago Press. Copyright © 1962 by The University of Chicago.

Armen A. Alchian and Reuben A. Kessel, "Redistribution of Wealth Through Inflation," is reprinted with permission from *Science* 130, no. 3375 (September 4, 1959): 535–39.

R. A. Kessel and A. A. Alchian, "The Meaning and Validity of the Inflation-Induced Lag of Wages Behind Prices," is reprinted with permission from *The American Economic Review* 50, no. 1 (March 1960): 43–66.

Reuben A. Kessel and Armen A. Alchian, "Real Wages in the North During the Civil War: Mitchell's Data Reinterpreted," is reprinted with permission from *The Journal of Law & Economics* 2 (October 1959): 95–113.

Reprinted by permission. Armen A. Alchian and Benjamin Klein, "On a Correct Measure of Inflation," *Journal of Money, Credit, and Banking* 5, no. 1 (Part 1, February 1973): 173–81. Copyright © 1973 by the Ohio State University Press.

Library of Congress Cataloging in Publication Data

Alchian, Armen Albert, 1914–
Economic forces at work.

Includes index.
1. Economics. 2. Property. 3. Cost. 4. Inflation (Finance) I. Title.
HB171.A43 330 77-1327
ISBN 0-913966-35-5

Contents

Introduction
by Ronald H. Coase

Economists treat their heroes well. All our great men have had their works collected in volumes which are treasured and studied. It was therefore to be expected that the economics profession would want to see Armen Alchian's major papers gathered together and published as a book. Such a collection makes it much more convenient for those who wish to study his thought (as many do, and will), but even more important, it exhibits in a way no single article can the essential character of his approach.

Keynes tells us that Edgeworth, after the publication of his *Collected Economic Papers*, was genuinely surprised, and pleased, to learn the extent of his international reputation. Armen Alchian will, I am sure, experience a similar surprise, and also pleasure. It was remarked by Sir James Mackintosh that he had known Adam Smith, Ricardo and Malthus, and that it said something for economics that "its three greatest masters were about the three best men I ever knew." It would be difficult to add some modern economists to this list without changing the wording. But this would not be necessary with Armen Alchian. He is classical in manners as well as thought. The publication of this book offers us an opportunity to pay honor to a colleague who has enriched our subject but who never stooped to conquer.

Armen Alchian was born on April 12, 1914, in Fresno, California. He was brought up in a tightly-knit Armenian community, a community which was subject to intense discrimination. This discrimination, which does not now exist, was not the result, Armen Alchian believes, of any natural unfriendliness or unreasonableness on the part of the other inhabitants of Fresno but was due to the strangeness of the Armenians' manners and customs, which, because they were unusual and not quickly altered, were not understood or tolerated initially. This personal experience with discrimination led Armen Alchian to distrust efforts to prevent or remove discrimination by political means.

Armen Alchian was educated in the Fresno school system and in 1932 went to Fresno State College. Two years later he transferred to Stanford, where he obtained his B.A. in 1936. He continued at Stanford for graduate work, obtaining his Ph.D. in 1943, the thesis topic being "The Effects of Changes in the General Wage Structure." Armen Alchian's teachers at Stanford included Elmer Fagan, Bernard Haley, Edward S. Shaw and Allen Wallis. While working for his Ph.D., Alchian was a teaching assistant in the Department of Economics from 1937 to 1940, held a Social Science Council Fellowship at the National Bureau of Economic Research and Harvard in 1940 and 1941, and, for a period in 1942, was an instructor in economics at the University of Oregon. In 1942, he joined the U. S. Army Air Forces, in which he served until 1946. From 1943 until the end of the war he was engaged in statistical work for the Air Forces.

The war over, Armen Alchian joined the economics department of the University of California, Los Angeles, where he has been ever since, becoming a full professor in 1958. In 1946, he also became associated, at the instigation of Allen Wallis, with the RAND Corporation, a connection which was to have a profound influence on his work in economics. It enabled him to see how economics could be used to illuminate and solve practical problems. It also brought him into close contact with Reuben Kessel, Jack Hirshleifer and William Meckling, and from his collaboration with them much important work sprang.

Armen Alchian's first publications were an outgrowth of his statistical work with the U. S. Army Air Forces. His later publications were undoubtedly influenced by his work at RAND and his interaction with his colleagues there. But it would be wrong to think of Armen Alchian's contribution to economics as a fortuitous result of the RAND connection. In 1950, he published his paper on "Uncertainty, Evolution and Economic Theory" (reprinted in this volume), a paper of striking originality, whose importance was immediately perceived and which gained him international recognition. It was clear that economics had a new master. The power which that article revealed would have served economics whatever the circumstances of Armen Alchian's life. But it was our good fortune that fate led him in the particular direction it did.

Armen Alchian has made important contributions to the economic analysis of inflation and unemployment, and to the theory of costs and of the firm. He has played the leading role in the development of a theory of property rights. His writing is distinguished by his ability to disentangle the essential from the trivial, and above all by his skill in showing how the same basic economic forces are at work in a wide variety of apparently completely different social settings. And if the operation of these forces seems sometimes to produce satisfactory and sometimes unsatisfactory results, this does not come about because the individuals concerned are better or worse but because the environment within which they make their choices is not the same. This is true whether one is dealing with discrimination in Fresno or the behavior of university teachers, government officials or businessmen.

Alfred Marshall considered that it was an essential task of an economist to demonstrate "the Many in the One, the One in the Many." No modern economist has been more successful in accomplishing this than Armen Alchian.

I am grateful to Mrs. Pauline Alchian, Dean William Meckling and Professors Wytze Gorter, Harold Demsetz and Jack Hirshleifer for their assistance in the preparation of this introduction.

Special thanks are also due to Professor Daniel K. Benjamin of the University of Washington, who selected the essays included in this volume.

Economic Forces at Work

I

Information, Uncertainty and the Allocation of Resources

1

Uncertainty, Evolution and Economic Theory[1]

A modification of economic analysis to incorporate incomplete information and uncertain foresight as axioms is suggested here. This approach dispenses with "profit maximization"; and it does not rely on the predictable, individual behavior that is usually assumed, as a first approximation, in standard textbook treatments. Despite these changes, the analytical concepts usually associated with such behavior are retained because they are not dependent upon such motivation or foresight. The suggested approach embodies the principles of biological evolution and natural selection by interpreting the economic system as an adoptive mechanism which chooses among exploratory actions generated by the adaptive pursuit of "success" or "profits." The resulting analysis is applicable to actions usually regarded as aberrations from standard economic behavior as well as to behavior covered by the customary analysis. This wider applicability and the removal of the unrealistic postulates of accurate anticipations and fixed states of knowledge have provided motivation for the study.

[1] I am indebted to Dr. Stephen Enke for criticism and stimulation leading to improvements in both content and exposition.

The exposition is ordered as follows: First, to clear the ground, a brief statement is given of a generally ignored aspect of "profit maximization," that is, where foresight is uncertain, "profit maximization" is *meaningless* as a guide to specifiable action. The constructive development then begins with an introduction of the element of environmental adoption by the economic system of a posteriori most appropriate action according to the criterion of "realized positive profits." This is illustrated in an extreme, random-behavior model without any individual rationality, foresight, or motivation whatsoever. Even in this extreme type of model, it is shown that the economist can predict and explain events with a modified use of his conventional analytical tools.

This phenomenon—environmental adoption—is then fused with a type of individual motivated behavior based on the pervasiveness of uncertainty and incomplete information. Adaptive, imitative, and trial-and-error behavior in the pursuit of "positive profits" is utilized rather than its sharp contrast, the pursuit of "maximized profits." A final section discusses some implications and conjectures.

I. "PROFIT MAXIMIZATION" NOT A GUIDE TO ACTION

Current economic analysis of economic behavior relies heavily on decisions made by rational units customarily assumed to be seeking perfectly optimal situations.[2] Two criteria are well known—profit maximization and utility maximiza-

[2] See, e.g., J. Robinson, *Economics of Imperfect Competition* (London, Macmillan), p. 6, for a strong statement of the necessity of such optimal behavior. Standard textbooks expound essentially the same idea. See also P. Samuelson, *Foundations of Economic Analysis* (Cambridge: Harvard University Press, 1946).

tion.[3] According to these criteria, appropriate types of action are indicated by marginal or neighborhood inequalities which, if satisfied, yield an optimum. But the standard qualification usually added is that nobody is able really to optimize his situation according to these diagrams and concepts because of uncertainty about the position and, sometimes, even the slopes of the demand and supply functions. Nevertheless, the economist interprets and predicts the decisions of individuals in terms of these diagrams, since it is alleged that individuals use these concepts implicitly, if not explicitly.

Attacks on this methodology are widespread, but only one attack has been really damaging, that of G. Tintner.[4] He denies that profit maximization even makes any sense where there is uncertainty. Uncertainty arises from at least two sources: imperfect foresight and human inability to solve complex problems containing a host of variables even when an optimum is definable. Tintner's proof is simple. Under uncertainty, by definition, each action that may be chosen is identified with a *distribution* of potential outcomes, not with a unique outcome. Implicit in uncertainty is the consequence that these distributions of potential outcomes are overlapping.[5] It is worth emphasis that each possible action has a *distribution* of potential outcomes, only one of which will materialize if the action is taken, and that one outcome cannot be foreseen.

[3] In the following we shall discuss only profit maximization, although everything said is applicable equally to utility maximization by consumers.

[4] "The Theory of Choice under Subjective Risk and Uncertainty," *Econometrica* 9 (1941): 298–304; "The Pure Theory of Production under Technological Risk and Uncertainty," *ibid.*, pp. 305–11; and "A Contribution to the Nonstatic Theory of Production," *Studies in Mathematical Economics and Econometrics* (Chicago: University of Chicago Press, 1942), pp. 92–109.

[5] Thus uncertainty is defined here to be the phenomenon that produces overlapping distributions of potential outcomes.

Essentially, the task is converted into making a decision (selecting an action) whose potential outcome *distribution* is preferable, that is, choosing the action with the *optimum distribution*, since there is no such thing as a *maximizing* distribution.

For example, let each of two possible choices be characterized by its subjective distribution of potential outcomes. Suppose one has the higher "mean" but a larger spread, so that it might result in larger profits or losses, and the other has a smaller "mean" and a smaller spread. Which one is the maximum? This is a nonsensical question; but to ask for the optimum distribution is not nonsense. In the presence of uncertainty—a necessary condition for the existence of profits—there is no meaningful criterion for selecting the decision that will "maximize profits." The maximum-profit criterion is not meaningful as a basis *for selecting* the action which will, in fact, result in an outcome with higher profits than any other action would have, unless one assumes nonoverlapping potential outcome distributions. It must be noticed that the meaningfulness of "maximum profits—a realized outcome which is the largest that could have been realized from the available actions"—is perfectly consistent with the meaninglessness of "profit maximization"—a criterion for selecting among alternative lines of action, the potential outcomes of which are describable only as distributions and not as unique amounts.

This crucial difficulty would be avoided by using a preference function as a criterion for selecting most preferred distributions of potential outcomes, but the search for a criterion of rationality and choice in terms of preference functions still continues. For example, the use of the mean, or expectation, completely begs the question of uncertainty by disregarding the variance of the distribution, while a "certainty equivalent" assumes the answer. The only way to make "profit maximization" a specifically meaningful action is to postulate a model containing certainty. Then the question of the predictive and explanatory reliability of the model must be faced.[6]

II. SUCCESS IS BASED ON RESULTS, NOT MOTIVATION

There is an alternative method which treats the decisions and criteria dictated by the economic *system* as more important than those made by the individuals in it. By backing away from the trees—the optimization calculus by individual units—we can better discern the forest of impersonal market forces.[7] This approach directs attention to the interrelationships of the environment and the prevailing types of economic behavior which appear through a process of economic natural selection. Yet it does not imply that individual foresight and action do not affect the nature of the existing state of affairs.

In an economic system the realization of profits is the criterion according to which successful and surviving firms are selected. This decision criterion is applied primarily by an impersonal market system in the United States and may be completely independent of the decision processes of individual units, of the variety of inconsistent motives and abilities, and

[6] Analytical models in all sciences postulate models abstracting from some realities in the belief that derived predictions will still be relevant. Simplifications are necessary, but continued attempts should be made to introduce more realistic assumptions into a workable model with an increase in generality and detail (see M. Friedman and L. Savage, "The Utility Analysis of Choices Involving Risks," *Journal of Political Economy* 56, no. 4 [1948]: 279).

[7] In effect, we shall be reverting to a Marshallian type of analysis combined with the essentials of Darwinian evolutionary natural selection.

even of the individual's awareness of the criterion. The reason is simple. Realized positive profits, not *maximum* profits, are the mark of success and viability. It does not matter through what process of reasoning or motivation such success was achieved. The fact of its accomplishment is sufficient. This is the criterion by which the economic system selects survivors: those who realize *positive profits* are the survivors; those who suffer losses disappear.

The pertinent requirement—positive profits through relative efficiency—is weaker than "maximized profits," with which, unfortunately, it has been confused. Positive profits accrue to those who are better than their actual competitors, even if the participants are ignorant, intelligent, skillful, etc. The crucial element is one's aggregate position relative to actual competitors, not some hypothetically perfect competitors. As in a race, the award goes to the relatively fastest, even if all the competitors loaf. Even in a world of stupid men there would still be profits. Also, the greater the uncertainties of the world, the greater is the possibility that profits would go to venturesome and lucky rather than to logical, careful, fact-gathering individuals.

The preceding interpretation suggests two ideas. First, success (survival) accompanies relative superiority; and, second, it does not require proper motivation but may rather be the result of fortuitous circumstances. Among all competitors, those whose particular conditions happen to be the most appropriate of those offered to the economic system for testing and adoption will be "selected" as survivors. Just how such an approach can be used and how individuals happen to offer these appropriate forms for testing are problems to which we now turn.[8]

[8] Also suggested is another way to divide the general problem discussed here. The

III. CHANCE OR LUCK IS ONE METHOD OF ACHIEVING SUCCESS

Sheer chance is a substantial element in determining the situation selected and also in determining its appropriateness or viability. A second element is the ability to adapt one's self by various methods to an appropriate situation. In order to indicate clearly the respective roles of luck and conscious adapting, the adaptive calculus will, for the moment, be completely removed. All individual rationality, motivation, and foresight will be temporarily abandoned in order to concentrate upon the ability of the environment to *adopt* "appropriate" survivors even in the absence of any adaptive behavior. This is an apparently unrealistic, but nevertheless very useful, expository approach in establishing the attenuation between the ex-post survival criterion and the role of the individual's adaptive decision criterion. It also aids in assessing the role of luck and chance in the operation of our economic system.

Consider, first, the simplest type of biological evolution. Plants "grow" to the sunny side of buildings not because they "want to" in awareness of the fact that optimum or better conditions prevail there, but rather because the leaves that happen to have more sunlight grow faster and their feeding systems become stronger. Similarly, animals with configurations and habits more appropriate for survival under prevailing conditions have an enhanced viability and will with higher probability be typical survivors. Less appropriately acting organisms of the same general class having lower probabilities

process and rationale by which a unit chooses its actions so as to optimize its situation is one part of the problem. The other is the relationship between changes in the environment and the consequent observable results, i.e., the decision process of the economic *society*. The classification used in the text is closely related to this but differs in emphasizing the degree of knowledge and foresight.

of survival will find survival difficult. More common types, the survivors, may appear to be those having *adapted* themselves to the environment, whereas the truth may well be that the environment has *adopted* them. There may have been no motivated individual adapting but, instead, only environmental adopting.

A useful, but unreal, example in which individuals act without any foresight indicates the type of analysis available to the economist and also the ability of the system to "direct" resources despite individual ignorance. Assume that thousands of travelers set out from Chicago, selecting their roads completely at random and without foresight. Only our "economist" knows that on but one road are there any gasoline stations. He can state categorically that travelers will *continue* to travel only on that road; those on other roads will soon run out of gas. Even though each one selected his route at random, we might have called those travelers who were so fortunate as to have picked the right road wise, efficient, foresighted, etc. Of course, we would consider them the lucky ones. If gasoline supplies were now moved to a new road, some formerly luckless travelers again would be able to move; and a new pattern of travel would be observed, although none of the travelers had changed his particular path. The really possible paths have changed with the changing environment. All that is needed is a set of varied, risk-taking (adoptable) travelers. The correct direction of travel will be established. As circumstances (economic environment) change, the analyst (economist) can select the types of participants (firms) that will now become successful; he may also be able to diagnose the conditions most conducive to a greater probability of survival.[9]

[9] The undiscerning person who sees survivors corresponding to changes in environment claims to have evidence for the "Lysenko" doctrine. In truth, all he may

IV. CHANCE DOES NOT IMPLY NONDIRECTED, RANDOM ALLOCATION OF RESOURCES

These two examples do not constitute an attempt to base all analysis on adoptive models dominated by chance. But they do indicate that collective and individual random behavior does not per se imply a nihilistic theory incapable of yielding reliable predictions and explanations; nor does it imply a world lacking in order and apparent direction. It might, however, be argued that the facts of life deny even a substantial role to the element of chance and the associated adoption principle in the economic system. For example, the long lives and disparate sizes of business firms and hereditary fortunes may seem to be reliable evidence of consistent foresighted motivation and nonrandom behavior. In order to demonstrate that consistent success cannot be treated as prima facie evidence against pure luck, the following chance model of Borél, the famous French mathematician, is presented.

Suppose two million Parisians were paired off and set to tossing coins in a game of matching. Each pair plays until the winner on the first toss is again brought to equality with the other player. Assuming one toss per second for each eight-hour day, at the end of ten years there would still be, on the average, about a hundred-odd pairs; and if the players assign the game to their heirs, a dozen or so will still be playing at the end of a thousand years! The implications are obvious. Suppose that some business had been operating for one hundred years. Should one rule out luck and chance as the essence of the factors producing the long-term survival of the enterprise?

---

have is evidence for the doctrine that the environment, by competitive conditions, selects the most viable of the various phenotypic characteristics for perpetuation. Economists should beware of economic "Lysenkois m."

No inference whatever can be drawn until the number of original participants is known; and even then one must know the size, risk, and frequency of each commitment. One can see from the Borél illustration the danger in concluding that there are too many firms with long lives in the real world to admit an important role to chance. On the contrary, one might insist that there are actually too few!

The chance postulate was directed to two problems. On the one hand, there is the actual way in which a substantial fraction of economic behavior and activity is effected. On the other, there is the method of analysis which economists may use in their predictions and diagnoses. Before modifying the extreme chance model by adding adaptive behavior, some connotations and implications of the incorporation of chance elements will be elaborated in order to reveal the richness which is really inherent in chance. First, even if each and every individual acted in a haphazard and nonmotivated manner, it is possible that the variety of actions would be so great that the resulting collective set would contain actions that are best, in the sense of perfect foresight. For example, at a horse race with enough bettors wagering strictly at random, someone will win on all eight races. Thus individual random behavior does not eliminate the likelihood of observing "appropriate" decisions.[10]

Second, and conversely, individual behavior according to some foresight and motivation does not necessarily imply a collective pattern of behavior that is different from the collective variety of actions associated with a random selection of actions. Where there is uncertainty, people's judgments and opinions, even when based on the best available evidence, will

[10] The Borél gamblers analogue is pertinent to a host of everyday situations.

differ; no one of them may be making his choice by tossing coins; yet the aggregate *set* of actions of the entire group of participants may be indistinguishable from a set of individual actions, each selected at random.[11]

Third, and fortunately, a chance-dominated model does not mean that an economist cannot predict or explain or diagnose. With a knowledge of the economy's realized requisites for survival and by a comparison of alternative conditions, he can state what types of firms or behavior relative to other possible types will be more viable, even though the firms themselves may not know the conditions or even try to achieve them by readjusting to the changed situation if they do know the conditions. It is sufficient if all firms are slightly different so that in the new environmental situation those who have their fixed internal conditions closer to the new, but unknown, optimum position now have a greater probability of survival and growth. They will grow relative to other firms and become the prevailing type, since survival conditions may push the observed characteristics of the set of survivors toward the unknowable optimum by either (1) repeated trials or (2) survival of more of those who happened to be near the optimum—determined ex post. If these new conditions last "very long," the dominant firms will be different ones from those which prevailed or would have prevailed under other conditions. Even if environmental conditions cannot be forecast, the economist can compare for given alternative potential situations the types of behavior that would have higher probability of viability or adoption. If explanation of past results rather

[11] Of course, the economic units may be going through a period of soul-searching, management training, and research activity. We cannot yet identify mental and physical activity with a process that results in sufficient information and foresight to yield uniquely determinate choices. To do so would be to beg the whole question.

than prediction is the task, the economist can diagnose the particular attributes which were critical in facilitating survival, even though individual participants were not aware of them.[12]

Fourth, the bases of prediction have been indicated in the preceding paragraph, but its character should be made explicit. The prediction will not assert that every—or, indeed, any—firm necessarily changes its characteristics. It asserts, instead, that the characteristics of the new *set* of firms, or possibly a set of new firms, will change. This may be characterized by the "representative firm," a purely statistical concept—a vector of "averages," one dimension for each of the several qualities of the population of firms. A "representative firm" is not typical of any one producer but, instead, is a set of statistics summarizing the various "modal" characteristics of the population. Surely, this was an intended use of Marshall's "representative firm."

Fifth, a final implication drawn from consideration of this extreme approach is that empirical investigations via questionnaire methods, so far used, are incapable of evaluating the validity of marginal productivity analysis. This is true because productivity and demand analyses are essential in evaluating relative viability, even though uncertainty eliminates "profit maximization" and even if price and technological changes were to have no consciously redirecting effect on the firms. To

[12] It is not even necessary to suppose that each firm acts as if it possessed the conventional diagrams and knew the analytical principles employed by economists in deriving optimum and equilibrium conditions. The atoms and electrons do not know the laws of nature; the physicist does not impart to each atom a willful scheme of action based on laws of conservation of energy, etc. The fact that an economist deals with human beings who have sense and ambitions does not *automatically* warrant imparting to these humans the great degree of foresight and motivations which the economist may require for his customary analysis as an outside observer or "oracle." The similarity between this argument and Gibbsian statistical mechanics, as well as biological evolution, is *not* mere coincidence.

illustrate, suppose that, in attempting to predict the effects of higher real wage rates, it is discovered that every businessman says he does not adjust his labor force. Nevertheless, firms with a lower labor-capital ratio will have relatively lower cost positions and, to that extent, a higher probability of survival. The force of competitive survival, by eliminating higher-cost firms, reveals a population of remaining firms with a new average labor-capital ratio. The essential point is that individual motivation and foresight, while sufficient, are not necessary. Of course, it is not argued here that therefore it is absent. All that is needed by economists is their own awareness of the survival conditions and criteria of the economic system and a group of participants who submit various combinations and organizations for the system's selection and adoption. Both these conditions are satisfied.[13]

As a consequence, only the method of use, rather than the usefulness, of economic tools and concepts is affected by the approach suggested here; in fact, they are made more powerful if they are not pretentiously assumed to be necessarily associated with, and dependent upon, individual foresight and adjustment. They are tools for, at least, the diagnosis of the operation of an economic system, even if not also for the internal business behavior of each firm.

V. INDIVIDUAL ADAPTING VIA IMITATION AND TRIAL AND ERROR

Let it again be noted that the preceding extreme model was designed to present in purest form only one element of the suggested approach. It is not argued that there is no purposive,

[13] This approach reveals how the "facts" of Lester's dispute with Machlup can be handled with standard economic tools.

foresighted behavior present in reality. In adding this realistic element—adaptation by individuals with some foresight and purposive motivation—we are expanding the preceding extreme model. We are not abandoning any part of it or futilely trying to merge it with the opposite extreme of perfect foresight and "profit maximization."

Varying and conflicting objectives motivate economic activity, yet we shall here direct attention to only one particular objective—the sufficient condition of realized positive profits. There are no implications of "profit maximization," and this difference is important. Although the latter is a far more extreme objective when definable, only the former is the sine qua non of survival and success. To argue that, with perfect competition, the two would come to the same thing is to conceal an important difference by means of a very implausible assumption. The pursuit of profits, and not some hypothetical and undefinable perfect situation, is the relevant objective whose *fulfillment* is rewarded with survival. Unfortunately, even this proximate objective is too high. Neither perfect knowledge of the past nor complete awareness of the current state of the arts gives sufficient foresight to indicate profitable action. Even for this more restricted objective, the pervasive effects of uncertainty prevent the ascertainment of actions which are supposed to be optimal in achieving profits. Now the consequence of this is that modes of behavior replace optimum equilibrium conditions as guiding rules of action. Therefore, in the following sections two forms of conscious adaptive behavior are emphasized.

First, wherever successful enterprises are observed, the elements common to these observable successes will be associated with success and copied by others in their pursuit of profits or success. "Nothing succeeds like success." Thus the urge for "rough-and-ready" imitative rules of behavior is accounted for. What would otherwise appear to be merely customary "orthodox," nonrational rules of behavior turns out to be codified imitations of observed success, e.g., "conventional" markup, price "followship," "orthodox" accounting and operating ratios, "proper" advertising policy, etc. A conventionally employed type of behavior pattern is consistent with the postulates of the analysis employed, even though the reasons and justifications for the particular conventions are not.[14]

Many factors cause this motive to imitate patterns of action observable in past successes. Among these are: (1) the absence of an identifiable criterion for decision-making, (2) the variability of the environment, (3) the multiplicity of factors that call for attention and choice, (4) the uncertainty attaching to all these factors and outcomes, (5) the awareness that superiority relative to one's competitors is crucial, and (6) the nonavailability of a trial-and-error process converging to an optimum position.

In addition, imitation affords relief from the necessity of really making decisions and conscious innovations, which, if wrong, become "inexcusable." Unfortunately, failure or success often reflects the willingness to depart from rules when conditions have changed; what counts, then, it not only imita-

[14] These constructed rules of behavior should be distinguished from "rules" which, in effect, do no more than define the objective being sought. Confusion between objectives which motivate one and rules of behavior is commonplace. For example, "full-cost pricing" is a "rule" that one cannot really follow. He can try to, but whether he succeeds or fails in his objective of survival is not controllable by following the "rule of full-cost pricing." If he fails in his objective, he must, of necessity, fail to have followed the "rule." The situation is parallel to trying to control the speed of a car by simply setting by hand the indicator on the speedometer.

tive behavior but the willingness to abandon it at the "right" time and circumstances. Those who are different and successful "become" innovators, while those who fail "become" reckless violators of tried-and-true rules. Although one may deny the absolute appropriateness of such rules, one cannot doubt the existence of a strong urge to create conventions and rules (based on observed success) and a willingness to use them for action as well as for rationalizations of inaction. If another untried host of actions might have been even more successful, so much the worse for the participants who failed, and even for those who missed "perfect success."

Even innovation is accounted for by imitation. While there certainly are those who consciously innovate, there are those who, in their imperfect attempts to imitate others, unconsciously innovate by unwittingly acquiring some unexpected or unsought unique attributes which under the prevailing circumstances prove partly responsible for the success. Others, in turn, will attempt to copy the uniqueness, and the imitation-innovation process continues. Innovation is assured, and the notable aspects of it here are the possibility of unconscious pioneering and leadership.

The second type of conscious adaptive behavior, in addition to imitation, is "trial and error." This has been used with "profit maximization," wherein, by trial and ensuing success or failure, more appropriate actions are selected in a process presumed to converge to a limit of "profit maximization" equilibrium. Unfortunately, at least two conditions are necessary for convergence via a trial-and-error process, even if one admits an equilibrium situation as an admissible limit. First, a trial must be classifiable as a success or failure. The position achieved must be comparable with results of other potential actions. In a static environment, if one improves his position relative to his former position, then the action taken is better than the former one, and presumably one could continue by small increments to advance to a local optimum. An analogy is pertinent. A nearsighted grasshopper on a mound of rocks can crawl to the top of a particular rock. But there is no assurance that he can also get to the top of the mound, for he might have to descend for a while or hop to new rocks. The second condition, then, for the convergence via trial and error is the continual rising toward some *optimum optimorum* without intervening descents. Whether decisions and actions in economic life satisfy these two conditions cannot be proved or disproved here, but the available evidence seems overwhelmingly unfavorable.

The above convergence conditions do not apply to a changing environment, for there can be no observable comparison of the result of an action with any other. Comparability of resulting situations is destroyed by the changing environment. As a consequence, the measure of goodness of actions in anything except a tolerable-intolerable sense is lost, and the possibility of an individual's converging to the optimum activity via a trial-and-error process disappears. Trial and error becomes survival or death. It cannot serve as a basis of the *individual's* method of convergence to a "maximum" or optimum position. Success is discovered by the economic system through a blanketing shotgun process, not by the individual through a converging search.

In general, uncertainty provides an excellent reason for imitation of observed success. Likewise, it accounts for observed uniformity among the survivors, derived from an evolutionary, adopting, competitive system employing a criterion of survival, which can operate independently of individual motivations. Adapting behavior via imitation and venturesome innovation enlarges the model. Imperfect imitators provide opportunity for innovation, and the survival criterion of the economy determines the successful, possibly because imperfect, imitators. Innovation is provided also by conscious willful action, whatever the ultimate motivation may be, since drastic action is motivated by the hope of great success as well as by the desire to avoid impending failure.

All the preceding arguments leave the individual economic participant with imitative, venturesome, innovative, trial-and-error adaptive behavior. Most conventional economic tools and concepts are still useful, although in a vastly different analytical framework—one which is closely akin to the theory of biological evolution. The economic counterparts of genetic heredity, mutations, and natural selection are imitation, innovation, and positive profits.

VI. CONCLUSIONS AND SUMMARY

I shall conclude with a brief reference to some implications and conjectures.

Observable patterns of behavior and organization are predictable in terms of their relative probabilities of success or viability *if* they are tried. The observed prevalence of a type of behavior depends upon both this probability of viability and the probability of the different types being submitted to the economic system for testing and selecting. One is the probability of appearance of a certain type of organization (mutation), and the other is the probability of its survival or viability, once it appears (natural selection). There is much evidence for believing that these two probabilities are interrelated. But is there reason to suppose that a high probability of viability implies a high probability of an action's being taken, as would be implied in a system of analysis involving some "inner directed urge toward perfection''? If these two probabilities are not highly correlated, what predictions of types of action can the economist make? An answer has been suggested in this paper.

While it is true that the economist can define a profit maximization behavior by assuming *specific* cost and revenue conditions, is there any assurance that the conditions and conclusions so derivable are not too perfect and absolute? If profit maximization (certainty) is not ascertainable, the confidence about the predicted effects of changes, e.g., higher taxes or minimum wages, will be dependent upon how close the formerly existing arrangement was to the formerly ''optimal'' (certainty) situation. What really counts is the various actions actually tried, for it is from these that ''success'' is selected, not from some set of perfect actions. The economist may be pushing his luck too far in arguing that actions in response to changes in environment and changes in satisfaction with the existing state of affairs will converge as a result of adaptation or adoption toward the optimum action that should have been selected, if foresight had been perfect.[15]

[15] An anomalous aspect of the assumption of perfect foresight is that it nearly results in tautological and empty statements. One cannot know everything, and this is recognized by the addendum that one acts within a ''given state and distribution of the arts.'' But this is perilously close, if not equivalent, to saying either that action is taken only where the outcome is accurately foreseen or that information is always limited. The qualification is inserted because one might contend that it is the ''*constancy* of the state and distribution of arts'' that is necessary as a *ceteris paribus*. But even the latter is no solution. A large fraction of behavior in a world of incomplete information and uncertainty is necessarily directed at increasing the state of arts and venturing into an unknown sphere. While it is probably permissible to start with a prescribed ''distribution of the knowledge of the arts,'' holding it constant is too restrictive, since a large class of important and frequent actions necessarily involves changes in the state and distribution of knowledge. The modification suggested here incorporates this search for more knowledge as an essential foundation.

In summary, I have asserted that the economist, using the present analytical tools developed in the analysis of the firm under certainty, can predict the more adoptable or viable types of economic interrelationships that will be induced by environmental change even if individuals themselves are unable to ascertain them. That is, although individual participants may not know their cost and revenue situations, the economist can predict the consequences of higher wage rates, taxes, government policy, etc. Like the biologist, the economist predicts the effects of environmental changes on the surviving class of living organisms; the economist need not assume that each participant is aware of, or acts according to, his cost and demand situation. These are concepts for the economist's use and not necessarily for the individual participant's, who may have other analytic or customary devices which, while of interest to the economist, serve as data and not as analytic methods.

An alternative to the rationale of individual profit maximization has been presented without exorcising uncertainty. Lest isolated arguments be misinterpreted, let it be clearly stated that this paper does not argue that purposive objective-seeking behavior is absent from reality, nor, on the other hand, does it endorse the familiar thesis that action of economic units cannot be expressed within the marginal analysis. Rather, the contention is that the precise role and nature of purposive behavior in the presence of uncertainty and incomplete information have not been clearly understood or analyzed.

It is straightforward, if not heuristic, to start with complete uncertainty and nonmotivation and then to add elements of foresight and motivation in the process of building an analytical model. The opposite approach, which starts with certainty and unique motivation, must abandon its basic principles as soon as uncertainty and mixed motivations are recognized.[16] The approach suggested here is intellectually more modest and realistic, without sacrificing generality. It does not regard uncertainty as an aberrational exogenous disturbance, as does the usual approach from the opposite extreme of accurate foresight. The existence of uncertainty and incomplete information is the foundation of the suggested type of analysis; the importance of the concept of a class of "chance" decisions rests upon it; it permits of various conflicting objectives; it motivates and rationalizes a type of adaptive imitative behavior; yet it does not destroy the basis of prediction, explanation, or diagnosis. It does not base its aggregate description on individual optimal action; yet it is capable of incorporating such activity where justified. The formalization of this approach awaits the marriage of the theory of stochastic processes and economics—two fields of thought admirably suited for union. It is conjectured that the suggested modification is applicable to a wide class of events and is worth attempts at empirical verification.[17]

[16] If one prefers, he may believe that the suggestions here contain reasons why the model based on certainty may predict outcomes, although individuals really cannot try to maximize profits. But the dangers of this have been indicated.

[17] Preliminary study in this direction has been very convincing, and, in addition, the suggested approach appears to contain important implications relative to general economic policy; but discussions of these are reserved for a later date.

2

Information Costs, Pricing and Resource Unemployment

Economic theory of exchange often appears to imply that demand changes induce instant wage and price adjustments to maintain full resource use. But unemployment, queues, rationing, and idle resources refute any such implication. And macroeconomic theory does not explain why demand decreases cause unemployment rather than immediate wage and price adjustments in labor *and* nonhuman resources. Instead, administered prices, monopolies, minimum wage laws, union restrictions, and ''natural'' inflexibilities of wages and prices are invoked.

This paper attempts to show that economic theory is capable of being formulated—consistently with each person acting as an individual utility, or wealth, maximizer without constraints imposed by competitors, and without conventions or taboos about wages or prices—so as to imply shortages, surpluses, unemployment, queues, idle resources, and nonprice rationing with price stability. The theory implies massive correlated fluctuations in employment of both labor and capital in response to aggregate demand decreases—in a context of open

Acknowledgment for substantial aid is made to the Lilly Endowment, Inc., grant to UCLA for a study in the behavioral effects of different kinds of property rights.

market, individual utility maximizing behavior. The theory is general in that it applies to nonhuman goods as well as to human services. Though my primary motivation to explain "unemployed" resources arose from labor market behavior, the analysis is best exposited initially without special reference to labor markets.

The key, which, till recently, seems to have been forgotten, is that *collating information about potential exchange opportunities* is costly and can be performed in various ways.[1] Nobody knows as much as he would like (at zero cost) about everyone else's offers and demands (including the properties of goods offered or demanded), but at a cost, more information can be acquired. Two questions guide our analysis. First, what are the means of providing information more efficiently? Second, given that information is costly, what kinds of substitute arrangements are used to economize on search costs?

I. THEORY OF EXCHANGE, UNEMPLOYMENT AND PRICE STABILITY

In equilibrium everyone has equal marginal rates of substitution, but how is that equilibrium equality approached? It is not rational to expect a person to exchange with the first person he happens to meet with a different subjective value. It will pay to seek a higher "bid" or a lower "ask." Discovery of the variety of bids and offers and the best path or sequence of actual exchange prices toward an "equilibrium" requires costly search over the population. Institutions facilitate and

[1] A study of Stigler [28] will reveal this paper to be a development and application of the fundamentals of that paper. See also, for earlier interest in this problem, Rees [21] [22]. Arrow and Capron [3] used the difficulty of knowing the true market demand and supply as a reason for individual delays in adapting to the equilibrating price and output.

economize on that search. The marketplace is an example. A large and costly portion of so-called marketing activity is information dissemination. Advertisements, window displays, sales clerks, specialist agents, brokers, inventories, catalogs, correspondence, phone calls, market research agencies, employment agencies, licensing, certification, aptitude testing services (to name a few) facilitate the spread and acquisition of knowledge about potential demanders and suppliers and their goods and about prices they can expect to see prevail.

Marketing includes many activities: (a) ''extensive'' searching for all possible buyers or sellers; (b) communication of information about characteristics of the goods of each party—the ''intensive'' search;[2] (c) contract information; (d) contract enforcement; (e) ''buffer inventories'' by sellers; (f) queueing of buyers, and (g) provision of price predictability. Two propositions about the costs of production or market opportunity information will be critical in the ensuing analysis.

(1) *Dissemination and acquisition (i.e., the production) of information conforms to the ordinary laws of costs of production—viz., faster dissemination or acquisition costs more*. A simple, fruitful characterization of the search for information is sampling from a distribution of ''offers'' (or ''bids'') with some mean and dispersion. As the sample is enlarged, the observed maximum value will increase *on the average* at a *diminishing* rate. Assuming search (sampling) at a constant rate, with time thereby measuring size of sample, the expected (mathematical expectation of the) maximum observed value will rise from the median at a diminishing rate toward the upper limit of the distribution.[3] That limit will

---

[2] This terminology is taken from Rees [21].

[3] For example, if potential prices are normally distributed with mean, m, and with variance, σ^2, then the expected maximum observed bid $W(n)$ at the n-th obser-

exceed the past actual price, since there is no necessity for the past sale to have been negotiated at the highest possible price (with exhaustive prior sampling, regardless of cost).

(2) *Like any other production activity, specialization in information is efficient. Gathering and disseminating information about goods or about oneself is in some circumstances more efficiently done while the good or person is not employed, and thus able to specialize (i.e., while specializing) in the production of information*. If seeking information about other jobs while employed is more costly than while not employed, it can be economic to refuse a wage cut, become unemployed, and look for job information.[4] The deeper the wage cut in the old job, the cheaper the choice of unemployment in order to ferret information. Without this proposition of *differential* search costs, the theory would not be able, consistently with wealth maximizing choices, to account for the fact that some people refuse to accept a low wage while acquiring and comparing job information.

The fact that being employed is itself a recommendation to a prospective employer does not deny that it may pay to forsake that recommendation in view of the large wage cut required to obtain it. The value of such a recommendation would imply

---

vation is approximately $m + \sigma(2 \log n)^{1/2}$. $W(n)$ starts at m and increases at a decreasing rate with n. If we assume one observation every λ units of time, then we can replace n by λt, and obtain W as a function of time of search.

$$W(t) = m + \sigma(2 \log \lambda t)^{1/2}$$

Further, if we increase expenditures on search, the rate of search can be increased per unit time, whatever is the environment of search; in other words, the effective λ is a function of the environment, V, and of the expenditures on search $E(t)$: $\lambda = f[V, E(t)]$. A larger expenditure implies a larger λ and if we let a larger V denote a more costly search environment, then a larger V implies a smaller λ.

[4] This proposition is added to those contained in Stigler and is crucial to much that follows.

acceptance of greater wage cuts to keep jobs. However, the question here is why anyone would choose to forsake that lower wage and accept unemployment—not why wages are sometimes cut to hold jobs.

Figure 1

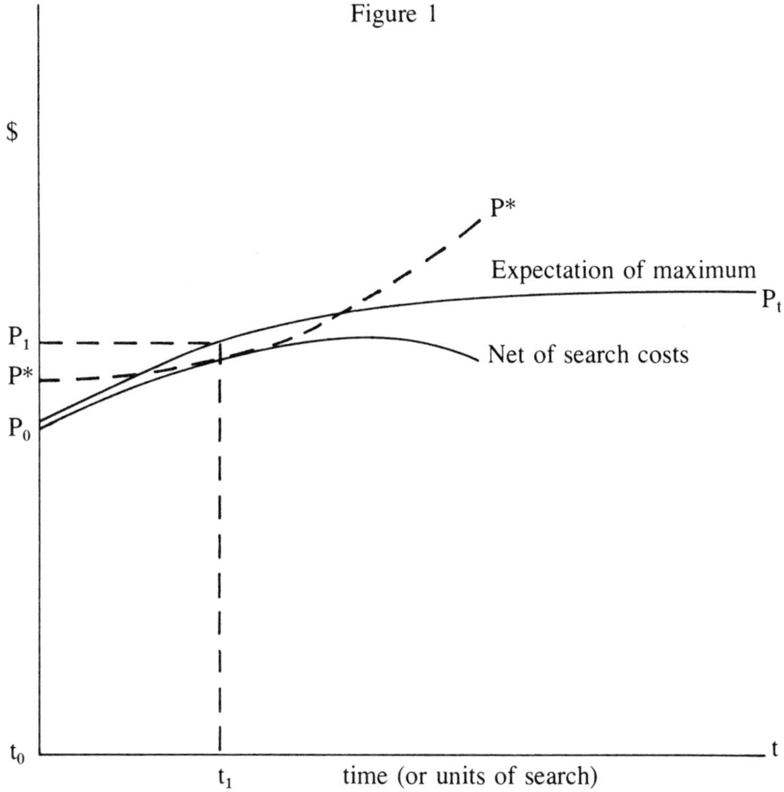

Our choice of words is deliberate when speaking of seeking "job-information" rather than seeking "jobs." Jobs are always easily available. Timely information about the pay, working conditions, and life expectancy of all available jobs is not cheap. In a sense, *this* kind of unemployment is self-employment in information collection.

This applies to nonhuman resources as well. For example, the automobile on a used car lot—out of "normal" service (unemployed)—facilitates cheaper information to potential buyers. Similarly, unoccupied apartments and houses (like cars and people) are cheaper to show to prospective clients.[5]

A graph of some characteristics of search and its costs is shown in Figure 1. Time is on the horizontal scale and price or wage on the vertical. For any constant rate of search over the population of potential buyers, time and scope of search can both be measured on the horizontal scale. If some good were sold to the first found offerer at t_0, the price would be P_0. The height of curve P_0P_t *is* the "expectation" of the maximum discerned available contract price found by time *t*—assuming discerned options do not disappear or decay with time. The line rises at a decreasing rate, rather than being horizontal at P_t, as it would be if information about all potential offers were costless (and if all people knew all the characteristics of the good). As the sample (information) increases the expected maximum discerned available price increases by successively smaller increments. In terms of costs, there are increasing marginal costs of unit increments of expected maximum ascertained price.[6] The curve for an unemployed searcher will be

[5] We can now identify a "perfect" market—one in which all potential bids and offers are known at zero cost to every other person, and in which contract enforcement costs are zero. Characteristics of every good need to be known perfectly at zero cost. A "perfect" market would imply a "perfect" world in which all costs of production, even of "exchanges," were zero. It is curious that while we economists never formalize our analysis on the basis of an analytical ideal of a perfect world (in the sense of costless production) we have postulated costless *information* as a formal ideal for analysis. Why?

[6] If we subtract the *cumulated* search costs over the search interval from the then best observed sales bid price, the *net* price line, now *net* of search costs, will hit a peak after which it will decrease, assuming no "decay" in value of earlier perceived options.

above that for an employed searcher—if unemployment is to occur. By identifying characteristics that will affect the shape and position of the curves we can reduce unemployment patterns.

Liquidity. The analogy to liquidity is obvious. Liquidity concepts can be portrayed by the same diagram. The ratio of P^* to P_t is one dimension of the liquidity *vector*. Another, for example, is the time to t_1.

The expectation of discerned maximum offers is a function of amount of expenditures (of all types) for acquiring information up to any moment. A potential (expected maximum discerned) *gross* price will be higher, as of any time t, if more is spent on hastening the information-acquiring process. The seller nets a reward equal to P_1 minus *his* search costs, and the buyer pays P_1 plus his search costs. A perfectly liquid asset is one for which P_0P_t is horizontal at height P_t with no search costs. Money is typically regarded as a resource fulfilling these criteria.[7] It enters into almost every exchange because it provides the most economical vehicle of exchange.

Brokers and Middlemen. The P_0P_t curve reveals an opportunity for exchange with an intermediary broker. Since this analysis is applicable to nonhuman goods as well as to labor, it will be profitable for a "middleman" or "broker" to offer at the initial moment, t_0, a price higher than P_0, if he believes the discerned resale value of the good (net of *his* search costs) will increase at a rate greater than the interest rate and greater than that of the existing possessor of the good. The price he would offer at t_0 would be, at most, the present value of the expected maximum discerned bid price for the time his discerned price line (*net* of *his* search costs) was rising at a rate equal to the

[7] For an illustration of the application of information and search costs to money and liquidity per se, see Miller [18].

interest rate. This can be illustrated by inserting an "iso-net-present value" P^*P^*, the height of which *at the vertical* axis ($t = 0$) shows the maximum *present net* discounted value as of t_0 of any future net amount available (net of the *middleman's* search costs). The price that would be offered now by the middleman is P^*. The difference between the present-value price P^*, and the future selling price, P_1, is essentially the retail-wholesale price spread, or the bid-ask spread of brokers, wholesalers or retailers. Since the middleman is a successful specialist in search, his search costs are, by definition, lower, and hence his P^* is higher than for a nonmiddleman, non-specialist [5].

Price Stability: Economizing on Information and Market Adjustment Costs. Aside from the obvious ways to produce information (e.g., advertising and specialist middlemen) there are less well recognized ways involving price stability, unemployed resources, and queues (in which costs are incurred to *reduce* search and other marketing costs even more). Inventories economize on costs of information. Inventories may appear to be idle, excess or unemployed resources, but they can be interpreted as an economical use of resources [26]. An oversimplified but suggestive example is the problem faced by a newsboy who sells an average of 100 copies of a daily paper—but not always 100 each day. The more accurately he tries to predict and the more quickly he adjusts to imperfectly predictable fluctuations in the flow of demand, the greater are the costs of his action. Potential customers may prefer that he stock an excessive number on the average with instant availability from inventories, despite higher costs caused by unsold copies. The higher cost may be manifested to customers as a lower quality of product, fewer sellers or a higher price. But this extra cost (of the unsold papers) will be less than if the newspaper sellers attempted to obtain complete information about demands at each future moment, or to make instantaneous adjustments in the number of papers without an inventory. In brief, the costs of unsold items are incurred to reduce even more the information costs in marketing.

Another option exists. The seller could change price instantly to always clear the market when demand fluctuates and thereby never have an inventory of unsold goods awaiting purchasers.[8] Retailers would not be awaiting buyers. Retailers could avoid reservations and queues by varying price instantly with the random fluctuations of appearance of customers. Why don't they? After all, that is what happens, or seems to happen, in the futures markets and stock markets.[9]

Consider the consequences. Patrons appear at random intervals, though the probability density of the rate may be predictable. Would patrons prefer to see the market instantly cleared with no queues whatsoever—but only with price fluctuations to do the rationing? Not necessarily. That might *induce more search elsewhere* than under queueing. Customers may prefer

[8] The expression "demand fluctuation" covers a great amount of mischievousness. For a more rigorous conceptualization, a "probability distribution of latent offers" is better. Reference to the mean and variance of that distribution of potentially discernible or revealed offers would provide some specification of the demand confronting a seller. Furthermore, there is not a *given* flow of *revealed* demanders. Offers could be emitted or received at a slower or faster rate. The analogy to emissions of particles from radioactive elements is apt. The emissions have a "mean" and a "range" of values (voltages) and a random time between emission, i.e., the "rate" of emission. These "randomly spaced" emissions of market offers can be characterized by a probability distribution. The *rate* at which offers are discerned by the seller can be increased or decreased by engaging more information activity (i.e., marketing activity). This paper is not trying to specify some special underlying distribution rigorously. Some progress toward this is to be found in Stigler [28].

[9] As a matter of fact, even on the futures markets and stock exchanges, there are specialists and "scalpers" who stabilize price by providing a buffer inventory [31].

more predictable prices with enhanced probability of some queues and less search. Unpredictable prices, as well as queues, impose costs on patrons; there is no reason why *only one* should be avoided regardless of the cost of the other. Retailers must balance (a) costs of search induced by unpredictable prices and of inventories against (b) costs of queues and of waiting in queues. If prices of all sellers were known, extensive persistent search could be reduced (there would still be search for small queues), and the gross cost could fall, even though the money price were higher. This is basically one of the economic defenses of manufacturer-imposed retail prices.

A seller who eliminates a nonpredictably fluctuating, transient, market-clearing price could offer his patrons a saving in costs of search. He could make price more predictable by carrying a larger inventory to buffer the transient demand fluctuations, and customers would reduce search costs with the assurance of a stable (i.e., predicted) price if they accepted some costs of waiting in a queue.

The queue length could vary with constant price so long as the *mean* rate of purchases is matched by the production rate. The greater the variance in the transient rate of appearance of shoppers, the greater will be the variation in the length of the queue and *also* the longer will be the average length of the line. An alternative to customer queues is "queueing" of an inventory as a buffer to eliminate customer queues while price is constant. Among these options—transient and instant price changes, customer queues, inventories and continued market search for better options—what determines the efficient extent of each?

Customers engage in repeat purchases; in making purchase plans, predictability of price is conducive to closer adjustment to optimal purchases. Revising purchase plans and actions is costly. If one finds a dinner price transiently and unexpectedly high because of randomly high demand at the moment he appears in the restaurant, he will have been led to inappropriate action. Ex post his action was not optimal. To avoid such losses, he will, thereafter, prior to concluding a purchase, engage in more search among sellers to discover unusually, transiently low prices. This extra search is less costly than taking one's chances as to what price he will face in a transiently fluctuating market.

In general, smaller and more frequent random fluctuations in demand (i.e., with a fixed expectation in the probability density function), greater search costs, greater value of the buyer's time, and less burdensome forms of queueing or rationing, all will increase the incidence of price stability. If the demand probability density function shifted *predictably*, prices would vary—as they do for daytime and evening restaurants and theaters for example. A lower cost of holding inventories relative to the value of the product will increase the relative size of inventories and increase price stability and shorten queues for any frequency and size of random demand fluctuations.[10]

Accordingly, we should expect to see some prices maintained relatively rigidly over time and among retail stores (with so-called Fair Trade Laws) as *manufacturers* seek to assure final customers of the lower *overall* costs of purchasing their items for high quality, but low value, items purchased by people whose time is relatively valuable (i.e., high wage groups).

An obvious application of the analysis is to shop hours. Stores are open during known hours and stay open even when there are no customers in sight. A store could have lower

[10] Had this paper been devoted also to the conditions that induce non-market-clearing prices, even with predictable demand, it would have included a discussion of forms of property rights in the goods being sold.

prices if customers were to ring a bell and wait for the owner to open the store, but this would impose waiting costs on the patrons. I presume the advantage to the store operator (with lower pecuniary prices to customers) in closing his store when no customers are in sight is smaller than the convenience to shoppers.

More apartment units are built than the owner expects on the average to rent. This, of course, assumes that *revealed* demand *to him* for his apartments is neither continuous nor costlessly and perfectly predictable. It pays to build more apartments to satisfy *unpredictable* vagaries in "demand fluctuations" if such demand fluctuations cannot be accommodated by costless reallocation among demanders or "no inconvenience" from immediate rent changes. The apartment owner could always keep apartments fully rented at a lower, quickly revised rental; or at higher stable rentals he could have vacancies part of the time. A landlord, faced with an empty apartment, could cut the rent sufficiently to induce immediate rental to the first person he happened to see, if he ignored marketing (including moving) costs. But in view of costs of transactions, contract revision and displaying and arranging for new higher paying tenants of already *occupied* premises, it sometimes yields greater wealth to forgo transient rent revision that would keep apartments *always* rented. In maintaining vacancies, he is responding to renters' preferences (a) to examine apartments, have rental predictability and move more spontaneously rather than (b) to continually adjust to rental changes or (c) to make plans and reservations in advance if there were price predictability *and no* inventory of vacant apartments. The "vacancies" serve as inventories; as such they do not warrant rent reductions.

If instant production were no more costly than slower production or adjustment, people could always produce whatever was wanted only at the moment it was wanted. In fact, however, producing in advance at a less hasty, less expensive rate *and* holding an "excess" for contingent demands economizes in having more services at a cost that is worth paying, taking into account the value of being able to adapt to changed demands without long, advance, "reservations-type" planning. The situation is the same for a home with enough bathrooms and dining space to accommodate more visitors than one will ordinarily have. To say there is "idle," "wasted," or "unemployed" bathroom or dining room capacity is to consider only the cost of that extra capacity while ignoring its infrequent-use value and the *greater* costs of other ways of obtaining equally high convenience or utility.

The foregoing considerations suggest that in a society with (a) costs of obtaining information about sellers' "asking" prices, (b) costs of sellers' obtaining information about customers' demand, and (c) a tendency for unpredicted price changes to induce extra search by buyers and sellers, the "ideal" market will *not* be characterized by prices that instantly fluctuate so as always to clear the market without queues by buyers or sellers. Instead, to reduce the losses consequent to unpredictable delivery times if prices were perfectly stable, it pays: (a) sellers to hold inventories, (b) buyers to accept some queueing—as means of purchasing at predictable prices and avoiding higher search costs that would be induced if with instant price adjustments there were no queues and inventories, and (c) sometimes to continue shopping before making a contract. The stable price, accompanied by queues and inventories will be slightly higher than if it were not stabilized by queues and inventories—but the higher pecuniary price can save on search and disappointed, incorrect price anticipations. This higher price to the buyer is lower than the sum of the average lower fluctuating price plus search and inconvenience costs to the buyer.

Before leaving the question of price stability as an information economizing device, it is useful to try to complete the catalogue of reasons for price stability in the sense that some prices are *persistently* below or above the market-clearing level. This can be done by introducing considerations of the property rights held by the allocator of the goods, of price controls, and of transaction-enforcement costs. Attenuated property rights as prevail in nonprofit enterprises, not-for-profit institutions, or publicly owned enterprises induce prices below the market-clearing level. They do so because the higher income or wealth derivable with a higher price at a market-clearing level does not become the private property of the allocator or principal to whom it may be responsible. Transactions costs also induce price inflexibility and rationing at a zero price. If the value of the item being rationed is less than the costs of collecting a fee and enforcing the contract (as in parking space or street use) the price will be chronically too low. Or if the change in price to a market-clearing level is less valuable than the costs of enforcing that changed price, the price will lag on non-market-clearing levels. See [1, pp. 153–79] [3] [8].

II. LABOR MARKETS

Though most analyses of unemployment rely on wage conventions, restrictions, and controls to retard wage adjustments above market-clearing levels, Hicks and Hutt penetrated deeper. Hicks suggested a solution consistent with conventional exchange theory. He stated that "knowledge of opportunities is imperfect" and that the time required to obtain that knowledge leads to unemployment and a delayed effect on wages [9, pp. 45, 58].[11] It is precisely this enhanced significance that this paper seeks to develop, and which Hicks ignored when he immediately turned to different factors—unions and wage regulations, placing major blame on both for England's heavy unemployment in the 1920s and 30s.

We digress to note that Keynes in using a *quantity*, instead of a price, adjusting theory of exchange, merely *postulated* a "slow" reacting price, without showing that slow price responses were consistent with utility or wealth maximizing behavior in open, unconstrained markets. Keynes' analysis was altered in the subsequent income-expenditure models where reliance was placed on "conventional" or "noncompetitive" *wage* rates. Modern "income-expenditure" theorists assumed "institutionally" or "irrationally" inflexible wages resulting from unions, money illusions, regulations or factors allegedly idiosyncratic to labor. Keynes did not assume inflexibility for only wages. His theory rested on a more general scope of price inflexibility.[12] The present paper may in part be viewed as an attempt to "justify" Keynes' presumption about price response to disturbances in demand.

In 1939 W. H. Hutt exposed many of the fallacious interpretations of idleness and unemployment. Hutt applied the analysis suggested by Hicks but later ignored it when discussing Keynes' analysis of involuntary unemployment and policies to alleviate it [10, pp. 165–69]. This is unfortunate, because Hutt's analysis seems to be capable of explaining and accounting for a substantial portion of that unemployment.

---

[11] And he added another type—"the unemployment of the man who gives up his job in order to look for a better."

[12] For a thorough exposition and justification of these remarks on Keynes, see Leijonhufvud [14].

If we follow the lead of Hicks and Hutt and develop the implications of ''frictional'' unemployment for *both* human and *nonhuman* goods, we can perceive conditions that will imply *massive* ''frictional'' unemployment and depressions in open, unrestricted, competitive markets with rational, utility maximizing, individual behavior. And some tests of that interpretation can be suggested.[13]

Unemployment. The preceding analysis shows why an employee will not necessarily accept a pay cut to *retain* a job, even though some current wage income is better than ''none.'' An employee correctly and *sensibly* believes he can, with some search and evaluation of alternatives, get approximately his old wage at some other job; after all, that is why he was getting what he did at his current job. If looking and ''finding out'' is more costly while employed, he may have reason to choose temporary unemployment as an efficient form of ''producing'' or investing in information.

There is reason for rejecting even a ''temporary'' wage cut. A subsequently restored demand will not be immediately revealed to the employee-seller at zero cost; he will continue at the lower wage than he could get elsewhere, if only he had incurred costs to ''find out.'' Of course, employer competition would not reveal subsequent demand increases instantly; employers also have costs of getting information about alternatives. The cost of learning about all potentially available bids and offers (for employers, as well as employees, and the attributes of the goods being offered) restricts the speed of price adjustments. In sum, a refusal to cut wages to retain continu-

[13] Many labor economists have used elements of this approach in their writings. In that sense, nothing said in the preceding is new. But we are attempting to collate and assemble these elements into a general theory of pricing and exchange of goods and service in which labor is included. For example, see [11], [19], [20], [23], [24], [27], [29].

ous present employment is neither nonoptimal behavior nor adherence to a convention as to "proper" wages.[14]

Any firm experiencing a demand decrease could try to lower costs (to maintain output) by offering less to its inputs. But if providers of inputs know, or believe, they have undiminished opportunities elsewhere they will not accept the cut.[15] It seems exceedingly unlikely that *all* providers of inputs would know that all their alternatives had deteriorated (if indeed, they had) so as to induce them to accept a cut sufficient to retain their current employment. The larger the portion of the providers of inputs who do not regard their alternative discoverable opportunities as having deteriorated, the larger is the required price cut an employer must ask the complementary inputs to accept if he is to continue their employment in current jobs.[16]

[14] For an indication of the difficulties in formulating as well as solving the optimal search problem, see [15, 16, and especially 17].

[15] A seller faced with decreased demand by a buyer does not regard it as a reliable indicator of similar changes in demand by all other demanders for that service. Yet such behavior has been described as an irrational holding of "less than unity (or even zero) elasticity of price expectation." A decrease in price available from *a* buyer does not mean all other buyers have reduced their offer prices. To the extent *we* see only a part of the potential "market" at any one time, it is rational to believe that a decrease in price here does not imply all potential offers will have fallen elsewhere. Keynes, in assuming inelastic price expectations, could have been arguing that a decrease in wages from a current employer or a small set of them is not sufficient to warrant the expectation they are lower every place as well. The contrast with securities is especially striking. Insofar as the securities market is a cheaper market—that is, insofar as it reflects more cheaply a larger, more complete sample of bids and offers of the population, any fall in an observed price is more likely indicative of a decrease in other potential offers as well; the elasticity of expectations about yet-to-be discerned available prices with search should be higher. Thus there is nothing inconsistent in assuming different price expectations elasticities in different markets; in fact there is much to be gained in detecting factors that make them different. See Tobin [30], Fellner [6, pp. 141–51] for examples of failures to make the distinction.

[16] The deeper the wage cut necessary to retain the old job, the greater the incentive to embark on job information search while unemployed. The greater the degree of seniority, the greater the wage cut that could be imposed before unemployment, for

Layoffs. There remains a phenomenon that obscures the present interpretation. For example, General Motors lays off men when demand for cars drops, without any negotiations about a temporary wage cut. It is tempting to blame unions or to conclude that no wage, however low, would enable GM profitably to maintain employment, or that lower wages were impossible because of pressure from those workers who are not laid off. But suppose there were no such pressure and no union contracts. What would evolve as the "sensible" response when GM's demand fell? Employers learn that wage cuts sufficient to justify profitable maintenance of the prior rate of output and employment would be too low to keep employees, given their beliefs about alternatives. And so layoffs are announced without fruitless wage renegotiations.

If there are job-switching costs, but a man's search costs are not far greater when he is employed than unemployed, a *temporary* wage cut is more likely to be acceptable. If the *temporarily* reduced wage offer is too low to make work worthwhile, the result is a "temporary layoff" taken without an intent of changing jobs. Insofar as onset and duration of "temporary" conditions are *predictable*, the situation is a recognition of normal working hours (e.g., not working at nights or on weekends) at *predictable* intervals because the worker prefers leisure to the wages available during those hours. If the onset of the decreased demand is unpredictable (building workers), but if its probability is believed known, this is again akin to weekend rest—and the wage rate is adjusted to reflect that. Building workers are an example; "casual" labor is another. If the demand reduction persists longer than expected, the person will begin a job-information search.

---

equally high seniority elsewhere cannot be obtained by a job change. The greater threatened wage cut is fought by the requirement that lower seniority men be dropped first.

If job-information costs depend upon whether one is employed or unemployed, then unemployment can occur (with or without moving costs). If there are moving costs also, the *length* of unemployment will be longer. But *differential* information costs are necessary for the incidence of unemployment. A *common* (i.e., *un*differentiated) cost of search and job switching would only mean a greater reduction of wealth of employees, not their unemployment as a result of unexpected demand decreases.[17]

Irrelevancy of Atomistic vs. Monopolistic Market Types. Resources sold in atomistic markets (devoid of all monopolistic or "impure" competition) experience unemployment. In any market—even in a price-taker's atomistic market, free of all price "administration" or constraints—if demand falls, some sellers will be unable immediately to sell their output at the price at which others are selling, because marketing (i.e., information) is costly. Although hazardous, it is tempting to push the analysis into the foundation of pure, perfect and monopolistic markets; the idealized polar extreme, pure competition market assumes zero costs of market-information and product identification. If costs of either are significant, some sellers would sell less at a higher price to cater to buyers who deem it not worthwhile looking further for lower price sellers—given the costs of canvassing the population. To attri-

[17] Some of the preceding ideas can be summarized in terms of general economic theory by explicitly treating information as a good that is demanded and supplied. The sum of excess demands and supplies for all goods should be zero by definition. We may say that during unemployment there is an increased demand for and supply of information about market opportunities. Or we may say the market for each good is in equilibrium, but the production of market-opportunity-information has increased, leaving other production at equilibrium rates lower than would have existed had resources not been diverted to production of more market-opportunity-information. This method of formulating the structure of the analysis saves Say's Principle that the sum of excess demand equals the sum of excess supplies—always.

bute unemployment to monopolistic markets or to administered conventional wages and prices is to assume that market information costs the same amount no matter how it is produced.

Job Vacancies: Search by Employers. Information is sought by employers also. Job vacancies, with search for best employees, are the counterpart to unemployment. An employer searching (i.e., competing) for more employees knows that a higher wage will get more employees—or that it costs more to more quickly find out who will work at the same wage with the same talent. Employer search activity will increase the incidence of job changes without the employees' having experienced unemployment, because employers will seek currently employed labor and offer better wages.

Uncertainty of the employer about the quality of a potential employee induces a lower initial wage offer. The best perceived offer to a prospective employee will reflect both the applicant's costs of canvassing all employers *and* the employers' cost of learning more about the applicant. The more homogeneous the class to which the employer believes the applicant belongs—or the less the variance of the possible marginal productivity of the applicant—the closer will the applicant's discerned offers be to the maximum. He will more quickly settle on a new job.

Interproduct Shift vs. "Depression" Unemployment. The greater the rate of interproduct demand shifts, the larger will be unemployment. We could talk of interproduct demand shift unemployment and also of aggregate demand decrease (depression) unemployment, without any reference to *full* employment [10, p. 35]. We shall occasionally use the term "full" employment to admit of unemployment in the absence of *aggregate* demand shifts. In such cases interproduct demand shifts will determine the degree of unemployment that is associated with "full" employment. That source of unemployment is usually called "frictional." But if aggregate demand changes, there is a change in the degree of unemployment, whatever it be called.

Output per Unit of Input. Faced with demand decreases that are regarded as transient, employers will retain employees and equipment because there is a cost of finding new employees as replacements. (Of course, any layoff probably involves loss of some employees.) Keeping "excessive" employees on the payroll is analogous to having empty apartments to allow for economic adjustment to transient unpredictable shifts in demand. Therefore, decreases in demand for an employer's products can imply a less than equivalent reduction in employment and a resultant apparent "higher cost" per output. This is more economical (efficient) than quickly adjusting the size of the work force.

"Depression" Unemployment. It is not necessary here to explain decreases in aggregate demand. Our purpose is to concentrate on the consequences of aggregate demand decreases without attention to feedback effects of unemployment on aggregate demand. A decrease in general demand causes an increase in unemployment because more people will accept unemployment to engage in search, and each unemployed person will look longer. Wage earning opportunities will diminish in the sense that lower wages are available elsewhere. People use time to *learn* that the failure to find other equally good job options as quickly as they thought they would, reflects *diminished* alternatives in general, not unlucky search. The discerned maximum offers will be lower than if the structure of alternatives had not decreased. The lower level and slower rate of rise of best observed options is at first taken as an unlucky

string of searches, and so unemployment is extended in the expectation of "shortly" finding that elusive best option. And with each person looking longer the total number of unemployed at any one time will be larger. (Incomes fall and feedback effects occur.) Each now has the added task of revising his whole pattern of expectations. Whereas he was formerly searching for a higher clearly formulated expected wage, now he must learn that the "best" has deteriorated.

If the decrease in aggregate demand is a continuing affair (induced, we shall assume for concreteness, by a continuing fall in the quantity of money) unemployment will persist at the higher level during the continuing decrease in demand, which must be continually "discovered." The greater the rate of decrease of general demand, the greater the extent and average duration length of unemployment. Thus a *continuing* decrease in the community's stock of money is associated with a continuing decrease in general demand and with continuing unemployment of human (and nonhuman) resources. Holding general demand at its *new* level would reduce unemployment. But the costs of that mode of recovery may be greater than action designed to increase aggregate demand back to the demand beliefs that people hold.

Conversely, if the rate of increase in the quantity of money accelerates (unanticipated), the general increase in demand will increase job vacancies, increase job information dispersal activity by employers, and increase the search by employers for information about available employable resources. "Jobs are easier to get . . ." meaning the alternatives are better than they (as well as the present job) formerly were thought to be.

Changes in aggregate demand confuse the public. Each seller notices a changed demand for his current product, but he cannot tell if that is a change also in aggregate demand which affects options elsewhere. Whether he should shift to another option, as he should not if the demand change is general, or stay where he is and change price, is the question to be answered. Should an employee switch jobs upon receipt of a superior offer or should he look over the market more fully? Given interproduct fluctuations, any person who refuses unemployment search for the best alternative option can be misled into accepting another job too soon. He will, because of increasing demand, more easily find a job with higher wages than he now gets. Yet he should have held out longer, since the upward shift means he could have done better. Unemployment will be less than "optimal"—*given* the extent of *interproduct* demand shifts and of the differential costs of knowing other job potentials. In speaking of "optimal" unemployment we are not suggesting that unemployment per se is desirable. We mean that *given the fact of differential search costs and demand shifts* it pays to engage in some search more economically while not employed. The opportunity to search while not employed is better than the lack of an opportunity to move to unemployment as a more efficient means of search. Given interproduct demand shifts, without unemployment the extent to which resources are in their most valuable uses is reduced, because the public is fooled into believing they have found the best available jobs, when in fact they have failed to invest in enough search to find "best" available jobs.

One cautionary note: Constant per capita aggregate demand is consistent with falling prices of final products. Falling consumer good prices in this case reflect lower costs of production, not reduced profitability of production. Resource prices will not fall. If there is an *un*anticipated inflation trend, the increased (unanticipated) aggregate demand (per capita) will reduce unemployment and maintain it at a lower level. If inflation is correctly anticipated, the change of unemployment implied for any given rate of change of aggregate demand will be lower than for unanticipated inflation, and it will be independent of the anticipated rate.

Lag of What Behind What? The analysis can be expressed more conventionally, but *not* as follows: "A reduction in demand involves a lag of wage rate decreases behind prices—which *is* a rise in real or relative wage rates. This rise implies lower employment because of diminishing marginal returns to labor inputs." That is not contained in the present analysis; wage rates and all other prices can fall at the *same* rate. But the lag that does occur is a lag of the *discernment* of the best available prices behind the new, as yet undiscerned, best (i.e., the new, unascertained lower *equilibrium*) prices which *when* discovered would restore employment. In Walrasian terms, the auctioneer does not instantaneously reveal the new equilibrium price vector. (Even in an actual auction, the time for bidders to reveal the best price is not trivial.) The "lag" is the *time for discovery*. The lag terminology tends to confuse a lag of wages behind other factor or product prices with the "lag" of discernment of the best opportunities behind the (undiscerned) equilibrating price—a price that is not freely or instantly revealed to the world. It follows that a general economywide demand decrease does not imply a correlation between real wage rates and depressions (and recoveries). Wage rates can fall as fast as other prices; *that* lag is not necessary for unemployment.[18]

[18] An intriguing, intellectual historical curiosum may be explainable by this theory, as has been brought to my attention by Axel Leijonhufvud. Keynes' powerful, but elliptical, definition of involuntary unemployment has been left in limbo. He said: men were involuntarily employed if,

> . . . in the event of a small rise in the price of wage-goods relative to the money-wage,

Reduced employment of human *and nonhuman resources* when coupled with the conventional production function implies nothing about real output per employed input. Suppose that resources when faced with a demand decrease in present jobs *immediately* accepted the first available job—forgoing search for a better job. Job allocations would be "inefficient." Better allocations could be discerned with search, at a cost. The destruction of a former equilibrium is not followed by a costless immediate new equilibrium. But the faster it is sought the greater the costs. There is some optimal rate. Insofar as re-

---

> both the aggregate supply of labor willing to work for the current money wage and the aggregate demand for it at that wage would be greater than the existing volume of employment [11, p. 15].

To see the power and meaning of this definition (not *cause*) of unemployment, consider the following question. Why would a cut in money wages provoke a different response than *if* the price level rose relative to wages—when both would amount to the same change in relative prices, but differ only in the money price level? Almost everyone thought Keynes presumed a money-wage illusion. However, an answer more respectful of Keynes is available. The price-level rise conveys *different information:* money wages everywhere have fallen relative to prices. On the other hand, a cut in one's own money wage does not imply options elsewhere have fallen. A cut only in one's present job is revealed. The money versus real wage distinction is not the relevant comparison; the wage in the present job versus the wage in all other jobs is the relevant comparison. This rationalizes Keynes' *definition* of involuntary unemployment in terms of price-level changes. If wages were cut everywhere else, and *if* employees knew it, they would not choose unemployment—but they would if they believed wages were cut just in their current job. When one employer cuts wages, this does not signify cuts elsewhere. His employees rightly think wages are not reduced elsewhere. On the other hand, with a rise in the price level, employees have less reason to think their current real wages are lower than they are elsewhere. So they do not immediately refuse a lower real wage induced by a higher price level, whereas they would refuse an equal money wage cut in their present job. It is the revelation of information about prospects elsewhere that makes the difference. And this is perfectly consistent with Keynes' definition of unemployment, and it is also consistent with his entire theory of market adjustment processes [12], since he believed wages lagged behind nonwage prices—an unproved and probably false belief [13]. Without that belief a general price-level rise is indeed general; it includes wages and as such there is no reason to believe a price-level rise is equivalent in real terms to a money-wage cut in a particular job.

sources take interim jobs, while "inefficiently" search for better jobs, or failing to search, the "total" output vector will be smaller. In other words there is an optimal rate of unemployment *given* the rate of demand changes and *given* the differential costs of search. Very low unemployment resulting from inflationary forces can be socially inefficient, because resources mistakenly accept new jobs with too little search for better ones.

III. POTENTIAL TESTS OF THE THEORY

Empirical tests of the theory can be sought by identifying characteristics of resources that increase the length and frequency of unemployment. Or situations in which the parameters of search conditions have changed can be compared to see if the implied changes in unemployment are observed. Since the class of alternative theories is open-ended, we shall simply indicate some implications of the present theory, letting the reader conjecture whether any alternative theory contains so broad a class of phenomena.

A discriminatory test of the theory lies not in its implication of "cyclical" labor unemployment fluctuations but in its implication of unemployment, price stability, and queueing for *all* types of resources—as suggested in the preceding pages.

One aggregative unemployment feature that is implied by this analysis is a positive correlation between extent of recovery in employment from a depression with the extent of the preceding decline; a *zero* correlation is implied between the magnitude of an expansion with the subsequent decline. Absence of tendencies to restore employment would imply no correlation between either pair of movements. There is in fact a positive correlation of magnitude of rises with the preceding decrease, and none between contractions and preceding rises [8].

Resources with *less differentiated* costs (while employed or unemployed) of obtaining or dispersing information will have lower incidence, as well as shorter periods, of unemployment. Since an employer knows more about his own employees than those of other employers, the probability of job changes (in tasks and grades) should be greater within a firm than among firms—especially in the upward direction. But the excess probability should decrease in the higher paid tasks, since extra search is more economic the higher the marginal product of an employee's position.

Readily (i.e., cheaply) recognizable, divisible (time, place, etc.), portable (more quickly moveable at a given cost), durable (more long-lived so as to reduce contracting costs) resources, should display shorter length of unemployment.[19] What characteristics of goods yield low costs of information? Market demands and offers of homogeneous goods ("easily and cheaply recognized") should be cheaper to survey. Tract houses built by one builder should be easier to sell or rent than custom-built houses. "Easier" to sell or buy means that for given cost of search the realized price is closer (more quickly) to the best possible price obtainable (i.e., to the price that would have resulted if every potential buyer or seller had been canvassed and if each had full information about the product). An observable magnitude correlated with search costs should be the bid-ask spread, or markup, between the buying and selling price [5]. Thus inventories should be a smaller ratio to sales for low than for high information cost items. Frequent,

[19] The preceding sentence reminds us of the attributes of money, and who can doubt that money has a very low "unemployment" rate? The suggestive analogy is in fact precisely to the point.

repeated purchases by buyers should be correlated with knowledge about the item and alternative sources of purchases so that the bid-ask spread is lower. Goods sold in a formal market should have lower price spreads, reflecting the lower cost of information provided by formal markets. For example, over-the-counter stocks should have a larger bid-ask spread than stocks on more organized markets [5]. New goods, we conjecture, involve higher information dispersal costs and hence inventories relative to sales and wider price spreads [4].

Apartments built in standard designs will have lower vacancy rates because their characteristics are more cheaply understood, being already commonly known. At one time in Southern California, homes with swimming pools were so unusual as to fall in the higher information cost category. Brokers' fees should therefore be larger in percentage terms.

Corporation stocks and bonds can be categorized by extent of knowledge by the public about the companies. If only a few people are informed, and unless they are more easily discovered, the market will be "thin," implying longer search periods or larger bid-ask spreads. The fewness of buyers or sellers is not per se a source of thinness or high information costs. Rather it is the higher cost of finding those few potential buyers among the larger population. Thus new "unseasoned" stocks and bonds should be markedly different in the bid-ask spread from older established stocks and bonds [5].

Price stability with transient demand fluctuations is provided in the commodity and stock exchanges by floor traders. They trade on the "uptick and downtick" out of personal inventories, so as to reduce the variance of prices in response to what these traders regard as transient, random fluctuations in revealed market demands and supplies [31].

The highest and the lowest priced variant of any class of

goods will have a longer inventory period and larger retail-wholesale price spread than the typical or modal variant. We assume the extremes are less familiar types; information acquisition and disbursing costs will be larger. Special purpose machinc tools should have a longer unemployment period than general purpose widely used types of equipment. Their inventory to sales ratio should be larger.

Standard types of used automobiles should have a shorter inventory interval (and lower ratio of inventory to sales) than do unusual used cars because information about the standard type car is more common among potential buyers.

The larger the dispersion of potential bid prices among buyers, the greater the gross gain from continued search. The *absolute* (not relative) increment of discerned maximum price is larger if the dispersion is larger. Assuming that more unusual items (like paintings or works of art) are subject to a larger variance in valuation by the population, we expect a longer search period or larger markup.

The fewer the major employers in any community the shorter will be the length and the lower will be the incidence of unemployment. Information about jobs is more readily available if there are fewer employers to search and to be told of one's talents. Wages should be more quickly adjusted in areas with only one employer. It has been suggested that the Negro in the South is faced with a fewer number of employers in the small towns than in the North and that he would therefore spend less time in job search in the South.[20]

If the highly skilled worker has a higher ratio of wages per hour to the value of self-generated income from extended job information search, then the highly paid laborer will resort

[20] Suggested by H. Gregg Lewis.

more to employment agencies to economize on his relatively valuable search time. And he will use private more than public employment agencies, because private agencies, by being able to charge higher fees for higher salaried employees, have an incentive to devote more resources to placement of such people than do public agencies. Public agencies are closer competitors of private agencies for lower wage job applicants. (This does not mean low wage workers are not served by private agencies.) Looking at the employment problem from the point of view of the buyer or employer, one implication is that job vacancies for the expensive, heterogeneous executive will be longer-lived than for lower productivity and standard types of laborers. Some evidence of this should be revealed by employment agency fees which, according to the present analysis, should be larger than for lower paying jobs.

Consider an employer looking for a manager and for a janitor. The value of a manager's services are higher than a janitor's, so a dollar spent for information about managers has a larger expected net marginal product. Because a better measure of the probability of the marginal product of high marginal product employees is worth more than a better measure of the probability of a lower marginal product employee, the employer will find it profitable to incur greater costs to get information about potential managers than for janitors. If skin color, eye shape, or sex is cheaply observable and believed to be correlated with quality or performance, the physical traits provide cheap (though incomplete) information about the quality of the person. For higher salaried jobs an extra dollar of costs for information about the potential employee is more likely to be profitable. The extra information will supplement the skin, eye, or sex indicator of quality. As a result, for higher paying jobs, the cheap information will be supplemented by other information. "Discrimination" solely according to only eye shape, sex, skin color, and ethnic group is less profitable and hence less probable in higher paying jobs.[21]

If the evidence were to conform to all the foregoing implications, could this interpretation be consistent with the events of 1929–39? There is no doubt that aggregate demand decreased rapidly from 1929–32. Money stocks fell by about fifteen percent in 1939, 1931 and 1932. That does imply decreasing aggregate demand and abnormal unemployment. But it is the prolonged high unemployment after 1932 and the slow recovery, when aggregate demand stopped decreasing that appears inconsistent with the theory. After 1932 national income and money stocks were increasing and it is hard to believe that the rate of unemployment should not have decreased more rapidly. Even if the money stock had not increased, the convergence toward the full equilibrium price vector should have progressed more rapidly, if one is allowed to make *ad hominem* conjectures as to the expected rate of recovery.[22]

---

[21] The example of this paragraph was developed by A. De Vany. The same principle applies to short- versus long-term employees. This test is not relevant for the *differentiated* (according to employed or unemployed) search cost, but instead is derived from presence of search costs as such. One index of discrimination is the extent to which similar types of people work in clusters. Janitors are more likely to be mostly of the same types, but managers are more likely to be of a mixed group. Discrimination by cheaply observed traits should be less frequent for managers. My impression is that, in fact, for lower paying jobs there is greater concordance or uniformity of physical types than in higher paying jobs.

[22] There is one restraining factor in the unrestored quantity of money. If the quantity of money is not increased, the recovery of output and employment will imply still lower "full employment" equilibrium prices. The increased real output with constant stock of money requires still lower prices. This continuing deflationary pressure on prices would retard the return of production and employment to "full-use" levels. A sufficient increase in money stocks would have avoided the necessity of a fall in prices and wages and thereby would have speeded the rate of

One thing that can save the proposed interpretation despite the prolonged unemployment is the imposition of arbitrary restrictions on permissible prices. Another factor that would help to explain the prolonged unemployment without rejecting the proposed interpretation is a sequential injection of depressing policy actions.

In other words a prolonged unemployment—without decreasing aggregate demand—would be consistent with the present interpretation of price behavior and unemployment if actual permissible (not the equilibrium) wages or prices were arbitrarily or exogenously increased. Events that support this interpretation have been chronicled by Roose [25, pp. 45–57] and Friedman [7, pp. 493–99]. A *sequence* of measures by the government (NIRA, Guffey Coal Act, agricultural price support, and the Labor Relations Act, minimum wages) arbitrarily and successively raised prices and wages over the period—not once and for all in 1932. In the absence of these autonomous factors pushing up permissible (though not the equilibrating) wages and prices, 1933–37 would have shown greater employment and output. Roose [25, pp. 45–57] attributes the low recovery to restrictive policies such as higher wages of NIRA codes, National Labor Relations Act, minimum wage enactments, imposition of social security taxes, and unemployment and old age security taxes on employment. In the same interval other policies involving new regulatory agencies are believed to have temporarily restrained capital goods production. Securities and exchange acts, separation of investment from commercial banking, public utility holding com-

---

resource reallocation and hence the restoration of employment and output, by eliminating the cost of discerning the continuing *reduction* of potentially available prices and wages in all other opportunities. This was, of course, Keynes' advocated policy.

pany restrictions, the encouragement of labor strikes, and a general attack on businessmen all contributed to lower capital goods equilibrating price—whatever their merits. To these factors add the 1937 monetary legal reserve debacle. If all of these factors had occurred once and for all in, say, 1932, the subsequent recovery rate should have been more rapid. But they in fact did occur in sequence over several years. If these considerations are accepted, the delayed recovery until 1941 in the face of nondecreasing aggregate demand is consistent with the differential-cost-of-information-about-best-available-job-opportunities theory of unemployment.

References

1. A. A. Alchian, and W. R. Allen. *Exchange and Production; Theory in Use*. Belmont, 1968.
2. A. A. Alchian and R. A. Kessel. "Competition, Monopoly, and the Pursuit of Pecuniary Gain," *Aspects of Labor Economics*. A Conference of the Universities—National Bureau Committee for Economic Research. New Jersey, 1962, 156–83.
3. K. J. Arrow, and W. M. Capron. "Dynamic Shortages and Price Rises: The Engineer Scientist Case," *Quart. Jour. Econ.* 73 (May 1959): 292–308.
4. H. Demsetz. "Exchange and Enforcement of Property Rights, *Jour. Law Econ*. 7 (October 1964): 11–26.
5. H. Demsetz. "The Cost of Transacting," *Quart. Jour. Econ.* 82 (February 1968): 33–53.
6. W. Fellner. *Monetary Policies and Full Employment*. Berkeley, 1946.
7. M. Friedman. *A Monetary History of the United States, 1867–1960*. Princeton, 1964.

8. M. Friedman. "The Monetary Studies of the National Bureau," *The National Bureau Enters Its Forty-Fifth Year, Forty-Fourth Annual Report*. Washington, 1964, 14–18.
9. J. R. Hicks. *The Theory of Wages*, 2d ed. London, 1963.
10. W. H. Hutt. *The Theory of Idle Resources*. London, 1939.
11. H. Kasper. "The Asking Price of Labor and the Duration of Unemployment," *Rev. Econ. Stat.* 49 (May 1967): 165–72.
12. R. A. Kessel, and A. A. Alchian. "The Meaning and Validity of the Inflation-Induced Lag of Wages Behind Prices," *Amer. Econ. Rev.* 50 (March 1960): 43–66.
13. J. M. Keynes. *The General Theory of Employment, Interest and Money*. London, 1936.
14. A. Leijonhufvud. *The Economics of Keynes and Keynesian Economics*. Oxford, 1968.
15. J. MacQueen, and R. G. Miller, Jr. "Optimal Persistence Policies," *Oper. Res. Jour.* 16 (March–April 1968): 362–80.
16. J. J. McCall. "The Economics of Information and Optimal Stopping Rules," *Jour. Bus.* 38 (July 1965): 300–17.
17. J. J. McCall. "Economics of Information and Job Search," RM-5745-OEO. Santa Monica, 1968.
18. H. L. Miller. "Liquidity and Transaction Costs," *Southern Econ. Jour.* 32 (July 1965): 43–48.
19. A. C. Pigou. *Lapses from Full Employment*. London, 1945.
20. R. V. Rao. "Employment Information and Manpower Utilization," *Manpower Jour.* 1 (July–September 1965): 7–15.
21. A. Rees. "Wage Determination and Involuntary Unemployment," *Jour. Pol. Econ.* 59 (April 1951): 143–44.

22. A. Rees. "Information Networks and Labor Markets," *Am. Econ. Rev., Supplement* 56 (May 1966): 559–66.
23. L. Reynolds. *Labor Economics and Labor Relations*, 4th ed. New Jersey, 1964.
24. A. M. Roose. "Do We Have a New Industrial Feudalism?" *Am. Econ. Rev.* 48 (December 1958): 903–20.
25. K. D. Roose. *The Economics of Recession and Revival*. New Haven, 1954.
26. T. L. Saaty, *Elements of Queueing Theory*. New York, 1961.
27. H. L. Sheppard, and H. A. Belitsky. *The Job Hunt: Job Seeking Behavior of Unemployed Workers in a Local Economy*. Kalamazoo, 1965.
28. G. J. Stigler. "Information in the Labor Market," *Jour. Pol. Econ., Supplement* 70 (October 1962): 94–105.
29. V. Stoikov. "Some Determinants of the Level of Frictional Employment: A Comparative Study," *Intl. Lab. Rev.* 93 (May 1966): 530–49.
30. J. Tobin. "Liquidity Preference as Behavior Towards Risk," *Rev. Econ. Stud.* 25 (October 1957): 65–86.
31. H. J. Working. "Test of a Theory Concerning Floor Trading on Commodity Exchanges," unpublished.

3

Production, Information Costs and Economic Organization

The mark of a capitalistic society is that resources are owned and allocated by such nongovernmental organizations as firms, households, and markets. Resource owners increase productivity through cooperative specialization and this leads to the demand for economic organizations which facilitate cooperation. When a lumber mill employs a cabinetmaker, cooperation between specialists is achieved within a firm, and when a cabinetmaker purchases wood from a lumberman, the cooperation takes place across markets (or between firms). Two important problems face a theory of economic organization—to explain the conditions that determine whether the gains from specialization and cooperative production can better be obtained within an organization like the firm, or across markets, and to explain the structure of the organization.

It is common to see the firm characterized by the power to settle issues by fiat, by authority, or by disciplinary action superior to that available in the conventional market. This is

This article was coauthored by Harold Demsetz. Acknowledgment is made for financial aid from the E. Lilly Endowment, Inc., grant to UCLA for research in the behavioral effects of property rights.

delusion. The firm does not own all its inputs. It has no power of fiat, no authority, no disciplinary action any different in the slightest degree from ordinary market contracting between any two people. I can "punish" you only by withholding future business or by seeking redress in the courts for any failure to honor our exchange agreement. That is exactly all that any employer can do. He can fire or sue, just as I can fire my grocer by stopping purchases from him or sue him for delivering faulty products. What then is the content of the presumed power to manage and assign workers to various tasks? Exactly the same as one little consumer's power to manage and assign his grocer to various tasks. The single consumer can assign his grocer to the task of obtaining whatever the customer can induce the grocer to provide at a price acceptable to both parties. That is precisely all that an employer can do to an employee. To speak of managing, directing, or assigning workers to various tasks is a deceptive way of noting that the employer continually is involved in renegotiation of contracts on terms that must be acceptable to both parties. Telling an employee to type this letter rather than to file that document is like my telling a grocer to sell me this brand of tuna rather than that brand of bread. I have no contract to continue to purchase from the grocer and neither the employer nor the employee is bound by any contractual obligations to continue their relationship. Long-term contracts between employer and employee are not the essence of the organization we call a firm. My grocer can count on my returning day after day and purchasing his services and goods even with the prices not always marked on the goods—because I know what they are—and he adapts his activity to conform to my directions to him as to what I want each day . . . he is not my employee.

Wherein then is the relationship between a grocer and his

employee different from that between a grocer and his customers? It is in a *team* use of inputs and a centralized position of some party in the contractual arrangements of *all* other inputs. It is the *centralized contractual agent in a team productive process*—not some superior authoritarian directive or disciplinary power. Exactly what is a team process and why does it induce the contractual form, called the firm? These problems motivate the inquiry of this paper.

I. THE METERING PROBLEM

The economic organization through which input owners cooperate will make better use of their comparative advantages to the extent that it facilitates the payment of rewards in accord with productivity. If rewards were random, and without regard to productive effort, no incentive to productive effort would be provided by the organization; and if rewards were negatively correlated with productivity the organization would be subject to sabotage. Two key demands are placed on an economic organization—metering input productivity and metering rewards.[1]

Metering problems sometimes can be resolved well through the exchange of products across competitive markets, because in many situations markets yield a high correlation between rewards and productivity. If a farmer increases his output of wheat by ten percent at the prevailing market price, his receipts also increase by ten percent. This method of organizing economic activity meters the *output directly*, reveals the marginal product and apportions the *rewards* to resource owners in

[1] Meter means to measure and also to apportion. One can meter (measure) output and one can also meter (control) the output. We use the word to denote both; the context should indicate which.

accord with that direct measurement of their outputs. The success of this decentralized, market exchange in promoting productive specialization requires that changes in market rewards fall on those responsible for changes in *output*.[2]

The classic relationship in economics that runs from marginal productivity to the distribution of income implicitly *assumes* the existence of an organization, be it the market or the firm, that allocates rewards to resources in accord with their productivity. The problem of economic organization, the economical means of metering productivity and rewards, is not confronted directly in the classical analysis of production

[2] A producer's wealth would be reduced by the present capitalized value of the future income lost by loss of reputation. Reputation, i.e., credibility, is an asset, which is another way of saying that reliable information about expected performance is both a costly and a valuable good. For acts of God that interfere with contract performance, both parties have incentives to reach a settlement akin to that which would have been reached if such events had been covered by specific contingency clauses. The reason, again, is that a reputation for "honest" dealings—i.e., for actions similar to those that would probably have been reached had the contract provided this contingency—is wealth.

Almost every contract is open-ended in that many contingencies are uncovered. For example, if a fire delays production of a promised product by *A* to *B*, and if *B* contends that *A* has not fulfilled the contract, how is the dispute settled and what recompense, if any, does *A* grant to *B*? A person uninitiated in such questions may be surprised by the extent to which contracts permit either party to escape performance or to nullify the contract. In fact, it is hard to imagine any contract, which, when taken solely in terms of its stipulations, could not be evaded by one of the parties. Yet that is the ruling, viable type of contract. Why? Undoubtedly the best discussion that we have seen on this question is by Stewart Macaulay.

There are means not only of detecting or preventing cheating, but also for deciding how to allocate the losses or gains of unpredictable events or quality of items exchanged. Sales contracts contain warranties, guarantees, collateral, return privileges and penalty clauses for specific nonperformance. These are means of assignment of *risks* of losses of cheating. A lower price without warranty—an "as is" purchase—places more of the risk on the buyer while the seller buys insurance against losses of his "cheating." On the other hand, a warranty or return privilege or service contract places more risk on the seller with insurance being bought by the buyer.

and distribution. Instead, that analysis tends to assume sufficiently economic—or zero cost—means, as if productivity automatically created its reward. We conjecture the direction of causation is the reverse—the specific system of rewarding which is relied upon stimulates a particular productivity response. If the economic organization meters poorly, with rewards and productivity only loosely correlated, then productivity will be smaller; but if the economic organization meters well productivity will be greater. What makes metering difficult and hence induces means of economizing on metering costs?

II. TEAM PRODUCTION

Two men jointly lift heavy cargo into trucks. Solely by observing the total weight loaded per day, it is impossible to determine each person's marginal productivity. With team production it is difficult, solely by observing total output, to either define or determine *each* individual's contribution to this output of the cooperating inputs. The output is yielded by a team, by definition, and it is not a *sum* of separable outputs of each of its members. Team production of Z involves at least two inputs, X_i and X_j, with $\partial^2 Z/\partial X_i \partial X_j \neq 0$.[3] The production function is *not* separable into two functions each involving only inputs X_i or only inputs X_j. Consequently there is no *sum* of Z of two separable functions to treat as the Z of the team production function. (An example of a *separable* case is $Z = aX_i^2 + bX_j^2$ which is separable into $Z_i = aX_i^2$ and $Z_j = bX_j^2$, and $Z = Z_i + Z_j$. This is not team production.) There exist pro-

[3] The function is separable into additive functions if the cross partial derivative is zero, i.e., if $\partial^2 Z/\partial X_i \partial X_j = 0$.

duction techniques in which the Z obtained is greater than if X_i and X_j had produced separable Z. Team production will be used if it yields an output enough larger than the sum of separable production of Z to cover the costs of organizing and disciplining team members—the topics of this paper.[4]

Usual explanations of the gains from cooperative behavior rely on exchange and production in accord with the comparative advantage specialization principle with separable additive production. However, as suggested above there is a source of gain from cooperative activity involving working as a *team*, wherein individual cooperating inputs do not yield identifiable, separate products which can be *summed* to measure the total output. For this cooperative productive activity, here called ''team'' production, measuring *marginal* productivity and making payments in accord therewith is more expensive by an order of magnitude than for separable production functions.

Team production, to repeat, is production in which (1) several types of resources are used and (2) the product is not a sum of separable outputs of each cooperating resource. An additional factor creates a team organization problem—(3) not all resources used in team production belong to one person.

We do not inquire into why all the jointly used resources are not owned by one person, but instead into the types of organization, contracts, and informational and payment procedures used among owners of teamed inputs. With respect to the one-owner case, perhaps it is sufficient merely to note that (a) slavery is prohibited, (b) one might assume risk aversion as a reason for one person's not borrowing enough to purchase all

[4] With sufficient generality of notation and conception this team production function could be formulated as a case of the generalized production function interpretation given by our colleague, E. A. Thompson.

the assets or sources of services rather than renting them, and (c) the purchase-resale spread may be so large that costs of short-term ownership exceed rental costs. Our problem is viewed basically as one of organization among different people, not of the physical goods or services, however much there must be selection and choice of combination of the latter.

How can the members of a team be rewarded and induced to work efficiently? In team production, marginal products of cooperative team members are not so directly and separably (i.e., cheaply) observable. What a team offers to the market can be taken as the marginal product of the team but not of the team members. The costs of metering or ascertaining the marginal products of the team's members are what call forth new organizations and procedures. Clues to each input's productivity can be secured by observing behavior of individual inputs. When lifting cargo into the truck, how rapidly does a man move to the next piece to be loaded, how many cigarette breaks does he take, does the item being lifted tilt downward toward his side?

If detecting such behavior were costless, neither party would have an incentive to shirk, because neither could impose the cost of his shirking on the other (if their cooperation was agreed to voluntarily). But since costs must be incurred to monitor each other, each input owner will have more incentive to shirk when he works as part of a team, than if his performance could be monitored easily or if he did not work as a team. If there is a net increase in productivity available by team production, net of the metering cost associated with disciplining the team, then team production will be relied upon rather than a multitude of bilateral exchange of separable individual outputs.

Both leisure and higher income enter a person's utility function.[5] Hence, each person should adjust his work and realized reward so as to equate the marginal rate of substitution between leisure and production of real output to his marginal rate of substitution in consumption. That is, he would adjust his rate of work to bring his demand prices of leisure and output to equality with their true costs. However, with detection, policing, monitoring, measuring, or metering costs, each person will be induced to take more leisure, because the effect of relaxing on *his realized* (reward) rate of substitution between output and leisure will be less than the effect on the *true* rate of substitution. His realized cost of leisure will fall more than the true cost of leisure, so he ''buys'' more leisure (i.e., more nonpecuniary reward).

If his relaxation cannot be detected perfectly at zero cost, part of its effects will be borne by others in the team, thus making *his* realized cost of relaxation less than the true total cost to the team. The difficulty of detecting such actions permits the private costs of his actions to be less than their full costs. Since each person responds to his private realizable rate of substitution (in production) rather than the true total (i.e., social) rate, and so long as there are costs for other people to detect his shift toward relaxation, it will not pay (them) to force him to readjust completely by making him realize the true cost. Only enough efforts will be made to equate the marginal gains of detection activity with the marginal costs of detection; and that implies a lower rate of productive effort and more shirking than in a costless monitoring, or measuring, world.

In a university, the faculty use office telephones, paper, and mail for personal uses beyond strict university productivity.

---

[5] More precisely, ''if anything other than pecuniary income enters his utility function.'' Leisure stands for all nonpecuniary income for simplicity of exposition.

The university administrators could stop such practices by identifying *the* responsible person in each case, but they can do so only at higher costs than administrators are willing to incur. The extra costs of identifying each party (rather than merely identifying the presence of such activity) would exceed the savings from diminished faculty "turpitudinal peccadilloes." So the faculty is allowed some degree of "privileges, perquisites, or fringe benefits." And the total of the pecuniary wages paid is lower because of this irreducible (at acceptable costs) degree of amenity-seizing activity. Pay is lower in pecuniary terms and higher in leisure, conveniences, and ease of work. But still every person would prefer to see detection made more effective (if it were somehow possible to monitor costlessly) so that he, as part of the now more effectively producing team, could thereby realize a higher pecuniary pay and less leisure. If everyone could, at zero cost, have his reward-realized rate brought to the true production possibility real rate, all could achieve a more preferred position. But detection of the responsible parties is costly; that cost acts like a tax on work rewards.[6] Viable shirking is the result.

What forms of organizing team production will lower the cost of detecting "performance" (i.e., marginal productivity) and bring personally realized rates of substitution closer to true rates of substitution? Market competition, in principle, could monitor some team production. (It already *organizes* teams.) Input owners who are not team members can offer, in return

[6] Do not assume that the sole result of the cost of detecting shirking is one form of payment (more leisure and less take home money). With several members of the team, each has an incentive to cheat against each other by engaging in more than the average amount of such leisure if the employer can not tell at zero cost which employee is taking more than average. As a result the total productivity of the team is lowered. Shirking detection costs thus change the form of payment and also result in lower total rewards. Because the cross partial derivatives are positive, shirking reduces other people's marginal products.

for a smaller share of the team's rewards, to replace excessively (i.e., overpaid) shirking members. Market competition among potential team members would determine team membership and individual rewards. There would be no team leader, manager, organizer, owner, or employer. For such decentralized organizational control to work, outsiders, possibly after observing each team's total output, can speculate about their capabilities as team members and, by a market competitive process, revised teams with greater productive ability will be formed and sustained. Incumbent members will be constrained by threats of replacement by outsiders offering services for lower reward shares or offering greater rewards to the other members of the team. Any team member who shirked in the expectation that the reduced output effect would not be attributed to him will be displaced if his activity is detected. Teams of productive inputs, like business units, would evolve in apparent spontaneity in the market—without any central organizing agent, team manager, or boss.

But completely effective control cannot be expected from individualized market competition for two reasons. First, for this competition to be completely effective, new challengers for team membership must know where, and to what extent, shirking is a serious problem, i.e., know they can increase net output as compared with the inputs they replace. To the extent that this is true it is probably possible for existing fellow team members to recognize the shirking. But, by definition, the detection of shirking by observing team output is costly for team production. Second, assume the presence of detection costs, and assume that in order to secure a place on the team a new input owner must accept a smaller share of rewards (or a promise to produce more). Then his incentive to shirk would still be at least as great as the incentives of the inputs replaced, because he still bears less than the entire reduction in team output for which he is responsible.

III. THE CLASSICAL FIRM

One method of reducing shirking is for someone to specialize as a monitor to check the input performance of team members.[7] But who will monitor the monitor? One constraint on the monitor is the aforesaid market competition offered by other monitors, but for reasons already given, that is not perfectly effective. Another constraint can be imposed on the monitor: give him title to the net earnings of the team, net of payments to other inputs. If owners of cooperating inputs agree with the monitor that he is to receive any residual product above prescribed amounts (hopefully, the marginal value products of the other inputs), the monitor will have an added incentive not to shirk as a monitor. Specialization in monitoring plus reliance on a residual claimant status will reduce shirking; but additional links are needed to forge the firm of classical economic theory. How will the residual claimant monitor the other inputs?

We use the term monitor to connote several activities in addition to its disciplinary connotation. It connotes measuring output performance, apportioning rewards, observing the

---

[7] What is meant by performance? Input energy, initiative, work attitude, perspiration, rate of exhaustion? Or output? It is the latter that is sought—the *effect* or output. But performance is nicely ambiguous because it suggests both input and output. It is *nicely* ambiguous because as we shall see, sometimes by inspecting a team member's input activity we can better judge his output effect, perhaps not with complete accuracy but better than by watching the output of the *team*. It is not always the case that watching input activity is the only or best means of detecting, measuring or monitoring output effects of each team member, but in some cases it is a useful way. For the moment the word performance glosses over these aspects and facilitates concentration on other issues.

input behavior of inputs as means of detecting or estimating their marginal productivity and giving assignments or instructions in what to do and how to do it. (It also includes, as we shall show later, authority to terminate or revise contracts.) Perhaps the contrast between a football coach and team captain is helpful. The coach selects strategies and tactics and sends in instructions about what plays to utilize. The captain is essentially an observer and reporter of the performance at close hand of the members. The latter is an inspector-steward and the former a supervisor manager. For the present all these activities are included in the rubric "monitoring." All these tasks are, in principle, negotiable across markets, but we are presuming that such market measurement of marginal productivities and job reassignments are not so cheaply performed for team production. And in particular our analysis suggests that it is not so much the costs of spontaneously negotiating contracts in the markets among groups for team production as it is the detection of the performance of individual members of the team that calls for the organization noted here.

The specialist *who receives the residual rewards* will be the monitor of the members of the team (i.e., will manage the use of cooperative inputs). The monitor earns his residual through the reduction in shirking that he brings about, not only by the prices that he agrees to pay the owners of the inputs, but also by observing and directing the actions or uses of these inputs. *Managing or examining the ways to which inputs are used in team production is a method of metering the marginal productivity of individual inputs to the team's output.*

To discipline team members and reduce shirking, the residual claimant must have power to revise the contract terms and incentives of *individual* members without having to terminate or alter every other input's contract. Hence, team members who seek to increase their productivity will assign to the monitor not only the residual claimant right but also the right to alter individual membership and performance on the team. Each team member, of course, can terminate his own membership (i.e., quit the team), but only the monitor may unilaterally terminate the membership of any of the other members without necessarily terminating the team itself or his association with the team; and he alone can expand or reduce membership, alter the mix of membership, or sell the right to be the residual claimant-monitor of the team. It is this entire bundle of rights: (1) to be a residual claimant; (2) to observe input behavior; (3) to be the central party common to all contracts with inputs; (4) to alter the membership of the team; and (5) to sell these rights, that defines the *ownership* (or the employer) of the *classical* (capitalist, free-enterprise) firm. The coalescing of these rights has arisen, our analysis asserts, because it resolves the shirking-information problem of team production better than does the noncentralized contractual arrangement.

The relationship of each team member to the *owner* of the firm (i.e., the party common to all input contracts *and* the residual claimant) is simply a "quid pro quo" contract. Each makes a purchase and sale. The employee "orders" the owner of the team to pay him money in the same sense that the employer directs the team member to perform certain acts. The employee can terminate the contract as readily as can the employer, and long-term contracts, therefore, are not an essential attribute of the firm. Nor are "authoritarian," "dictational," or "fiat" attributes relevant to the conception of the firm or its efficiency.

In summary, two necessary conditions exist for the emergence of the firm on the prior assumption that more than pecuniary wealth enters utility functions: (1) It is possible to increase productivity through team-oriented production, a production technique for which it is costly to directly measure the marginal outputs of the cooperating inputs. This makes it more difficult to restrict shirking through simple market exchange between cooperating inputs. (2) It is economical to estimate marginal productivity by observing or specifying input behavior. The simultaneous occurrence of both these preconditions leads to the contractual organization of inputs, known as the *classical capitalist firms* with (a) joint input production, (b) several input owners, (c) one party who is common to all the contracts of the joint inputs, (d) who has rights to renegotiate any input's contract independently of contracts with other input owners, (e) who holds the residual claim, and (f) who has the right to sell his central contractual residual status.[8]

Other Theories of the Firm

At this juncture, as an aside, we briefly place this theory of the firm in the contexts of those offered by Ronald Coase and Frank Knight.[9] Our view of the firm is not necessarily inconsistent with Coase's; we attempt to go further and identify refutable implications. Coase's penetrating insight is to make more of the fact that markets do not operate costlessly, and he relies on the cost of using markets to *form* contracts as his basic explanation for the existence of firms. We do not disagree with the proposition that, *ceteris paribus*, the higher is the cost of transacting across markets the greater will be the comparative advantage of organizing resources within the firm; it is a difficult proposition to disagree with or to refute.

[8] Removal of (b) converts a capitalist proprietary firm to a socialist firm.

[9] Recognition must also be given to the seminal inquiries by Morris Silver and Richard Auster, and by H. B. Malmgren.

We could with equal ease subscribe to a theory of the firm based on the cost of managing, for surely it is true that, *ceteris paribus*, the lower is the cost of managing the greater will be the comparative advantage of organizing resources within the firm. To move the theory forward, it is necessary to know what is meant by a firm and to explain the circumstances under which the cost of "managing" resources is low relative to the cost of allocating resources through market transaction. The conception of and rationale for the classical firm that we propose takes a step down the path pointed out by Coase toward that goal. Consideration of team production, team organization, difficulty in metering outputs, and the problem of shirking are important to our explanation but, so far as we can ascertain, not in Coase's. Coase's analysis insofar as it had heretofore been developed would suggest open-ended contracts but does not appear to imply anything more—neither the residual claimant status nor the distinction between employee and subcontractor status (nor any of the implications indicated below). And it is not true that employees are generally employed on the basis of long-term contractual arrangements any more than on a series of short-term or indefinite length contracts.

The importance of our proposed additional elements is revealed, for example, by the explanation of why the person to whom the control monitor is responsible receives the residual, and also by our later discussion of the implications about the corporation, partnerships, and profit sharing. These alternative forms for organization of the firm are difficult to resolve on the basis of market transaction costs only. Our exposition also suggests a definition of the classical firm—something crucial that was heretofore absent.

In addition, sometimes a technological development will

lower the cost of market transactions while, at the same time, it expands the role of the firm. When the "putting out" system was used for weaving, inputs were organized largely through market negotiations. With the development of efficient central sources of power, it became economical to perform weaving in proximity to the power source and to engage in team production. The bringing in of weavers surely must have resulted in a reduction in the cost of negotiating (forming) contracts. Yet, what we observe is the beginning of the factory system in which inputs are organized within a firm. Why? The weavers did not simply move to a common source of power that they could tap like an electric line, purchasing power while they used their own equipment. Now team production in the joint use of equipment became more important. The measurement of marginal productivity, which now involved interactions between workers, especially through their joint use of machines, became more difficult though contract negotiating cost was reduced, while managing the *behavior* of inputs became easier because of the increased centralization of activity. The firm as an organization expanded even though the cost of transactions was reduced by the advent of centralized power. The same could be said for modern assembly lines. Hence the emergence of central power sources expanded the scope of productive activity in which the firm enjoyed a comparative advantage as an organizational form.

Some economists, following Knight, have identified the bearing of risks of wealth changes with the director or central employer without explaining why that is a viable arrangement. Presumably, the more risk-averse inputs become employees rather than owners of the classical firm. Risk averseness and uncertainty *with regard to the firm's fortunes* have little, if anything, to do with our explanation although it helps to explain why all resources in a team are not owned by one person.

That is, the role of risk taken in the sense of absorbing the windfalls that buffet the firm because of unforeseen competition, technological change, or fluctuations in demand are not central to our theory, although it is true that imperfect knowledge and, therefore, risk, in *this* sense of risk, underlie the problem of monitoring team behavior. We deduce the system of paying the manager with a residual claim (the equity) from the desire to have efficient means to reduce shirking so as to make team production economical and not from the smaller aversion to the risks of enterprise in a dynamic economy. We conjecture that "distribution-of-risk" is not a valid rationale for the *existence* and organization of the *classical* firm.

Although we have emphasized team production as creating a costly metering task and have treated team production as an essential (necessary?) condition for the firm, would not other obstacles to cheap metering also call forth the same kind of contractual arrangement here denoted as a firm? For example, suppose a farmer produces wheat in an easily ascertained quantity but with subtle and difficult to detect quality variations determined by how the farmer grew the wheat. A vertical integration could allow a purchaser to control the farmer's behavior in order to more economically estimate productivity. But this is not a case of joint or team production, unless "information" can be considered part of the product. (While a good case could be made for that broader conception of production, we shall ignore it here.) Instead of forming a firm, a buyer can contract to have his inspector on the site of production, just as home builders contract with architects to supervise building contracts; that arrangement is not a firm. Still, a firm might be organized in the production of many products wherein no team production or jointness of use of separately owned resources is involved.

This possibility rather clearly indicates a broader, or complementary, approach to that which we have chosen. (1) As we do in this paper, it can be argued that the firm is the particular policing device utilized when joint team production is present. If other sources of high policing costs arise, as in the wheat case just indicated, some other form of contractual arrangement will be used. Thus to each source of informational cost there may be a different type of policing and contractual arrangement. (2) On the other hand, one can say that where policing is difficult across markets, various forms of contractual arrangements are devised, but there is no reason for that known as the firm to be uniquely related or even highly correlated with team production, as defined here. It might be used equally probably and viably for other sources of high policing cost. We have not intensively analyzed other sources, and we can only note that our current and readily revisable conjecture is that (1) is valid, and has motivated us in our current endeavor. In any event, the test of the theory advanced here is to see whether the conditions we have identified are necessary for firms to have long-run viability rather than merely births with high infant mortality. Conglomerate firms or collections of separate production agencies into one owning organization can be interpreted as an investment trust or investment diversification device—probably along the lines that motivated Knight's interpretation. A holding company can be called a firm, because of the common association of the word firm with any ownership unit that owns income sources. The term firm as commonly used is so turgid of meaning that we can not hope to explain every entity to which the name is attached in common or even technical literature. Instead, we seek to identify and explain a particular contractual arrangement induced by the cost of information factors analyzed in this paper.

IV. TYPES OF FIRMS

A. Profit-Sharing Firms

Explicit in our explanation of the capitalist firm is the assumption that the cost of *managing* the team's inputs by a central monitor, who disciplines himself because he is a residual claimant, is low relative to the cost of metering the marginal outputs of team members.

If we look within a firm to see who monitors—hires, fires, changes, promotes, and renegotiates—we should find him being a residual claimant or, at least, one whose pay or reward is more than any others correlated with fluctuations in the residual value of the firm. They more likely will have options or rights or bonuses than will inputs with other tasks.

An implicit "auxiliary" assumption of our explanation of the firm is that the cost of team production is increased if the residual claim is not held entirely by the central monitor. That is, we assume that if profit sharing had to be relied upon for *all* team members, losses from the resulting increase in central monitor shirking would exceed the output gains from the increased incentives of other team members not to shirk. If the optimal team size is only two owners of inputs, then an equal division of profits and losses between them will leave each with stronger incentives to reduce shirking than if the optimal team size is large, for in the latter case only a smaller percentage of the losses occasioned by the shirker will be borne by him. Incentives to shirk are positively related to the optimal size of the team under an equal profit-sharing scheme.[10]

[10] While the degree to which residual claims are centralized will affect the size of the team, this will be only one of many factors that determine team size, so as an approximation, we can treat team size as exogenously determined. Under certain assumptions about the shape of the "typical" utility function, the incentive to avoid shirking with unequal profit sharing can be measured by the Herfindahl index.

The preceding does not imply that profit sharing is never viable. Profit sharing to encourage self-policing is more appropriate for small teams. And, indeed, where input owners are free to make whatever contractual arrangements suit them, as generally is true in capitalist economies, profit sharing seems largely limited to partnerships with a relatively small number of *active*[11] partners. Another advantage of such arrangements for smaller teams is that it permits more effective reciprocal monitoring among inputs. Monitoring need not be entirely specialized.

Profit sharing is more viable if small team size is associated with situations where the cost of specialized management of inputs is large relative to the increased productivity potential in team effort. We conjecture that the cost of managing team inputs increases if the productivity of a team member is difficult to correlate with his behavior. In "artistic" or "professional" work, watching a man's activities is not a good clue to what he is actually thinking or doing with his mind. While it is relatively easy to manage or direct the loading of trucks by a team of dock workers where input activity is so highly related in an obvious way to output, it is more difficult to manage and direct a lawyer in the preparation and presentation of a case. Dock workers can be directed in detail without the monitor himself loading the truck, and assembly line workers can be monitored by varying the speed of the assembly line, but detailed direction in the preparation of a law case would require in much greater degree that the monitor prepare the case himself. As a result, artistic or professional inputs, such as lawyers, advertising specialists, and doctors, will be given

[11] The use of the word *active* will be clarified in our discussion of the corporation, which follows below.

relatively freer reign with regard to individual behavior. If the management of inputs is relatively costly, or ineffective, as it would seem to be in these cases, but, nonetheless if team effort is more productive than separable production with exchange across markets, then there will develop a tendency to use profit-sharing schemes to provide incentives to avoid shirking.[12]

B. Socialist Firms

We have analyzed the classical proprietorship and the profit-sharing firms in the context of free association and choice of economic organization. Such organizations need not be the most viable when political constraints limit the forms of organization that can be chosen. It is one thing to have profit sharing when professional or artistic talents are used by small teams. But if political or tax or subsidy considerations induce profit-sharing techniques when these are not otherwise economically justified, then additional management techniques will be developed to help reduce the degree of shirking.

For example, most, if not all, firms in Yugoslavia are owned by the employees in the restricted sense that all share in the residual. This is true for large firms and for firms which employ nonartistic, or nonprofessional, workers as well. With a decay of political constraints, most of these firms could be expected to rely on paid wages rather than shares in the residual. This rests on our auxiliary assumption that general sharing in the residual results in losses from enhanced shirking by the monitor that exceed the gains from reduced shirking by

[12] Some sharing contracts, like crop sharing, or rental payments based on gross sales in retail stores, come close to profit sharing. However, it is gross output sharing rather than profit sharing. We are unable to specify the implications of the difference. We refer the reader to S. N. Cheung.

residual-sharing employees. If this were not so, profit sharing with employees should have occurred more frequently in Western societies where such organizations are neither banned nor preferred politically. Where residual sharing by employees is politically imposed, as in Yugoslavia, we are led to expect that some management technique will arise to reduce the shirking by the central monitor, a technique that will not be found frequently in Western societies since the monitor retains all (or much) of the residual in the West and profit sharing is largely confined to small, professional-artistic team production situations. We do find in the larger scale residual-sharing firms in Yugoslavia that there are employee committees that can recommend (to the state) the termination of a manager's contract (veto his continuance) with the enterprise. We conjecture that the workers' committee is given the right to recommend the termination of the manager's contract precisely because the general sharing of the residual increases "excessively" the manager's incentive to shirk.[13]

C. The Corporation

All firms must initially acquire command over some resources. The corporation does so primarily by selling promises of future returns to those who (as creditors or owners) provide financial capital. In some situations resources can be acquired in advance from consumers by promises of future delivery (for

---

[13] Incidentally, investment activity will be changed. The inability to capitalize the investment value as "take-home" private property *wealth* of the members of the firm means that the benefits of the investment must be taken as annual income by those who are employed at the time of the income. Investment will be confined more to those with shorter life and with higher rates or payoffs if the alternative of investing is paying out the firm's income to its employees to take home and use as private property. For a development of this proposition, see the papers by Eirik Furobotn and Svetozar Pejovich, and by Pejovich.

example, advance sale of a proposed book). Or where the firm is a few artistic or professional persons, each can "chip in" with time and talent until the sale of services brings in revenues. For the most part, capital can be acquired more cheaply if many (risk-averse) investors contribute small portions to a large investment. The economies of raising large sums of equity capital in this way suggest that modifications in the relationship among corporate inputs are required to cope with the shirking problem that arises with profit sharing among large numbers of corporate stockholders. One modification is limited liability, especially for firms that are large relative to a stockholder's wealth. It serves to protect stockholders from large losses no matter how they are caused.

If every stock owner participated in each decision in a corporation, not only would large bureaucratic costs be incurred, but many would shirk the task of becoming well informed on the issue to be decided, since the losses associated with unexpectedly bad decisions will be borne in large part by the many other corporate shareholders. More effective control of corporate activity is achieved for most purposes by transferring decision authority to a smaller group, whose main function is to negotiate with and manage (renegotiate with) the other inputs of the team. The corporate stockholders retain the authority to revise the membership of the management group and over major decisions that affect the structure of the corporation or its dissolution.

As a result a new modification of partnerships is induced—the right to sale of corporate shares without approval of any other stockholders. Any shareholder can remove his wealth from control by those with whom he has differences of opinion. Rather than try to control the decisions of the management, which is harder to do with many stockholders than with only a few, unrestricted salability provides a more acceptable escape to each stockholder from continued policies with which he disagrees.

Indeed, the policing of managerial shirking relies on across-market competition from new groups of would-be managers as well as competition from members within the firm who seek to displace existing management. In addition to competition from outside and inside managers, control is facilitated by the temporary congealing of share votes into voting blocs owned by one or a few contenders. Proxy battles or stock purchases concentrate the votes required to displace the existing management or modify managerial policies. But it is more than a change in policy that is sought by the newly formed financial interests, whether of new stockholders or not. It is the capitalization of expected future benefits into stock prices that concentrates on the innovators the wealth gains of their actions if they own large numbers of shares. Without capitalization of future benefits, there would be less incentive to incur the costs required to exert informed decisive influence on the corporation's policies and managing personnel. Temporarily, the structure of ownership is reformed, moving away from diffused ownership into decisive power blocs, and this is a transient resurgence of the classical firm with power again concentrated in those who have title to the residual.

In assessing the significance of stockholders' power it is not the usual diffusion of voting power that is significant but instead the frequency with which voting congeals into decisive changes. Even a one-man owned company may have a long term with just one manager—continuously being approved by the owner. Similarly a dispersed voting power corporation may be also characterized by a long-lived management. The question is the probability of replacement of the management if it behaves in ways not acceptable to a majority of the stockholders. The unrestricted salability of stock and the transfer of proxies enhances the probability of decisive action in the event current stockholders or any outsider believes that management is not doing a good job with the corporation. We are not comparing the corporate responsiveness to that of a single proprietorship; instead, we are indicating features of the corporate structure that are induced by the problem of delegated authority to manager-monitors.[14]

[14] Instead of thinking of shareholders as joint *owners*, we can think of them as investors, like bondholders, except that the stockholders are more optimistic than bondholders about the enterprise prospects. Instead of buying bonds in the corporation, thus enjoying smaller risks, shareholders prefer to invest funds with a greater realizable return if the firm prospers as expected, but with smaller (possibly negative) returns if the firm performs in a manner closer to that expected by the more pessimistic investors. The pessimistic investors, in turn, regard only the bonds as likely to pay off.

If the entrepreneur-organizer is to raise capital on the best terms to him, it is to his advantage, as well as that of prospective investors, to recognize these differences in expectations. The residual claim on earnings enjoyed by shareholders does not serve the function of enhancing their efficiency as monitors in the general situation. The stockholders are "merely" the less risk-averse or the more optimistic member of the group that finances the firm. Being more optimistic than the average and seeing a higher mean value future return, they are willing to pay more for a certificate that allows them to realize gain on their expectations. One method of doing so is to buy claims to the distribution of returns that "they see" while bondholders, who are more pessimistic, purchase a claim to the distribution that they see as more likely to emerge. Stockholders are then comparable to warrant holders. They care not about the voting rights (usually not attached to warrants); they are in the same position in so far as voting rights are concerned as are bondholders. The only difference is in the probability distribution of rewards and the terms on which they can place their bets.

If we treat bondholders, preferred and convertible preferred stockholders, and common stockholders and warrant holders as simply different classes of investors—differing not only in their risk averseness but in their beliefs about the probability distribution of the firm's future earnings, why should stockholders be regarded as "owners" in any sense distinct from the other financial investors? The entrepreneur-organizer, who let us assume is the chief operating officer and sole repository of control of the corporation, does not find his authority residing in common stockholders (except in the case of a take over). Does this type of control make any difference in the way the firm is conducted? Would it make any difference in the kinds of behavior that would be tolerated by competing managers and

D. Mutual and Nonprofit Firms

The benefits obtained by the new management are greater if the stock can be purchased and sold, because this enables *capitalization* of anticipated future improvements into present

---

investors (and we here deliberately refrain from thinking of them as owner-stockholders in the traditional sense)?

Investment oldtimers recall a significant incidence of nonvoting common stock, now prohibited in corporations whose stock is traded on listed exchanges. (Why prohibited?) The entrepreneur in those days could hold voting shares while investors held nonvoting shares, which in every other respect were identical. Nonvoting shareholders were simply investors devoid of ownership connotations. The control and behavior of inside owners in such corporations has never, so far as we have ascertained, been carefully studied. For example, at the simplest level of interest, does the evidence indicate that nonvoting shareholders fared any worse because of not having voting rights? Did owners permit the nonvoting holders the normal return available to voting shareholders? Though evidence is prohibitively expensive to obtain, it is remarkable that voting and nonvoting shares sold for essentially identical prices, even during some proxy battles. However, our casual evidence deserves no more than interest-initiating weight.

One more point. The facade is deceptive. Instead of nonvoting shares, today we have warrants, convertible preferred stocks all of which are solely or partly "equity" claims without voting rights, though they could be converted into voting shares.

In sum, is it the case that the stockholder-investor relationship is one emanating from the *division* of *ownership* among several people, or is it that the collection of investment funds from people of varying anticipations is the underlying factor? If the latter, why should any of them be thought of as the owners in whom voting rights, whatever they may signify or however exercisable, should reside in order to enhance efficiency? Why voting rights in any of the outside, participating investors?

Our initial perception of this possibly significant difference in interpretation was precipitated by Henry Manne. A reading of his paper makes it clear that it is hard to understand why an investor who wishes to back and "share" in the consequences of some new business should necessarily have to acquire voting power (i.e., power to change the manager-operator) in order to invest in the venture. In fact, we invest in some ventures in the hope that no other stockholders will be so "foolish" as to try to toss out the incumbent management. We want him to have the power to stay in office, and for the prospect of sharing in his fortunes we buy nonvoting common stock. Our willingness to invest is enhanced by the knowledge that we can act legally via fraud, embezzlement and other laws to help assure that we outside investors will not be "milked" beyond our initial discounted anticipations.

wealth of new managers who bought stock and created a larger capital by their management changes. But in nonprofit corporations, colleges, churches, country clubs, mutual savings banks, mutual insurance companies, and "coops," the future consequences of improved management are not capitalized into present wealth of stockholders. (As if to make more difficult that competition by new would-be monitors, multiple shares of ownership in those enterprises cannot be bought by one person.) One should, therefore, find greater shirking in nonprofit, mutually owned enterprises. (This suggests that nonprofit enterprises are especially appropriate in realms of endeavor where more shirking is desired and where redirected uses of the enterprise in response to market-revealed values is less desired.)

E. Partnerships

Team production in artistic or professional intellectual skills will more likely be by partnerships than other types of team production. This amounts to market-organized team activity and to a nonemployer status. Self-monitoring partnerships, therefore, will be used rather than employer-employee contracts, and these organizations will be small to prevent an excessive dilution of efforts through shirking. Also, partnerships are more likely to occur among relatives or long-standing acquaintances, not necessarily because they share a common utility function, but also because each knows better the other's work characteristics and tendencies to shirk.

F. Employee Unions

Employee unions, whatever else they do, perform as monitors for employees. Employers monitor employees and similarly employees monitor an employer's performance. Are correct wages paid on time and in good currency? Usually, this is extremely easy to check. But some forms of employer performance are less easy to meter and are more subject to employer shirking. Fringe benefits often are in nonpecuniary, contingent form; medical, hospital, and accident insurance, and retirement pensions are contingent payments or performances partly in *kind* by employers to employees. Each employee cannot judge the character of such payments as easily as money wages. Insurance is a contingent payment—what the employee will get upon the contingent event may come as a disappointment. If he could easily determine what other employees had gotten upon such contingent events he could judge more accurately the performance by the employer. He could "trust" the employer not to shirk in such fringe contingent payments, but he would prefer an effective and economic monitor of those payments. We see a specialist monitor—the union employees' agent—hired by them and monitoring those aspects of employer payment most difficult for the employees to monitor. Employees should be willing to employ a specialist monitor to administer such hard-to-detect employer performance, even though their monitor has incentives to use pension and retirement funds not entirely for the benefit of employees.

V. TEAM SPIRIT AND LOYALTY

Every team member would prefer a team in which no one, not even himself, shirked. Then the true marginal costs and values could be equated to achieve more preferred positions. If one could enhance a common interest in nonshirking in the guise of a team loyalty or team spirit, the team would be more efficient. In those sports where team activity is most clearly exemplified, the sense of loyalty and team spirit is most strongly urged. Obviously the team is better, with team spirit and loyalty, because of the reduced shirking—not because of some other feature inherent in loyalty or spirit as such.[15]

Corporations and business firms try to instill a spirit of

[15] *Sports leagues:* Professional sports contests among teams is typically conducted by a *league* of teams. We assume that sports consumers are interested not only in absolute sporting skill but also in skills *relative* to other teams. Being slightly better than opposing teams enables one to claim a major portion of the receipts; the inferior team does not release resources and reduce costs, since they were expected in the play of contest. Hence, absolute skill is developed beyond the equality of marginal investment in sporting skill with its true social marginal value product. It follows there will be a tendency to overinvest in training athletes and developing teams. "Reverse shirking" arises, as budding players are induced to overpractice hyperactively relative to the social marginal value of their enhanced skills. To prevent overinvestment, the teams seek an agreement with each other to restrict practice, size of teams, and even pay of the team members (which reduces incentives of young people to overinvest in developing skills). Ideally, if all the contestant teams were owned by one owner, overinvestment in sports would be avoided, much as ownership of common fisheries or underground oil or water reserve would prevent overinvestment. This hyperactivity (to suggest the opposite of shirking) is controlled by the league of teams, wherein the league adopts a common set of constraints on each team's behavior. In effect, the teams are no longer really owned by the team owners but are supervised by them, much as the franchisers of some product. They are not full-fledged owners of their business, including the brand name, and can not "do what they wish" as franchises. Comparable to the franchiser, is the league commissioner or conference president, who seeks to restrain hyperactivity, as individual team supervisors compete with each other and cause external diseconomies. Such restraints are usually regarded as anticompetitive, antisocial, collusive-cartel devices to restrain free open competition, and reduce players' salaries. However, the interpretation presented here is premised on an attempt to avoid hyperinvestment in team sports production. Of course, the team operators have an incentive, once the league is formed and restraints are placed on hyperinvestment activity, to go further and obtain the private benefits of monopoly restriction. To what extent overinvestment is replaced by monopoly restriction is not yet determinable; nor have we seen an empirical test of these two competing, but mutually consistent interpretations. (This interpretation of league-sports activity was proposed by Earl Thompson and formulated by Michael Canes.) Again, athletic teams clearly exemplify the specialization of monitoring with captains and coaches; a captain detects shirkers while the coach trains and selects strategies and tactics. Both functions may be centralized in one person.

loyalty. This should not be viewed simply as a device to increase profits by *over*working or misleading the employees, nor as an adolescent urge for belonging. It promotes a closer approximation to the employees' potentially available true rates of substitution between production and leisure and enables each team member to achieve a more preferred situation. The difficulty, of course, is to create economically that team spirit and loyalty. It can be preached with an aura of moral code of conduct—a morality with literally the same basis as the ten commandments—to restrict our conduct toward what we would choose if we bore our full costs.

VI. KINDS OF INPUTS OWNED BY THE FIRM

To this point the discussion has examined why firms, as we have defined them, exist? That is, why is there an owner-employer who is the common party to contracts with other owners of inputs in team activity? The answer to that question should also indicate the kind of the jointly used resources likely to be owned by the central-owner-monitor and the kind likely to be hired from people who are not team owners. Can we identify characteristics or features of various inputs that lead to their being hired or to their being owned by the firm?

How can residual-claimant, central-employer-owner demonstrate ability to pay the other hired inputs the promised amount in the event of a loss? He can pay in advance or he can commit wealth sufficient to cover negative residuals. The latter will take the form of machines, land, buildings, or raw materials committed to the firm. Commitments of labor-wealth (i.e., human wealth), given the property rights in people, are less feasible. These considerations suggest that residual claimants—owners of the firm—will be investors of resalable capital equipment in the firm. The goods or inputs more likely to be invested, than rented, by the owners of the enterprise, will have higher resale values relative to the initial cost and will have longer expected use in a firm relative to the economic life of the good.

But beyond these factors are those developed above to explain the existence of the institution known as the firm—the costs of detecting output performance. When a durable resource is used it will have a marginal product and a depreciation. Its use requires payment to cover at least use-induced depreciation; unless that user cost is specifically detectable, payment for it will be demanded in accord with *expected* depreciation. And we can ascertain circumstances for each. An indestructible hammer with a readily detectable marginal product has zero user cost. But suppose the hammer were destructible and that careless (which is easier than careful) use is more abusive and causes greater depreciation of the hammer. Suppose in addition the abuse is easier to detect by observing the way it is used than by observing only the hammer after its use, or by measuring the output scored from a hammer by a laborer. If the hammer were rented and used in the absence of the owner, the depreciation would be greater than if the use were observed by the owner and the user charged in accord with the imposed depreciation. (Careless use is more likely than careful use—if one does not pay for the greater depreciation.) An absentee owner would therefore ask for a higher rental price because of the higher *expected* user cost than if the item were used by the owner. The expectation is higher because of the greater difficulty of observing specific user cost, by inspection of the hammer after use. Renting is therefore in this case more costly than owner use. This is the valid content of the misleading expressions about ownership being more economical than renting—ignoring all other factors that may work in the opposite direction, like tax provision, short-term occupancy and capital risk avoidance.

Better examples are tools of the trade. Watch repairers, engineers, and carpenters tend to own their own tools especially if they are portable. Trucks are more likely to be employee owned rather than other equally expensive team inputs because it is relatively cheap for the driver to police the care taken in using a truck. Policing the use of trucks by a nondriver owner is more likely to occur for trucks that are not specialized to one driver, like public transit busses.

The factor with which we are concerned here is one related to the costs of monitoring not only the gross product performance of an input but also the abuse or depreciation inflicted on the input in the course of its use. If depreciation or user cost is more cheaply detected when the owner can see its use than by only seeing the input before and after, there is a force toward owner use rather than renting. Resources whose user cost is harder to detect when used by someone else, tend on this count to be owner-used. Absentee ownership, in the lay language, will be less likely. Assume momentarily that labor service cannot be performed in the absence of its owner. The labor owner can more cheaply monitor any abuse of himself than if somehow labor services could be provided without the labor owner observing its mode of use or knowing what was happening. Also his incentive to abuse himself is increased if he does not own himself.[16]

[16] Professional athletes in baseball, football, and basketball, where athletes having sold their source of service to the team owners upon entering into sports activity, are owned by team owners. Here the team owners must monitor the athletes' physical condition and behavior to protect the team owners' wealth. The athlete has *less* (not, *no*) incentive to protect or enhance his athletic prowess since capital value

The similarity between the preceding analysis and the question of absentee landlordism and of sharecropping arrangements is no accident. The same factors which explain the contractual arrangements known as a firm help to explain the incidence of tenancy, labor hiring or sharecropping.[17]

VII. FIRMS AS A SPECIALIZED MARKET INSTITUTION FOR COLLECTING, COLLATING, AND SELLING INPUT INFORMATION

The firm serves as a highly specialized surrogate market. Any person contemplating a joint-input activity must search and detect the qualities of available joint inputs. He could contact an employment agency, but that agency in a small town would have little advantage over a large firm with many

---

changes have less impact on his own wealth and more on the team owners. Thus, some athletes sign up for big initial bonuses (representing present capital value of future services). Future salaries are lower by the annuity value of the prepaid "bonus" and hence the athlete has *less* to lose by subsequent abuse of his athletic prowess. Any decline in his subsequent service value would in part be borne by the team owner who owns the players' future service. This does not say these losses of future salaries have no effect on preservation of athletic talent (we are not making a "sunk cost" error). Instead, we assert that the preservation is reduced, not eliminated, because the amount of loss of wealth suffered is smaller. The athlete will spend less to maintain or enhance his prowess thereafter. The effect of this revised incentive system is evidenced in comparison of the kinds of attention and care imposed on the athletes at the "expense of the team owner" in the case where athletes' future services are owned by the team owner with that where future labor service values are owned by the athlete himself. Why athletes' future athletic services are owned by the team owners rather than being hired is a question we should be able to answer. One presumption is cartelization and monopsony gains to team owners. Another is exactly the theory being expounded in this paper—costs of monitoring production of athletes; we know not on which to rely.

[17] The analysis used by Cheung in explaining the prevalence of sharecropping and land tenancy arrangements is built squarely on the same factors—the costs of detecting output performance of jointly used inputs in team production and the costs of detecting user costs imposed on the various inputs if owner used or if rented.

inputs. The employer, by virtue of monitoring many inputs, acquires special superior information about their productive talents. This aids his *directive* (i.e., market hiring) efficiency. He "sells" his information to employee-inputs as he aids them in ascertaining good input combinations for team activity. Those who work as employees or who rent services to him are using him to discern superior combinations of inputs. Not only does the director-employer "decide" what each input will produce, he also estimates which heterogeneous inputs will work together jointly more efficiently, and he does this in the context of a privately owned market for forming teams. The department store is a firm and is a superior private market. People who shop and work in one town can as well shop and work in a privately owned firm.

This marketing function is obscured in the theoretical literature by the assumption of homogeneous factors. Or it is tacitly left for individuals to do themselves via personal market search, much as if a person had to search without benefit of specialist retailers. Whether or not the firm arose because of this efficient information service, it gives the director-employer more knowledge about the productive talents of the team's inputs, and a basis for superior decisions about efficient or profitable combinations of those heterogeneous resources.

In other words, opportunities for profitable team production by inputs already within the firm may be ascertained more economically and accurately than for resources outside the firm. Superior combinations of inputs can be more economically identified and formed from resources already used in the organization than by obtaining new resources (and knowledge of them) from the outside. Promotion and revision of employee assignments (contracts) will be preferred by a firm to the hiring of new inputs. To the extent that this occurs there is reason to expect the firm to be able to operate as a conglomerate rather than persist in producing a single product. Efficient production with heterogeneous resources is a result not of having *better* resources but of *knowing more accurately* the relative productive performances of those resources. Poorer resources can be paid less in accord with their inferiority; greater accuracy of knowledge of the potential and actual productive actions of inputs rather than having high productivity resources makes a firm (or an assignment of inputs) profitable.[18]

VIII. SUMMARY

While ordinary contracts facilitate efficient specialization according to comparative advantage, a special class of contracts among a group of joint inputs to a team production process is commonly used for team production. Instead of

---

[18] According to our interpretation, the firm is a specialized surrogate for a market for team use of inputs; it provides superior (i.e., cheaper) collection and collation of knowledge about heterogeneous resources. The greater the set of inputs about which knowledge of performance is being collated within a firm the greater are the present costs of the collation activity. Then, the larger the firm (market) the greater the attenuation of monitor control. To counter this force, the firm will be divisionalized in ways that economize on those costs—just as will the market be specialized. So far as we can ascertain, other theories of the reasons for firms have no such implications.

In Japan, employees by custom work nearly their entire lives with one firm, and the firm agrees to that expectation. Firms will tend to be large and conglomerate to enable a broader scope of input revision. Each firm is, in effect, a small economy engaging in "intranational and international" trade. Analogously, Americans expect to spend their whole lives in the United States, and the bigger the country, in terms of variety of resources, the easier it is to adjust to changing tastes and circumstances. Japan, with its lifetime employees, should be characterized more by large, conglomerate firms. Presumably, at some size of the firm, specialized knowledge about inputs becomes as expensive to transmit across divisions of the firms as it does across markets to other firms.

multilateral contracts among all the joint inputs' owners, a central common party to a set of bilateral contracts facilitates efficient organization of the joint inputs in team production. The terms of the contracts form the basis of the entity called the firm—especially appropriate for organizing team production processes.

Team productive activity is that in which a union, or joint use, of inputs yields a larger output than the sum of the products of the separately used inputs. This team production requires—like all other production processes—an assessment of marginal productivities if efficient production is to be achieved. Nonseparability of the products of several differently owned joint inputs raises the cost of assessing the marginal productivities of those resources or services of each input owner. Monitoring or metering the productivities to match marginal productivities to costs of inputs and thereby to reduce shirking can be achieved more economically (than by across market bilateral negotiations among inputs) in a firm.

The essence of the classical firm is identified here as a contractual structure with: (1) joint input production; (2) several input owners; (3) one party who is common to all the contracts of the joint inputs; (4) who has rights to renegotiate any input's contract independently of contracts with other input owners; (5) who holds the residual claim; and (6) who has the right to sell his central contractual residual status. The central agent is called the firm's owner and the employer. No authoritarian control is involved; the arrangement is simply a contractual structure subject to continuous renegotiation with the central agent. The contractual structure arises as a means of enhancing efficient organization of team production. In particular, the ability to detect shirking among owners of jointly used inputs in team production is enhanced (detection costs are reduced) by this arrangement and the discipline (by revision of contracts) of input owners is made more economic.

Testable implications are suggested by the analysis of different types of organizations—nonprofit, proprietary for profit, unions, cooperatives, partnerships, and by the kinds of inputs that tend to be owned by the firm in contrast to those employed by the firm.

We conclude with a highly conjectural but possibly significant interpretation. As a consequence of the flow of information to the central party (employer), the firm takes on the characteristic of an efficient market in that information about the productive characteristics of a large set of specific inputs is now more cheaply available. Better recombinations or new uses of resources can be more efficiently ascertained than by the conventional search through the general market. In this sense inputs compete with each other within and via a firm rather than solely across markets as conventionally conceived. Emphasis on interfirm competition obscures intrafirm competition among inputs. Conceiving competition as the *revelation and exchange* of knowledge or information about qualities, potential uses of different inputs in different potential applications indicates that the firm is a device for enhancing competition among sets of input resources as well as a device for more efficiently rewarding the inputs. In contrast to markets and cities which can be viewed as publicly or nonowned market places, the firm can be considered a privately owned market; if so, we would consider the firm and the ordinary market as competing types of markets, competition between private proprietary markets and public or communal markets. Could it be that the market suffers from the defects of communal property rights in organizing and influencing uses of valuable resources?

References

M. Canes. ''A Model of a Sports League, unpublished doctoral dissertation, UCLA, 1970.

S. N. Cheung. *The Theory of Share Tenancy*, Chicago, 1969.

R. H. Coase. ''The Nature of the Firm,'' *Economica* 4 (November 1937): 386–405; reprinted in G. J. Stigler and K. Boulding, eds., *Readings in Price Theory*, Homewood, 1952, pp. 331–51.

E. Furobotn, and S. Pejovich. ''Property Rights and the Behavior of the Firm in a Socialist State,'' *Zeitschrift für Nationalökonomie* 30 (1970): 431–54.

F. H. Knight. *Risk, Uncertainty and Profit*, New York, 1965.

S. Macaulay. ''Non-Contractual Relations in Business: A Preliminary Study,'' *Amer. Sociological Rev.* 28 (1968): 55–69.

H. B. Malmgren. ''Information, Expectations and the Theory of the Firm,'' *Quart J. Econ.* 75 (August 1961): 399–421.

H. Manne. ''Our Two Corporation Systems: Law and Economics,'' *Virginia Law Rev.* 53, no. 2 (March 1967): 259–84.

S. Pejovich. ''The Firm, Monetary Policy and Property Rights in a Planned Economy,'' *Western Econ. J.* 7 (September 1969): 193–200.

M. Silver, and R. Auster. ''Entrepreneurship, Profit, and the Limits on Firm Size,'' *J. Bus. Univ. Chicago* 42 (April 1969): 277–81.

E. A. Thompson. ''Nonpecuniary Rewards and the Aggregate Production Function,'' *Rev. Econ. Statist.* 52 (November 1970): 395–404.

4

Why Money?

Ignorance of availability of goods and of their terms of trade and attributes will provoke efforts to reduce that ignorance in order to achieve more trade. Several institutions have evolved to reduce those costs: money, specialist middlemen who are experts in assessing attributes of goods and who carry inventories and whose realiability of assurance is high, specialized market places, and even unemployment. This paper concentrates on the way in which that ignorance leads to the use of money and how money requires concurrent exchange with specialist, expert middlemen of high reputability. It will be seen that the use of money does not rest on a bookkeeping, debt-recording function. The recording function could be done by any good without specialized markets if goods were perfectly and costlessly identifiable in all relevant,

Reprinted by permission from the *Journal of Money, Credit, and Banking* 9, no. 1 (Part 2, February 1977): 133–40.

The best way I can indicate respect for my long association with Karl Brunner and admiration for his work is to report as a secretary-reporter the gist of some ancient joint discussions when we were willing to admit we had a lot to learn. My hope is that he will find the report faithful, while others may find it interesting and instructive. Brunner cannot be absolved from blame for errors nor credit for merit.

present and future, attributes including future terms of trade. We mean by money a commodity used in all or a dominant number of exchanges.

Imagine society to be composed of people with different goods but without costlessly perfect knowledge of characteristics or attributes of each good. Any exchange proposed between two parties with two goods will be hindered (be more costly) the less fully informed are the two parties about the true characteristics of the proffered goods. We assume: Interpersonal differences exist in degrees of knowledge about different goods—either by fortuitous circumstance or by deliberate development of such knowledge. Goods differ in the costs of determining or conveying to others their true qualities and attributes. Reputability of people as sources of reliable information about goods differ and their ranking is different among goods. People differ in their costs of not only assaying goods but in searching out potential profferers of the good. These differences may be fortuitous or may be developed in response to economic motives, a point to which we shall return. With these conditions it can be shown that:

(a) People will specialize in certain goods in providing information and availability to searching buyers.
(b) Specialist purveyors (or buyers) of goods will be reputable (low variance) sources of estimates of the quality of what is being purchased from or sold to that specialist.
(c) People who have developed lower costs of identifying characteristics of goods will be specialists in selling, buying, inventorying, and giving information about the good.
(d) Trade between a specialist and a novice will involve lower transactions costs than trade between two nonexperts.
(e) If some good were sufficiently and most cheaply identifiable so that everyone were like an expert in it, exchange

TABLE 1

Single Party After Inspection Value		Net Value After Exchanges: *Novices* *D*	*O*	*W*	*C*	*Experts* *D*	*O*	*W*	*C*
		.2	*.4*	*.6*	*.95*	*.85*	*.90*	*.95*	*.99*
Novices									
D	.2	.04	.08	.12	.19	.85	.18	.19	.20
O	.4	.08	.16	.24	.38	.34	.90	.38	.40
W	.6	.12	.24	.36	.57	.51	.54	.95	.59
C	.95	.19	.38	.57	.90	.81	.86	.90	.99
Experts									
D	.85	.85	.34	.51	.81	1	1	1	1
O	.90	.18	.90	.54	.86	1	1	1	1
W	.95	.19	.38	.95	.90	1	1	1	1
C	.99	.20	.40	.59	.95	1	1	1	1

cost of that good for any other good would be less than if a more costly to identify good were offered, and it would become a money.

Consider a world of four goods: diamonds, wheat, oil, and the one called just C. Not all are immediately identifiable in all their true characteristics at insignificant costs, and some are more expensive to identify than others. The community consists of people most of whom are novices, or nonspecialists, in these goods. Imagine (and this begs a question initially) four people are experts respectively in one of the four goods.

Prior to completing an exchange of diamonds for oil between two novices in diamonds and oil, each will incur costs of identifying the other's product attributes, including legal entitlements, quantity, and all aspects defining the rights and the quality and quantity of the good being transferred. The net value transfer after subtracting those costs will be less than if they knew costlessly the true characteristics of these goods.

Table 1 shows the proportions of value *remaining* after "transactions" costs between all pairs of traders with various goods. For example, if a novice in diamonds were to trade some of his diamonds (no matter why!) for the diamonds of another novice in diamonds, only four percent of the (perfect knowledge) value would be remaining, as stated in row 1. Why? Each party knows the quality only of his own diamonds. Each would assess the quality of the other's diamonds. Assume the costs of the assay amount to 80 percent of the diamonds tested—a sort of destructive test in which four out of five good diamonds were destroyed for each one determined to be good. Instead of a destructive test, one can think of the costs of determining the quality as being equal to 80 percent of the value of the diamond. If offered 100 diamonds on a one for one basis (prior to tested quality), then *net* of examination costs he is receiving 20 proven diamonds for his 100. The second party, also a novice, will incur the same costs in examining the first party's stones. He will net only 20 of the 100 diamonds he would receive. So, knowing his own proffered diamonds are good, the first party would be willing to offer only 20 of his diamonds for thc 100 untested ones of the other party. The second, who would receive 20 untested diamonds, would end up with four tested, proven diamonds after he incurs his tests. So the second party would have given 100 of his diamonds to get back four tested ones—a loss from exchange of 96 percent of the value of what he gave up. An exchange is not likely.

If a pair of novices were to make an agreeable exchange of a diamond for some oil, their costs of ascertaining the qualities of the two products to be purchased would, according to Table 1, amount to 92 percent of the value of the goods. Only eight cents on the dollar would be remaining. Unless at least one of the parties had a very high marginal personal value for one of those goods, no trade would occur. A very large part of that net potential gain would be dissipated in the transactions costs.

If a diamond novice were to trade his diamond for wheat from a wheat novice, 12 percent of the value of the two goods remains.

By definition of C, trade between a novice in diamonds and one in C would lose less than between novices trading diamonds and any other good, as can be seen from the first row, left side. The first row is pertinent to a novice in diamonds who proposes to sell a diamond. The right half of the row is the result of trades made by our diamond novice with experts in diamonds, oil, wheat, or C. An expert is defined as one who has a lower cost function for identifying attributes of a good. (We temporarily beg the question of why some are more expert than others.)

A transaction with an expert will cost less, if the novitiate buyer of the product from the expert will rely on the expert's word. The expert's word will have value if he develops a reputation for honesty and reliability in his assessment. Experts will then sell their knowledge at a price lower than the cost for a buyer to get such information in other ways. It is not necessary that the expert be the seller of the good in which he has expertise. He could be an independent assayer, but for reasons to be discussed later, experts will tend to be dealers in the commodity in which they are experts—and dealers will tend to be experts in the goods in which they deal.

The righthand half of row one indicates that a diamond novice trading with a jeweler (diamond expert) where the novice trades his diamond for some from the expert (no matter why such a trade would be made) will experience a lower loss of value than if the diamond were sold to an expert of any other good. A diamond for a diamond will get better terms because the expert is an expert in both what he is getting and giving (here just one kind of good), whereas though a diamond by a novice for oil from an oil expert will save on oil identification costs, it will not save on diamond identification. Hence the costs of transactions between a novice and an expert in the same commodity are less than those between a novice and an expert in a different good.

The matrix is completed, with some redundancy, by filling in the row cells in the bottom half, representing sales by experts in diamonds, wheat, oil and C to novices (in the lefthand half of those rows). Exchanges between pairs of experts, one in each commodity, are represented in the lower righthand half. We assume experts are perfectly knowledgeable in the commodities in which they specialize and are 100 percent honest. This assumption may be too strong, but we make it.

Less loss occurs with trade between two novices where one

exchanges diamonds for C than when he trades diamonds for wheat. It may be tempting, but erroneous, to conclude that trades should occur of diamonds for C, and then with the C to buy wheat. That is not quite correct.

To test that, try to find how a *novice* in one good could trade for another good with a novice and gain by going through an intermediary good. It can't be done in the upper lefthand portion of the table because the costs of recognizing the intermediate good are an added cost incurred by use of an intermediary trading good. The costs of identifying the two "basic" goods are not reduced, while an extra cost identifying the intermediate good is added.

Using the specialist expert involves an extra exchange, a cost of identification of another good—the one offered to him, in which he is not an expert. An expert is an expert in one good only, not in all *pairs* of goods. Hence the problem of identification costs persists. Now, if there is some good in which identification costs are both (a) *low* and (b) low for *everyone*, that will permit purchase of product identification information cheaply from the specialized intermediary expert. If his costs of identifying that offered (money) good are less than the reductions in costs by using the specialist for information about the basic goods, the total costs of identification can be reduced.

The cost of identifying that intermediary good is less than the reduced costs by use of a specialist who provides information about the basic good at a low cost. That double event, (1) a low identification cost to everyone about the intermediate commodity *and* (2) specialist-experts who provide quality assurance and information more cheaply than novices can provide for themselves, explains the use of a low identification cost commodity as a general intermediary medium of exchange—money. It permits purchase of information from lower cost sources, a cost reduction that exceeds the added cost of using an intermediary good for indirect exchange. No double coincidence of wants is pertinent. Indeed, it is a general prevalence of double coincidence of information by both parties that would avoid use of money.

The matrix illustrates the above propositions. For example, consider some alternative routes of exchange for a novice with diamonds, who wants some wheat.

(1) Diamonds to wheat, novice to novice ($D_n \rightarrow W_n$). A diamond novice exchanges diamonds for wheat with a wheat novice. The net value obtained by the diamond novice, according to the matrix of information-transaction costs, is .12.

(2) Diamonds to oil to wheat, all through novices ($D_n - O_n - W_n$), yield .0196 ($= 1 \times .08 \times .24$). This is less than .12 because of an extra pair of identification costs of oil.

(3) Diamonds to C (cash) to wheat, all through novices ($D_n - C_n - W_n$). The result is a net value of .108 ($= 1 \times .19 \times .57$). Though better than through any other mediary because cash, C (because identification costs are less than for oil), it is not as cheap as either direct barter or route 2.

(4) Diamond novice to wheat with wheat specialist. The net result is .19. Contrasting this with the prior route shows the gain from using the specialist for wheat. The difference is the saving to the diamond novice in identifying the wheat, because the wheat specialist offers him "wheat assurance" at a lower cost. And the wheat specialist's word, his reputable reliability, is a source of income. A dishonest specialist would lose a source of income if he destroyed his credibility. So an established wheat mer-

chant has more incentive to make honest statements about the quality of his wheat than does a transient novice.

(5) Interposing the intermediary good, C, into route 4 will worsen matters because the costs of identifying an intermediary good, C, are added to the process, with no reductions in any other costs. For example, going from a diamond novice through a C novice—or even a C expert—rather than through a diamond expert first won't help. Some buyer of the novice's diamonds still has to value them. Whether a wheat specialist or anyone else (except a diamond specialist) does so won't reduce costs. And introduction of C as another good only adds another identification cost. The net value of a route from diamond novice through C through a wheat specialist is .1715, compared to .19 for a direct barter via route 4 without intermediate goods.

(6) A gain would arise if the lower cost services of a *diamond* expert could be used in the exchange process. So what does permit further lowering of costs through an intermediary good is the use of *two* specialists—in wheat and in diamonds. The diamond novice sells to a diamond expert (who assesses qualities more cheaply than any other buyer could), and then our novice takes the proceeds of C and purchases wheat from a wheat specialist, relying on the specialists' reputations and knowledge as a cheaper substitute for the demand and wheat assessment costs by novices. The extra costs of using C are offset by the expert's lower diamond assessment costs.

In our matrix we can compute the net value (.767) of the intermediate good, two middlemen route wherein a diamond novice goes to a diamond specialist and then to a wheat specialist using the good C as the medium between specialists.

The value is .767, as the product of .85 × .9025, the values respectively of (a) the diamond specialist who receives C, and (b) the entry in the cell for the C novice (the former diamond novice who now offers C to the wheat specialist) selling C to the wheat specialist.[1] This increase in value to .767 is the result of ability to get quality assurance at a lower cost from the diamond specialist and from the wheat specialist without imposing on them the higher costs of identifying goods other than C, in which most people are nearly experts.

The feature emphasized here (without excluding others) is the use of the pair of specialists in diamonds and wheat to reduce information costs. With only one specialist no intermediary good helped. (See route 2, 3.) The intermediary good C would be of no use in this context if *two* (or more) specialists were not used as economical sources of quality assurance. It is both (1) the presence of *more* than one specialist and (2) the generally low identification cost good, C, that enable indirect exchange to reduce quality ascertainment costs. Use of C as the intermediary good with the lowest *general* identification costs enables obtaining the conveying information more cheaply from several specialists.

What properties of the matrix of information costs are critical? First, specialists permit lower costs, as indicated by the larger numbers in the cells in the upper righthand or lower lefthand quadrants. Second, the row and column of C for novices is larger uniformly than any other row or column and

[1] Where does the diamond specialist get C to pay the diamond novice who offers diamonds? From a C specialist. The diamond specialist will have an inventory of C on hand because that will economize on the novice's information costs the novice induces with the wheat specialist when the novice purchases wheat from the wheat specialist. Of all the intermediary goods to be used by a novice between successive specialists, the best is C, a generally easily recognizable good. Try interposing others and the poorer results will be demonstrated with the data of the matrix.

the corresponding rows and columns for experts are also dominant. It is the dominance of the *row* of C both for the novice and for the experts in other goods that seems critical. The ability of everyone to assess the qualities of C enables it to be used as a low cost means of purchasing information about other goods from specialists without imposing offsetting high costs on the experts to identify the good C.

An alternative view of the reason for use of a common medium of exchange is in its presumed role of avoiding the necessity of a double coincidence of wants. But any commodity used as an intermediary would do that. If goods were perfectly identifiable at zero costs, rights to goods could be transferred and any commodity would serve as measure of debt. This would then leave some goods as presumably less volatile in value so that the exchange value of units of those goods would be preferred. But this confuses the store of value with the medium of exchange. The two need not be the same good.

Another presumed rationale is the case of search over the population of potential demanders of a good. If everyone uses a good, it is more likely that it could be a medium of exchange. But again everyone uses bread or milk. Generality of use aids, but is neither a sufficient nor a necessary precondition. Generality here is a result of people using it as a medium of exchange, not a cause of the good becoming a medium. For example, chocolate candy and nylons became a near money during price controls in the absence of other "money." The items were cheaply identifiable by many people—not necessarily consumed by everybody.

Costs of identifying qualities of a good are what counts. If costs for some good are low and generally low across members of society, the good will become a medium through which information costs can be reduced and exchange made more economical. But it will rise only with the rise of chains of specialists in various goods and commodities, who know the goods cheaply, whose reputation for reliability of evaluation is high, who because of that knowledge and cheapness of assurance to buyers become specialist middlemen in the good both as inventory carriers and buying and selling agents. Other explanations of the occurrence and use of money are silent or vacuous on the existence of specialists and their reliability and activities.

This analysis explains the use of money, which good becomes money, why it is not necessarily also the store of value, the existence of two or more specialists in the sequence of exchanges with money, the reputability of specialists as an integral part of their capital values, and the reason specialists are also dealers.

This model is also consistent with the explanation of unemployment as a search and selection process for best work opportunities during demand shifts among potentially performed activities. Commodities or services that are more difficult to assess in qualities will experience greater losses or changes in values consequent to demand shifts. That higher cost tends to act like specificity of a good to particular tasks. The higher costs of assessing their attributes are like a tax on transfer. Hence the larger gains (or avoidance of loss) from more expensive search in the event of a demand shift (with a large change or high variance of next best known opportunities), induce greater or longer search. It is not simply a task of searching out best opportunities, but also a search for potential demanders to assess productive qualities. Those costs of becoming informed about what a good or service or rented good will do, raise transfer costs and also reward longer or greater searching activity by potential buyers or employers. Commodities or services with qualities that have high costs for other people to ascertain will tend to be held longer in inventories awaiting sale and will suffer greater costs of exchange—as evident by larger bid-ask spreads, wholesale-retail spreads, or "unemployment" lengths. Since the commodity used as money will have low cost in these respects, we conclude money will have the lowest "unemployment" rate.

It is not the absence of a double coincidence of wants, or of the costs of searching out the market of potential buyers and sellers of various goods, or of record keeping, but the costliness of information about the attributes of goods available for exchange that induces the use of money in an exchange economy—if some good has low recognition costs for a large segment of the population, while other goods do not. A result is the use not only of money but of knowledgeable experts, with high reputability, who deal in the goods in which they are specialists.

Because most of the formal economic models of competition, exchange, and equilibrium have ignored ignorance and lack of costless full and perfect information, many institutions of our economic system, institutions that are productive in creating knowledge more cheaply than otherwise, have been erroneously treated as parasitic appendages. The explanation of use of money, expertise with dealing in a good as a middleman specialist with a trademark or brandname, reputability or goodwill, along with advertising of one's wares (and even unemployment) is often misunderstood. All these can be derived from the same information cost factors that give rise to use of an intermediary medium of exchange.

II

Property Rights and Economic Behavior

5

Some Economics of Property Rights

1. SCARCITY, COMPETITION, AND PROPERTY

In *every* society, conflicts of interest among the members of that society must be resolved. The process by which that resolution (not elimination!) occurs is known as competition. Since, by definition, there is no way to eliminate competition, the relevant question is what kind of competition shall be used in the resolution of the conflicts of interest. In more dramatic words designed to arouse emotional interest, What forms of discrimination among the members of that society shall be employed in deciding to what extent each person is able to achieve various levels of his goals? Discrimination, competition, and scarcity are three inseparable concepts.

2. CONSTRAINTS

That list of concepts can be expanded—scarcity, competition, discrimination, constraints, property. In other words,

Preparation of this paper was facilitated by a grant from the Lilly Endowment of Indianapolis, Indiana, to the University of California, Los Angeles, for a study of various forms of property rights.

constraints exist that prevent our individually achieving a level of want-fulfillment beyond which none of us wants more. In still other words, these constraints, even though imposed by nature, include also the constraints imposed by other people who because they achieve certain levels of want fulfillment leave other people with lower levels. (I do not mean that *all* activities that enable one person to have a greater level of goal fulfillment will also necessarily mean less for someone else; we know that some forms of exchange permit joint increases. But we also know that cooperative action is possible, and also that competitive action is also present.) If we concentrate attention on constraints and classes of permissible action we find ourselves studying the *property* aspect of behavior.

Economists are, I think, too prone to examine exchange as a cooperative act whereby the buyer and seller each act in an effort to reach a more desired position. Yet I find it more interesting (now that I understand the cooperative aspect of exchange) to examine the competitive, or property, aspect of exchange. The act of exchange is a means whereby the buyer is able to compete against other claimants for the goods being obtained from the seller. The kinds of offers, forms of competition and behavior that the members of society can employ in an endeavor to get more of the goods that would otherwise go to other people, is brought more into the focus of attention. More directly, the forms and kinds of property rights sanctioned in a society define or identify the kinds of competition, discrimination, or behavior characteristic of that society.

Yet if we look at the "fields" of economics, say as presented by the American Economic Association's classification of areas of interest or specialization, we find no mention of the word "property." Either we can infer that the profession is so obviously aware of the pervasiveness of the effects of various forms of property rights that property rights can not sensibly be regarded as merely a subfield; or else we can infer that economists have forgotten about the possibility of subjective rigorous systematic coherent analysis of the various forms of property rights. My conviction is that the latter inference is the more valid one. As evidence I cite that the only systematic analysis of choice among "goods" postulates utility maximization subject to a budget or *wealth* constraint, wherein the constraint is almost invariably a *private* property type of wealth constraint.

3. PROPERTY RIGHTS

If, in what follows, I talk as if the property rights were enforced by formal state police power, let me here emphasize that such an interpretation, regardless of what I may later say, is gross error. It seems to be a fact that individuals will not stand by idly while some other person's property is stolen. It seems to be a fact that *private* property rights are rights not merely because the state formally makes them so but because individuals want such rights to be enforced, at least for a vast, overwhelming majority of people. And yet if I recognize the number of socialist states, I must admit to some confusion (I appeal for edification).

The rights of individuals to the use of resources (i.e., property rights) in any society are to be construed as supported by the force of etiquette, social custom, ostracism, and formal legally enacted laws supported by the states' power of violence or punishment. Many of the constraints on the use of what we call private property involve the force of etiquette and social ostracism. The level of noise, the kind of clothes we wear, our intrusion on other people's privacy are restricted not merely by laws backed by the police force, but by social acceptance, reciprocity, and voluntary social ostracism for violators of accepted codes of conduct. The use of arabic numbers rather than roman, the use of certain types of clothing, or styles of speech and address, of printing from left to right and top to bottom, rather than the reverse, or keeping our garden up with Jones', all are subject to the force of social opprobrium. No laws require such behavior. Yet each of us (or nearly every one of us) will punish in one way or another those who violate these rules. Surely it is not the important rules that are left to the formal state power of enactment and compulsion. Obviously there is heated dispute as to which forms of behavior should be "enforced" by social voluntary ostracism and which by formal state police action.

By a system of property rights I mean a method of assigning to particular individuals the "authority" to select, for specific goods, any use from a nonprohibited class of uses. As suggested in the preceding remarks the concepts of "authority" and of "nonprohibited" rely on some concept of enforcement or inducement to respect the assignment and scope of prohibited choice. A property right for me means some protection against other people's choosing against my will one of the uses of resources, said to be "mine."

Often the idea or scope of *private* property rights is expressed as an assignment of exclusive authority to some individual to choose any use of the goods deemed to be his private property. In other words the "owners," who are assigned the right to make the choice, have an unrestricted right to the choice of use of specified goods. Notice, that we did not add—"so long as the rights of other people are similarly respected." That clause is redundant in strict logic. Private property owners can use their goods in any way they choose. If some of these chosen uses involve the use or destruction of other people's private property, it follows that the private property system is being violated, for this use has denied to other people the control of use over the goods classed as private property. To say I have private property rights is to say that no one else has the right to make the choice of use of that good (contained in the class of private property). This means that if I select a use for the goods said to be my private property, the selection must not affect the physical attributes of your goods. If I own some iron, I can make window frames or fence posts out of it, but if I shove a piece of iron through "your" glass window, I shall be denying you the right of choice of the physical attributes of your private property. However, if I convert the iron to a special kind of good that other people are willing to buy instead of buying what you are selling, you may find that the reduced exchange value of your goods imposes a greater loss of exchange power (wealth) than if I had simply broken your window.

Although private property rights protect private property from physical changes chosen by other people, no immunity is implied for the exchange value of one's property. Nor does it imply that my use of my goods, which may not in any way affect your goods, cannot be a use that you find objectionable on moral or emotional grounds. If I use my resources to make lewd pictures for my own use or for exchange with other people, you may find your "utility" much affected. You may be more upset, annoyed, distressed, or hurt by my action than if I had broken your window or stolen some of your wealth.

Private property, as I understand it, does *not* imply that a person may use his property in any way he sees fit so long as no one else is "hurt." Instead, it seems to mean the right to use goods (or to transfer that right) in any way the owner wishes so long as the physical attributes or uses of all other people's private property is unaffected. And that leaves plenty of room for disturbance and alienation of affections of other people. If I open a restaurant near yours and win away business by my superior service, you are as hurt as if I had burned part of your building. If I open a restaurant and pour smells and smoke over your neighboring land then I have changed the physical attributes of your property; I have violated your private property rights—incidentally, a form of violation very common in most societies.

But if the right for me to open a business were denied, this could, if it also were part of a system in which your rights to enter into various businesses were similarly restricted, be considered by you to be an undesirable restriction and one that did you more harm than would be encountered by you in a less restrictive environment.

In sum, it is only the choice over physical attributes that is constrained to owners, not the value-in-exchange effects nor the psychological, emotional effects that you may suffer in the knowledge that I am behaving in what you consider improper ways (short of changing the physical attributes of your property).

4. PARTITIONING OF PROPERTY RIGHTS

Whether or not the preceding suggested definition is useful, we examine another issue. What are the effects of various partitionings of use rights? By this I refer to the fact that at the same time several people may each possess some portion of the rights to use the land. A may possess the right to grow wheat on it. B may possess the right to walk across it. C may possess the right to dump ashes and smoke on it. D may possess the right to fly an airplane over it. E may have the right to subject it to vibrations consequent to the use of some neighboring equipment. And each of these rights may be transferable. In sum, private property rights to various partitioned uses of the land are "owned" by different persons.[1]

A lease or rental agreement partitions the rights so that the renter gets the right to make decisions about particular uses of the item by the "owner." Normally the rights of the renter to decide where the furniture will be placed or when it will be sat on, etc., are not thought of as ownership rights, because they are so frequently allocated to the renter, and because the ultimate value consequence rests on the "owner." However, our main point here is that the rights can be partitioned, divided, and reallocated on a temporary—or even on a permanent—basis, so that the "ownership" rights are partitioned among two or more persons. This kind of division is not necessarily a cross-sectional division with each owner now having equal parts of all the ownership rights. Instead it is a selective partitioning with all of some of the subrights staying with the "owner" and all of some other rights being transferred temporarily at least to the "renter." Even though this is called a rental or leasing agreement, it does contain transfers of some of the rights that are included in ownership. The fact that these partitionings of owner are temporary makes it easy to decide who is the "owner" in the conventional sense.

The partitioning of various types of rights to use, has been

[1] A different form of interpersonal sharing of rights is that in which all rights are possessed in common and jointly by the group, but the decision as to any use must be reached by the group. Rights to each different kind of use are not separated and possessed by different people. Instead the rights are commonly owned; and the problem is in devising or specifying some choice process which will "declare" the decision of the "group" of joint owners.

explored by Ronald Coase.[2] He notes that what are commonly called nuisances and torts apply to just such situations in which rights are partitioned and the exercise of one owner's rights involves distress or nuisance for the owners of other rights. For example, if a railroad spreads sparks and ignites fires in wheatfields near the tracks, the wheat grower can pay the railroad not to spread sparks (if the law gives the railroad the right to spread such sparks). On the other hand, if the right to decide about such land use is reserved to the farmer, the railroad could pay him for the right to drop sparks on the land (and save costs of spark screens, etc.). If there were no costs of *negotiating* such exchanges of rights and policing them, the initial partitioning of rights would not affect the way resources are used. (Of course, wealth would be redistributed in accord with the initial assignment of the partitioned rights.)

But when we recognize that transaction costs do exist, it seems clear that the partitioned rights will be reaggregated into more convenient clusters of rights. If so, there should be an evolutionary force toward survival of larger clusters of certain types of rights in the sanctioned concept of property rights. But I am at a loss to formulate this more precisely, meaningfully, and fruitfully. Except for rare studies like those of Glanville Williams on the development of the laws of trespass and the two-volume work of Maitland and Pollack on the development of law (and property rights) in the 12th through 14th centuries, I suspect our main alternative is to initiate studies of our own.[3] For example, a study of the property rights in Ireland during the past three hundred years and of

[2] "The Problem of Social Costs," *Journal of Law and Economics* (1960): 1–5.

[3] Frederick Pollock and Frederic Maitland, *The History of English Law Before the Time of Edward I*, 2nd ed. (Cambridge, 1952); Glanville Williams, *Liability for Animals* (Cambridge: Cambridge University Press, 1939).

water law in the United States may (and I believe, will) enable us to discover more rigorous formulation of the laws of development of property law.

5. SHARING PROPERTY RIGHTS

At this point there is a temptation to start classifying various partitioning of property rights, e.g., private, public, bailments, easements, leases, licenses, franchises, inheritances, etc. This temptation is easy to avoid, because the task is so difficult. Another temptation is to list the various ways in which property rights of owners—ownership rights, as they are called hereafter—whatever they may be, can be shared among people as joint owners or as a partnership. Or corporations can be created as a means of sharing property rights of owners among voluntary sharers. Or public property may amount to everyone having a share—although, as we shall see, I think this is not the crucial difference between public and private ownership.

The ability of individuals to enter into mutually agreeable sharing of the rights they possess is evident from the tremendous variety of such arrangements, e.g., corporations, partnerships, nonprofit corporations, licenses, bailments, nonvoting common stock, trusts, agencies, employee-employer relationships, and marriages.

Should we be surprised that the government refuses to enforce some voluntary proposed sharing of legitimate property rights among owners? Presumably the "undesirable" effects justify the refusal to sanction some of the ownership sharing. For example, at one time, the state refused to enforce corporate ownership—even though all the members of the corporation entered voluntarily. Will it enforce every voluntary sharing and partitioning of ownership rights among individuals?

The variety of joint sharing of property and ownership rights is a testimony to man's ingenuity. But if one asked what the difference was between any two of them, say public and private ownership, he would find the answer not so easy. In one sense it is adequate to say that the public is the owner as contrasted to a private group. But that is not very helpful if one is interested in discovering what difference it makes for behavior and use of resources. Compare a privately owned golf course with a publicly owned course (or auditorium, bus service, water service, garbage collection, airport, school, or even spaghetti factory). There are differences in the way they are operated; at least anyone who has ever compared them will think so. Why do these differences occur? Are the objectives different? Is it because the kind of people who operate one are different from those who operate the other? Is it because of the form of ownership?

I believe (on the basis of something more than casual observation) that behavior under each institution is different, not because the objectives sought by organizations under each form are different, but, instead, because even with the same explicit organization goals, the costs-rewards system impinging on the employees and the "owners" of the organization are different. And I suspect that these differences are implied by economic theory, if the trouble is taken to apply the theory. Further, preliminary speculation suggests, for example, that the difference between a privately owned corporation with 1,000 owners and a state-owned entity in a democracy with 1,000 citizens is quite significant, because the 1,000 individuals are furthering their own individual interests in each entity under two different systems of property rights, i.e., the rewards-costs schedules differ.

6. PRIVATE AND PUBLIC OWNERSHIP

How do private and public ownership rights differ? To sharpen the issue, consider a small-town theater owned by 1,000 corporate shareholders (each with one share) and an auditorium owned by the 1,000 residents as public property. This eliminates the difference of sharing and differences in the number of joint "owners." Every activity conducted at one could, in principle, just as well be held at the other building. Assume also, the city auditorium is operated to make money, not to subsidize some group, and so is the private theater.

The public auditorium and the private theater both serve the public. It is not the case that the former is designed to provide a public service and the latter not. The privately owned theater will survive only if it can provide services that the public wants at the price asked. It is a source of public service, even though its purpose from the owners' point of view is to make money. But what about the publicly owned auditorium? Is its end that of public service or to make money for the public owners? Suppose its end is public service. This does not *require* that its means of action be any different than if its ends were profits to the owners—public or private. Furthermore, assume in both cases the managers and employees were induced to take their jobs only because the salary enhances their own wealth or well-being. They take the jobs—not because they want to provide a public service or wealth for the owners; but instead because they want a better living for themselves. We can assume that those resident citizens who "own" the auditorium and voted for it did so because each felt it would make his own situation preferable—not because he wanted to benefit someone else as a charity device.

But there are differences, and we conjecture the proposition that the differences between public and private ownership arise from *the inability of a public owner to sell his share of public ownership* (and the ability to acquire a share without a purchase of the right). But let us be clear about this. We are not yet asserting that there are no other differences, nor that this difference has not been noticed before. Instead we are emphasizing the *unique* importance of this difference in the ownership rights.

We are not begging the issue by assuming away one general difference—the profit incentive or criterion. Both public and private property can seek profits. The desire to avoid or suppress the effects of the profit-making incentive is, however, often the reason society resorts to public ownership. However, the objectives sought by public ownership cannot merely be announced to the managers or operators with expectation that exhortation will be either sufficient or necessary to achieve the objective. Since our general postulate is that people, as individuals, seek to increase their utility and that wealth is a source of utility, we cannot expect people to change their goals or desires. Instead, we rely upon changes in the rewards-costs structure to redirect their activities as they seek to increase their utility or level of satisfaction of their desires.[4] And we shall try to show that many differences, that do exist between behavior in public and privately owned institutions, reflect this ownership difference—viz., the presence or the absence of the right to sell a share of ownership to someone else.

The difference can be put somewhat less euphemistically.

---

[4] Friends of Adam Smith will recognize this as the major postulate of his *Wealth of Nations*, a postulate which seems to have served economists well when not forgotten.

Public ownership *must* be borne by all members of the public, and no member can divest himself of that ownership. Ownership of public property is not voluntary; it is compulsory as long as one is a member of the public. To call something "compulsory" usually is a good start towards condemning it.

A person must move from one town to another to change his ownership in public property. In one sense it is not compulsory because it is not compulsory that one lives in a particular community. But so long as one does live in any community with public property he is a public owner and cannot divest himself of public ownership; but he can sell and shift private property ownership rights without also having to leave the community.

It is tempting to emphasize the possibility, under public ownership, of someone joining the community and thereby acquiring a share of public ownership, without payment to any of the existing owners. This dilution of a person's share of ownership is presumably absent in private ownership. In fact, a community could close off immigration; but public ownership would continue even if this dilution effect were an important problem. Furthermore, many corporations issue new shares without preemptive rights to former owners. Presumably this is done only when the receiver of the new shares pays the corporation something of at least equivalent value. And it is a safe assumption that the management deems the *quid pro quo* to have been worthwhile so far as present purposes are concerned. Still, it is sufficient that even if dilution of public ownership were eliminated by restriction of entry, the inability to sell one's share of public ownership remains a potent factor in the costs-reward system impinging on all members of the public and on the employees and administrators of the publicly owned institution.

7. SOME IMPLICATIONS OF TRANSFERABILITY

To see what difference is made by the right to transfer ownership shares, suppose public ownership could be sold. It would be possible for me to sell to someone else my share in the publicly owned water, or bus or garbage, or parks, or school system. To separate out the fact that public ventures are usually run without the intent of making a profit, let us suppose that the water or bus system had been instructed to be as profitable as it could. Now that its ownership has become salable, with capitalized profits or losses accruing to the owners, will incentives be any different?

The answer is suggested by two implications of the specialization of "ownership" which is similar to the familiar specialization of other kinds of skills or activities. The two derivative implications are: (1) concentration of rewards and costs *more* directly on each person responsible for them, and (2) comparative advantage effects of specialized applications of (a) knowledge in control and (b) of risk bearing.

Degree of Dependency. The greater concentration of rewards and costs means simply that each person's wealth is more dependent upon his own activities. This is brought about as follows: the more he concentrates his wealth holding in particular resources, the more will his wealth respond to his own activities in those areas. Consider the following example: Suppose there are 100 people in a community, with 10 separate enterprises. Suppose that each person, by devoting one tenth of his time to some one enterprise as an owner, could produce a saving or gain of $1,000. Since the individual is a 1/100 part owner he will acquire $10. Suppose, further, that he does this for each of the 10 different enterprises, in each of which he owns 1/100 part. His total wealth gain will be $100, with the rest of the product, $9,900, going to the 99 other people. If the 99 other people act in the same way, he will get from their activities an increase of wealth of $990,000/100=$9,900, which gives him a total of $10,000. This is exactly equal to his product most of which was spread over the other owners.

However, if everyone each owns 1/10 part of *one* enterprise only (which means that ownership has been reshuffled from pro rata equal shares in all enterprises to a concentration in one enterprise by each person, although with the same total number of enterprises), the individual will now be assumed to devote his whole time during one year to the one enterprise, so he again produces $10,000. (We assume that his productivity is proportional to the number of hours of work, and that it is the same for everyone. Other assumptions will change the arithmetic, but will not destroy the main principle being elaborated.) Of this he gets $1,000. The remainder, $9,000, goes to the owners of the other 9/10 share. Like them, he too receives portions of the other owners' products, and if all are assumed to be exactly alike, then he gets from the 9 other joint owners of his enterprise $9,000 for a total of $10,000—precisely the same as in the preceding example. The difference is that now $1,000 of this is dependent upon his own activities whereas formerly only $100 was. Or more pertinently, the amount dependent upon the activities of other people is reduced from $9,900 to $9,000.

If we go to the extreme where the 10 enterprises are divided into 100, with each person as the sole owner of one enterprise, then all $10,000 of his year's wealth increase will depend upon his own activities. The first of these three examples corresponds to public ownership, the second to corporate joint private ownership, and the third to sole proprietorship.

If public ownership rights were made salable, they would in effect become private ownership rights and there would be a movement toward concentration of ownership of the type in the second example, at least. Why? In the second case, the wealth a person can get is more dependent upon his own activities than in the first case. Many people may prefer to let the situation stay as in example 1, hoping to collect a major portion of their wealth gain from other people's activities. If this were the case, the total wealth gain would decrease since everyone would have less incentive to work. But it suffices that there be at least one person who prefers to make himself less dependent upon other people's activities than in example 1 and who prefers at least some more wealth to some more leisure. He will then be prepared to buy up some ownership rights and pay a higher price for them than they are worth to some other people. That he values them more highly is precisely another way of saying that he values independence more than they do, or that he prefers more wealth to less wealth—even if it requires some work by him.

Comparative Advantage in Ownership: Control. The preceding example did not involve interpersonal differences of abilities, knowledge, or attitude toward risk. But if people differ in any of these respects, as they in fact do, it can be shown that specialization in various tasks—including that of owning a business—will increase wealth. This demonstration is simply the logical theorem of gains from comparative advantage, which we shall not explain here.

Usually the illustrations of comparative advantage are based on "labor" productivities with no reference to "ownership" productivities. But people differ in their talents as owners. Owners bear the risk of value changes, make the decisions of how much to produce, how much to invest, and how it shall be produced and who shall be employed as laborers and managers. Ownership ability includes attitude toward risk bearing, knowledge of different people's productive abilities, foresight and, of course, "judgment." These talents differ among people according to the particular industry, type of product, or productive resource one is considering. The differences in skills of people as owners make pertinent the principle of comparative advantage through specialization in ownership. If ownership rights are transferable, then specialization of ownership will yield gains. People will concentrate their ownership in those areas in which they believe they have a comparative advantage, if they want to increase their wealth. Just as specialization in typing, music, or various types of labor is more productive, so is specialization in ownership. Some people specialize in electronics industry knowledge, some in airlines, some in dairies, some in retailing, etc. Private property owners can specialize in knowledge about electronics, devoting much of their effort and study to learning which electronic devices show promise, which are now most efficient in various uses, which should be produced in larger numbers, where investment should take place, what kinds of research and development to finance, etc. But public ownership practically eliminates possibilities of specialization among owners—though not of employees in the publicly owned venture.

A person who is very knowledgeable about woodworking and cabinet or furniture building would have an advantage as an owner of a furniture company. He would, by being a stockholder, not necessarily make the company any better, but instead he would choose the better company—as judged by his knowledge—as one in which to own shares. The relative rise in the price of such companies enables the existing owners to issue new shares, borrow money more readily, and retain control. In this way the differences in knowledge enable people to specialize in the application of that knowledge to the management and operation of the company—albeit sometimes by indirect lines.

Comparative Advantage in Ownership: Risk Bearing. A second aspect of ownership specialization is risk bearing. People's attitudes toward risk differ. If various ventures or resources represent different prospects of values, then exchange of ownership will enable a reallocation of risks among people, leading to greater utility in the same sense that exchange of goods does. This risk-bearing difference reflects not only attitudes toward risk but beliefs about the prospects of future values of the assets whose ownership can be transferred. Differences in "knowledge" can be used not only in an effort to be more productive but also as a means for distinguishing different risk situations. For example, I may be the top administrator of the Carnation Milk Company, but I may choose to hold stocks in some electronic company because I prefer the risk pattern provided by that stock to that provided by ownership in Carnation. In this way a person can separate the productivity of knowledge and effort in what he owns from the risk bearing. He can, if he wants, combine them by holding stock in a company in which he is active. This possibility of separating the *control* (effective administration or operation of the company—an activity which rewards comparative superiority in ability and knowledge) from *risk bearing* is, of course, regarded as an advantage by those who act as employed managers or administrators, and by those who choose to act as corporate stock owners without also bothering to exercise their vote or worry about control. Yet, it is often criticized as undesirable.

Not all of the owners have to think of themselves as owners who are going to exercise their voting rights so effectively as to exert an influence on management. Most of the owners may go along simply because they believe the prospects for profits and losses are sufficiently promising relative to other assets they could own. If losses eventuate, their only alternative is to sell out. To whom? To other buyers who, because of the reduced profit prospects, will offer only a lower price. These "nonactive" owners perform a very important function in that they provide the willingness to bear some of the value consequences, at least. So long as scarce resources *exist*, value changes will occur. The question left is then which particular members are to bear the reduced value. Someone has to bear them. Those changes cannot be eliminated.

Often it is said that joint ownership in the modern corporation has separated ownership and control. What this means is that risk bearing and management are more separate. This is correct in that each owner does not have the kind of control he would as the sole owner. But it is a long logical leap to decrying this. It can be a good thing. Specialization in risk bearing and in management or decision-making about particular uses of resources is now possible. Complete separation does not exist for every joint owner, for to the extent that some share owners are inactive or indifferent to alternative choices or management problems, other stockholders (joint owners) will be more influential. In effect, the "passive" owners are betting on the decisions of "active" owners; "betting" in the sense that they are prepared to pay other people for any losses produced by these "activists" and in turn collect the profits, if any. In the absence of any right to buy and sell shared ownership rights voluntarily everyone would have to bet on the activists as a group (the case of public property). The right to sell concentrates this betting on these who are prepared to pay the most (or demand the least) for the right to do so. And it concentrates the control or management with those who believe they are relatively most able at that task—and these beliefs can be tested with the less able being eliminated more surely in private ownership than in public because (1) the evidence of poor management and the opportunity to capture wealth gains by eliminating it is revealed to outsiders by the lower selling price of the ownership rights, (2) the specialization of ownership functions is facilitated, and (3) the possibility of concentrating one's wealth in certain areas permits greater correlation of personal interest and effort in line with wealth holdings.

We conjecture from the preceding discussion the theorem: *Under public ownership the costs of any decision or choice are less fully thrust upon the selector than under private property*. In other words, the cost-benefit incentives system is changed toward lower costs. The converse of this implication is that the gains to any owner resulting from any cost-saving action are less fully effective. These do not mean that the true costs are reduced. The looser correlation between the costs borne by any chooser and the costs of the particular choices he makes is what is implied. Similarly, the capturable gains to the owners of their actions are reduced.

They are *less* fully borne than they would be if the same action were taken in a private property institution, with a similar number of owners.[5] From this theorem one would expect that public agencies would, in order to offset or counterbalance this reduced cost bearing, impose special extra costs or constraints on public employees or agents. Public agents who

[5] In other words, this difference between public and private ownership does not flow from differences in numbers of owners.

are authorized to spend public funds should be more severely constrained with extra restrictions precisely because the costs of their actions are less effectively thrust upon them. And of course these extra constraints do exist. Because of these extra constraints—or because of the "costs" of them—the public arrangement becomes a higher cost (in the sense of "less efficient") than that for private property agencies.

For example, civil service, nepotism restrictions, tenure, single-salary structures for public schoolteachers, sealed bids, and "lineitem" budget controls, to name a few, are some of the costly devices used.

But it is not easy—indeed impossible—in many instances to impose "corrective" costs as offsets. How would one impose full costs upon a city manager who decided to have a garbage collection system (that turned out to be a big money loser) that the city would tolerate? By not reelecting him. But this cost is less than that borne by the private owner who decides (erroneously) to start a garbage collection system. He loses his job *and* the sunk costs. Similarly, how do we make a voter bear the costs of bad judgment in his votes? Are the prospects of costs that may be imposed on a voter equivalent to the cost-prospects that will be laid on a private owner (with share rights) voting in a private corporation? Not according to the theorem derived from our analysis.

I should, I suppose, avow at random intervals that all this is not a condemnation of public ownership any more than certain "deficiencies" of marriage, the human eye, the upright position of the human being, or smoking are to be regarded as condemnations of marriage, eyes, walking on two feet, or smoking. The "lesser" evils in some institutions—and they exist in all—are borne for the greater good in some of them. We are not arguing that private property even in its purest form is perfect in the cost-bearing sense. No standard of perfection is available. All of our statements have been comparative in degrees of cost bearing.

The converse of this "apologia" is that one should not speak of the imperfections of the marketplace, either. Nor should one assume in those instances where the marketplace is inferior in certain respects to, say, public ownership or government control, that we ought to switch from the private property market to the government. The presence of one kind of relative deficiency does not justify a switch to another agency—which has other kinds of deficiencies.

8. WE SUMMARIZE

As we suggested earlier, public and private ownership are used for different purposes, and in some cases *because* of these different behavioral implications. If public ownership in some government activity were converted to private property, the method of achieving the government objectives would be changed. If city and national parks, or golf courses owned by cities were converted to private property, they would no longer be operated as subsidies for certain groups. If the fire and police department rights were converted to private property rights, vast changes would occur in their operation. And the same goes for the postal system, the garbage collection system, the bus lines, streets, the federal mortgage insurance companies, and the army, the navy, and the air force. When "we" do not want (whatever that means) these changes to occur, these activities are conducted via public ownership instead of privately. And if the effects of greater dependence of benefits and costs on one's own actions are not wanted, resort is made to government activity. Which is not to say that government activity is therefore for that reason good or bad. The extent to which ''society'' reduces risks that must be individually borne and instead has them borne by society at large—thus reducing the correlation between choice of action and consequences for people as individuals—the greater is the extent of public property. How much this depends upon a *choice* to socialize certain risks, and how much reflects the voting and decision-making *process* are questions I cannot answer.

6

Competition, Monopoly and the Pursuit of Money

THE PROBLEM

Generally speaking, the observations of economists on the subject of monopoly fall into two classes. One set of observations, which flows directly from monopoly theory, is that resources in the competitive sector of the economy would be underutilized if used by monopolists. The other, which does not arise as an implication of either monopoly or competitive theory, consists of a series of observations of empirical phenomena: that monopolistic enterprises, by comparison with competitive enterprises, are characterized by rigid prices, stodgy managements, and relaxed, easygoing working conditions. Alternatively, it is alleged that employees of competitive enterprises work harder, managements are more aggressive and flexible, and pricing is more responsive to profit opportunities.[1]

This article was coauthored by Reuben A. Kessel.

[1] Hicks concludes: "The best of all monopoly profits is a quiet life." This conclusion appears in a theoretical paper on monopoly; yet it does not flow from the theory presented.

Preceding the foregoing quotation is: "Now, as Professor Bowley and others have pointed out, the variation in monopoly profit for some way on either side of the

To regard this second class of observations as not an implication of either monopoly or competitive theory is only partly correct. More correctly, these observations are inconsistent with the implications of the standard profit or wealth maximization postulate. For analyzing the behavior described by Hicks, the pecuniary wealth maximization postulate is clearly inappropriate and should be replaced by a utility maximization postulate.

UTILITY MAXIMIZATION, NOT WEALTH MAXIMIZATION

That a person seeks to maximize his utility says little more than that he makes consistent choices. In order to employ this postulate as an engine of analysis, one must also specify what things are regarded as desirable. This is the class that includes all those things of which a person prefers more rather than less: money, wealth, love, esteem, friends, ease, health, beauty, meat, gasoline, etc.[2] Then, assuming that a person is willing to

highest profit output may often be small (in the general case it will depend on the difference between the slopes of the marginal revenue and marginal cost curves); and if this is so, the subjective costs involved in securing a close adaption to the most profitable output may well outweigh the meager gains offered. It seems not at all unlikely that people in monopolistic positions will often be people with sharply rising subjective costs; if this is so, they are likely to exploit their advantage much more by not bothering to get very near the position of maximum profit, than by straining themselves to get very close to it. The best of all monopoly profits is a quiet life.'' John R. Hicks, ''Annual Survey of Economic Theory: The Theory of Monopoly.'' *Econometrica*, January 1935, p. 8.

[2] The following impression is not uncommon. ''To say that the individual maximizes his satisfaction is a perfectly general statement. It says nothing about the individual's psychology of behavior, is, therefore, devoid of empirical content.'' T. Scitovsky, ''A Note on Profit Maximization and Its Implications,'' *Review of Economic Studies*, 1943, pp. 57–60. But this is also true of profit or wealth maximization—unless one says what variables affect profit or wealth and in what way. And so in utility maximization, one must similarly add a postulate stating

substitute among these variables, that is, he will give up wealth in return for more peace and quiet, or better-looking secretaries, or more cordial employees, or better weather, the behavior described by Hicks can be analyzed.

Economics cannot stipulate the exchange value that these things have for any particular person, but it can and does say that, whatever his preference patterns may be, the less he must pay for an increase in one of them, the more it will be utilized. This principle, of course, is merely the fundamental demand theorem of economics—that the demand for any good is a negative function of its price. And price here means not only the pecuniary price but the cost of whatever has to be sacrificed.

For predicting the choice of productive inputs by business firms, where only the pecuniary aspects of the factors are of concern, the narrower special-case postulate of pecuniary wealth is usually satisfactory. But this special-case postulate fails when a wider class of business activities is examined. Therefore we propose to use the general case consistently, even though in some special cases simpler hypotheses, contained within this more general hypothesis, would be satisfactory.[3]

---

what variables affect satisfaction or utility. This leads to meaningful implications refutable, in principle, by observable events. For example, an individual will increase his use of those variables that become cheaper. Utility maximization, like wealth maximization, is not a mere sterile truism.

[3] Failure to give adequate heed to the special-case properties of wealth maximization may have been responsible for some complaints about the inadequacy of economic theory and may even have led to the curious belief that people themselves change according to which postulate is used. For example, Scitovsky says (*ibid.*):

"The puritan psychology of valuing money for its own sake, and not for the enjoyments and comforts it might yield, is that of the ideal entrepreneur as he was conceived in the early days of capitalism. The combination of frugality and industry, the entrepreneurial virtues, is calculated to insure the independence of the entrepreneur's willingness to work from the level of his income. The classical

An example of the power of the generalized utility maximizing postulate is provided by Becker.[4] He shows that under the more general postulate a person, deliberately and even in full knowledge of the consequences for business profits or personal pecuniary wealth, will choose to accept a lower salary or smaller rate of return on invested capital in exchange for nonpecuniary income in the form of, say, working with pretty secretaries, nonforeigners, or whites. The difference in money return between what an entrepreneur could earn and what he does earn when he chooses to discriminate is an equalizing

economists, therefore, were justified in assuming that the entrepreneur aims at maximizing his profits. They were concerned with a type of businessman whose psychology happened to be such that for him maximizing profits was identical with maximizing satisfaction.

"The entrepreneur today may have lost some of the frugality and industry of his forefathers; nevertheless, the assumption that he aims at maximizing his profits is still quite likely to apply to him—at least as a first approximation. For this assumption is patently untrue only about people who regard work as plain drudgery; a necessary evil, with which they have to put up in order to earn their living and the comforts of life. The person who derives satisfaction from his work—other than that yielded by the income he receives for it—will to a large extent be governed by ambition, spirit of emulation and rivalry, pride in his work, and similar considerations, when he plans the activity. We believe that the entrepeneur usually belongs in this last category."

Aside from the dubious validity of (1) alleged differences between the entrepreneurs of the "early days" of capitalism and those of today, and (2) the allegation that the early entrepreneur was one whose utility function had only a single variable—wealth—in it, the more general analysis obviates the urge to set up two different and inconsistent behavior postulates, as if people were schizophrenic types—utility maximizers when consumers and wealth maximizers when businessmen.

The special-case property of the wealth maximizing postulate has been noted by M. W. Reder ("A Reconsideration of the Marginal Productivity Theory," *Journal of Political Economy* [October 1947]: 450–58). But in suggesting alternatives he did not postulate the more general one, which includes the valid applications of the special-case postulate as well as many more, without leading to the invalid implications of the special-case postulate.

[4] Gary S. Becker, *The Economics of Discrimination* (University of Chicago Press, 1957).

difference that will not be eliminated by market pressures. If these persisting, equalizing differences exist, their size, and consequently the extent of discrimination, will differ when institutional arrangements lead to differences in the relative costs of income in pecuniary form relative to income in non-pecuniary form. Thus, if one can determine the direction in which relative costs are affected by activities or variables that enhance a person's utility, then it should be possible to observe corresponding differences in behavior.

MONOPOLISTIC VERSUS COMPETITIVE BEHAVIOR

The wealth-maximizing postulate seems to imply that both competitive and monopolistic enterprises pursue profits with equal vigor and effectiveness, that their managements are equally alert and aggressive, and that prices are just as flexible in competitive as in monopolized markets. Both the competitive and monopoly model imply that the assets of an enterprise, be it a monopolist or competitive firm, will be utilized by those for whom these assets have the greatest economic value. One might object to this implication of similarity between competition and monopoly by arguing that, when a monopolistic enterprise is not making the most of its pecuniary economic opportunities, it runs less risk of being driven out of business than a similarly mismanaged competitive enterprise. The answer to this is that despite the absence of competition in product markets, those who can most profitably utilize monopoly powers will acquire control over them: competition in the capital markets will allocate monopoly rights to those who can use them most profitably. Therefore, so long as free capital markets are available, the absence of competition in product markets does not imply a different quality of management in monopolistic as compared with competitive enterprises. Only in the case of nontransferable assets (human monopoly rights and powers like those commanded by Bing Crosby) does classical theory, given free capital market arrangements, admit a difference between competition and monopoly with respect to the effectiveness with which these enterprises pursue profits.[5]

The preceding argument implies that there is no difference in the proportion of inefficiently operated firms among monopolistic as compared with competitive enterprises. (Inefficiency here means that a situation is capable of being changed so that a firm could earn more pecuniary income with no loss in nonpecuniary income or else can obtain more nonpecuniary income with no loss in pecuniary income.) As Becker has shown, discrimination against Negroes in employment is not necessarily a matter of business inefficiency. It can be viewed as an expression of a taste, and one's a priori expectation is that discrimination is characterized by a negatively sloped demand curve. From this viewpoint, discrimination against Negroes by business enterprises, whether competitors or monopolists, would not lessen even if managements were convinced that discrimination reduced their pecuniary income. Presumably, the known sacrifice of pecuniary income is more than compensated for by the gain in nonpecuniary income. But if discrimination does not constitute business inefficiency, then the frequency of discrimination against Ne-

[5] For a statement of this position, see Becker, *The Economics of Discrimination*, p. 38. Becker argues that, insofar as monopoly rights are randomly distributed and cannot be transferred, there are no forces operating to distribute these resources to those for whom they are most valuable. Consequently monopolists, when rights are nontransferable, would be less efficient, on the average, than competitive firms.

groes ought to be just as great in competitive as in monopolistic enterprises, since both are presumed to be equally efficient. This implication is apparently inconsistent with existing evidence. Becker's data indicate that Negroes are discriminated against more frequently by monopolistic enterprises.[6] But why do monopolistic enterprises discriminate against Negroes more than do competitive enterprises? One would expect that those who have a taste for discrimination against Negroes would naturally gravitate to those economic activities that, for purely pecuniary reasons, do not employ Negroes. Free choice of economic activities implies a distribution of resources that would minimize the costs of satisfying tastes for discrimination. Consequently the managements of competitive enterprises ought to discriminate against Negroes neither more nor less than those of monopolistic enterprises.

If there is greater discrimination by monopolists than by competitive enterprises, and if it cannot be explained by arguing either that people with tastes for discrimination also have special talents related to monopolistic enterprises or that monopolists are in some sense less efficient businessmen, what, then, explains Becker's data and similar observations? More generally, what is the explanation for the contentions that monopolists pursue pecuniary wealth less vigorously, do not work as hard, have more lavish business establishments, etc.? It is to this problem that this paper is addressed.

MONOPOLY AND PROFIT CONTROL

Stigler and others have pointed out that monopolies, both labor and product, are creatures of the state in a sense which is

[6] *Ibid.*, p. 40, Table 2.

not true of competitive enterprises.[7] Monopolies typically are protected against the hazards of competition, not simply by their ability to compete, but by the state's policy of not permitting competitors to enter monopolized markets. Laws are enacted that encourage and lead to the creation of monopolies in particular markets. Monopolies so created are beholden to the state for their existence—the state giveth, the state taketh away. Accordingly, they constrain their business policies by satisfying the requirements that they shall do what is necessary to maintain their monopoly status.

Public utilities are an example. Under this head one should include not only gas, electric, and water companies, but all franchised and licensed industries. Railroads, busses, airlines, and taxis fall in this category of business for which permission of a public authority is required, and for which rate and profit regulation exists. For many other businesses, entry regulation exists: commercial and savings banks, savings and loan associations, insurance companies, and the medical profession. All these are formally regulated monopolies, since they are licensed and operated with the approval of the state. Their cardinal sin is to be too profitable.[8] This constraint upon monopolists does not exist for firms operating in competitive markets. This difference in constraints implies differences between the business policies of competitive firms and those of

[7] George J. Stigler, "The Extent and Bases of Monopoly," *American Economic Review* (June 1942), Supplement Part 2, p. 1; H. Gregg Lewis, "The Labor Monopoly Problem: A Positive Program," *Journal of Political Economy* (August 1951): 277; C. E. Lindbloom, *Unions and Capitalism* (Yale University Press, 1949), p. 214; and Milton Friedman, "Some Comments on the Significance of Labor Unions for Economic Policy," in *The Impact of the Union*, ed. David M. Wright (Harcourt Brace, 1951), p. 214.

[8] The notorious suggestion of the medical profession that doctors not drive around town in expensive Cadillacs when visiting patients is an example of the point being made.

monopolies. The remainder of this paper is devoted to indicating specifically the character of the constraints that are postulated and exploring the observable implications of this postulate.

Even a firm that has successfully withstood the test of open competition without government protection may manifest the behavior of a protected monopoly. Thus a firm like General Motors may become very large and outstanding and acquire a large share of a market just as a protected monopoly does. If, in addition, its profits are large, it will fear that public policy or state action may be directed against it, just as against a state-created monopoly. Such a firm constrains its behavior much in the style of a monopoly whose profit position is protected but also watched by the state. This suggests that the distinction between publicly regulated monopolies and non-regulated monopolies is a false distinction for this problem. As the possibility of state action increases, a firm will adapt its behavior to that which the state deems appropriate. In effect, state regulation is implicitly present.

The cardinal sin of a monopolist, to repeat, is to be too profitable. Public regulation of monopolies is oriented about fixing final prices in order to enable monopolists to earn something like the going rate of return enjoyed by competitive firms. If monopolists are too profitable, pressures are exerted to reduce profits through lowering prices. Only if monopolists can demonstrate to regulatory authorities that they are not profitable enough are they permitted to raise prices.

IMPLICATIONS

If regulated monopolists are able to earn more than the permissible pecuniary rate of return, then "inefficiency" is a free good, because the alternative to inefficiency is the same pecuniary income and no "inefficiency." Therefore this profit constraint leads to a divergence between private and economic costs. However, it is easy to be naive about this inefficiency. More properly, it is not inefficiency at all but efficient utility maximizing through nonpecuniary gains. Clearly one class of nonpecuniary income is the indulgence of one's tastes in the kind of people with whom one prefers to associate. Specifically, this may take the form of pretty secretaries, of pleasant, well-dressed, congenial people who never say anything annoying, of lavish offices, of large expense accounts, of shorter working hours, of costly administrative procedures that reduce the wear and tear on executives rather than increasing the pecuniary wealth of the enterprise, of having secretaries available on a moment's notice by having them sitting around not doing anything, and of many others. It is important to recognize that to take income in nonpecuniary form is consistent with maximizing utility. What is important is not a matter of differences in tastes between monopolists and competitive firms, but differences in the terms of trade of pecuniary for nonpecuniary income. And given this difference in the relevant price or exchange ratios, the difference in the mix purchased should not be surprising.[9]

[9] Usually in economics consumers are presumed to maximize utility subject to fixed income or wealth. What is the wealth or income constraint here? In one sense it is not merely wealth or income that is the pertinent limitation. Many people have access to the use and allocation of resources even though they don't own them. An administrator can assign offices and jobs; he can affect the way company or business resources are used. In all of these decisions, he will be influenced by the effects on his own situation. Therefore to gauge his behavior by the usual wealth or income limitation is to eliminate from consideration a wider range of activities that do not fall within the usual "wealth" or ownership limitation. By straining it is possible to incorporate even this kind of activity with the wealth constraint but we

If wealth cannot be taken out of an organization in salaries or in other forms of personal pecuniary property, the terms of trade between pecuniary wealth and nonpecuniary business-associated forms of satisfaction turn against the former. More of the organization's funds will now be reinvested (which need not result in increased wealth) in ways that enhance the manager's prestige or status in the community. Or more money can be spent for goods and services that enhance the manager's and employees' utility. There can be more luxurious offices, more special services, and so forth, than would ordinarily result if their costs were coming out of personal wealth.

For the total amount of resources used, these constrained expenditure patterns necessarily yield less utility than the unconstrained. The man who spends a dollar with restrictions will need less than a dollar to get an equivalent satisfaction if he can spend it without the restriction. This constrained optimum provides the answer to the question: If a person does spend the wealth of a business as business-connected expenditures for thick rugs and beautiful secretaries, can they not be treated simply as a substitute for household consumption, since he can be regarded as voluntarily choosing to spend his wealth in the business rather than in the home? The answer is that business spending is a more constrained, even if voluntary, choice. This whole analysis is merely an illustration of the effects of restricting the operation of the law of comparative advantage by reducing the size of the market (or range of alternatives).

Employment policies will also reflect the maximization of

---

find it more convenient for exposition not to do so. In this paper, in a sense, we are discussing the institutional arrangements which determine to what extent constraints are of one type rather than another.

utility. Assume that an employer prefers clean-cut, friendly, sociable employees. If two available employees are equally productive, but only one is white, native born, Christian, and attractive, the other will not get the job. And if the other employee's wages are reduced to offset this, it will take a greater cut or equilibrating difference to offset this in a monopoly. Why? Because the increase in take-home profits provided by the cost reduction is smaller (if it is increased at all) in the monopoly or state-sheltered firm. Thus one would expect to find a lower fraction of "other" employees in "monopolies" and other areas of sheltered competition.

What this means is that the wages paid must be high enough to attract the "right" kind of employees. At these wages the supply of the "other" kind will be plentiful. A rationing problem exists, so that the buyer, when he offers a higher price than would clear the market with respect to pecuniary productive aspects clears the market by imposing other tests, like congeniality, looks, and so on. For the right kind of employee the price is not above the market clearing price. In a competitive situation this price differential would not persist because its elimination would all redound to the benefit of the owners, whereas in monopoly it will persist because the reduction in costs cannot be transformed into equally large take-home pecuniary wealth for the owners.

The question may be raised: Even if all this is true of a regulated monopoly like a public utility, what about unregulated, competitively superior monopolies? Why should they act this way? The answer is, as pointed out earlier, that the distinction between regulated and unregulated monopolies is a false one. All monopolies are subject to regulation or the threat of destruction through antitrust action. And one of the criteria that the courts seem to consider in evaluating whether or not a firm is a "good" monopoly is its profitability.[10] It behooves an unregulated monopoly, if it wants to remain one, not to appear to be too profitable.

The owners of a monopoly, regulated or "not," therefore have their property rights attenuated because they do not have unrestricted access to or personal use of their company's wealth. This suggests that the whole analysis can be formulated, not in terms of monopoly and competition, as we have chosen to for present purposes, but in terms of private property rights. There is basically no analytic difference between the two since an analysis made in terms of monopoly and competition identifies and emphasizes circumstances that affect property rights. The same analysis can be applied to nonprofit organizations, governments, unions, state-owned, and other "nonowned" institutions, with almost identical results.

One word of clarification—the contrast here is between monopoly and competition, not between corporate and noncorporate firms. We are analyzing differences in implications for behavior that arise from factors other than the corporate structure of the firm. Although there may be differences between corporate, diffused ownership firms and single proprietorships that may affect the many kinds of behavior discussed in this paper, we have been unable to derive them from the corporate aspect. Nor are those features derived from considerations of size per se—however much this may affect behavior.[11]

[10] See Aaron Director and Edward H. Levi, "Trade Regulation," *Northwestern Law Review* (1956): 286 ff.

[11] We were originally tempted to believe that the same theory being applied here could be applied to corporate versus noncorporate institutions, where the corporate form happens to involve many owners. Similarly the size factor could also be

The preceding propositions stated that more of some forms of behavior would be observed among monopolies. But more than what and of what? More than would be observed in competitive industries. It is not asserted that every monopolist will prefer more than every competitor; instead, it is said that, whatever the relative tastes of various individuals, all those in a monopolistic situation pay less for their actions than they would in a competitive contest. And the way to test this is not to cite a favorable comparison based on one monopolist and one competitor. Rather the variations in individual preferences must be allowed to average out by random sampling from each class.

TESTS OF THE ANALYSIS

What observable populations can be compared in testing these implications? One pair of populations are the public utilities and private competitive corporations. Public utilities are monopolies in that entry by competitors is prohibited. Yet, as indicated earlier, the utility is not allowed to exercise its full monopoly powers either in acquiring or in distributing pecuniary wealth as dividends to its owners. The owners therefore have relatively weak incentives to try to increase their profits through more efficient management or operation beyond (usually) six percent. But they do have relatively strong incentives to use the resources of the public utility for their own personal interests, but in ways that will count as company costs. Nor does the public utility regulatory body readily detect such activities, because its incentives to do so are even weaker than those of the stockholders. The regulatory body's

analyzed via the effects on the costs and rewards of various choice opportunities. Subsequent analysis suggests that many of the appealing differences between corporate, dispersed ownership and individual proprietorship proved to be superficial.

survival function is the elimination of publicly detectable inefficiencies. Furthermore, the utility regulatory board has a poor criterion of efficiency because it lacks competitive standards.

Public utility managements, whether or not they are also stockholders, will engage in activities that raise costs even if they eat up profits. Management will be rational (i.e., utility maximizing and efficient) if it uses company funds to hire pleasant and congenial employees and to buy its supplies from salesmen who have these same virtues. They cost more, of course, but how does the regulatory commission decide that these are unjustifiable expenditures—even though stockholders would prefer larger profits (which they aren't allowed to have) and customers would prefer lower product prices? Office furniture and equipment will be of higher quality than otherwise. Fringe benefits will be greater and working conditions more pleasant. The managers will be able to devote a greater part of their business time to community and civic programs. They will reap the prestige rewards given to the "statesman-businessman" class of employers. Vacations will be longer and more expensive. Time off for sick leave and for civic duties will be greater. Buildings and equipment will be more beautiful. Public utility advertising will be found more often in magazines and papers appealing to the intellectual or the culturally elite, because this is a low "cost" way of enhancing the social status of the managers and owners. Larger contributions out of company resources to education, science, and charity will be forthcoming—not because private competitors are less appreciative of these things, but because they cost monopolists less.[12]

[12] We could compare a random sample of secretaries working for public utilities with a random sample of secretaries working for competitive businesses. The

Job security, whether in the form of seniority or tenure, is a form of increased wealth for employees. Since it makes for more pleasant employer-employee relations, it is a source of utility for employers. The incentive or willingness of owners to grant this type of wealth to employees and thereby increase their own utility is relatively strong because profits are not the opportunity costs of this choice. The owners of a competitive firm, on the other hand, would have to pay the full price either in profits or in competitive disadvantage. Therefore the viability of such activities is lower in that type of firm. The relative frequency or extent of job security should be higher in monopolies and employee turnover rates lower. Also, the incidence of tenure in private educational institutions will be less than in nonprofit or state-operated educational institutions—if the foregoing analysis is correct.[13]

The relative incidence of employee cooperatives will also

---

former will be prettier—no matter whom we select as our judges (who must not know what hypothesis we are testing when they render their decision). The test, however, really should be made by sampling among the secretaries who are working for equal-salaried executives in an attempt to eliminate the income effect on demand. Another implication is that the ratio of a secretary's salary to her supervisor's salary will be higher for a public utility—on the grounds that beauty commands a price. Other nonpecuniary, desirable attributes of secretaries also will be found to a greater extent in public utilities (as well as in nonprofit enterprises) than in private competitive firms. In a similar way, all of the preceding suggested implications about race, religion, and sex could be tested.

Another comparison can be made. Consider the sets of events in the business and in the home of the public utility employee or owner having a given salary or wealth. The ratio of the thickness of the rug in the office to that of the rug at home will be greater for the public utility than for the private competitive firm employee or owner. The ratio of the value of the available company car to the family car's value will be higher for the public utility than for the private competitive firm. And similarly for the ratios of secretary's beauty to wife's beauty, decorations in the office, travel expenses, etc.

[13] See Armen A. Alchian, "Private Property and the Relative Cost of Tenure," *The Public Stake in Union Power*, ed. P. Bradley (University of Virginia Press, 1958), pp. 350–71.

provide a test. Some employee cooperatives are subsidized by employers. This subsidy often takes the form of free use of company facilities and of employees for operating the cooperative. For any given set of attitudes of employers towards employee cooperatives, costs are lower for monopolists with "excess" profits. Consequently their frequency will be greater among these enterprises.

Inability to keep excess profits in pecuniary form implies that monopolists are more willing than competitive enterprises to forgo them in exchange for other forms of utility-enhancing activities within the firm. Fringe benefits, cooperatives, and special privileges for certain employees will be more common. Employees whose consumption preferences do not induce them to use the cooperatives or fringe benefits are not necessarily stupid if they complain of this diversion of resources. But their complaints do reflect their differences in tastes and their ignorance of the incentives and reward patterns that impinge upon owners and administrators. Instead of complaining, they might better seek benefits of special interest to themselves. But since this involves a power play within the firm, the senior people are likely to be the ones who win most often. Hence one would expect to find such benefits more closely tailored to the preferences of the higher administrative officials than would be observed in a competitive business.

Wage policies will also differ in monopoly and non-monopoly enterprises. If business should fall off, the incentive to resort to fringe or wage reductions (unpleasant under any circumstances), will be weaker for a public utility because the potential savings in profits, if profits are not below the maximum permissible level, cannot be as readily captured by the management or stockholders. One would expect to find wages falling less in hard times, and one would also expect a smaller turnover and unemployment of personnel. The fact that these same implications might be derived from the nature of the demand for the utility's product does not in itself upset the validity of these propositions. But it does make the empirical test more difficult.

Seniority, tenure, employee cooperatives, and many other fringe benefits—instead of increased money salaries or payments—can be composed of mixtures of pecuniary and nonpecuniary benefits, though the inducement to adopt them despite their inefficiency is enhanced by the relatively smaller sacrifice imposed on the owners of organizations in monopolistic situations, as defined here. The relative cost of take-home wealth for the owners is higher; hence they are more willing to utilize other consumption channels.[14]

Constraints on the opportunity to keep profits that are above the allowable limit reduce the incentive to spend money for profitable expansion of services. An upper limit on profits, with strong protection from competition but no assurance of protection from losses of overexpansion, will bias the possible rewards downward in comparison with those of competitive business. An implication of this is "shortages" of public utility services. Despite the fact that prices are above the cost of providing some services, the latter will not necessarily be available. It is better to wait until the demand is already existent and expansion is demanded by the authorities. The possible extra profits are an attenuated inducement.

[14] The other commonly advanced reasons for such benefits or "inefficiencies" are the income tax on pecuniary wealth and the influence of unions. The former force is obvious; the latter is the effect of desires by union officials to strengthen their position by emphasizing the employee members' benefits to the union administration, as is done in many fringe benefits. But whether or not these latter factors are present, the one advanced here is an independent factor implying differences between monopoly and competition.

But these implications hold only if the public utility is earning its allowable limit of profits on investment. If it is losing money—and there is no guarantee against it—stockholders' take-home pay will be curtailed by inefficiency. Until profits reach the take-home limit, profitable and efficient operations will be desirable. If the state regulatory commission is slow to grant price increases in response to cost increases, the utilities should find their profits reduced below the allowable limit during a period of inflation. As a result there should be a tightening up or elimination, or both, of some of the effects predicted in the preceding discussion.[15] One would expect the opposite to occur during periods of deflation.

The present analysis also suggests that there may be an economic rationale for the "shock theory" of wage adjustments. This theory asserts that the profit-reducing wage increases imposed by labor will shock management into greater efficiencies. Suppose that monopolies are induced to trade pecuniary wealth (because they are not allowed to keep it) for nonpecuniary forms of income financed out of business expenditures. This means that, under the impact of higher wage costs and lower profits, the monopolies can now proceed to restore profit rates. Since some of their profit possibilities have been diverted into so-called nonpecuniary forms of income, higher labor costs will make realized profits, broadly interpreted, at least a little smaller. In part, at least, the increased pe-

[15] This analysis suggests that, with the decline in profitability of railroads, the principle of seniority advancement in railroad management has become relatively less viable. Similar arguments are applicable for other fringe benefits. With respect to negotiation with unions, it implies that railroad managements will more vigorously resist giving the unions extravagantly large concessions because these costs are being borne by owners.

The analysis also implies that unions do better in dealing with monopolistic as contrasted with competitive industries.

cuniary wages will come at the expense of nonpecuniary benefits, which will be reduced in order to restore profit levels. Actually, the shock effect does not produce increases in effiency. Instead, it revises the pattern of distribution of benefits. Left unchanged is the rate of pecuniary profits—if these were formerly at their allowable, but not economic, limit.

Evidence relevant for testing the hypothesis presented here has been produced by the American Jewish Congress, which surveyed the occupations of Jewish and non-Jewish Harvard Business School graduates. The data consist of a random sample of 224 non-Jewish and a sample of 128 Jewish MBAs.[16] The 352 Harvard graduates were classified by ten industry categories: (1) agriculture, forestry, and fisheries, (2) mining, (3) construction, (4) transportation, communication, and other public utilities, (5) manufacturing, (6) wholesale and retail trade, (7) finance, insurance, and real estate, (8) business services, (9) amusement, recreation, and related services, and (10) professional and related services.

Categories (4) and (7) must be regarded as relatively monopolized. Therefore, if the hypothesis presented here is correct, the relative frequency of Jews in these two fields is lower than it is for all fields combined.[17] The relative frequency of Jews in all fields taken together, in the entire sample, is 36 percent. These data show that the frequency of Jews—74 MBAs—in the two monopolized fields is less than

[16] The existence of these data became known to the authors as a result of an article that appeared in the *New York Times* on the first day of the conference at which this paper was presented. Subsequently the American Jewish Congress released a paper, ''Analysis of Jobs Held by Jewish and by Non-Jewish Graduates of the Harvard Graduate School of Business Administration,'' which contains the data reported here.

[17] Similarly, one would expect Jews and Negroes to be underrepresented among enterprises supplying goods and services to monopolists for the same reason that they are underrepresented as employees.

18 percent. If a sample of 352, of whom 36 percent are Jews, is assigned so that 74 are in monopolized and 278 in nonmonopolized fields, the probability that an assignment random with respect to religion will result in as few as 18 percent Jews in monopolized fields (and over 41 percent in nonmonopolized fields) is less than 0.0005. This evidence, therefore, is consistent with the hypothesis presented.

One might object to classifying all finance, insurance, and real estate as monopolized fields. This classification includes the subcategories of banking, credit agencies, investment companies, security and commodity brokers, dealers and exchanges, other finance services, insurance, and real estate. Of these, only insurance and banking are regulated monopolies. If only these two subcategories are used, then there are 6 Jews among a group of 39 or a frequency of less than 15 percent. If a sample of 352, of whom 36 percent are Jews, is assigned so that 39 are in monopolized and 313 in nonmonopolized fields, the probability that an assignment that is random with respect to religion will result in as few as 15 percent Jews in the monopolized fields (and over 39 percent in the nonmonopolized fields) is less than 0.005. This evidence is also consistent with the hypothesis presented.

APPLICATIONS TO LABOR UNIONS

This application of monopoly analysis need not be restricted to public utilities. Any regulated activity or one that regulates entry into work should show the same characteristics. Labor unions, because of their control over entry or because of exclusive union representation in bargaining, have monopoly potential. Insofar as a union is able to use that potential to raise wages above the competitive level, unless the jobs are auctioned off, the rationing problem is a nonprice one. A "thoroughly unscrupulous" agent could, in principle, pocket the difference between the payment by the employer and the receipts to the employee, where this difference reflects the difference between the monopolistic and the competitive wage. The moral pressures and the state regulation of union monopoly operate against the existence of thoroughly unscrupulous union officers. But so long as the fruits of such monopoly are handed on to the employed members of the union, the state seems tolerant of monopoly unions. Because of the absence of free entry into the "union agent business," competitive bidding by prospective union agents will not pass on the potential monopoly gains fully to the laborers who do get the jobs.

The necessity of rationing jobs arises because the union agents or managers do not keep for themselves the entire difference between the monopoly wage and the lower competitive wage that would provide just the number of workers wanted. If they did keep it, there would be equilibrium without nonprice rationing. If any part of that difference is captured by the laborers, the quantity available will be excessive relative to the quantity demanded at the monopolized wage rate. The unwillingness of society to tolerate capture of all that difference by the union agents means that either it must be passed on to the workers, thus creating a rationing problem, or it must be indirectly captured by the union agents—not as pecuniary take-home pay, but indirectly as a utility derived from the expenditure of that difference in connection with union business.

To the extent that the monopoly gains are passed on, the preceding rationing problem and its implications exist. But to the extent that they are not, the union agents or persons in control of the monopoly organization will divert the monopoly gains to their own benefit, not through outright sale of the jobs to the highest bidder, but through such indirect devices as high initiation fees and membership dues. This ties the monopoly sale price to the conventional dues arrangement. Creation of large pension funds and special service benefits controlled by the unions redounds to the benefit of the union agents and officers in ways that are too well publicized as a result of recent hearings on union activities to need mention here.[18]

The membership of monopoly unions will tolerate such abuses to the point where the abuses offset the value of monopoly gains accruing to the employed members. We emphasize that these effects are induced by *both* the monopoly rationing problem and by the desire to convert the monopoly gains into nonpecuniary take-home pay for the union officers or dominant group. We conjecture that both elements are present; part of the monopoly gain is passed on to the workers, and part is captured as a nonpecuniary source of utility. When the former occurs the rationing problem exists, and the agents or those in the union will exclude the less desirable type of job applicants—less desirable not in pecuniary productivity to the employer but as fellow employees and fellow members of the union. Admission will be easier for people whose cultural and personal characteristics conform to the interests of

[18] Relevant for the analysis of monopoly power is the character of the protection afforded by the state. For utilities the state actively and directly uses its police powers to eliminate competition. For other monopolies—and this is especially relevant for union monopoly—the state permits these monopolies to use private police power to eliminate competition. The powers of the state passively and indirectly support these monopolies by refusing to act against the exercise of private police power. This suggests that there ought to exist a link between those who have a comparative advantage in the exercise of private police powers (gangsters), and monopolies that eliminate competition through "strong-arm" techniques.

the existing members.[19] And admission will be especially difficult for those regarded as potential price cutters in hard times or not to be counted on as faithful members with a strong sense of loyalty to the union. Minority groups and those who find they must accept lower wages because of some personal or cultural attribute, even though they are just as productive in a pecuniary sense to the employer, will be more willing to accept lower wages if threatened with the loss of their jobs. But these are the very types who will weaken the union's monopoly power. All of this suggests that young people, Negroes, Jews, and other minority or unorthodox groups will be underrepresented in monopolistic unions.[20]

There exists a symmetry in effects between nonprice rationing of admission to monopolistic trade unions and the allocation of rights to operate TV channels, airlines, radio stations, banks, savings and loan associations, public utilities, and the like. In the absence of the sale of these rights by the commission or government agency charged with their allocation, nonprice rationing comes into play. This implies that Negroes, Jews, and disliked minority groups of all kinds will be underrepresented among the recipients of these rights. The symmetry between admission to monopolistic trade unions and the allocation of monopoly rights over the sale of some good or

[19] If the employer is the nonprice rationer, i.e., if the employer does the hiring and not the union, as is true for airplane pilots, he too will display a greater amount of discrimination in nonpecuniary attributes than with a competitive wage rate. If the wage rate has been raised so that he has to retain a smaller number of employees, he will retain those with the greater nonpecuniary productivity. If the wage rate would have fallen in response to increased supplies of labor but instead is kept up by wage controls, then the supply from which he could choose is larger, and again he will select those with the greater nonpecuniary attributes—assuming we are dealing with units of labor or equal pecuniary productivity.

[20] See Reuben A. Kessel, "Price Discrimination in Medicine," *Journal of Law and Economics* (1958): 46 ff.

service by a government agency is not complete. The rights allocated by the government, but not by trade unions, often become private property and can be resold. Therefore this analysis implies that entrance into these economic activities is more frequently achieved by minority groups, as compared with the population as a whole, through the purchase of outstanding rights.

The chief problem in verifying these implications is that of identifying relative degrees of monopoly power. If the classification is correct, there is a possibility of testing the analysis. A comparison of the logic of craft unions with industrywide unions suggests that the former have greater monopoly powers. Therefore if this classification is valid, the preceding analysis would be validated if the predicted results were observed.

For classic economic reasons, we conjecture that the craft unions are more likely to have monopolistic powers than industrywide unions. Therefore we would expect to observe more such discrimination in the first type of union than in the second. And included in the category of craft unions are such organizations as the American Medical Association, and any profession in which admission involves the approval of a governing board.[21]

CONCLUSIONS AND CONJECTURES

This analysis suggests that strong nonrestrained profit incentives serve the interests of the relatively unpopular, unorthodox, and individualistic members of society, who have

[21] For evidence of the existence of discrimination, see H. R. Northrup, *Organized Labor and the Negro* (New York: Harper, 1944), chap. 1; and Kessel, *op. cit.*, pp. 47 ff.

relatively more to gain from the absence of restrictions. Communists are perhaps the strongest case in point. They are strongly disliked in our society and, as a matter of ideology, believe that profit incentives and private property are undesirable. Yet if this analysis is correct, one should find communists overrepresented in highly competitive enterprises. Similar conclusions hold for ex-convicts, disbarred lawyers, defrocked priests, doctors who have lost their licenses to practice medicine, and so forth.

The analysis also suggests an inconsistency in the views of those who argue that profit incentives bring out the worst in people and at the same time believe that discrimination in terms of race, creed, or color is socially undesirable. Similarly, those concerned about the pressures toward conformity in our society, i.e., fears for a society composed of organization men, ought to have some interest in the competitiveness of our markets. It is fairly obvious that the pressures to conform are weaker for a speculator on a grain or stock exchange than they are for a junior executive of AT&T or a university professor with or without tenure.

7

Private Property and the Relative Cost of Tenure

Private property and consumer sovereignty have effects that can be more vividly revealed by case studies than by a statement of principles. I should like, therefore, to examine a special labor market whose product is regarded as unique, so that special employment relations are necessary to preserve the quality of that product. I am speaking of the collegiate market for professors. The special employment relations in the professors' market is tenure, whereby the professor has job security except for immoral acts, loss of mental competence, or financial disability by the college. The professor is assured of his job security so long as his teaching reflects his search for the truth. I shall pass over the questions of how one determines dishonest expounding of the search for the truth and how incompetence and immorality are established. And I shall not dispute the meaning of financial inability. But assuming they are answerable questions, we can concentrate on the question of why tenure is desirable and viable.

Why is this kind of security deemed necessary for the professor? That is, for what is it necessary? Let me quote some of the arguments. I quote first from the Statement of Principles of the American Association of University Professors, a statement endorsed by many other academic professional associations.

> Institutions of higher education are conducted for the common good and not to further the interest of either the individual teacher or the institution as a whole. The common good depends upon the free search for truth and its free exposition. Academic freedom is essential to these purposes and applies to both teaching and research.
>
> Tenure is a means to certain ends; specifically: (1) freedom of teaching and research and of extramural activities, and (2) a sufficient degree of economic security to make the profession attractive to men and women of ability. Freedom and economic security, hence tenure, are indispensable to the success of an institution in fulfilling its obligations to its students and to society.[1]

I give another quotation.

> The modern university . . . is a unique type of organization. For many reasons it must differ from a corporation created for the purpose of producing a salable article for profit. Its internal structure, procedures, and discipline are properly quite different from those of business organizations. It is not so closely integrated and there is no such hierarchy of authority as is appropriate to a business concern; the permanent members of a university are essentially equals. . . .
>
> Free enterprise is as essential to intellectual as to economic progress. *A* university [my italics] must therefore be hospitable to an infinite variety of skills and viewpoints, relying upon open competition among them as the surest safeguard of truth. *Its* [my italics] whole spirit requires investigation, criticism, and presentation of ideas in an atmosphere of freedom and mutual confidence. This is the real meaning of "academic" freedom. It is essential to the achievement of its ends that the faculty be guaranteed this freedom by its governing board, and that the reasons for the guarantee be understood by the public.
>
> When the [scholar's] opinions challenge existing orthodox points of view, his freedom may be more in need of defense than that of men in other professions. The guarantee of tenure of professors of

[1] American Association of University Professors, "Academic Freedom and Tenure," *AAUP Bulletin* 42, no. 1 (Spring 1956): 42.

> mature and proven scholarship is one such defense. As in the case of judges, tenure protects the scholar against undue economic or political pressure and ensures the continuity of the scholarly process.[2]

What are the reasons for tenure? Apparently it is necessary to insure efficient searching for the truth because of the special nature of the product, truth, and because the university is different from ordinary business entities. However, my conclusion is that the reason for the general acceptance of tenure is not that the search for truth has some special characteristics which distinguish it from other products, but that, instead, its acceptance springs from the special ownership arrangement and financial structures of our colleges. Economic analysis has driven me to this conclusion, that it arises from an absence of the ordinary kind of property rights that exist in profit-seeking businesses.

What is the economic analysis or what are the theorems that yield this conclusion? The simplest and most fundamental postulates and theorems of economics are sufficient. The first theorem says individuals act so as to further their own interest, even when acting as members of a group. The second fundamental theorem of economics says the lower the relative price of any good or source of satisfaction the more will be purchased. These are called the first and second fundamental theorems of economics to suggest that their power is comparable to that of the first and second fundamental theorems of physics.

A person can further his interest—or as we say in the jargon of economics, he can increase his utility—in many different ways. He can increase his pecuniary wealth and personal con-

[2] Association of American Universities, *The Right and Responsibilities of Universities and Their Faculties* (March 1953); reprinted in the *University Bulletin* of the University of California 1, no. 33 (April 20, 1953): 162–64.

sumption expenditures. He can further his interests or satisfaction by having more pleasant working conditions, a bigger and plushier office, a more beautiful and cooperative secretary, a jovial, friendly, and lenient employer, cleaner and more elaborate wash rooms, more convenient and automatic equipment with which to work, music in the factory, or if he is the employer he might have more responsible employees with desirable personal and cultural characteristics. The lower the costs that must be paid for any of these the more he will buy them, in exactly the same way that a person revises his purchases of types of food in response to their prices. A person will always spend some of his personal wealth on his job environment, but every dollar so spent means a dollar less for expenditure at home. If the costs of things bought for home consumption were to rise relative to costs of business connected sources of personal satisfaction he would buy more of the latter.[3]

What this all says is that a person has at least two ways to spend money. He can take it out of the business, if he owns it, and spend it at home and wherever he pleases. Or he can spend it in the business not merely for the sake of increasing the net profits or income of the business but for the personal benefits he gets in the course of his income earning activity. He can always take a smaller salary or profits in exchange for better working conditions or for greater job security. The less of any one of these things he must sacrifice to get the other, the more of the other he will take. The more the personal, take-home wealth he must sacrifice to get pleasanter working conditions, the poorer will be his working conditions. For example, if he sacrificed no profits or salary he would indulge in job choices exclusively on the basis of security and working conditions.

[3] For an excellent illustration of this see G. S. Becker, *The Economics of Discrimination* (Chicago, 1957).

People differ in their preferences for various ways to spend their personal wealth at home and they differ in their business-connected expenditures. Some will be willing to buy more in the way of attractive working surroundings than will other people in the same wealth position. Some will want their business-connected sources of personal satisfaction more in the form of congenial employees and others will place a greater emphasis on physical surroundings. It all depends upon their personal preference patterns. But if the cost of beautiful secretaries should rise, everyone will be induced to cut down somewhat on the amount of beautiful secretarial services, regardless of his relative preferences for beauty and efficient secretarial work. Of course it is possible that some employers may attach no significance to degree of beauty, but as long as some do, the effect will be noted. Only if employers attached no value whatsoever to beauty—perhaps such as might happen if the employer's wife were in some way to be in control of secretarial hiring—would it not follow that more would be bought at a lower price.

To be more explicit, suppose that a certain secretary was capable of producing $ .80 of pecuniary income per hour. At $1.00 an hour the employer would have to sacrifice $ .20 of personal profits which he could have used in any way he saw fit in or out of the business. Let us suppose that he decided the extra attractions of the secretary were not worth the $ .20 per hour sacrifice of profits that he could have taken home and devoted to, say, his wife's beauty. Now, modify the system so that he is not allowed to take home all the profits. As an extreme, suppose that he can take home only one fourth, $ .05 per hour. Now the attraction of the secretary, formerly not worth $ .20 per hour, need be compared only with $ .05 of sacrificed domestic expenditures. The cost to him of business-connected satisfaction has fallen from $ .20 per hour to $ .05 per hour. The employer will find his satisfaction enhanced if he spends more in the business, getting a larger portion of this personal satisfaction through business-connected expenditures or costs. Not only will he hire a prettier secretary but he will enlarge all business costs that in any way provide personal satisfaction.

A word of caution: it has not been said that he would have spent nothing for secretarial beauty before a tax or confiscation of profits. All that is implied is that he would have bought *less* of it before, not none of it. Everyone always is willing to buy some pleasantness of working environment depending upon the costs of domestic consumption. What is being said here is that more will be bought as the domestic consumption sacrifice or price is made lower. And not only will secretarial beauty be more extensively purchased, but *every* source of personal satisfaction obtainable through business-connected costs will be increased. And the increase will be greater, the greater is the cost of taking profits home.

Significant also is that there is inefficiency when his profits are taxed. The business is using up $1.00 worth of resources to provide a benefit worth less than $1.00. The business owner is spending a dollar to get $ .80 worth of pecuniary service via typing and $ .05 worth of extra pleasure of beauty. Formerly he got $1.00 worth of typing services, whereas now he gets a total satisfaction worth only $ .85, a loss of $ .15. But that loss is not imposed on him. Instead it is borne by the whole of society as a consequence of not using resources in their most valuable ways as judged by consumers. It is possible to have provided just as much typing service and beauty and still have other things too. This, of course, is merely the well-known efficiency aspect of the competitive, free price system under private property.

The task to which we turn now is to see what affects the relative prices of these various sources of satisfaction, some of which are domestic, business-free expenditures and others of which are business-connected cost-covered expenditures. In particular, we shall consider the effects of profit-seeking privately owned institutions as compared to nonprofit organizations on the cost ratios of various forms of business-connected sources of satisfaction, and the particular form of business-connected source of satisfaction to which we shall devote most of our attention is tenure.

An ordinary privately owned profit-seeking business, whether it sells shoes or news, whether it be proprietorship or a corporation, is operated for the sake of increasing the wealth of the owners and not for the common good. That the business will survive only if it benefits other people as a consequence of its owner's search for personal profits does not deny this latter objective. In other words, the test of survival of such a business is not that it intend to serve the public interest or common good, but instead that it produce profits—which the owner can take out of the business if he wishes. To make profits the business must be taking resources from less useful alternative activities and putting them to work in more valuable channels. From this difference in usefulness, as judged by the consumers, arise the profits. If the owner fails to satisfy this condition, he will suffer a loss in his personal wealth which will compensate other people for the reduction in the value of output which he has caused. Thus the owner is forced to bear through smaller profits or through losses the true economic costs of his actions. Losses of personal wealth are a powerful dissuader, while profits are a powerful persuader to pay heed to other people's preferences.

Any employer who may be induced by an employee to produce a service inefficiently will find that consumers punish him by making him bear the costs through losses. And this dissuades the employer from supporting inefficient behavior. But no one employer can prevent the employee from continuing his inefficient activities elsewhere if any other member of the community will agree to bear the costs out of his personal wealth. In summary, the profit-seeking owner who satisfies the consumer best makes profits and he can use the profit in any way he likes, at home or in the business. His range of choice of places and ways in which he can spend the income of the business is not confined to business avenues or working conditions only.

This kind of private ownership or private property right, common as it is, is not universal. A non-profit-seeking business is the name usually given to an entity or institution administered by individuals acting in the capacity of trustees and who *cannot* appropriate the net wealth gains directly to themselves as profits nor completely as higher salaries. Nor can anyone else take the wealth out of the business as an owner could and spend it on as wide a range of alternatives as he could with his own personal wealth. The administrator is a trustee and not for any particular person's private wealth. There is no owner in the conventional sense; there are merely managers, administrators and operators. This does *not* mean that no one can further his own interest through the ways the wealth of the organization is spent. But what it does mean is that since there is no residual owner who can spend the net profits more efficiently at home and in the business than in the narrower range of business associated sources of personal benefits, the inducement to increase profits is reduced. In fact, it is turned into an inducement to reduce them to zero, but not into losses. Avoidance of losses is still a binding, effective constraint on the activities of a non-profit-seeking institution that relies upon sales to consumers for its income.

In a non-profit-seeking enterprise, the administrator must spend all the income in the business for salaries, materials, building, etc. Some of the expenditures will contribute to future income and some will be spent in ways to enhance the working environment or to acquire personal satisfaction through business cost expenditures. This all is merely an application of the earlier stated principle about buying more of these things that are cheaper and less of those that become more expensive. It is more expensive in a nonprofit organization to take the profits home, and the ruse of raising the administrator's salary to equal the profits is not completely available. If it were, then the nonprofit organization would be the same as a profit-seeking institution. But the fact which we have to accept is that the profits cannot all be taken out in this way as cheaply as in a privately owned profit-seeking organization. And so in conformity with the second fundamental theorem of economics, a greater portion of the business expenditures will be spent for business-connected sources of personal satisfaction than in a profit-making organization. Of course, the particular kinds of business associated or business cost activities that will in any case be *most* increased depends upon the particular tastes and preference patterns of the administrators. But whatever ones are increased most, all will be increased.

It is easy to cite many examples. Medical insurance in the business, especially if it is proportional to salaries or status, becomes more attractive since this substitutes for domestic, personally purchased medical aid. Life insurance for all the employees is now a cheaper way of getting it for the administrator—without sacrificing so much profits. And if the key officials like coffee, the coffee break is longer and more elaborate. If they like baseball, the company will have a box at the ballpark for its employees, with you-know-who going most often. Company cars will be newer. Athletic facilities in the plant will be more common because their cost via the business has fallen relative to take-home profits. The administrator can devote more of his time to community affairs and act more like a statesman and less like a grubbing profit seeker. Some, or even all of these things, will be found in a profit-seeking business, but since their cost is even less in a nonprofit organization relative to profits, these things will be more common and on a larger scale.

For example, an administrator of an automobile company, if non-profit-seeking, would find it more in his interest (than in a profit-seeking business) to lower prices and sacrifice some revenue and profits, in order to create a backlog of orders, or as they say—a waiting list. His production scheduling and inventory problems would be eased. Prestige and personal benefits could be gained by his being able to favor and obtain various acceptable favors from certain customers by special priorities. He would be willing also to increase costs and lower profits if in that way he could reduce internal management nuisances and employee relations problems. Unproductive but congenial workers who would be fired in a profit-seeking business will be more readily kept. Firing a person is an unpleasant task, but in a profit-seeking business it is even more unpleasant not to fire them.

His employment policy will be *less* closely related to productivity in a pecuniary sense and more oriented toward satisfying his own welfare through nonpecuniary forms, e.g., employees who agree with his point of view, or employee cultural characteristics, or special employment arrangements which are conducive to administrative ease. But insofar as employment policies reflect considerations other than productivity in the business, some employees without these side characteristics will feel unjustly discriminated against if they are not promoted or are fired when doing what they think is consistent with the avowed purposes of the enterprise. They will demand less "arbitrary" hiring, firing and employment policies and will seek to protect themselves from the inefficient practices of the employer. But the policies they seek will reduce efficiency. Weakened as the consumer controls are on the employer because of the elimination or reduction of the available profits, they are even weaker on the employees. The less such policy costs the administrator-employer the more he will be induced to accept it. He will be more ready to accept employment policies that mean a quieter, more peaceful, even if less profitable life. And one of the forms of employment policy that will be pressed on him and more willingly brought now is greater job security for the employees.

At any given wage rate, the greater the job security an employee can get, the better for him and the worse for the employer. An employer who grants a long term contract must bear the consequences of changes in the employee's productivity. If the employee proves to be less productive than anticipated, the employer suffers and the employee is the gainer. If the employee proves to be better than anticipated, the employee can quit his job and go elsewhere and get a higher pay. The risks are not symmetrical. Hence at the same wage rate an employer prefers shorter-term to longer-term contracts. And since the employer cannot revise wages downward, else the whole objective of security would be negated, he will offer a lower wage guarantee than he expects the employee's productivity to be.

If we look at our private colleges and universities we find that they are typically non-profit-seeking institutions. Whatever the attitude of the administrator of the college toward academic freedom and exposition of the truth, his ability to impose his own standards of acceptable employee behavior are enhanced above those in a profit-seeking enterprise. His actions do, of course, affect the status of the college and the attraction it has for students or for donors. Yet since he does not have a right to keep the profits for personal expenditures he is not so severely affected by the loss of profits caused by the unpopularity of his decisions. Of all the forces that can be brought to bear on him, one is now weakened and this one is the personal wealth effect. Students and their parents are less able to punish him so severely for behavior not in conformity with their desires, since the profits incentive is attenuated, as it is *not* in a profit-seeking owned institution. As said earlier, it is in just such situations that the administrator will more frequently evidence arbitrariness in hiring and firing people. And similarly, in just such institutions would we expect employees to react most strongly and seek protection from this apparently capricious behavior by the college administrator who seems to be paying even less attention to the criterion of truthful teaching. It is perfectly true, however, that those administrators who already stand for the truth are even more willing to retain teachers of the truth who present the unpleasant truth. But what all this means is that those who would defend such teachers from discharge by keeping them despite their statements are more easily able—that is, at lower cost to themselves—to grant tenure. Those who do not want such teaching are more insulated from the pressure of their customers' withdrawal of purchases since the losses of profits are not all imposed on him as his costs. But whatever his degree of opposition and whatever his attitude toward the truth, the cost imposed on him for granting tenure is lower in a nonprofit organization. Therefore, because the demand for it is larger and because the gains to the employer from opposing it get smaller, the probability of tenure is increased in nonprofit organizations.

It is not necessarily the college president or board of governors whose capricious behavior is made cheaper as a source of personal satisfaction. Many college staffs have attempted to protect themselves from this by having fellow faculty members decide on new appointments, retentions and promotions. This is called democracy, but it is not clear that this makes any difference. Who is to protect the individual faculty member from the equally cheap-to-exercise personal preferences of his colleagues when they assume the administrative powers?

Everyone wants security, if the cost is zero. And the higher the cost the less they will want. But there is a particular set of employees who will most desire tenure. These are older people, whose productivity is nearing or past its peak. By securing tenure at existing current wages they will be assured of continuing employment, despite declining productivity, at a high wage rate. At the same time all current employees on short-term contracts will be happy to switch to a tenure contract if no cut in pay is involved, for then it would appear as though they had obtained job security without any cost to themselves with all the cost being dumped on the employer. An employer will, of course, resist this, but the extent will depend upon the cost, and in a nonprofit institution the costs imposed on the administrator are lower than the same person would bear in the same kind of business if it were a profit-seeking enterprise. Hence the extent to which employers are induced to resist this demand is reduced and tenure is more likely to exist, as are other forms of inefficiency.

But it should not be assumed that all the costs of tenure will be shifted by the employer to society at large. Actually they have also been shifted onto *some* of the employees. Nothing is guaranteed in a tenure contract as to the rate of advance of pay. The employer, once he has granted tenure, may subsequently resist pay increases until the margin between pay and productivity reflects the risk-bearing aspect mentioned earlier. As a partial defense the employees insist on provisions about the rate at which pay will advance. But the beginning rate under tenure will be lower than under nontenure as a result of the risks of long-term contracts. In such arrangements, who prove to be gainers and losers—since this is essentially a vast insurance-type gamble? Individuals who live longest and turn out to be below average in productivity growth gain at the expense of the short-lived in this profession and whose productivity increases the most. Those who had short lives received less of their total productivity. The risk the employer bore was that they, later in life, would be less productive and at that time their wages would not be decreasing. Hence in the earlier part of his career the employee is underpaid in the gamble that later he will overcollect.

Another gamble also occurs. Those who proved to be most productive will have received less than they would have received without tenure, even though they earn more than the average worker. And those who turn out to be below average in productivity growth will earn more than they would have got without tenure, but still they earn less than the average of better workers.

Mobility is penalized because every new job means the task of resolving some doubt in the new employer's mind. This implies that older and less able people, who are now getting a reward more than they are worth, will find very few new job offers elsewhere at equivalent or better wages since no new employer is likely to induce a person to leave a job at which he is currently being overpaid. On the other hand, the better men will be paid less than they are worth and so should be receiving offers from other employers who will offer to narrow the gap.

This does not mean that new employers want to hire only the best people, rather it means that they will find the better people are more willing to move because of the discrepancy of their wages and productivity. Tenure benefits the older, less able people at the expense of the younger, more able and shorter-lived individuals.

If one goes one step farther and assumes that in such a nonprofit organization the older people are in authority, as seems likely by virtue of the weaker pecuniary productivity rewards because "profits" are less efficiently used, one would expect the interests of older people to be given greater consideration than those of younger people. This would be evident in the way facilities and privileges were rationed among the many employees.

The drive for tenure involves compelling most, but not all, employees to accept the tenure system. In many colleges all staff members must acquire tenure—as it is euphemistically stated—at the end of a fixed number of years outside the tenure system. Any member who wants to continue without tenure at a higher wage for a nontenure appointment is not allowed to do so. To permit this would undermine the position of those in the tenure situation exactly in the same way that a nonmember of a cartel is able to undermine the cartel.

Furthermore, if wages are tied to rank, and rank to tenure, it becomes impossible for the younger, more able men to bargain for higher pay without tenure. They are prevented from forgoing tenure in the interests of a higher current wage. In this way tenure is harder to break. If this is so, why should anyone be allowed to teach without tenure? For two reasons: in the first place, a trial period gives the administrator and his colleagues a better idea of what a person's productivity will be—or was. Also, they can get a better idea of whether he will be a compatible, docile, agreeable colleague, or will be obstreperous and overly competitive in what he seeks to do. And if one's colleagues are involved in determining appointment and promotion these questions become even more pertinent. This system has been called democratic. Indeed it is democratic, along the same lines of democracy that would prevail if auto manufacturers were to be the democratic deciders as to who could make cars, or as in fact the medical profession does in deciding who can be a doctor. The question of democracy is a red herring. The correct question is whose tastes and preferences are to be satisfied and who is to bear the gains and the costs, the consumer or one's fellow employees? The second reason for not insisting on tenure for every member is that a nonprofit institution may become a "loss" institution and will then have to curtail expenditures. This will mean cutting the staff. But who is to go if all have tenure? To protect those who do have tenure, a buffer, nonpermanent group is created to absorb the possible shock.

There is one more institutional factor that also enhances tenure's viability. In addition to student fees, colleges get income from current gifts and from current income from past gifts—the endowment. Consider the extreme of endowed income, where the income is dependent upon how well the endowment is invested and not upon current activities of teaching and research, which do affect student fees and current gifts. Colleges with endowments can and do sell their services at prices less than the cost of the education received by the student. No longer is the old constraint of no losses binding on the administrator. It will be recalled that under a profit-seeking owned institution increments in profits are sought, but under a nonprofit institution costs are magnified until they equal income. In each of those cases the extent to which profit or income was sought depended upon their costs relative to other sources of satisfaction that could be obtained with the money available to the institution. Now as we introduce another feature, that of a source of income independent of how well one uses the money to enhance current income, it will be even more in the administrator's interest to devote some more of the income of the institution to sources of satisfaction that do not bring the pecuniary income. In addition, he can more cheaply devote more of his own time to nonpecuniary income-obtaining activities and more to leisure or statesmanship. He can be consciously or unconsciously less efficient in the way he spends the organization's money. Of course, he is still efficiently pursuing his own interests at the new relative costs of various activities. He can use more assistants; he can delegate out to assistants tasks that he would have performed himself; he can also delegate to less able persons and committees. The faculty can be brought more and more into administrative work if they complain about the way he is doing things. He can let them do it, and even if it is more inefficient in the usual sense it will give him a quieter, more placid life among more friendly fellows. And tenure will again be still less costly and the demand for it will be still greater, exactly as outlined earlier. Activities which would not be tolerated by consumers are now more viable, hence more common.

How can the validity of the preceding analysis be established? That it follows directly from the simplest and most powerful economic theorems is subject to a logical test. But more pertinent, for present purposes, is the question, Is it empirically valid? What empirically observable results, if observed, would refute the analysis and what would be consistent with it? First, non-profit-seeking schools will be observed to have a higher incidence of tenure than will private profit-seeking schools. And there are both types, so this can be checked. There are hundreds, if not thousands, of privately owned profit-seeking schools. Some survive entirely from student fees. Some of our best accounting and engineering schools are profit-seeking, financed entirely from student fees, as are some girls' colleges. Schools of advertising, art, music, theater, television, design, secretarial work, foreign languages, law, nursing, beautyshop work, barbering are straight profit-seeking institutions. Here student consumer sovereignty exists jointly with the explicity imposed costs of inefficient behavior. If tenure is not more frequent in nonprofit educational institutions the analysis is refuted.

Second, the preceding analysis implies that the incidence of tenure is correlated with the ratio of total income that is covered by endowed income. If such a test were made and the evidence refuted this empirical proposition, the immediately preceding analysis would be conceded to be wrong. However, nothing is implied to the effect that teaching or research will be better or worse as a larger fraction of the income is endowed nor is anything said about the quality of teaching between private profit-seeking and nonprofit organizations. The relationship in that respect may be positive, negative, or zero and still be consistent with the preceding analysis, even if there were agreement on a measure of good teaching and good research.

It is implied also that tenure should be observed more frequently where rank and pay are tied to tenure than where rank and pay are not tied to tenure. I have not gathered these observable pieces of evidence, but I can illustrate the idea by noting that the extension service at my university teaches much the same courses as the regular university and in it we find full cost pricing for the student and no tenure, nor is pay related to age. The summer session which operates on the same basis also operates with no tenure. Furthermore, it does not invite full professors to teach because they don't earn their way compared with the younger, lower-salaried men. The truth is sometimes concealed by asserting that the young men "need" the jobs.

Purposely excluded from this discussion have been the state-owned schools, not because I teach at one and presented this analysis at another one. Rather, I can't decide whether the taxpayers should be regarded as customers or as endowers. I *conjecture* that they are close to endowers and so would predict that tenure would be more common than a profit-seeking private and in nonprofit private schools that are wholly supported by tuition fees, and I would expect tenure to be less frequent than in the most heavily endowed private schools.

Another, and possibly humorous, implication is that the eagerness with which the administrators devote themselves to seeking new sources of revenue, as distinct from gifts, should be inversely related to the fraction of the total income that is endowed. Although less eager, because less rewarding than in a private profit-seeking institution, it will still pay the nonprofit-seeking institution to spend some of its money so as to enhance its total revenue. Recall that this was not denied earlier, instead it was merely stated that the rewards obtained from it were less captureable, hence less valuable, than in a private profit-seeking institution. Now, if I may indulge in a bit of byplay, I would predict that football would be more avidly used as a source of income, the smaller the fraction of income covered by endowment. But I shall not pursue that further here.

Other lines of reasoning have been advanced for tenure. It is not entirely clear whether these other reasons attempt to explain why tenure ought to exist, or why it does exist. The analysis presented so far sought to explain why it developed and why it continues to persist. It did not seek to justify tenure. Essentially the analysis said that it developed because it was one way to further the interests of people working for nonprofit institutions. However, some proponents of tenure argue that it ensures a higher probability of the truth being taught, or that it gets more of it taught. And some argue that it is necessary if the truth is to be sought and taught. With respect to the first argument, more truth may in fact be taught, but the reason is that if tenure is granted more resources are devoted to teachers than would otherwise be diverted to them. But by what criterion is this judged desirable—except that of inducing a greater demand for one's services?

Or maybe the argument is that greater job security enhances the teaching of the truth. It certainly does, but it also induces one to take his job less carefully and to devote more time to one's politics or social ambitions. The net effect is by no means necessarily, nor even more probably, favorable to greater truth. Neither theoretical analysis nor empirical evidence suggests that result, nor is there anything in economics to imply that compulsory lifetime contracts are more efficient than shorter-term voluntary contracts. In truth quite the contrary is implied.

Could it not be argued alternatively that it is indeed fortunate that colleges are not privately owned profit-seeking enterprises, for then tenure would not have survived and without it the search for the truth would have been dissuaded? Therefore these arrangements have grown up in order that the inefficiencies of tenure can be borne in order to preserve the exposition of truth. This would make a virtue of a necessity, if tenure were necessary. To argue that it is, is to ignore the relevance and effect of competition. If there were but one employer of teachers from whose decision there could be no escape, then suppression of the truth would be cheap. With alternative available employers, suppression by one would not prevent other employers from hiring the intimidated individual and paying him to speak his piece. It would pay another employer to hire him if what he had to say were wanted by other people. A new employer may pay less than the former employer. However much this may be distressing to the employee, there is no cause for anyone else to be concerned. No one has any right to compel another person to support him in the style he would like to have, merely because he is, or believes he is, seeking the truth. And yet that is exactly the position taken when one argues that no person ought to be discharged for teaching the truth.

The news industry is an excellent example of the effect of competition. Any newspaper or radio station owner who prints or broadcasts false news will be hurt by other competitors who reveal the truth—not just the polite superficial truth, but all the truth in its most lurid details. While the *New York Times* may be justly proud of its wide coverage, it is debatable as to whether it prints as much truth in depth as some of the more sensational papers, which are sensational primarily because they print more of the facts of some events. Competition among newspapers for profits by catering to the customers' pocketbooks brings out the truth. A news agency could suppress honesty and truth only if it were a protected monopoly, but it would not succeed in the face of competitors who would seek profits by appealing to the consumer's desire for the truth. The truth in news reporting is not the result of tenure for reporters or editors, nor of a code of ethics, and by no stretch of my imagination can I understand why reporters are not just as much in search of the truth as are teachers.

Competition does exist among our schools. Schools that do not satisfy students' desires will lose their students; the repute of the school will decline among those people who want honesty in teaching. People who do have different ideas about the truth or who care more for indoctrination in some other ideal will support schools that satisfy their demands, as they are entitled to do. We must acknowledge that such schools have a valid place in our society unless we were to seek to impose our tastes on everyone—a position somewhat incompatible with voluntaristic, individualistic principles.

A criticism of this substitution of competition for tenure is that students and parents can't tell good from bad teaching. I do believe they have ways of discerning good from bad: they can also tell the difference between hard and easy, interesting and dull. And they reveal their choices unmercifully, but in accord with the rules of success that are imposed on them by the colleges that ask of them only grade points unweighted by difficulty or severity or importance of material. As long as we weigh grades only by hours of class work, we should hesitate to say that students cannot discern good from bad or truth from falsity. Furthermore, to the extent that students pay less in fees or tuition than the course is worth, to that extent will they sensibly tolerate inefficiency and bad teaching. Would one say that students who go to Massachusetts Institute of Technology or California Institute of Technology do so without knowledge of the best engineering schools? If the students can't tell good from bad teaching, one has to wonder how they manage to choose among colleges?

It may be true that some students can't tell a true theorem from a false one. But so long as some students can detect the difference, they will challenge the teacher. And, furthermore, a teacher will challenge his colleague's teaching when he thinks he detects error in it. The ethic of not criticizing one's colleagues, or competitors, in the fashion of the medical profession, is a very dangerous one to the discernment of the truth. Of course, some of the ideas taught are incapable of being proven true or false. They are recital of doctrines and preferences, and economists certainly are not free of this fault. We shouldn't be alarmed if we then find students unable to detect truth from falsity; there may be none to detect. There may be just accuracy of note taking.

What if consumers do not want the truth and instead want romance and illusion? The theater and the movies are much more efficient at that than the teachers are. Fiction writers may have outclassed teachers for many centuries. And in any event, so much the worse for tenure, for then those who want tenure to foster the truth, if such it did, would be trying to impose their preference on other people. To assert that some college officials do not always want the truth and that some alumni or outsiders criticize the teacher and seek to get him fired is certainly true—and commendable. If the truth harms or offends some people, in a free society why should they not have the right to use their resources to combat it? Others may desire the truth even more, and be willing to pay for it. When I buy a house, the fact that I outbid the other bidders means that someone else did not get what he otherwise would have got. And so it is with the bidding for the truth. If someone prefers to buy up the time of teachers to induce them not to speak the truth he is entitled to do so. And if he tries to buy up a college president in order to persuade him not to continue to hire a certain teacher he is entitled to do so. Teachers have no claim on the resources of society or of any person. The crucible of the truth is open competition among ideas, although ideas are costly.

A question still hangs over my head. Why do non-profit-seeking subsidized schools exist if they are less efficient, as revealed by the willingness to make inefficient labor contracts. The answer, I think, lies in two places. One is our state school system, in which the state, through its taxing power, not only subsidizes education but also administers the state schools on a non-full-cost tuition basis. Even the most efficient private profit-seeking business would have a difficult time surviving, if survival is possible, in any endeavor where the taxing power is used to support a competitor. The nonstate, nonowned private schools can survive only if they too are given subsidies. If the tax-supported education were instead given to students as tuition grants in the fashion of the G.I. educational benefits, there would be a chance for the private profit-seeking school to provide us with a test of efficient education and truth seeking.[4] But barring that change in our educational structure there seems little hope for avoiding the inefficiencies of the non-profit-seeking nonowned educational system. The efforts of many people to help education will take the form of grants to institutions if they are nonprofit, whereas such grants would not occur if they were profit-making. If they were profit-seeking, the grant would merely go into the owners' pockets. Under a private profit-seeking school arrangement, givers would be induced to give to students or to set up charities for students rather than for schools, much on the lines of the Guggenheim and Carnegie grants. But if nonprofit institutions exist, it will be possible to aid education via grants to schools,

[4] M. Friedman, "The Role of Government in Education," in R. Solo, ed., *Economics and the Public Interest* (New Brunswick, N.J., 1955).

although such grants will be less efficient than direct grants to students.

The answer lies, second, in that special and legal advantages given to a nonprofit institution have enabled it to grow and survive, and with it the particular feature developed in this analysis. The persistence of the nonprofit college arises, not from its ability to support tenure and the search for the truth, but, rather, from legal and tax advantages given it, and the granting of gifts to the college rather than to students. And even with these aids it is highly doubtful that it will be able to survive against the tax-subsidized support of the state schools. Admittedly, these last remarks about the reasons for the existence of nonprofit schools are based on personal conjecture.

In sum, the conclusion suggested is that tenure is neither necessary nor efficient. Its survival depends upon the absence of private ownership and also is encouraged by subsidization of education by noncustomer income sources. Without a private profit-seeking system and without full-cost tuition, the demand for tenure increases and the cost of granting it appears to be cheaper because the full costs are not imposed on those granting it. Competition among schools, teachers, and students provides protection to the search for the truth without tenure. Just as in the dissemination of news, the exposition of the search for the truth is tested in the open market for ideas and empirical verification. Truth is not something given the stamp of authority or validity by appointed persons. Authority cannot establish what people will believe is the truth. The individual must do that. Truth then is no higher an objective than that of voluntary individualism. The two are not incompatible. Indeed, what does one mean in the absence of the other?

As a test of whether or not my exposition has been even

moderately successful, let me quote a passage from a far better than average defense of tenure. If the passage now appears humorous or transparent I will have passed the test.

> The demand we of the academic world make for academic freedom is not made primarily for our own benefit. We enjoy the exercise of freedom; but the purposes of liberty lie, in a democracy, in the common welfare. It has recently been said, "With regard to some occupations, it is eminently in the interest of society that the men concerned speak their minds without fear of retribution. . . . The occupational work of the vast majority of people is largely independent of their thought and speech. The professor's work consists of his thought and speech. If he loses his position for what he writes or says, he will, as a rule, have to leave his profession, and may no longer be able effectively to question and challenge accepted doctrines or effectively to defend challenged doctrines. And if *some* professors lose their positions for what they write or say, the effect on many other professors will be such that their usefulness to their students and to society will be gravely reduced."
>
> We ask then for the maintenance of academic freedom and of the civil liberties of scholars, not as a special right, but as a means whereby we may make our appointed contributions to the life of the commonwealth and share equitably, but not more than equitably, in the American heritage.[5]

[5] American Association of University Professors, "Academic Freedom and Tenure in the Quest for National Security, Report of a Special Committee," *AAUP Bulletin* 42, no. 1 (Spring 1956): 54–55.

The Economic and Social Impact of Free Tuition

Rarely do educational issues provoke as much passion as the proposal to raise tuition fees in California colleges. Unfortunately, the passion has not been matched by reason—it is hard to find a clear statement of the consequences of or reasons for a zero tuition or a high tuition fee. It is hard to determine from the public comments whether the antagonists differ about what the consequences of alternative tuition arrangements would be or have different preferences with respect to well perceived consequences. Some defenders of zero tuition have asserted that zero tuition is necessary for aid to poorer students, for the maintenance of our great system of higher education, for the preservation of free and prosperous society, for achievement of great social benefits, for educational opportunity for all, is a hallowed century-old tradition, and that tuition is a tax on education. Some proponents of tuition fees have argued, for example, that the university and colleges are harboring delinquents who

Acknowledgment is made to the Lilly Endowment, Inc., for a research grant to UCLA during which the present article was written. The opinions expressed here in no way reflect any conditions of that research grant.

would not be there with full tuition, the poor are aiding the rich, students should pay tuition in order to appreciate their education, taxes are excessive, and low tuition requires exploitation of an underpaid faculty, to cite a few. Most of these arguments are so patently fallacious or nonsensical or irrelevant that they do disservice to the more intelligent arguments. But there are some propositions that merit closer examination. To evaluate them it is first necessary to identify at some length the issues that are involved in analyzing and thereby choosing among the alternatives—and in the process make clear my own preferences. If I overlook significant objectives or consequences, perhaps others will be stimulated to fill the gaps.

The issues represent a classic topic for applied economics—the effects of different means of allocating scarce resources among competing claimants. A rational analysis of the consequences of tuition systems requires separation of two questions: (1) Who should bear the costs of education? (2) If someone other than the student should pay for his education, in what form should the aid be given?

Unless the distinction between these two issues is grasped, confusion is inevitable. The case for zero tuition is *not* established by demonstrating that aid to students is desirable. Full tuition may still be desirable, with the desired aid taking the form of explicit grants-in-aid or scholarships from which the student pays the tuition fee of his chosen school.

The issue of the most desirable form of aid should be separated from still another closely related question: What is the desired method of financing and controlling *colleges*—as distinct from financing *students?* For example, aid to students in the form of zero tuition means also that the state finances the colleges' activities directly by legislative appropriations with the students and their parents having less influence on financing and controlling the activities of colleges. Where student aid is in the form of grants-in-aid or scholarships, students and parents paying full tuition to their chosen colleges have a greater role in determining which colleges shall be financed and rewarded for superior performances. Recognition of these differences in effect explains why some people have asserted the administrators and members of state universities and colleges, which are currently financed by direct legislative appropriation, have sought from self-interest, rather than educational interest, to maintain the impression that zero tuition is the only feasible or sensible means of aid to students—in order to repress student influence and control over the colleges while retaining the influence of politicians.

Advocates of subsidization of college students (regardless of the method) assume that if each student bore the full cost there would be too little college education as well as a decrease of educational opportunity. What makes it desirable to have more education than if students pay full costs? Several arguments are advanced. Let us discuss these in ascending order of sophistication.

(1) "Although the costs of education are less than the gains to the students themselves, some are unable to finance their education now. A subsidy would provide educational opportunity to the poor." (2) "Cultural education, though not profitable in market earnings, and hence not capable of being paid for out of enhanced earnings, is nevertheless desirable." (3) "Even if every student acquires as much education as is worthwhile to him, he would take too little, because the individual ignores the beneficial social gains indirectly conferred on other members of society—giving what some people call 'external social effects.' Therefore, society at large should

induce students to take more education than indicated by their private interests."

The argument that the poor cannot afford to pay for a profitable college education is deceptive. What is meant by a "poor" person. Is he a college-caliber student? All college-caliber students are rich in both a monetary and nonmonetary sense. Their inherited superior mental talent—human capital—*is* great wealth. For example, the college-caliber student is worth on the average about $200,000, and on the average, approximately $20,000-$50,000 of that has been estimated as the enhanced value derived from college training, depending upon his major field and profession.

Failure to perceive this inherent wealth of college-caliber students reflects ignorance of two economic facts. One is the enormous human wealth in our society. Every good educator recognizes that inanimate capital goods are not the only forms of wealth. The second fact is the difference between current earnings and wealth. For example, a man with a million dollars' worth of growing trees, or untapped oil is a rich man—though he is not *now* marketing any of his wealth or services. So it is with the college-caliber student. Though his *current* market earnings are small, his wealth—the present wealth value of his future earnings—is larger than for the average person. This is true no matter what the current earnings or wealth of his parents. It is *wealth*, not current earnings nor parent's wealth, that is the measure of a student's richness. College-caliber students with low current earnings are not poor. Subsidized higher education, whether by zero tuition, scholarships, or zero-interest loans, grants the college student a second windfall—a subsidy to exploit his initial windfall inheritance of talent. This is equivalent to subsidizing drilling costs for owners of oil-bearing lands in Texas.

There remains an even more seriously deceptive ambiguity—that between the subsidization of college education and provision of educational *opportunity*. Educational *opportunity* is provided if any person who can benefit from attending college is enabled to do so despite smallness of *current* earnings. Nothing in the provision of full educational *opportunity* implies that students who are financed during college should not later repay out of their enhanced earnings those who financed that education. Not to ask for repayment is to grant students a gift of wealth at the expense of those who do not attend college or who attend tuition colleges and pay for themselves. This is true because, for one reason, our tax bills do not distinguish between those directly benefited by having obtained a zero-tuition educational subsidy and those not so benefited. Alumni with higher incomes pay more taxes, but they do not pay more than people with equal incomes who financed their own education or never went to college.

Many discussions about educational opportunity refer to proportions of students from poorer and richer families at tuition-free colleges. However strong the emotional appeal, the proportion of rich and poor family students is relevant only to the separate issue of wealth redistribution, per se, consequent to state-operated zero-tuition education. It has nothing to do with the extent of educational opportunity. Though data for California colleges and taxes suggest that lower-income groups provide a smaller proportion of students than of taxes to support education, such comparisons are irrelevant, so far as provision of educational *opportunity* is concerned. These data tell how much wealth redistribution there is among the less educated, the poor, the educated, and the rich. That wealth redistribution is good or bad depending upon whether one believes the educational system should be used as a device to redistribute wealth as well as to enhance wealth, knowledge, and educational opportunity. No matter how zero tuition in tax-supported schools may redistribute wealth, the provision of full educational opportunity does *not* require redistributions of wealth. Yet, it seems to me, many people confuse these two entirely separate issues or think the latter is necessary for the former. To think that college-caliber students should be given zero tuition is to think that smart people should be given wealth at the expense of the less smart.

When some zero-tuition university alumni say that without zero tuition they could not have attended college, they should have a modest concern for the implications of that statement. One poor, "uneducated" resident of Watts, upon hearing Ralph Bunche say that he could not have had a college education unless tuition were free, opined, "Perhaps it's time he repay out of his higher income for that privilege granted him by taxes on us Negroes who never went to college." That reply spots the difference between educational opportunity and a redistribution of wealth.

Full educational *opportunity* would be provided if college-caliber students could borrow against their future enhanced earnings. Students could repay out of their enhanced future earnings. Although, currently, loans are available from private lenders and also from publicly supported loans, a subsidy could provide a state guarantee of repayment of educational loans exactly as housing loans are guaranteeed for veterans. Students could select among optional repayment methods. Some could contract to repay in full with interest; others could opt for a sort of insurance system, whereby the amount repaid was related to their income, with upper and lower limits to amounts repaid being specified. A host of possibilities are available. In fact today with income taxes, the college alumni are repaying part of the educational costs via taxes (but so are others who did not attend college).

Some people are impressed by the size of the debt that a college graduate would have to repay, but they should be impressed with the fact that the debt is *less* than the enhanced earnings he has thereby obtained and is an indication of the wealth bonanza given the student who is subsidized by society.

There remains one more facet of the educational opportunity argument. Even if a college education may be a very profitable investment for some person, he may, because of inexperience or lack of confidence, not appreciate his situation or be willing to borrow at available rates of interest. This presumably is an argument for subsidizing those students who lack confidence or understanding of their possibilities, and it may be a meaningful argument on its own ground, but it is not an argument for subsidizing "poor" students.

Pleas are made for subsidizing *cultural* education which, though it may add nothing to the student's future market earnings, will enhance his general welfare. But a person's welfare is increased if he gets more food, housing, recreation, beer drinking, and fancier cars. It would seem therefore that the relevant argument for helping students is one of helping them regardless of whether they wish their welfare increased via cultural education or better food. A grant of money to be spent as the recipient deems appropriate is an efficient form of aid—as judged by the recipient. Subsidized cultural education rather than money gifts could be justified if the giver knows better than the recipient what is good for the recipient. I cannot make that leap of faith for the collegiate student, although other people do it easily and confidently.

A case can be made for subsidizing the poor *and* the rich to take more education—more than a person would take when motivated by his own interests alone. It is often said there are privately unheeded, net social benefits, so each person will underinvest in education from the social point of view, regardless of whether he is rich or poor; but we must separate the illusory from the real external available gains.

Education makes a person more productive, as a doctor, lawyer, merchant, or engineer. Other people benefit from his greater productivity, because more engineers enable lower costs of engineering services for the rest of society. Engineers, looking only to their private gain would, it is said, undervalue the total benefit of having more engineers; too few people would seek sufficient engineering education. If this sounds persuasive, economics can teach you something. The increased supply of engineers reduces the prices of engineering services—even if by only a trivial amount—and thereby reduces the income of *other* engineers. Their income loss is the gain to the rest of society. This is a *transfer* of income from existing engineers to nonengineers; it is *not* a net social gain. The benefited parties gain at the expense of existing members of the engineering profession, who lose some of their scarcity value as more educated people are created. This is a transfer from the more educated to the less educated. A striking awareness of this effect is evident in the advocacy by labor groups of immigration restriction. Restricting the inflow of laborers of particular skills prevents reductions in wages of incumbent workers with similar skills and prevents a transfer of wealth from them to the rest of American society. An immigrant or a more educated person would have provided an increased product and he would have obtained that value by the sale of his services, but the lower wages to that *type* of services would have transferred some of the incomes of similar workers to the rest of society. This external *transfer* effect is not a net contribution to social output. It is not a reason for subsidizing education.

For external effects to serve as a valid basis for more education two conditions must be satisfied: (1) There must be a net social *gain* (not transfer) unheeded by the student. The ability to read reduces dangers and inconvenience to other people; ability to be sanitary enhances health of other people, or economic education may—but probably will not—prevent passage of socially detrimental, special-interest legislation. These are examples of education with external social gains, which we shall assume are not heeded by the student in his private actions because they do not affect the marketable value of his services. Professional education of doctors, engineers, lawyers, economists, mathematicians, etc., has not been shown to fit in that category. Perhaps education at the undergraduate collegiate level in the elements of law, psychology, political science, mathematics, economics may make for better *nonmarket* decisions or actions.

I confess to a strong suspicion that such education is most significant at the grade school level, diminishes at higher levels, and disappears for professional or cultural, artistic, personal satisfaction courses, and is possibly *reversed* at graduate levels (by overtraining and insistence on excessively high standards of training for granting of licenses to practice in some professions—though this is a point the validity of which is not crucial to the main issue here).

(2) The second condition is that there must be *further* external gains unheeded by students at the college level. The fact of having *achieved* net external gains is not sufficient to warrant

subsidization. The crucial condition is the failure to achieve still further available *incremental* net social gain from *further* education. Before concluding that they exist because of a tendency for people to ignore them, we should note that people attend college for reasons other than financial marketable gain. College attendance for personal reasons includes cultural, artistic education, and attendance to find mates. All these tend to extend education beyond maximizing one's market wealth and possibily even beyond that yielding unheeded social gains. But the facts are not conclusive in *either* direction.

Incidentally, an especially common but erroneous contention, presumably relying on the external effect, is that the growth, prosperity, and unusual position of California depend upon the free-tuition, higher education system. What does this mean? If this means that free tuition has contributed to higher wealth for the educated then this is no argument for either free tuition or more education. If it means the prosperity and growth of aircraft, electronics, motion picture, or agricultural industries in California are dependent upon free tuition, the contention remains unsupported by any analytic or factual evidence, and in fact can be falsified by comparisons with other states. Even if it could be demonstrated that *subsidized* higher education was responsible, the issue of *free* tuition would still not be touched. If this means that free tuition did attract some people to seek their education in California, they proceeded to reap the gain in their own higher income. If they provided a real net social benefit, it should have exceeded the extent of their subsidization to be justifiable. The same proposition holds for residents of California. If this argument is accepted, it is difficult to justify charging newcomers a full tuition while permitting existing residents a "free tuition." Yet, we have seen no proponent of zero tuition advocate zero tuition for all newcomers from all other states. If this means that the higher incomes for more people increase tax receipts, then the relevance of that completely escapes me. If this means California has a larger population, then this means higher land prices. But in so far as benefits to "California" have any relevance, I believe they should be viewed as benefits to people in California rather than as benefits to owners of a geographically identified piece of land, unless by "California" one means "landowners or politicians," who indeed do prefer larger populations as a source of political power and higher land values.

To induce students to take more education than is privately worth their while—in order to obtain the otherwise unheeded external gains—does call for payments to students. If a student were paid for doing what he would have done anyway, or if his education were subsidized to increase *his* wealth, he would be receiving a gift. But a payment (whether as zero tuition or a money payment) to the student to *extend* his education, for the sake of achieving *real*, external benefits that he otherwise would have not produced, is a payment for services, much as if he were to build houses, for the benefit of the rest of society. Such payments may well be independent of the income or future income of the student as well as of his parents. Though there is nothing that says the rich would provide less real external effects from more education, my conjecture is that the rich would in any event take more education than the poor for cultural reasons and would therefore require a smaller inducement to take the "optimal" extra amount of education for external social benefits. This can form a basis for advocating more educational inducements to the poor than to the rich, but not necessarily by a zero-tuition inducement to rich and poor alike.

It should be noted however that there is already subsidization of higher education by private philanthropy on a scale that staggers the imagination. The endowment funds of colleges and philanthropic foundations aiding education run into the scores of billions. Even if only half that were used to subsidize education (and the rest for research), the amount can not be regarded as minor, on any standard.

No matter what your beliefs about the validity or relevance of the preceding consideration, let us accept them, for the sake of analysis of alternative *means* of providing aid, for full educational opportunity, cultural aid, or extra inducements to education. (Of course, those who think the preceding arguments are too weak to warrant taxpayers' giving aid to college students can ignore all that follows, for to them there is no case for any state action, nor of zero tuition.) The rest will want to ask, "What is the best form of aid or inducement?"

We can enable or induce students to take more education with the following offer: "On the condition that you take certain kinds of education, we shall bear enough of the costs to induce you to do so." The costs he would have borne are the income forsaken and the tuition costs. (Food and living costs can be ignored for he would be incurring them no matter what he did.) Which of the following is the preferred way of extending that aid to potential students? (1) We pay directly the costs of extra education by operating the school to provide the extra education; this is the zero-tuition system. (2) We pay him an equal amount on the condition he take the additional, specified type of education, but he decides which school to attend and he pays the tuition to the school. This is an educational voucher or G.I.-type educational bill-of-rights (used after World War II for veterans).

The first requires *also* that the state directly finance and operate the school providing the education; the second permits the student to choose from competing schools and direct payment to the school he chooses. These two alternatives are sufficient to illustrate the major implications of zero versus high tuition modes of subsidy. The wealth effect for the student is superficially the same in either case, and the financial cost to the subscriber can be the same in each case, once it is decided how much education to subsidize for whom. The costs to the subscriber may be the same, but the results are not.

In the California state system of higher education, the tuition fee is zero for *all* state schools and for *all* kinds of training, regardless of whether it contributes to a net social gain or not, and regardless of how rich the student is.

Zero tuition implies that the appropriate aid or subsidy for every student of a state school is exactly equal to the tuition cost no matter what subject he takes. No basis for zero tuitions as being the proper amount has ever been presented; maybe the aid should be even larger, to compensate for forsaken earnings.

Because low- or zero-tuition schools are believed to have a larger proportion of less wealthy students than high-tuition colleges, zero-tuition schools are believed to do a better job of providing educational opportunity for less wealthy students. But this entails the earlier confusion between provision of *opportunity* and provision of a wealth *bonanza*; zero-tuition schools give bigger wealth gifts to the mentally able students than do the high-tuition schools.

Of course, higher tuition will, *other things left unchanged,* reduce the number of financially insecure students attending tuition colleges. The case for raising tuition is not that aid should be denied but instead that "zero-tuition" is a less desirable means of providing aid to students; it entails undesirable controls and political interference with education and lowers the quality of education. Yet there is another method of providing full educational opportunity *and* at the same time improving the quality and quantity of education and reducing political controls. The alternative is a system of full tuition supplemented by grants-in-aid to those who qualify as financially insecure and deserving students.

It is important to note that the financing of *colleges* to provide education is different from subsidizing *students*. The zero tuition is a subsidy to the *college* as well as to the student. Subsidies to *students* alone can be provided with a full-tuition system: in fact they are now being so provided by many private schools that do charge full tuition.

The alternative to the zero-tuition method of providing educational opportunity or giving aid is tuition, *with* loans or with grants of money. The critical difference, in my opinion, between no tuition and tuition, under these circumstances, is that the former lets the state politician and college administrator and faculty directly exert more control over education whereas the latter enables the student to exercise more power by his choice of college.

Subsidies to whatever extent desired could be provided by a system of grants-in-aid via scholarships. That would appear to be more expensive *administratively* (but only administratively) than zero tuition, precisely because an effort is made to eliminate the haphazard bonanzas in the zero-tuition system. The presumption is that the cost of selecting the students to be subsidized is less than the savings from the avoidance of subsidies to all students.

Tuition with grants-in-aid to students is not visionary. It is proven, practical, economical and currently used. New York

State already has a large system of Regents scholarships. California has a smaller scale system with about 2,000 scholarships. After World War II, the federal government granted millions of veterans educational vouchers for tuition, books, and incidental expenses under an enormously successful act known as the G.I. Bill. All these granted aid regardless of the student's current financial status. In California the university and state colleges now receive about $500 million annually directly from the legislature. That would finance 250,000 scholarships of $2,000 each. The university's budget would finance 125,000 students, more than the number now attending.

At present many arrangements exist whereby private colleges take into account the financial status of students in deciding how much tuition to charge each student. Even more efficient would be a system of loans with interest to be repaid after graduation out of the student's enhanced earnings. Under a loan system, the problem of filtering rich students from the financially distressed would be reduced to trivial dimensions, since the rich would have little, if anything, to gain by borrowing. This would provide full educational opportunity with little need for a means test.

Full tuition does not in any way restrict the achievability of full education opportunity. That can be achieved explicitly and openly by the scope of grants and subsidized loans. Just as social security and welfare payments are made in money with the recipient choosing his purchases from competing producers, so a full-tuition system with grants-in-aid or loans would enable separation of the issue of the amount, if any, of the subsidy from that of the best means of providing and controlling education.

Under a system of full-tuition fees, with whatever loans and scholarship voucher grants are deemed desirable, students could choose their education from the whole world. Any accredited college or educational institution whether it be for barbers, television technicians, beauty operators, mechanics, butchers, doctors, lawyers, or historians could serve. Ours would then really be the best educational system in the world; no longer would Californians be confined to California state-operated schools. Whatever one's beliefs about the desirable degree of subsidy for more education, and whatever his beliefs about who should get it, the full tuition voucher coupled with scholarships and loans would magically open a new, larger world of choice.

An alternative form of aid to students is a tax-credit allowance whereby parents, or students, could later receive a tax offset to their payments for tuition. This would put private college students on a more equal basis with low tuition public colleges. In my opinion, this would be equality at the wrong level of equality. Rather than give tax credits as a means of maintaining zero tuition, I would prefer placing a tax *liability* on students attending public colleges with low or zero tuition. Whereas the tax credit provides subsidies and aid to all students at the expense of nonstudents, the tax-liability assessment places the costs of providing the education more squarely on those who benefit from the education. A tax credit gives *equal* treatment to private and public college students—at the expense of nonstudents. A tax liability gives equality to private and public college students and to college and noncollege people, with each bearing only the costs of service provided for their benefit. If tax-liabiiity assessments are out of the question politically, the tax credit would be the next best; but it would not achieve one of the major purposes of a full tuition system.

With full-cost tuition, competition among California colleges, and even among academic departments would change. Instead of competition for funds being negotiated among university committees, deans, regents, state college boards, and legislators, competition would rely more on classroom behavior of instructors who would be more dependent on student attendance *vis-à-vis* other departments and other colleges. This would enormously enhance the power of the student in the former zero-tuition colleges. Giving students more attention and influence in the university would indeed occur, exactly as the customer exercises more power at the grocery—by his purchases and choice among competing products and stores, but not by leaping over the counter and insisting on power to run the store, as occurs with current protest. Currently at the grade school level many parents are turning to private schools precisely because the parents can choose more fully the kind of education given their children—via the power of the purse. The poorer people do not have that option—but they would with a tuition-grant system.

Since the producer usually knows more about what he is producing than does the consumer, the producer illogically tends to conclude that he is a better judge about the appropriate quality and quantity for the consumer. This tendency is especially rewarding if the producer can thereby obtain a sheltered competitive position in the production of the good. He would tend to produce a quality and quantity in a style related more to that which enhances his welfare and less to what students and parents prefer.

It is easy to see that with zero tuition the university faculty benefits from research and graduate activity that builds an impressive publication record and research status, with the currently less rewarding teaching of undergraduates being relegated to the less "distinguished," lower-ranking faculty or graduate students. The "publish or perish" rule would be less powerful under full tuition, because teaching would become a more important source of student directed funds. Survival of the better teachers who are weak in publication would be enhanced. It is interesting and amusing to note, incidentally, that students at the University of California are now attempting to protect some members of the faculty from being dropped because of inadequate research and publication. The protection comes by the students "donating" funds to hire the man to give classes; this *is* a voluntary, spontaneous full-tuition system. If allowed to expand, students would determine who was on the staff and who got the bigger incomes, just as they now decide which restaurants shall survive and prosper.

This is a simple application of the old, powerful, fundamental principle of behavior. The lower the price at which goods are distributed, relative to the market value, the greater the degree of discrimination and arbitrary criteria that the "seller" will display. Its corollary is that the lower the seller's right to the monetary proceeds, the greater his gain from underpricing the goods. The gains to the university administration and faculty from low tuition are classic examples, first expounded in Adam Smith's *The Wealth of Nations*. The greater the portion of a college's funds coming from tuition fees, the greater the power of the students and the greater the role teaching will play in the survival and prosperity of the members of the faculty. The less will the faculty choose which students shall attend, how they shall behave, etc. The lower is the ratio of tuition payments, the greater the power of the faculty over the students because the students are less able to exert significant effects on the financing of schools or departments as a reward for "good" performance—as they can with restaurants. The faculty says "education is different" and students are poor judges of good education; students are swayed by popular, theatrical teachers and do not appreciate the more valuable scholarly teachers. One wonders how students happen to go to the better and possibly tougher schools in the first place. The faculty of any college prefers lower tuition—until the budget expenditures can not be met from nontuition sources. And even then there is conflict of interest within the college between those who are threatened by the budget cut and those with tenure who are not. If the cut, or loss of income, would mean merely fewer undergraduates and fewer *new* teachers, clearly the least difficult resolution from the current faculty's interest is the reduction in new students, rather than an increase in tuition.

With zero tuition the state schools have expanded relative to higher-tuition private colleges, and the state university with its higher-salaried teachers and more expensive education is more attractive to students than the state colleges and junior colleges. The ex-president and the administrators of zero-tuition institutions correctly insist that *zero* tuition is the great principle underlying the *growth* of the university; but it is not a source of better education for California students. We should not confuse the *amount* of money with the *way* the money is obtained. More and better education, as judged by students, could be obtained at the same, or less, cost with the full tuition control of colleges coupled to loans and whatever grants-in-aid are desirable.

With full-cost tuition, the less expensive junior colleges would attract students and income from the university and colleges. Predictably, the few administrative voices heard in favor of higher tuition seem, from my observation, to come from junior college administrators—who believe they would outperform the university if put on a quality-cost basis of competition for students.

A counter argument to the preceding propositions is that junior college education is "inferior" to university education. Although the quality of the university as a research institution is high, not as much can be established for its quality as a teaching institution to educate college students. The move to junior colleges with full tuition would occur if the more expensive university education were not matched by the higher quality as judged by students and parents. The university would have to improve its teaching to hold students at its higher costs. If it could not, the results would constitute evidence that the high-cost and high-quality combination was not a superior combination of quality, cost, and quantity. A Rolls-Royce gives higher-quality transportation than a Ford, but it does not follow that more Rolls should be produced than Fords. *Education* must be judged by the quality, quantity, and costs, rather than in terms of only those who are educated at the highest, most expensive levels.

Yet, despite this patent fact of life, when faced with a budget cut the administrators of the state university plump four square for "quality at all costs"—for maintenance of quality education for a selected few regardless of how many must be turned away and given instead an "inferior" education. On what criterion is it established that it is better to maintain the level of quality of education for fewer students at the cost of sacrificing education for others? Would one argue that in the event of a social security reduction, we should reduce the *number* of recipients in order to maintain the quality of those lucky enough to keep getting social security payments? But analogies aside, the elite, authoritarian arguments by university administrators and faculty for a given level of quality, regardless of the sacrifices imposed on excluded students or on taxpayers, are sobering evidence of the seductiveness of self-interest pleading.

The faculty and administration of higher education in California have evolved in the zero-tuition environment, with appropriately adapted behavioral traits. They have learned to use that political structure; they have learned how to appeal to the political processes and to legislators and governors for more financing. They have been almost exclusively reliant on the political process. They praise politicians for statesmanlike, responsible behavior when the university budget is increased; but if it is decreased, they cry of political interference. Having accepted almost exclusive dependence on financing directly from the political and legislative processes, they should not complain of "political interference" when that same political process examines more intently the budget and the operations of the university. Are they really surprised that the venerable law "He who pays, controls" still is effective?

Legislators generally tend to favor direct state legislative financing of education coupled with no tuition, rather than full tuition with grants-in-aid. The closer the tuition approaches full cost, the less the power of the legislators over the educational institutions. It is not entirely accidental that Congress used a grant-in-aid system for veterans; there was no federal college system.

We must constantly remember the difference between paternalism and independence. Independence from the competition of political processes and politicians' interests can be enhanced by full tuition, but it will bring greater dependence on competition among educators in satisfying students' whims and interest. Either the students pay and control, or the political processes and politicians do. Yet some of the faculty seem to think they can avoid both. For educators there is no free lunch nor "free" tuition.

The situation reminds one of the Russian plight. Dissatisfaction with the quality of goods produced by Russian firms is sparking attempts to restore market prices as reflections of consumers' interests. While the Russian economists and consumers advocate more control via the market, producers and politicians show far less interest in weakening their power by moving away from socialism.

There remains a subtle, but effective means whereby full tuition would lead to *more* education than if directly provided by government at zero tuition. As matters stand now, an education at a tuition school may be worth $2,000, or say, $500 *more* than the education at zero-tuition state schools. For that superior education worth $500 *more*, the student would have to pay the full-tuition cost of $2,000. He gets no relief for not using state schools. If education were on a full-tuition basis, this obstacle to more and higher quality education would be removed. We should not assume that spending more by government for *direct* provision of education necessarily yields more education. This phenomenon, I conjecture, is powerful at all levels of education.

A preference for full tuition implies nothing whatsoever about the desirable extent of aid or subsidy to students. Unfortunately much of the debate has erroneously assumed that zero tuition is a necessary or a preferred method of aid while full tuition is a device to avoid aid to students. No matter how much aid, if any, should be given to students, the case for full tuition does not rest on a denial of aid. It rests on the premise that, whether or not aid is given to students, the financing of schools should be controlled more directly by students and their parents because the kind of education thereby made available is deemed to be better—by those who advocate full tuition.

Full tuition, plus grants-in-aid to whatever extent one believes is justified, directs educational activities more to the interest of students and less to that of the university staff. And after all, is it not the students whose interests are fundamental rather than the university's as an institution? Is it the students' interests as reckoned by students and parents rather than the convenience to the educators that is a better guide? My choice of answers is obvious. I suspect that these are the crucial issues on which advocates of zero tuition will differ with me.

My opposition to zero tuition arises because I do not like the way it redistributes wealth, nor do I like the totality of the effects of the kinds of competition it induces relative to that which would prevail under full tuition, supplemented by grants and loans. The latter yields more variety of educational opportunities and just as much educational opportunity and presumptively, greater detectability and survival of superior education. It reduces the producers' control over the products that the customers can have. The influence of selecting their colleges and controlling payments is a trait with high survival in the world outside of academia and which should be cultivated. The decreased role of the state and political activity in administering education is also a consequence I find congenial. Higher tuition would improve the quality of education rather than reduce it. The quantity would be affected not by either a zero or a high tuition, but by how much is spent for education. Zero tuition does not mean more is spent for education, nor that more poor people can attend. To believe it does is to think zero tuition is the only or best way to subsidize or aid students—and that contention begs the fundamental question of what is the best way.

All these consequences seem to work against my interests as a member of a zero-tuition college. If I thought this one exposition of economic analysis and one man's preferences really were capable of converting our system of educational subsidies from the zero-tuition to a full-tuition system with scholarships, loans, and vouchers, I might be less willing to expose it, for the price may be high enough to make me join with those who, whatever may be their reason, prefer the Holy Zero (excuse me, the *free*) tuition system.

9

Corporate Management and Property Rights

Though we know securities regulation is what securities regulators do, we may not know the "why." Why should exchange of corporate property rights be permitted only under restricted conditions, whereas exchanges of noncorporate rights are not equally regulated—such as rights to nonprofit corporations, or to proprietorships in houses and lands? What is there about corporate rights that calls for distinctive treatment?

Varied answers can be offered by economists. Securities in a corporation are homogeneous and purchased by many people; each potential stockholder in a corporation would bear a cost of independently discovering essentially the same information about the firm—a cost repeated for each potential buyer in some degree. If this information is required from each firm and made public, information search costs are reduced. For houses, or privately owned noncorporate enterprises the turnover of identical rights is sufficiently small that potential costs savings are insufficient to justify the costs of compulsory revelation of "all" material and relevant data.

One may wonder why we insist that all public, corporate firms reveal information. Why not let those that choose to do so file "full-disclosure" reports; potential buyers could then ignore those which do not. Stockholders could then decide whether the change in stock values consequent to reduced information costs about the corporation is worth the cost of general disclosure. This would permit buyers to act on less information if they wish. It is hard to see how one can argue against such optional behavior unless he takes a paternalistic attitude—a position not without its advocates.

Another argument for compulsory disclosure is the reduction in fluctuation in security prices (as distinct from later or earlier fluctuation), but strong theory or evidence to support that proposition—or indeed even to deny it—is lacking.

Another basis for regulation of conditions under which corporate securities may be sold rests in the ingenious phrase "separation of ownership and control," which allegedly implies something about behavior in the corporate world. Writers who have tried to put content in that phrase have elaborated by saying "no group of stockholders would be able under ordinary circumstances to muster enough votes to challenge the rule of management."[1] Or "barring blatant incompetence, management can count on remaining in office. . . . [S]o long as management possesses the confidence of the board (of directors), that body will usually not actively intervene to dictate specific policies."[2] "Control lies in the individual or group who have the actual power to select the board of directors" and these presumably are some group other than the stockholders.[3]

---

[1] R. J. Larner, "The 200 Largest Nonfinancial Corporations," *American Economic Review* (September 1966): 779.

[2] P. A. Samuelson, *Economics*, 7th ed. (New York: McGraw-Hill, 1966), pp. 89–90.

[3] A. Berle and G. Means, *The Modern Corporation and Private Property* (New York: Macmillan, 1933), p. 69.

Competition is said to be so restricted by the market power of large corporations as to change the role of competition; behavior by managers and employers is so insulated from the wealth-increasing interests of the owners that the conventional view of managers operating to increase owners' wealth is no longer germane.[4]

Though these pronouncements lack empirically refutable content, their emotional impact rivals that of a national anthem.

The empirical evidence for the "separation" theme, if we judge by the data brought to bear, is the dispersion of stockholdings in our largest corporations, combined with management advantages in a proxy fight. Recent data suggest the dispersion of stockholdings over holders with small proportional amounts has increased.[5] Yet surely the music about separation of ownership and control requires more lyrics than that stockholding is dispersed among many stockholders with no holders having, say, ten or more percent of the holdings. If that were all there were to the theme, it would mean merely that the expression "separation of ownership from control" had replaced the expression "dispersion of stockholdings." I would have thought that anyone propounding or testing a phenomenon to be called the separation of ownership from control would identify it with more than a measure of degree of stock ownership dispersion.

The expression probably was meant to convey behavioral implications. What are they? Is it that more dispersed holdings give less certainty to any one holder that his preferred use of the corporate resources will be the actual one? Or that the

4 C. Kaysen, "Another View of Corporate Capitalism," *Quarterly Journal of Economics* (1965): 43.

5 Larner, *op. cit.*

agent he prefers as the manager is not the one who is? Or that the probability that a *private* proprietor of $10,000 of goods can determine the use of those resources is higher than the probability that the preferred decision of an individual with a $10,000 interest in a million-dollar enterprise will be the one executed. But note that though his power of decision-making on $10,000 is reduced, it is increased over the remaining $990,000. Any of these might denote the behavioral phenomenon implicit in the expression ''separation of ownership from control.'' But I suspect that is not what is meant.

For clues to the meaning, we can note that a necessary attribute of ownership is the bearing of the value consequences of resources. We can interpret control to mean the authority to control decisions that will affect the value of resources. What must be meant by those who speak of separation of control from ownership is a reduced ability of the owners to revoke and reassign delegations of decision-making authority that will affect value.

In other words, it is assumed that the probability that any majority can be formed *to reassign* authority is lower the greater the dispersion of stock ownership. This may rest on two factors: (1) Knowledge of negligence or inefficiency by an agent will be more expensive to disperse over a majority. (2) The knowledge of harmful managerial decisions will be less influential on each stockholder, as the proportionate interest of the largest stockholders is smaller and the number of stockholders is greater. In this sense, a manager's deviations from stockholders' interests are less likely to be ''policed.'' This is one empirically meaningful interpretation of the expression greater separation of control from ownership.[6]

[6] Notice that one of the premises underlying this was *not* that in a group decision process one subgroup can exploit another, such as occurs in political voting, for, say, a tariff or licensing restriction on entry into a profession.

But some features of group ownership cut against this argument. A greater number of owners implies a greater variety of owners, some with more knowledge of the particular business. We can not assume legitimately that when there is one stockholder, he is the person most able to detect deviant behavior. Specialization of knowledge is not to be ignored; the corporate form enables a greater utilization of specialization of expert business knowledge. Despite the difficulty in reconciling several points of view, the variety of talents, and special knowledge, may more than compensate. Committees are not entirely vehicles for blocking action.

Corporate voting mechanisms are frequently alluded to both as a principal cause and as "evidence" of a separation of stockholders from "control," as the management with its accessibility to proxy rights at corporate expense is alleged to dominate the voting.[7] No minority group can be formed to fight the management. The picture is completed with an etching of a monolithic management group with common interests, no interpersonal conflicts of interest, and capable of perpetuating itself in office. (One is reminded of the naive cartel theory in which a group of erstwhile competitors agree to share a market, apparently with no conflicts of interests to be resolved and suppressed.)

But in fact, if a management group is exploiting stockholders by operating an enterprise in a diversionary manner, within the group opportunities will arise for some to gain personally by eliminating that "inefficient" behavior. Management cannot be adequately analyzed if it is regarded as a single person; there is competition within the management; managers can move to new jobs; and they compete for jobs by superior performance on present jobs. For example; few of us

---

[7] Berle and Means, *op. cit.*, p. 139.

at the University of California strive to produce superior products in research and teaching because the taxpayers of California are uppermost in our interests. It is the appeal we offer to other potential employers that induces us to act as if we were trying to satisfy our present employer's interests. Only if my future were irrevocably tied, like that of a slave, to my present employer would my behavior match that of the folklore indolent manager.

While we can leap from a monolithic view of management to the idea of effective separation of management from stockholder interest and control, we can not do so if we recognize other significant management constraints. If that leap were valid, then I conjecture the tenure of office of management in "management-controlled" corporations, as they are called, should be greater than in other corporations. Is the management more able to stay in office at unaffected salaries? Are stockholder profits in such corporations smaller? Is management compensation greater? Is the transition probability matrix of larger dispersed corporations different from others? I know of no empirical tests of these possible implications. Yet they are, I suspect, testable. And testing is precisely what should be done. Is what I have called the superficial analysis of the "separation" thesis incorrect, or is the alternative which does not dismiss so readily the competitive forces valid? Absent any empirical evidence in favor of the former, I shall, perhaps mistakenly, not reject the latter.

In sum, demonstration of greater dispersion of stockholdings, along with our proxy system, does not establish that bearing-of-value consequences have been separated from the effective control of the decision-maker, nor that the wealth of the stockholder is less well guarded.

There seems to have been an embarrassing delay or unwillingness to formulate the thesis in such a way as to make it refutable or testable. One would have expected the advocates to have presented evidence. But in thirty years, we remain with almost no empirical evidence. *So, presumed implications still remain to be validated by empirical study*, and I know of none . . . except one—the survival test—which is given almost no attention.

Since we observe an increased dispersion in corporate ownership, we should wonder why stockholders whose interests are less heeded by the top management would purchase stock in such corporations. Perhaps other advantages of the corporate form more than offset losses to stockholders imposed by the increased divergence of managers from stockholders' interests. This could be correct, but the fact that the dispersed ownership has increased certainly does not lend *support* to the implications of the general thesis that managerial activity in these situations will be less consistent with the shareholders' interests. However, although absence of a theory does not prove the phenomena are absent, the concomitance of unspecified implications, little evidence and inadequate logic is certainly not conducive to confidence.

WEAKNESSES IN THEORY OF NEW CORPORATE ECONOMY

Some analytical and conceptual mistakes have been committed in attempts to deduce a "distortion" in managerial behavior. It has been said that profits accrue to those who bear risks and make innovative decisions. Indeed, you can find economists who have referred to profits as rewards or penalties for innovative activity, with the value effects serving to induce such innovation (or eliminate it) by rewarding the risk-takers.

But it is something else to say that managers who select the innovative uses are those who bear or should bear consequent value effects. Whether or not they do depends upon prearranged contractual relationships with respect to property rights.

The economic concept of "profits" refers to a particular value phenomenon—unpredicted value changes. Whoever has the title to goods is the person who bears the profits and losses. The owner is the name given to that person and he is bearer of the profits or losses. It does not advance rigorous analysis to talk about profits as the "reward" both to the owners *and* to managers who exercise delegated decision authority in determining uses of resources. This careless conjunction, common in the lay literature, leads to sentences like. ". . . if the courts, following the traditional logic of property, seek to insure that all profits reach or be held for the security owners, they prevent profits from reaching the very group of men (managers) whose action is most important to the efficient conduct of enterprise. Only as profits are diverted into the pockets of control do they, in a measure, perform their second function" (i.e., inducing innovation).[8]

To believe that employed managers, with delegated authority to determine uses of someone else's resources, are the bearers of resultant profit or loss is to lose sight of the essential attributes of the ownership-agency relation. Managers do *not* bear those realized profit gains or losses. Owners do. The manager does not acquire those realized profits any more than does the designer or builder of a profitable apartment house acquire or share in the realized profits—all of which go to the apartment owner. Profits (or losses) from the construction of

[8] *Ibid.*, p. 350.

an apartment house are borne by the owner, not the architect or builder. The profits they initiated are not theirs and are not distributed to them unless they initially had a contract to share in them—i.e., unless they initially had become co-owners in the assets. Yet, although that is true, it does not follow that the wealth or income of the architect or builder is unaffected or that he is left unrewarded. A profitable apartment brings more demand for its architect or builder. This increased demand leads to higher incomes for the architects and builders or managers.

It is one thing for agents with delegated authority to be rewarded for creating profits for owners; it is a far different thing for delegated agents to share *in those* profits. Profit receivers do not give up any of their accrued profits when their agents are subsequently paid higher incomes for future services. The *past, realized* profits are not redirected or redivided to the managers in the form of new subsequent contractual terms. Rather, the initial realized profits of the resource owners were smaller because people anticipate that the wages of the superior manager will be bid up in efforts to obtain his services. No *prior* contractual provision explicitly arranged between the parties is necessary for the superior manager to realize a gain for superior services. His revealed superiority is reflected in his higher market value.

I conjecture that confusion has arisen from the impression that a person gets what he produces—a manifestly false, if not empty, proposition. Instead he may get, via a contract, in the context of competition for his services, an amount commensurate with the most optimistic employer's belief of what he is *expected* to produce. If he prefers a different kind of contractual reward, viz., one in which his reward is contingent upon realized results, then he can become a co-owner of the resources whose values are to be affected and part of which value is to be his.

In sum, the fact that delegated agents are paid to produce value changes in goods by the way they use them, does not in any sense imply that the agents deserve or will obtain part of *that* value change. This stands even though their subsequent contracts reflect their earlier performance in successfully producing past profits.

Belief that earlier realized profits must be shared among the owners and the so-called responsible superior managers or innovators results from a failure to recognize anticipatory capitalization in the market's valuation of resources. If the manager had to be rewarded by a payment out of the initial profits realized by the initial employer, then those who worry about separation of ownership and management functions would indeed have pointed out a problem.[9] But that is not the way a market values resources.

Neither is that the logic of economic theory or the logic of conventional profit theory, despite some assertions to the contrary.[10] The conventional and still valid wisdom presumes competitive market capitalization of foreseeable future events and assumes that once a manager displays evidence of a superior activity, the market (i.e., other people) will not ignore the implications about the future demand and costs for his services. Ignoring or denying the forces of open competitive market capitalization is, in my opinion, a fundamental error in the writing about ownership and control and about the modern corporate economy. Neither the role of competition in the markets for capital goods and services, nor its logic, is upset

[9] Note that I refer to a separation of *functions*, not a separation of interests or a loss of control.

[10] Berle and Means, *op. cit.*, pp. 341–51.

by the presence of large corporations with dispersed ownership.

Not only is market valuation ignored in the misinterpretation of the role of profits, but it is ignored also in the contention that the modern stockholder's wealth is less well protected in the dispersed than in the concentrated ownership corporation. We have only to ask if anyone would pay as much for a share of stock in a corporation with dispersed ownership if he knew his wealth would be given less diligent interest by corporate managers. He would pay less in the knowledge he was to get less. The lower bid prices for stock would protect investor-owners from the foreseeable losses anticipated from less diligent concern for their wealth. Yet, corporations have thrived, and they would not have if the dispersed ownership corporation suffered from this value discounting.

Resolution of these two conflicting interpretations lies in the possibility that either (1) the alleged greater diversionary activity is a myth, or (2) the dispersed large corporation is so advantageous in other respects that the diversionary tactics of the managers are financed out of those advantages while the stockholders get as much as they would in less dispersed corporations. If the former were true, the whole issue would collapse. If the latter were true, it would imply only that the *forms* (but not value) of managerial behavior and of rewards in the dispersed ownership corporation are different and more costly (inefficient), but the managers would reap no extra gain. The consumer of products of those corporations would be paying a higher price than he otherwise would (but still, a price lower than if there were *no* dispersed ownership corporations). But could it not still be argued that the stockholders could have received a larger return? It would seem not, for if they could have, the number of dispersed corporations would have increased, thus lowering returns to the equivalent of what is being obtained in less dispersed ownership corporations. Let me elaborate on these points.

Managers do not reap some special or additional gain or economic rent from their ability to engage in diversionary tactics. Awareness of greater diversionary capability by managers or employees results in lower pecuniary salaries as managers and employees compete for the jobs permitting diversionary tactics.[11] Competition among managers and employers in seeking attractive, easy, or secure jobs implies a lower pecuniary reward in those jobs. A job with more leisure yields a lower wage; one with greater security yields a lower wage; one with more leisure and a given wage will have its security competed down. Substitution among the various facets of jobs occurs so that, on *net* of all considerations, the advantage of one job over another is competed away. All the various facets constitute ''forms'' of payment to the employee, whether the facets be leisure, wages, types of colleagues, working hours, vacation provisions, extent of surveillance by the employer, etc. Pecuniary salary will be lower for the same reasons that salaries of people working in factories or shops in more pleasant surroundings will be lower than they would have been with less attractive working conditions. Stockholders need not be activists in bringing this about.

This argues that the dispersed ownership corporation implies a difference in the vector or form of payments to managers and employees. But not all forms of ''compensation'' to employees are equally costly. The form of compensation in a

[11] Unless you believe, with Kaysen (*op. cit.*), that executive compensation is not within control of the stockholders. If I knew what that really meant, I might test it. If it means what I suspect it was intended to mean, I think it is wrong. But then, ask yourself, Does an owner ''have control'' of the wages he pays—in any kind of firm?

dispersed corporation may indeed represent a higher cost vector to the corporation, but if the corporation can earn enough because of its advantages, it can in equilibrium bear this higher cost vector of a managerial "salary." This does not mean the employees or managers are getting a more valuable or preferable return than in less dispersed corporations. Instead they are being paid with a different, higher cost (i.e., less efficient), vector of rewards—one that costs more to provide but is no more preferable on net than in other corporations or businesses. It is different simply because the cost of controlling the various facets of the vector and changing it to a different one (say one with higher wages and less leisure) is greater than the saving. The higher costs of such vectors (of given attractiveness to employees) can be financed out of the advantages of this type of corporation. If the costs of these forms of rewards to managers had not been higher, one might think there would have been larger earnings for the owners. But this would not be an entirely correct conclusion, for the number and scope of such corporations would have been greater, with consequent lower prices to consumers. The higher cost salary vectors, if indeed they are more costly, simply mean a sacrificed output potential for consumers—evidenced by higher prices than would have been paid for the larger output if the dispersed ownership corporation could police and control its managers' and employees' behavior as efficiently as is alleged for a smaller, less dispersed, corporation.

To repeat, all this argues that the dispersed corporation changes the *forms* (and efficiency) of payment to employees and managers. It does *not* imply lower wealth for the stockholders, nor higher earnings for employees and managers, than in less dispersed corporations. If employees tend to be thieves, and if employers or employees are aware of this tendency, contractual money salaries will be adjusted so that part of the total salary is taken as legitimatized "theft." The employers do not necessarily lose. The higher policing costs are borne by (i.e., discounted to lower wage offers to) the employees whose past conduct determines their present reputation and beliefs about future behavior. Similarly, if dispersed corporate ownership permits managers greater scope for anti-stockholder activity and if the stockholders *or* the employees are aware of this tendency, the terms of employment compensation will be adjusted.

The resultant implication is that in large, dispersed-ownership, for-profit corporations, we should expect different types of managerial and employee behavior and rewards than in small and closely held corporations. The large corporate pattern should reflect the greater costs of policing and revising delegated authority, but *without* necessarily resulting in lower wealth for the stockholder than in less dispersed corporations. These effects, insofar as they are foreseen or predictable, on the average will be reflected in anticipatory behavior, and therefore in the valuation of initial capital investments or in stock prices on subsequent stock transfers. The stockholders are not any the poorer or their wealth less well secured.

How valid is this competitive, market equalization process in reality? We do not know. But that does not mean that we can gratuitously assume it is absent or weak, as does most of the writing on the "ownership and control separation" theme. Nor can we cavalierly assume the opposite.

Do dispersed ownership firms have historically lower rates of growth of stockholders' wealth (allowing for dividends and capital value growth) than less dispersed ownership firms? I have yet to see a test of this, though it appears this should be a feasible evaluation. With attention to the "regression phenomenon'' and with controls for types of industry, this should make a fine project for several doctoral dissertations . . . several, because of the value of replication and competitive testing of results.

Let us consider the presumed monolithic structure of management in the business firm. In reality, the firm is a surrogate of the marketplace, but differs in that longer-term general service contracts exist without continuous renegotiations at every change of type of service. To analyze the firm as a single-operator institution within which it is assumed there is not the competition that exists in markets is to miss a significant portion of the competitive processes. Though a firm may continue with unchanged name, and possibly even the same stockholders, the internal shifting of personnel within, as well as among, firms is market competition. The many people within a firm competing with each other and with people in other firms should suggest that the unit of analysis for competitive activity is the individual rather than an institution, which serves as an internalized market. Top management of a firm engages in screening employees, techniques, and proposals for new products which, if performed externally by separate firms, would be clearly evident as market functions. But when these functions are performed within the firm, the competitive market forces are hidden from obvious view and mistakenly ignored by careless analysts.

More significant than the rise and fall of firms, for purposes of behavioral analysis, is the rise and fall of individuals within firms. For many purposes (though not all) we can think of a firm (call it General Electric) as a marketplace, as if it were a city, within which individuals engage in atomistic competition. Competition among cities takes the form of individuals moving among cities and exporting ideas that have passed the test of profitability. While it is not correct to carry this analogy too far—and just how far "too far" is, I don't yet know—the analogy is very good in some respects. The long survival of some firm or of a few firms can not be interpreted as evidence of a lack of market competition either within or between firms.

If it be argued that corporations with dispersed ownership or with so-called management control have separated the interests of stockholders from those of managers, we should expect differences in the rates of transition of individual employees within and between firms. We should perhaps expect a lower turnover of management in the dispersed corporation. Do we have any evidence of it? I am embarrassed to admit I have been unable to find that evidence. However, I shall cite some evidence later for implying different types of behavior. For example, to continue to speak of a mythical firm called General Electric, the directors and president are quick to fire or demote a division chief whose profit record shows inferiority to some other potential division head. Replacement of an inefficient division head *may* be quicker within General Electric than if the division manager owned the division. The internal capital and personnel market *may*, nay *is*, more efficient than the external open market. That assertion I make in complete confidence, as a challenge to anyone who with equal aplomb asserts the contrary. I could go on and assert that there is greater mobility of managers and technical personnel within General Electric than among firms in an atomistic market economy, that new ideas are internally evaluated more quickly, cheaply, accurately, and on a broader scale than in a society made up of several firms aggregating the same size. I could assert that the labor market within General Electric is superior to the atomistic, so-called, pure competitive market and is superior because there are specialists within General

Electric who are rewarded more fully for collecting and evaluating information about people. Thus the usual outside employment agencies that specialize in providing personnel information would be less efficient than the personnel employment agencies operating within General Electric. But what the truth is, I do not know.

Further, the investment funds (capital) market *within* General Electric is fiercely competitive and operates with greater speed to clear the market and to make information more available to both lenders and borrowers than in the external "normal" markets. In fact I conjecture that the wealth growth of General Electric derives precisely from the superiority of its internal markets for exchange and reallocation of resources—a superiority arising from the greater (cheaper) information about people and proposals. Many "knowledge effects" that would be externalistic in an ordinary market are converted into beneficial internalities within the firm as incentives and rewards to those producing them.

The foregoing is intended to suggest that the traditional theory of profits, of private property, markets, and competition is not obsolete, and also that the "separation of ownership from control" theme still lacks validly deduced and established implications about exploitation of stockowners' wealth. Long prior to the wide dispersal of stockholdings in a corporation, potential conflicts of interest among stockholders were recognized. Political theory if not legal history tells us much about the probability of subgroups exploiting the remainder by the group decision process. Furthermore, the conflict of interest between principals and their agents has long been recognized, though I presume, quite safely, that it is not that idea which the "separation of ownership and control" is supposed to designate.

If I appear to be defending the old theory as adequate, let me beg off. Inadequacies in the old theory exist, but they derive from its use of a wealth instead of a utility-maximizing postulate. The wealth-maximizing postulate is usually appropriate (or less inappropriate) when applied to the "firm" as a unit of analysis. But in seeking to explain individual behavior *within* the firm, utility-maximizing criteria are more general and powerful than wealth-maximizing criteria. But this, I believe, would be equally true for the old-fashioned small firm.

Instead of a change in the modern society, it is the change in the objectives of economic theory that points up inadequacies in the old theory. We want now to interpret individual behavior, not merely firm survival as an entity. Although I say this is a change in objectives, I should be the first to assert that good old Adam Smith did exactly that in his *Wealth of Nations*. The adherents of the theme of a new modern corporate economy are saying what Smith said about corporations. Yet they are denying that the old competition theory is applicable. A somewhat strange twist, indeed.

There have been changes in our economy. But I do not believe that the idea of a replacement of a competitive era by an era of "market-power" large firms will enrich our theory or understanding of behavior.

My impression is that moves toward an economy with less open-market competition reflect a diversion of competition to the political processes, as resort is made to greater governmental control over economic access to markets and terms of exchange. Much of what passes for the new corporate economy should more accurately be called the new mercantilist, or the new "political" or politically regulated, economy, since it involves more political competition and the greater use of political rewards and penalties. And this move to political influence has occurred in both small and large firm industries. The "solution" (if such a "political" economy is a problem) usually is more political controls and political competition. This is beneficial to those most adept at political competition, for they would benefit from increased demand for their services as political competition displaces market competition in controlling economic activity. All this is of course what the "obsolete" economic theory implies.

SUGGESTED AND TESTED BASES FOR ANALYSIS: HIERARCHICAL CONTROL AND TYPES OF PROPERTY RIGHTS

Advances in economic theory could be obtained by more explicit recognition of the political rewards-penalties structure in our economy. Advance could also be made with recognition and analysis of two other features—the hierarchical control task within a firm and the types of property rights prevailing in the firm. The hierarchical control structure has been analyzed in the context of a utility-maximizing criterion by O. Williamson.[12] For fear of flattering him justifiably, though unnecessarily, I shall merely note that the problem of inducing workers at the various hierarchical levels to gear their work to a specified common goal, as against individual interests, becomes more severe as the number of hierarchical layers or number of coworkers increases. The problem of surveillance, information handling, and filtering is a difficult one even when there is perfect consonance of goals among the workers. Since large enterprises are usually of a corporate form with more dispersed ownership, it is easy to confound the effects of dispersed own-

[12] O. Williamson, "Managerial Discretion and Business Behavior," *American Economic Review* (December 1963): 1032–57.

ership with the problem of hierarchical control, and I conjecture this has been done.

Property Rights

But even if the confusion between stockholder dispersion and hierarchical controls is avoided, hierarchical control objectives are different in nonprofit or publicly owned enterprises (e.g., government agencies) from those in privately owned corporations. One objective—profitability—or effects on wealth of the owners will be given less weight in the former group. Profitability, combined with rights to profits, provides a clearer and stronger criterion for behavior of subordinates in for-profit corporations than in government agencies or not-for-profit enterprises. Absent that criterion and absent the "property" right to capture profits, resort is made to more detailed operating procedures and internal regulations.

The theme of separation of ownership and control in large dispersed corporations has been illustrated with public utilities and transportation companies, as well as with unregulated firms. The corporate manager's behavior has been characterized as resembling that of administrators of universities, philanthropic foundations, nonprofit corporations, unions, and government agencies. This suggests, and economic theory does indeed imply, that in corporations which are *not* profit-seeking or are *not* privately owned (at least in the sense of having salable, marketable shares of ownership) behavior will deviate from that in a profit-seeking corporation. It deviates because "stockholders" in nonprofit or public utility corporations have less incentive (costs of doing so aside) for responding to market, competitive pressures for "efficient" or profit-making types of behavior. I shall try to elucidate this relatively neglected *basis for analysis* of the *kinds* of property rights and their relationship to economic and cultural behavior, because I believe something can be deduced and verified about the relationship between behavior and the types of property rights.

Crudely and broadly, let me identify one attribute of property rights in goods as being the probability of the effectiveness of my decisions about the use of those goods. That is, the greater the uses for a given good *and* the greater the probability that my decision about uses will be effective, the greater are my property rights in that good. Rights will be weaker if they have not been specified or explicitly recognized or if they have a small probability of being enforced by society.

Specification and identification of rights is not costless. For example, water is a good to which property rights are loosely specified, in part, because of the high costs of doing so. But costs are high or low only *relative* to the value of the rights which could be specified. If the value of some right to a good rises, as that of rights to fresher water has during recent decades, the costs of specification, identification, and assignment of rights become more worth incurring. In general, the higher the value of potential rights to a good relative to costs of specifying those property rights, the greater will be the clarity of specification, identification, and assignment of rights in that good.

This proposition, that the increase in value of potential rights to goods leads to a stronger specification of rights, does not indicate what form the specification and identification will take, or to whom the rights will be assigned initially, or whether they will be transferable. It does not say whether title will be taken by the state or will be assigned to individuals as private property; it does not say whether the rights will be transferable among people or whether the goods are transferable among alternative uses.

You will rightly regard the proposition as obvious insofar as it is precise enough to have meaning. Anyone knows it doesn't pay to keep track of worthless things, while for more valuable goods greater safeguarding costs are more worth incurring. But the influence of this proposition on our legal evaluation or development of property rights structures is by no means obvious and direct. The development of water law in the several states well illustrates the tortuous and hesitant progress toward more explicit specification and clear assignments of rights over water. The hold of precedent is rightly strong; adaptation to the changed values of rights and changed costs of specification is often inordinately delayed—or so it would seem from an examination of individual cases. Let me cite an example. In California, billions of dollars of wealth are being wasted simply because of the slowness in the adaptation of water law to changes in values of potential rights over water. A multi-billion-dollar aqueduct, Northern to Southern California, is being built *now*, ostensibly to bring water to Southern California. But, in fact, the aqueduct is being built now not to bring more water to Southern California but to establish or *identify now* who is to have *rights* over Northern California water in the distant future. Building the aqueduct now to capture the present flow of water is justifiable only as a means of *presently* establishing one's *right* to the *future* flow of water. All that cost could be deferred if rights to water use were legally established and made transferable by paper records rather than by concrete and steel devices.

With but slight imagination we can perceive what would have happened had rights to future lumber, oil, gas, iron ore, and coal been assigned and controlled in that way. No imagination is required for what has happened to our radio-frequency spectrum, where a government board controls the use; private rights which had begun to arise in common law and which evoked judicial protection for exclusive use and exchange were thwarted by government agents who denied this policing activity and the legality of exchangeability. Small wonder that the resultant mess occurred. Federal allocative authority over assignment and use was established instead of property rights enforcement via market competition. The alternative of exclusive, exchangeable, private rights, facilitated by state enforcement, to portions of that scarce valuable property—radio-frequency spectrum—was not allowed to be established.

As you may know, lumber rights once were acquired not by title to standing trees, but by cutting the trees into lumber. If trees were not cut, the landowner could not count on clear title to the lumber. In some agricultural areas, land title could be established only after the claimant had stripped the trees from the land, in order to manifest its *use* for agricultural purposes, as a legal precondition to title acquisition. Small wonder we stripped some of our midwestern forest lands.

Yet these results have been interpreted by famous historians as failures in the private property, capitalistic competitive system. In fact, these results occurred where we did *not* have private property, capitalist market, competitive controls over those resources. The law did not permit the title acquisition and exchange rights that would enable economic competition to induce economic use of resources. As I view that history, the symptoms were not those of a private property, capitalist, competitive system, but of a different legal system of distributing and identifying rights which granted rights that induced "undesirable" behavior. Use values (of water or lumber) for future times or for different people and in different ways simply could not be realized; current possessors or competitors seeking rights in the resources were told they could not retain or capture rights to those future higher valued uses.

This suggests that while we endeavor to regulate people's

activities by imposing more regulation, with consequent enhancement of the role of political competition, it would be wise to examine the behavioral effects of the legal system of establishing, identifying, and transferring various types of property rights. For example, in a "not-for-profit" organization, the so-called owners or trustees do not have the right to decide to use or divide the wealth of the organization for their personal use—a right which *is* held by stockholders of a for-profit private property corporation. And in mutuals or cooperatives, while the "members" can vote to dissolve the enterprise and divide the proceeds among the members, they often cannot sell their rights. They can only abandon their interests in return for the initial investment, in contrast with private, for-profit corporate stockholders who can sell rights at open-market prices. Whereas the present capital value—or wealth effect—is thrust on a stockholder as the value of his salable stock changes, in a "nonprofit" or "mutual" or "cooperative" enterprise, a member without transferable capital value rights bears the future consequences of current decisions only if he remains a member until the time of the future consequence.

In a for-profit private property corporation, current stockholders gain or lose wealth when the future consequence is anticipated and reflected in stock values. If members consume capital or are less diligent in preserving the future earning power, they bear more of the cost immediately. These problems are present also in mutual associations and nonprofit organizations, since their managers do not have to answer to anyone whose capitalizable wealth is at stake. Absent property rights that permit capitalization of future events into present market values, stockholders have less incentive to be concerned with potential capital value effects and so the manager is less responsive to implicit capital value effects.

To avoid misunderstanding, let me emphasize that the proposition is that the capitalization of future effects into present values, combined with the ability to *capture* that market wealth by selling to a second party, provides an effective stimulus to the control of actions that affect present capital values.

There is a difference in incentive effects between a capitalizable, salable wealth right and a right to a stream of future receipts which will be obtainable only if one retains the claim into the future. For example, a mutual shareholder in a savings and loan association, or an "owning" managing-director of a nonprofit institution, can legally reap the future rewards for present action only by remaining with the enterprise, whereas a stockholder could immediately capitalize and reap the gain by selling his interests. Market capitalization and sale provide a different reward or punishment for present actions than is the case in the absence of capitalization possibilities. In sum the wealth-effects are more immediate to the stockholder than to the mutual shareholder or owner of an enterprise without capitalizable, salable, property rights.

Before discussing noncapitalizable rights, let us consider a situation in which stockholders' rights to capture profits are restricted. The profits of a public utility are usually controlled by the state and limited to some maximum set by a regulatory agency. The *managers* will have incentives to strive for profits above the legal limit if the managers can conceal them from the regulators and capture them. And they can, to some extent. Higher earnings might be absorbed into cost-enhancing activities easing the life of the managers. Better offices, more congenial colleagues, and a more relaxed business operation with shorter hours are means of "converting" potential profits into "higher cost" activities. Or, also, the managers can engage in discriminatory hiring practices, by heeding more the race, creed, and color of potential colleagues.[13]

This higher cost activity in a public utility is a form of profit conversion, and is a form of activity which would reduce survival prospects for firms with less restricted property rights. We should expect to see greater clusterings of employees according to race, creed, and religion, for example, in not-for-profit enterprises than in for-profit private enterprises. Empirical studies provide corroborative evidence. In sum, legal limitations on profits or on access to markets harm the interests of the relatively unpopular, unorthodox, or individualistic members of society. Given this fact, there is an inconsistency in the view of those who argue that market competition brings out the worst in people, if they also believe that discrimination in terms of race, creed, and color is undesirable.

The reason is simple. Any open-market competitors who were to discriminate in this high-cost way would be outcompeted by others who did not engage in such discrimination. But if the explicit net earnings are already at the upper legal limit in a public utility, there is less to gain by avoiding discrimination in favor of less productive, but more popular, colleagues. Remove the prospect for stockholders capturing *greater* capitalizable profit, and the incentive to use lower cost, less discriminatory production techniques is reduced. No escape from this same *implication* is obtained by reliance on a regulatory body, for its members also lack the possibility of capturing capitalized wealth increments.

All this, though obvious, bears exposition because some of the "separation of ownership from control" discussion seems to be drawn from observations on behavior in public utilities.

[13] A. Alchian and R. G. Kessel, "Competition, Monopoly and the Pursuit of Money," *Aspects of Labor Economics* (Princeton, 1962), pp. 157–83.

Here it is not the "widely dispersed ownership," but a legally imposed profit restriction, which induces stockholders to permit more management behavior deviating from the wealth interests of the stockholder.

If, with restrictions on capturable profits, we combine restricted or licensed *entry* into the market, as is typically the case for public utilities, then monopoly rent appears as a supplement to competitive economic profits. Monopoly rent, which regulatory folklore says belongs to the consumer, will be captured in the form of taxes or as an easier, more convenient, and better life for employees, managers, and regulators, or even possibly with higher than competitive wages. Unions, for example, find these public utilities relatively easy pickings insofar as the union can share in the monopoly rent. It follows also that public utilities will display more discrimination by race, creed, color, and age; they will display greater tenure of job, fewer firings, and other attributes at the cost of the consumers who could otherwise have had lower prices. And for this there is empirical corroborative evidence.

In addition to profit-limited firms, with or without market entry restrictions, there is another class of property arrangements that manifest similar behavior. These are the nonowned firms without stockholders known as nonprofit institutions, mutual associations, cooperatives, union-type associations, governmental enterprises. All lack private ownership rights in the enterprise; there are no capitalizable, alienable shares or rights. There are people who make decisions as to how certain resources shall be used *in the enterprise* and within the scope of activities of the enterprise, but no one nor any group has the right to divert the wealth of the organization to their personal benefit by taking it out of the enterprise. And furthermore, although rights to manage that enterprise can be bestowed on other parties, they are not salable. The implications are profound.

A nonprofit (i.e., not-for-profit) enterprise may be successfully originated by some organizer-managing director. But increases in his wealth can not be extracted from the enterprise for use outside the enterprise, nor can he sell his management rights. His only way to convert profits to his personal benefit is appropriately to use the enhanced wealth *in* the enterprise. Again, fancier offices, better-looking secretaries, more on-the-job fringe benefits, very liberal expense-accounts policies, and higher salaries all have served as conversion tactics. If he were the owner, he would have capitalized that net-earnings stream into a presently capturable wealth. Since he cannot, he dissipates the potential profitability via business-connected expenditure to obtain more nonpecuniary, non-take-home sources of utility. He substitutes on-the-job advantages for personal, at-home consumption.

Nonprofit, or not-for-profit, enterprises differ from profit-restricted enterprises in two respects. First, in the former profits are not legally restricted; these enterprises just "happen" to make profits, according to the legal fiction of the situation. Second, there is no restriction on entry. The nonprofit enterprise is entitled to retain any available economic profits in the face of open-market competition. But neither the organizer nor anyone else can capitalize the profits into personal take-home wealth. However, the self-perpetuative, organizing-director, trustees, or board of directors can take higher salaries or put profits into an endowment if profits accrue more rapidly than the director-manager can ethically divert them to personal benefit. Had it been a for-profit enterprise, with salable stock, the present *and future anticipated* earnings could have been distributed or, if retained, captured by the initial stockholders via the higher market value of salable stock. We would expect nonprofit enterprises, insofar as they are profitable, to manifest and distribute their net earnings via business-connected costs. Their "costs" may appear to be higher, but in fact those "costs" may be distributions of profits; the higher "costs" are not necessarily signs of inefficiency or higher real costs.

Mutual associations, of the sort that exist in the savings and loan business and in insurance, provide evidence of the effects of an absence of private property rights. The legal fiction is that depositors or insurees are mutual "owners." The mutual shareholders acquire shares that often cannot be liquidated by redemption, and there is no possibility of marketing them at a value reflecting the profitability of the mutual organization. Mutual shareholders are limited in their voting power to a maximum number of votes, usually a very small percentage of all votes. Proxies can be solicited, but no one can start with a large or significant base of his own votes. There is less gain in raiding a mutual association or waging a proxy battle to put in new management as a means of improving profitability, because if such an attempt were successful, the potential gains would not be reflected in capitalized market values of salable shares. The winner of a proxy battle would have to take on some managerial position and reward himself by a salary collected during his tenure of office. Not only is his salary subjected to a higher tax rate, but, more fundamentally, a series of future net earnings is a less powerful incentive than the choice between that course and capturing the currently capitalized present value.

However, the organizing manager-directors of mutual associations do have some means, even if roundabout, by which some of the profits can be capitalized. One way is for the operator-organizer to own private, for-profit accessory companies selling insurance and other complementary services to the mutual. The mutual's purchases of such services can be made from these side companies which charge higher than competitive rates, thereby siphoning off the net earnings and enabling their conversion into capitalizable stock values of the service companies.

Market competition by other potential managers for the mutual manager's job will be ignored because the director, to whom an appeal must be made, is the manager himself. And any potential savings from the more efficient potential manager would be given little weight, since the present director cannot capitalize the value of the potential savings. I am not asserting that mutual shareholders are incapable of controlling the managers, just that their costs of doing so are greater and the gains are smaller than for privately owned corporate institutions.

Evidence for this "higher cost" or "aberrant" activities of mutuals (not necessarily indicative of less able, efficient, or alert management) has been obtained by A. Nicols in a study of mutual and private-stock savings and loan associations.[14] Reported costs per dollar of new loans, turnover of management, nepotism, and responsiveness of interest rates to changed market conditions show that the mutuals had higher costs, higher nepotism, smaller management turnover, and slower response via interest rate changes.

This does not mean that the managers are less alert or informed of the possibilities. They exploit those possibilities in ways that yield benefits they can capture; the wealth potential

[14] A. Nicols, "Stock versus Mutual Savings and Loan Associations: Some Evidence of Differences in Behavior," *American Economic Review* (May 1967): 337–46.

is being exploited in ways other than take-home, capitalizable wealth for nonexistent stockholders.[15]

[15] A study of this is provided by B. Weisbrod in his investigation of nonprofit hospitals. He identifies what he regards as nonprofit maximizing behavior, and the analysis is rather suggestive. A stronger test could be provided if one were to make a similar study of proprietary hospitals. B. Weisbrod, "Some Problems of Pricing and Resource Association in a Non-Profit Industry—The Hospitals," *The Journal of Business* (January 1965): 18–28.

Electrical Equipment Collusion: Why and How

Man sensibly tries to collude with other people to avoid mutually costly competition. At the same time he tells himself that he should rise above the collusive habit and shun it. For example, the recently revealed collusion among sellers of heavy electrical equipment to the government has evoked sermonizing condemnations of business transgression. But, perhaps fortunately, collusion is as immune to preaching as is sex.[1]

At the birth of economics as a formal science, Adam Smith explicitly recognized the incentive to collude. But Smith went on to indicate some places wherein the economic system makes collusion difficult and wherein it makes it easy—aside from laws and doctrines of immorality. Smith showed how

This paper is the result of some luncheon discussions among W. Meckling, N. Breckner, G. Becker, and A. Alchian, and represents another stride forward in the effort to blame "government" for all evils of the world as an antidote to the strawmen who praise it for all virtue. Alchian is the reporter because the rest were employees of only one public agency, but he accepts no liability or responsibility for any misstatements of fact or logic.

[1] "The catastrophe resulting from the destruction of the instinct to collude would be second only to that resulting from the elimination of the sexual urge" (Y. Hamparsoom, *The Origins of Near-Eastern Philosophy* [Erevan, 1886], p. 137).

some forms of property rights or institutions make collusion less viable or profitable. Is there a similar explanation that will suggest why the "electrical equipment" collusion was tempting? Is there some reason why the instinct to collusion was provided with especially favorable environment? Or was it that the particular sellers involved were simply less "moral" or more predisposed toward lawbreaking than the mass of the rest of us?

The purpose of this note is to see how economic theory implies that the viability of collusion is stronger among sellers who are selling to an institution not characterized by private property and in particular one that is characterized by public ownership. In the present instance, the buyers against whom the collusion was *successful* were almost always governments, government agencies, or governmentally owned public utilities. What is interesting is that economic theory implies that one should expect a greater chance of effective collusion precisely in these cases.

By an involved line of analysis it can be shown that gains and the viability of collusion are greater for sellers to governments than for collusion among buyers in selling to private businesses. The reasoning is not based on any antagonism toward the government by the sellers. Instead it reflects the fact that the rewards and costs of public administrators of public property are less correlated with their cost-cutting, dollar-saving, careful-buying activities than are those of counterpart administrators or owners of privately owned businesses. Quickly, we insist that this does not mean that owners and administrators of private property are more intelligent, or alert, or more honorable than public administrators. No difference is assumed in these respects. We shall skip over the chain of logic that shows how all this can be derived from the fundamental law of economics—"the lower the cost of any source of personal gain, the more will that source be utilized" (or its converse, "the higher the cost of some source of personal utility the less will that source be utilized").

What is embarrassing about all this to an economist is that although this general understanding permeates economics, its import seems not to be widely enough appreciated. Perhaps I am wrong in saying it has not gained wide acceptance. But I certainly confess to a lack of evidence of such a state.

Perhaps the easiest way to put meat on the bare bones of the analysis is to ask why governments typically use the sealed-bid system of buying, *and* no private firms use it. One would think that if the sealed-bid system were so good, the private firms would use it, too. Or that if it really weren't good, that the government would abandon it and imitate the private firms.[2]

In the absence of a sealed-bid system, a public administrator could easily tell a "friendly" seller what were the best bids so far received and then give the sale to the friend at one dollar less. The advantage of being the last bidder—*and* knowing what the other bidders have offered—is obvious. Each competitor would like to be last, and he would like to make sure that no concealed bidders were around to take advantage of a friendly administrator who thereby could gain in nondirect, and possibly nonpecuniary, ways. Remember, we do not postulate that public administrators are "bad guys" or "good guys." Instead they are like me . . . and you. Both taxpayers and competing sellers have incentives to insist that the bidding be open, that each bidder have equal opportunity to make his best offer and that the public administrator buyer take the lowest offer.

[2] We say no private firms use it—which means obviously that we know of no cases where they do.

It would appear that the sealed bid is a wonderful device. For example, each competing seller would state the minimum price he would take. If he didn't, he might lose the contract. Thus it would seem that this system is very effective in squeezing the competing sellers. However, there are two flaws with that line of reasoning. In the first place, a private buyer without sealed bids can get equally effective "squeezes" simply by asking the potential seller to name a price, and then all the buyer has to do is (1) make it clear that he is a serious buyer, i.e., he is not just trying to decide whether or not to buy at all, and (2) tell each competing seller that he does not intend to return to report his best price from among the various sellers. At least he is under no compulsion to do so. As the buyer walks out the door, the seller knows he must make his best bid. This "seller" may try to play it coy in the belief that the buyer will not get better offers elsewhere. Notice, however, that exactly the same kind of "game" can be played with the sealed bid. And this is the second flaw in the preceding argument. There is no reason to presume that the sealed bid prices are really the minimum selling prices of each seller. Each competing seller can use some strategy and try to beat out merely the conjectured next best price. In sum, it is no trick at all for a private buyer to duplicate all the merits of the sealed bid—and then some. He can resort to even further attempted squeezes of the lowest bidder, who may not know he is already lowest.

The sealed bid, then, is a device to compensate for a well-recognized problem in government arising from public ownership—that of making the administrator act as aggressively and effectively in watching costs and performance as a private owner, or even of the administrator or manager of a privately owned business. Private property owners (and the capital markets enable private property owners more effectively to) induce their agents to act in ways consonant with the interest of the owners. We say *more* effectively (not with perfect or complete effectiveness) than for public property owners.[3]

The sealed bid is, unfortunately, only a crutch. Even with it, the public property owners—the governments—can't run as fast as private owners. Given the desire to collude, collusion is more viable against the government than against privately owned firms, even with the sealed bid. The reason is not hard to see. Although the sealed bid makes conniving by the public property administrators with the seller more difficult, it does not change the basic structure of the incentive system in public ownership and governments as compared to private ownership. Illegal activity by public administrators in conniving with competing sellers is thwarted by the sealed-bid system, but it does not offset the weaker incentives and lesser rewards for aggressive, price-conscious, dollar-saving activity. For example, the authors act quite differently in their capacities as public employees and as private individuals. When buying a typewriter for themselves they shop more extensively, and exert more effort to obtain the best price—in order to keep the savings for alternative personal uses.[4]

How much of the saving will accrue to the public employee

---

[3] We skip over the derivation of the implication that we are using as a premise here, namely that private property ownership implies more effective inducements and incentives than does public ownership to watch for the interests of the "owners." Some may take this on faith, and others by logical implication. We care not which at the present moment. And we simply ask the reader to accept it for purposes of the present exposition. If it be wrong, in fact, then our entire analysis collapses. And of course what we are leading up to is the fact that this premise implies such collusion as was observed will occur more frequently in sales to the government.

[4] Veterans of the military will remember well the sudden transformation that followed the expression, "You're on your own time."

or to his supervisor or even to his "boss" if he, by extra effort, manages to save extra dollars? They revert to the general fund, not to him. Where they do revert to his own budget, he will act more carefully. But the reduced incentive is clear cut. And furthermore, with the sealed-bid system it is improper for the buyer to continue negotiations and efforts to find still lower prices—even if he were to have as much incentive to do so. What the sealed-bid system and public ownership accomplishes is the *avoidance* of that kind of activity, as well as of conniving. It puts purchasing on a plateau of uninspired routine mediocrity. The councilman, the politician, or the bureaucrat in responding to prices suggested for paving a road, building a sewer, a school building, or an electric circuit does not respond to the prospects of "savings" by extra unpleasant laborious activity. Not to the extent he would if it were his own road, sewer, building, or electric circuit.

The sellers are not fools. They know that the initiative, care, perspicuity, and incentive on public agents are quite different from those on private purchasers. Care in being ethical, conformity with the rules, not bargaining hard (to avoid the appearance of trying to connive as well as because of reduced incentive) are manifest symptoms of public agencies. Any experienced salesman of computing machines, automobiles, furniture, paper, knows how the public agency buyers differ from the private buyer.

But, at this point the thoughtful reader will be impatient to interject that even though the buyers may be different, we have overlooked the fundamental nature of competition. Competition does *not* pit buyer against seller (whether it be electrical equipment, paper, or labor). Instead, it is the competition *among the sellers themselves* in trying to get business away from each other that aids the buyer. It is not the buyer who somehow by some mystical ''bargaining'' power makes a seller cut prices. Instead, it is the other sellers who make better offers that the buyer reflects back to still other sellers and that make the latter sellers compete. It simply is not seller against buyer. It is seller against seller. It is not the nasty, aggressive, loud, ''pushy,'' threatening buyer who gets prices down. It is competition among sellers. A person who wants to buy a car need not go into a showroom and start trying to be a hard, tough bargainer. He need merely let it be known he intends to buy and is willing to listen to all offers and will then take the one that is best for him.[5] The sellers can think up more devices or special devices to attract his business than the buyer could ever think up.

But if this is true, have we not destroyed our earlier argument? Will not sellers compete among themselves and destroy the collusive agreement, if the attitude of the buyer is irrelevant. We did not say the buyer's attitude was irrelevant. In fact, it is responsible for whatever effectiveness there may have been. What is being said is that the competition among sellers is intensive *to the extent that it will pay* each seller to be competitive. And this reflects the incentive and *ability* of the buyer to accept special competitive offers from sellers. To see why, ask the question: What will enable a collusive agreement to be effective? Or to put it conversely, What prevents collusive agreements from being viable?

A collusive agreement to restrict competition means that the members believe they can divide up this larger income so each gets more than he would in the absence of the agreement. Some people believe that our laws against collusion prevent such collusions. Perhaps they do, just as they prevent gam-

[5] Allen F. Jung, ''Price Variations Among Automobile Dealers in Metropolitan Chicago,'' *Journal of Business* 33, no. 1 (January 1960): 31–42.

bling. But there is another more powerful force that destroys collusive agreements even in the absence of laws. First, there is an incentive for each and every member secretly and individually to violate the agreement. We need not belabor this point except to state that policing agreements is extremely difficult and expensive—sometimes so expensive as to consume all the potential gains of the collusion.[6]

Secret rebates, extra service, and better quality are illegal if offered to the public agency administrators (let alone the problem of keeping them secret). Judgments of quality and service are easy for a private buyer to make and defend as compared to the defense which a public buyer must put up for buying from one seller rather than another at the same or higher price. As we indicated earlier, sellers will, when they know that buyers are more likely to be responsive to special or secret inducements, be very adept at devising methods for secretly offering better terms to the buyers. In public buying, such secrecy is illegal and unethical, as well as difficult to keep secret; whereas it is legal, ethical, and easier to keep secret (from other sellers) in private buying. This means that in bidding for public contracts the incentives to collusive agreements—which are always present—are less likely to be thwarted by secret terms between buyers and sellers.

But there is another potent force against viability of collusive agreements. Outsiders who are capable of producing the items being sold collusively will be attracted by the lure of profits. To admit them into the collusion would mean sharing

[6] A classic, though not widely understood, example of collusion beset with secret violations is the collusive agreement among colleges not to pay the free market price for talented athletes. This collusive agreement is the foundation of the National Collegiate Athletic Association. The violations of the agreement form the main items on the agenda of all of its meetings. We leave the question open as to how this collusive agreement manages to survive—although we think we know the answer. In many other areas collusion is *aided* by laws. Guess where!

the profits with so many newcomers that the gains would be (quickly?) dissipated. If admission is denied, they can undersell the conspirators and take away their sales directly. Since this *can* happen when the collusion is against a government, why is it assumed not to be present or weaker as a force in the case of collusion against the government than against private buyers? Here is where the buyer's incentives and attitudes are critical. A private buyer will have more incentive to detect collusion, and he will have more to gain by encouraging *new* producers. Even if he is not aware of the collusion, the incentives on the private buyer to seek out and stimulate new sources of supply are greater than for the public buyer. The private property buyer has more to gain by exerting effort and ingenuity in attracting *new* competitors than does a public property agent. In fact, a public property agent runs the risk of criticism in seeking out new firms to produce something for fear that such favoritism can be interpreted as conniving. And basically his rewards are less for such actions. In purest formal terms, the spread of information about the collusion is more rapid under private property than under public property. And information is not a free good; it costs something to disseminate it, or obtain it. Commitments can be made by private buyers to new potential suppliers—whereas a public agency would be readily accused of seeking special favors from special firms. Any politician or government employer or administrator will provide illustrative stories.

To put the issue bluntly. If the buying agent of a private firm failed to thwart a collusion, he would not survive as long as would a buyer in a government agency faced with the collusion. Can you see how behavior in the two cases would be different? Can you see why a buyer would be fired in the first case? And let alone in the second? This implies that if one examines the record in the electrical-equipment case, he will find that the public buyers who were paying the "cartel" prices were regarded as completely blameless, innocent parties, or even praised if they brought the collusion to the attention of the Federal Anti-Trust Division. But the buyer for a private firm would be criticized and demoted if he failed to quickly detect *and* circumvent the collusion.

We summarize. Collusion against the government is more viable because two things are reduced: (1) the possibility of secret violations, and (2) the extent to which information about the collusion will be disseminated and used as an inducement to outsiders to enter into competition and thwart the collusion. The attenuation of these forces reflects the existence of public ownership and is inevitably present.

None of this says that public ownership should be abandoned on this count alone, any more than marriage should be abandoned because of some of its inherent disadvantages relative to bachelorhood. But at least the faults or weaknesses should be discerned if understanding of the real world is desired.

How would one verify these implications of economic theory? In the first place, the fact of sealed bids serves as verifying implication—if they are present in public property agencies more than in private buying. In the strongest form, we would assert they are to be observed *only* in public property agencies (or for reasons basically similar, also in nonprofit firms and profit-regulated government firms—e.g., public utilities). But we prefer to leave out this embellishment.

Second, it should be observed that of all the collusions that have been recorded, more of them are directed against government than private property firms—after allowing for the relative proportion of government and private buying activity. However, there might seem to be one biasing factor in this particular piece of evidence, namely, that a collusion will be destroyed without legal action by private firms. But this is, of course, exactly what the preceding analysis implies. There is, however, a complicating factor that does have a biasing weight: legal suits involve costs—in the one case borne by the private firm, whereas in the government case it is borne by the public at large. However, this biasing effect can be overcome by the third testable implication. And this is that the life length of such collusions, as are verified to have existed, should be greater for those directed against the government than against private firms. This life-length test may appear to be biased *against* the preceding analysis by the fact that the public bears the legal prosecution costs in the public agency case.

Government agencies would resort to legal suit more readily—since they don't have to bear the economic costs. Hence, the life of such collusions should be shorter because legal suits are more likely to be used to destroy them—*if* one believes that private firms have to resort to suit to break collusion. But the preceding analysis denies this. Suits are clumsy, expensive, and less effective for private firms as devices to break collusion than are direct market operations or secret "deals."

We do not deny the birth of collusive agreements in the private sphere, nor do we assert that they last forever, or for a *long* time, in the public sphere. Just how long is long? We can't answer that question, but we note only that there is no necessity of proving immortality of certain forms of life to show why those forms will prosper in one area relative to another area. It suffices to show that collusion is *more* viable among sellers to governments than to private property institutions. Even then, whether collusion will survive very long or be profitable will depend upon economic costs for outsiders to enter the business—barring legal obstacles such as government licensing or union restrictions.

III

The Nature of Cost

Costs and Outputs [1]

Obscurities, ambiguities, and errors exist in cost and supply analysis despite, or because of, the immense literature on the subject. Especially obscure are the relationships between cost and output, both in the long run and in the short run. Propositions designed to eliminate some of these ambiguities and errors are presented in this paper. More important, these suggested propositions seem to be empirically valid.

COSTS

Costs will be defined initially as the change in equity caused by the performance of some specified operation, where, for simplicity of exposition, the attendant change in income is not included in the computation of the change in equity. Suppose that according to one's balance sheet the present value of his assets were $100, and suppose that at the end of the operation

[1] Indebtedness to William Meckling of the RAND Corporation, who gave many long hours to discussion of the points raised herein, even before the first of several drafts, is very great. Although my egoism prevents sharing the authorship with him, I cannot absolve him from responsibility for any errors that still remain and likewise for any merit the paper may have.

one year later the value of his assets were expected to be $80, not counting the sale value of the product of the operation. The present value of $80 a year hence (at 6 percent) is $75.47, which yields a cost in present capital value (equity) of $24.53. Because of logical difficulties in converting this present value concept into a satisfactory rate (per unit of time) concept, we defer a discussion of this problem and, for convenience, measure costs in units of present value or equity. Hereafter, the unmodified expression "costs" will always mean the present worth, capital value concept of cost, i.e., the change in equity.

OUTPUT

All the characteristics of a production operation can affect its cost. In this paper we want to direct attention to three characteristics:

1. The rate of output is typically regarded in economic analysis as the crucial feature. But it is only one feature, and concentration on it alone has led to serious error, as we shall see.

2. Total contemplated volume of output is another characteristic. Is accumulated output volume of 10,000 or 100 or 1,000,000 units being contemplated? Whatever may be the rate of output, the total volume to be produced is a distinct feature with important effects on cost. Of course, for any rate of output, the larger the total accumulated volume to be produced, the longer the operation will continue. Hence, incorporated in this description of total output is the total time length of the programmed production. Will it span one month or one year, or (at the other extreme) is the contemplated total volume so large that at the rate of output an indefinitely long time is allowed to the production run?

3. The programmed time schedule of availability of output is a further characteristic. For a point output, the programmed date of the output availability is sufficient, but for outputs which continue over time, the time profile (delivery schedule) of the output replaces a single date. We shall call these three distinct aspects the output *rate*, the contemplated *total volume*, and the programmed delivery *dates*.

These three characteristics can be summarized in the following definition, which also defines a fourth characteristic, m, the total length of the programmed schedule of outputs:

$$V = \sum_{T}^{T+m} x(t)\,dt.$$

In this expression V is the total contemplated volume of output, $x(t)$ the output rate at moment t, T the moment at which the first unit of output is to be completed, and m the length of the interval over which the output is made available. Of these four features, only three are independently assignable; the fourth is then constrained. Unless specific exception is made, in the following we shall always discuss changes in only one of the features, V, $x(t)$, and T, assuming the other two to be constant and letting the full compensatory adjustment be made in m.[2]

PROPOSITIONS ABOUT COSTS AND OUTPUT

Our task is now to make some propositions about the way costs are affected by changes in these variables. Letting C

[2] We note that time or dating enters in a multitude of ways: there is the date at which the delivery of output is to begin; there is the period of time used as a basis for the measure of the rate of output, i.e., so many units per day, per week, or per year; and there is the total time over which the output is to be made available.

denote costs (i.e., the change in equity), we have

$$C = F\,(V, x, T, m)$$

subject to the definition of V, which constrains us to three degrees of freedom among the four variables.

Proposition 1:

$$\left.\frac{\partial C}{\partial x\,(t)}\right|_{\substack{T = T_0 \\ V = V_0}} > 0$$

The lefthand expression is the derivative of the costs with respect to x, when T and V are held constant, letting m make up the adjustment. It shows the change in costs when the rate of output is increased without increasing V and without changing the delivery date, but with an appropriate reduction of m. Proposition 1 states that the faster the rate at which a given volume of output is produced, the higher its cost. We emphasize that cost means the change in equity, not the *rate* of costs.

Proposition 2:

$$\left.\frac{\partial^2 C}{\partial x^2}\right|_{\substack{V = V_0 \\ T = T_0}} > 0$$

The increment in C is an increasing function of the output rate. This is a proposition about increasing marginal cost in present value measure, and is usually derived as an implication of efficient allocation of scarce heterogeneous resources among alternative uses.

Its validity, however, does not depend upon the validity of the premises of the classical model. For example, inventories need not increase in proportion to the rate of output if the variance of random deviations in output rates does not increase more than proportionally to the expected output rate. In this event, a sufficient condition for Proposition 2 as derived by the classical model would be upset. But destruction of sufficient conditions does not eliminate the possibility of all necessary conditions being fulfilled; thus, even if the classical model's assumptions are upset, the proposition could still be true. Whether or not it is, in fact, true cannot be settled by an examination of the model from which it is derived. For present purposes, Proposition 2 can be regarded, if one wishes, as a postulated proposition.[3]

Proposition 3:

$$\left.\frac{\partial C}{\partial V}\right|_{\substack{x = x_0 \\ T = T_0}} > 0$$

C increases with V for given x and date of initial output, T. At a constant output rate, for example, this will require a longer program of production, a larger m.

[3] See T. M. Whitin and M. H. Peston, "Random Variations, Risk and Returns to Scale," *Quarterly Journal of Economics* 68 (November 1954): 603–14, for a longer discussion of some forces that could reverse the inequality of Proposition 2. Some of their suggested forces, e.g., relation between stocks of repairmen and number of machines, are circumvented by the ability to buy services instead of the agents themselves. Another weakness is the association of size of output with the number of independent random forces.

Proposition 4:

$$\left.\frac{\partial^2 C}{\partial V^2}\right|_{\substack{x = x_0 \\ T = T_0}} < 0$$

Increments in C diminish as V increases, for any rate of output, x, and initial output date, T. Thus, for any constant rate of output, as the total planned output is increased by uniform increments, costs (changes in equity) will increase by diminishing increments. The "reasons" for this proposition will be given later.

Proposition 4 also implies decreasing cost *per unit* of total volume, V. We shall state this as a separate proposition.

Proposition 5:

$$\left.\frac{\partial C/V}{\partial V}\right|_{\substack{x = x_0 \\ T = T_0}} < 0$$

GRAPHIC AND NUMERICAL ILLUSTRATIONS OF PROPOSITIONS 1–5

1. *Graphic Illustration*

The above properties are shown by the cost surface in Figure 1. Proposition 1 describes the slope of a slice on the cost surface where the slice is parallel to the Cx plane. Proposition 2 states that the slope of the path of such a slice on the cost surface increases with x. Proposition 3 is portrayed by the slope of a slice along the surface parallel to the CV plane—going back into the page. The slope of this slice decreases as V increases. Proposition 4 describes the decreasing rate at which

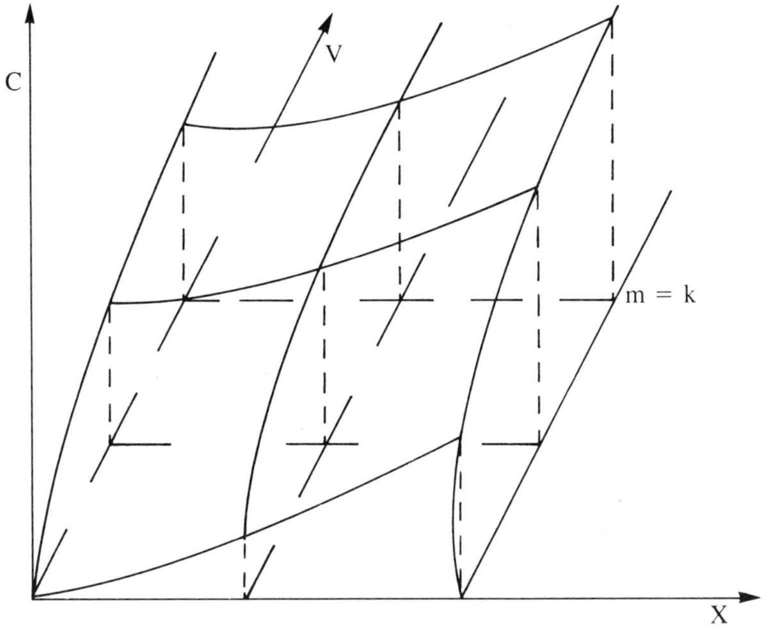

Figure 1. Cost Surface as Function of x and V

this surface of costs increases along this slice. Movements in other directions can be visualized. For example, one possible path is to start from the origin and move out some ray. This gives costs as a function of proportional increase in both the rate and the total output for a fixed interval of production, m, but the behavior of the cost slope of this slice, except for the fact that it is positive, cannot be derived from these propositions.

2. *Tabular, Arithmetic Illustration*

TABLE 1

Costs, Volume of Output, and Rates of Output

Rate of Output, x (per year)	Volume of Output 1	2	3	4
1	100	180	255	325
2	120	195	265	330
3	145	215	280	340
4	175	240	300	355

For an output rate, x, of one per year, beginning at some specified T, production must continue for one year to get a total volume, V, of 1, for two years to get 2, three years for 3, etc. For a production rate of two per year, production must last one year to get 2 units, two years to get a total of 4, etc. The present value of costs for an output rate, $x(t)$, of two a year for a total V of 4 in two years is \$330 (which, at 6 percent, is equal to a two-year annuity of \$180 a year).

Proposition 1 is illustrated by the increase in the numbers (costs) in cells down a given column. *Proposition 2* is illustrated by the increases in the differences between these cell entries. These differences increase as the rate of output increases, for a given total output. This represents increasing marginal costs (remember that cost is a present-value capital concept) for increments in the rate of output. *Proposition 3* is illustrated by the behavior of costs along a row (given output rate) as total volume of planned output changes. *Proposition 4* states that the increment in C is a diminishing increment as one moves across a row, i.e., as total volume of output is larger. For example, in the first row, the output *rate* is one a year. The first cell is therefore an output operation lasting one year, because only one is produced, at the rate of one a year. The total cost is \$100. For a total contemplated output of two units, at a rate of one per year, the operation will take two years and the cost is \$180. The marginal cost of one more unit of total volume of output—not of one unit higher *rate* of output—is \$80. For a total output of three units in three years the cost is \$255, an increment of \$75, which is less than the previous increment of \$80. Here the increments in cost are associated not with increments in rates of output, but with increments in total volume of output. *Proposition 5* is illustrated by dividing the cell entries in a row by the output quantities at the head of each column. The quotient, cost per unit of output quantity, decreases as V increases.

3. *Economic Illustration*

A comparison that could be made is the following: Imagine a person to contemplate a total volume of output of one unit at the rate of one a year. But he subsequently revises his plans and produces one more in the next year at the rate of one a year, again planning to produce a total volume of just one unit. Compare the total costs of that operation with an operation in which two units of total output were initially planned at the rate of one a year. Both take two years, but the cost of the latter is \$180 while the former's present value is \$100 plus \$100 discounted back one year at 6 percent, or a total of \$194. Thus it is cheaper to produce from a *plan* for a two-year output of two units at the rate of one a year than to produce two by repetition of methods which contemplate only one total unit of output at the same rate of one a year.

From this example it would appear that a reason for Proposition 4 is that better foresight enables one to see farther into the future and make more accurate forecasts; but this is not the reason, however helpful better foresight may be. A larger planned *V* is produced in a different way from that of a smaller planned *V*. A classic example is the printing press. To get three hundred copies of a letter in one day may be cheaper with mimeograph than with either typewriter or offset printing. The mimeograph method may be so much superior that, even if the rate of output were stepped up to 300 in an hour (instead of in a day), mimeographing might still be cheaper than typing. This does not deny that higher rates of output imply higher costs, as for example that 300 in an hour will cost more than 300 in two hours. The method of production is a function of the volume of output, especially when output is produced from basic dies—and there are few, if any, methods of production that do not involve "dies." Why increased expenditures on more durable dies should result in more than proportional increase of output potential is a question that cannot be answered, except to say that the physical principles of the world are not all linear (which may or may not be the same thing as "indivisible").[4] Different methods of tooling, parts design, and assembly are the usual explanation given in the production engineering literature.

Proposition 4 seems not to be part of current economic principles. Yet it may be the key to seeing the error in some attempts to refute Proposition 2, which applies to increased *rates* of output for constant total volume of output (or, as we shall see later, for perpetuity durations of output). Propositions 2 and 4 refer to two counterforces, rate of output and total

[4] Could it be that the term "indivisibility" has been meant to cover this phenomenon? A yes or no answer to that question is impossible because of the extreme vagueness and ambiguity with which the term has been used. Furthermore, the question is probably of little, if any, significance.

planned volume of output. What would be the net effect of increases in both cannot be deduced from the present propositions. All that can be said is that if the rate of output is increased for a given total contemplated volume of output, the increment in cost will be an increasing function of the rate of output. Proposition 4, on the other hand, implies diminishing increments as V increases, and it implies a lower per-unit cost for a larger total volume of output. Thus, we have the possibility that higher rates of production might be available at lower unit costs if they are associated with a larger volume of output, because this latter factor may be sufficient to overcome the effects of the higher output rate.

A larger volume of output could, of course, be obtained by both longer time and faster rates of production, but the relationship between time and volume should not be allowed to mask the fact that it is total contemplated volume of output—not the longer duration of output—that is here asserted (maybe erroneously) to be the factor at work in Propositions 3 and 4.

If both the *volume* and the *rate* of output change in the same direction, the two effects on costs are not in the same direction, and neither the net effect on the rate of change of *increments* in the cost nor even the effect on the costs per unit of total volume of output is implied by these or any other accepted postulates. It has been said, for example, that if some automobile manufacturer were to cut V, the volume of cars produced of a given year's model, from one million to a half million, costs per car would increase. This statement could refer either to a reduction in V achieved by producing for half the number of months at an unchanged monthly rate of output or to a simultaneous and parallel reduction in both V, the volume, and x, the monthly rate of output. If it refers to the former, it is a restatement of Proposition 5; if it refers to the latter, it is a statement that cannot be deduced from our propositions, which imply merely that costs would be lower if both V and x were reduced than if V alone were lowered.

Even returns to scale seem to have been confused with the effect of size of output. It is conjectured that a substantial portion of the alleged cases of increasing returns to scale in industries or firms is the result of ignoring the relation of costs to volume (rather than to rate) of output. The earlier discussions of automobile production and printing costs are simple illustrations of how this confusion can occur.

How many of the cases of alleged decreasing costs to *rates* of output are really decreasing costs to *volume* of output is an open question. Is it too much to expect that all of them can be so explained? Or that the realm of such cases can be greatly reduced by allowing for V, instead of letting x be the only variable? But that dirty empirical task is left for later and more ambitious efforts.

The observed concentration on a standardized model, e.g., four or five different sizes of tractors as distinct from a much greater possible range, is explained by the effect of volume of output on cost. Although an infinite range is possible, the concentration on a smaller set of fewer alternatives is more economical for most problems. The only way economic theory heretofore could explain this apparent anomaly was to invoke a falling cost curve for small output rates, in turn dependent upon some kind of unidentified indivisibility or returns to scale. Now the explanation may be contained in Propositions 4 and 9.

MORE PROPOSITIONS

Four more propositions remain. Proposition 6 is given in a footnote because its implications will not be suggested in this paper.[5] Propositions 7 and 8 concern the effects of changes in T, the time between the decision to produce and the delivery of output.

Proposition 7:

$$\left.\frac{\partial C}{\partial T}\right|_{\substack{x = x_0 \\ V = V_0}} < 0$$

[5] Proposition 6:

$$\left.\frac{\partial^2 C}{\partial x \, \partial V}\right|_{T=T_0} < 0$$

This says that the marginal present value-cost with respect to increased rates of output decreases as the total contemplated output increases. This can be regarded as a conjectural proposition, whose implications will not be developed in this paper. And the same proposition can be re-expressed as

$$\left.\frac{\partial^2 C}{\partial V \, \partial x}\right|_{T=T_0} < 0$$

This states that marginal present-value costs of increased quantity of output decrease as the rate of output increases.

Of interest is the relationship between these postulates and the implied shape of the production possibility function, where the rate and the volume of output are the two output alternatives. The cost isoquant with x and V as the arguments can be convex or concave. Usually a concave function is implied when rates of output of two different products are the arguments. However, J. Hirshleifer ("Quality vs. Quantity: Cost Isoquant and Equilibrium," *Quarterly Journal of Economics* 64 [November 1955]: 596–606) has pointed out that convex production possibilities are implicit in many engineering cost functions when quality and quantity are the alternative outputs. Hirshleifer, as it seems from his context, is really discussing cases where his quantity variable refers to volume and not to rate of output. Had he really meant rate of output rather than volume, his results might not have been so "reasonable." The convexity or concavity of the cost isoquant, it may be recalled, is given by the sign of

$$\frac{d^2x}{dV^2} = \frac{FxxFy^2 - 2\,FxvFxFv + FvvFx^2}{Fv^3}$$

Substituting our postulated conditions shows that the expression may be of any sign, hence the indeterminacy of the concavity or convexity property. However, concavity of the cost isoquant where the two arguments are rates of production for two different products is still implied.

This is not shown in the graph or in the table, but it says that the longer the time between decision to produce and delivery of output, the less the cost.

If we think of a single output point, then T is relatively unambiguous. If the output is to be made available over a period of time, then T could be defined as the beginning moment of output. But many different output programs are possible, even when they all extend over the same interval. One might be tempted to use some sort of average T, say, the date of output weighted by the rate of output. However, such an average T cannot be used for our purposes, because any particular value of T can be identified with an infinite variety of output patterns. Since we are talking about partial derivatives, the whole problem is easily avoided. All we need do is to state that, if one moves any output program or schedule closer to the present (or farther into the future) by a simple time shift, T will have decreased (or increased). Whatever the shape of the output schedule, a reduction of the interval between the present moment and the beginning of the output date (a sort of uniform timewise shifting) will increase cost. A more deferred output schedule (whatever its unchanged shape) will mean a lower cost.

Proposition 7 is really a corollary of Proposition 2. The slower the rate at which inputs are purchased, the lower their price because the lower are the costs to the seller, when Proposition 2 is applied to the seller.

Not only do the supply curves of inputs fall (or shift to the right) as more time is allowed, but the rates of shifting differ among inputs. The supply curves of some inputs are more elastic than those of others; and the rate at which the price elasticity of supply increases with T differs among inputs. Thus, while in an immediate period the price elasticity of supply of input x may be low relative to that of input y (and it may always be lower than that of y), the *ratio* of the costs of increments in y to the costs of increments in x may change with deferred purchase. If the ratio decreases, deferred purchases of y relative to purchases of x will be economical. In other words, it is not merely the slope of the supply curve or the price elasticity of supply that determines which inputs are going to be increased earliest. Rather, it is the rate at which these price elasticities *change* with deferred purchase that is critical. Thus, as stated earlier, the input x with a very low price elasticity of supply will vary more in the immediate period than the input of y with a higher price elasticity if the deferment of purchases by, say, a month would lower the cost of y more than that of x. As an extreme, if the supply curves of two inputs, x and y, were both horizontal, the input of one of them would be increased less if with deferred purchase the price or supply curve would become lower—though still horizontal. That input whose price would become lower with a deferred purchase would be increased in quantity later, with the relatively heavy present increase concentrated on that input whose deferred purchase price would not be as much lower.

Proposition 8:

All the derivatives in Propositions 1–5 are diminishing functions of T, but not all diminish at the same rate. This proposition asserts a difference in the extent to which inputs will be varied in the immediate, the short, and the longer period.

Short and long run. Statements to the effect that certain inputs are fixed in the short run are frequent and characteristic. In fact, there is no such fixed factor in any interval other than the immediate moment *when all are fixed*. Such statements may represent a confusion between revealed choice and technological constraints. There are no technological or legal restraints preventing one from varying any of his inputs. Even in Viner's classic statement of the short- and long-run cost curves, the short run is defined in terms of some *fixed* inputs and other inputs which can be varied as desired.[6] He stated that the long run is the situation in which all the inputs are "freely" variable. One need only ask, "What do the desires to adjust depend upon in the short run?" and, "What does 'freely' variable mean?" The first is answered by "costs" and potential receipts of the variations, and the second by noting that "freely" does not mean that costs of changes are zero. The fact is that the costs of varying the inputs differ among inputs, and the ratios of these costs vary with the time interval within which the variation is to be made. At any *calendar* moment, T, the producer will choose which input to vary according to *economic costs* and not because of technical or legal fixities that prevent the changing of some inputs.[7]

Debate over definitions or postulates is pertinent only in the light of their purpose. The purpose of the short- and long-run distinction is, presumably, to explain the path of prices or output (x or V?) over time in response to some change in demand or supply. The postulate of fixed inputs, and others more variable with the passing of time, does imply a pattern of responses that seems to be verified by observable evidence. On that count, the falsity of the postulate is immaterial. But if there are other implications of such a postulate that are invali-

---

[6] J. Viner, "Cost Curves and Supply Curves," *Zeitschrift fur Nationalökonomie* 3, no. 1 (1931): 23–46.

[7] The nearest, but still different, presentation of the immediate, short run, and long run found by the author is that contained in Friedman's unpublished lecture notes. Other statements may exist; an exhausting search of the literature failed to clarify exactly what is meant by the long run and short run.

dated by observable evidence, the postulate becomes costly. The question arises, therefore, whether it is more convenient and useful to replace the fixity postulate by a more general one that yields all the valid implications that the former one did and more besides, while at the same time avoiding the empirically false implications. It appears that the proposed alternative is cheaper in terms of logical convenience, more general, and more valid in its implications. But that is a judgment which is perhaps best left to the reader.

The differences between a short-run (near T) and a long-run (distant T) operation imply differences in costs, and these costs are pertinent to an explanation of the path of prices or costs over time in response to a lasting change in demand or factor availabilities. For example, for a lasting increase in demand, the output made available at more distant dates is producible at a lower cost; this means that the supply at a given cost will be larger and the price lower in the more distant future as the longer-run operations begin to yield their output. These outputs, having been planned for a later T date, are lower in cost. Output will be larger for a given price, thus reducing price in the market. This longer-run lower cost is the phenomenon whose explanation has usually been sought by resort to fixity of some particular inputs in the short run. The above argument suggests that this phenomenon can be explained without the fixity assumption that in turn leads to other, empirically wrong, implications.

The implication of our proposition is worth emphasizing here. It is that we define a "short run" and a "long run" not as differing in the fixity of some inputs; instead, we use T as the length of the run, and then from Proposition 8 derive the implications that were sought by the fixity assumption.

Most important, however, Proposition 8 makes it clear that

there is not both a "long-run" and a "short-run" cost for any given output program. For any given output program there is only *one* pertinent cost, *not* two. Unambiguous specification of the output or action to be costed makes the cost definition unambiguous and destroys the illusion that there are two costs to consider, a short- and a long-run cost for any given output. There is only one, and that is the *cheapest* cost of doing whatever the operation is specified to be. To produce a house in three months is one thing, to produce it in a year is something else. By uniquely identifying the operation to be charged there results one cost, not a range of costs from immediate to short- to longer-run costs. There is a range of operations to be considered, but to each there is only *one* cost. The question is not, What are the long-run or short-run costs of some operation? but, instead, How do total, average, and marginal costs vary as the T of the operation is changed? Answer: They decrease as T increases, according to Propositions 7 and 8.

The significance of this should be evident in the debate about marginal cost pricing policies for "optimal" output. Also the use of short-run and long-run costs as alternatives in public utility pricing appears to be a ripe area for clarification of concepts.

What the relationship is between the presently suggested effects of T, which we have just called a short- or long-run effect, and the common short run or long run in the standard literature is not entirely clear. Rather vague and imprecise implications about short and long run are available. Hence, rather than assert that the T effect is here being proposed as a substitute for the standard short-run analysis, the reader is left free to supply his own interpretation of the conventional "run" and to supplement or replace it, however he chooses, with the present proposition.

Proposition 9:

The preceding propositions refer to costs of outputs for a given distribution of knowledge, *F*, at the present moment, to situations where technology is held constant.[8]

Proposition 9 is "As the total quantity of units produced increases, the cost of *future* output declines." The cost per unit may be either the average cost of a given number of incremental units of output or the cost of a specific unit. This is not identical with the earlier Proposition 4 referring to the effects of the larger planned *V*. There the effect was a result of varying *techniques* of production, not of changes in technology. Here we are asserting that knowledge increases as a result of production—that the cost function is lowered. It is not simply a matter of a larger *V*, but rather a lower cost for any subsequent *V*, consequent to improved knowledge. This distinction should not be attributed necessarily to all the explanations of the learning curve. Some describers of the learning curve bring in the effect of different techniques consequent to different-sized *V*. Others also mention that, as output is produced and experience acquired, improved knowledge is acquired. Thus, even if one continually planned to produce small batches of output, so the *V* was constant but repeated, the costs would nevertheless be falling. In the present presentation we have chosen to separate these two effects in logic and principle, attributing the first effect, that of technique, to changes in planned *V* but with a given state of knowledge (as in Proposition 4), while the second effect, that of increased knowledge consequent to accumulated production experience, is isolated in Proposition 9. A review of industrial

[8] Technology, the state of distribution of knowledge, is different from techniques of production, which can be changed at any time, even with a constant technology.

and production management literature will show that both effects are adduced and incorporated in the learning curve discussion, contrary to our decision to separate them. This proposition about the rate of change in technology is accepted in industrial engineering. Usually the proposition is known as the "learning curve" or "progress curve."[9]

Several factors have been advanced as a rationale for this proposition: job familiarization, general improvement in coordination, shop organization and engineering liaison, more efficient subassembly production, and more efficient tools. An extensive literature on this proposition has been developed, but it seems to have escaped integration with the rest of cost theory in economics.[10]

Nevertheless, the proposition is a well-validated proposition and is widely used in industrial engineering. The significant implication of this proposition is that, in addition to rate of output, an important variable in determining total costs is the total planned output, for two reasons: first, because of changes in technique via Proposition 4, and, second, because the larger is the planned and ultimately realized output, the greater is the accumulated experience (technology) and knowledge at any point in the future via Proposition 9. Thus, the average cost per unit of output will be lower, the greater is the planned and ultimately experienced output. A more complete discussion of

---

[9] Sometimes the curve is called an 80 percent progress curve, because it is sometimes asserted that the cost of the 2*n*th item is 80 percent of the cost of the *n*th item. Thus the fortieth plane would involve only 80 percent of the direct man hours and materials that the twentieth plane did.

[10] See W. Hirsch, "Manufacturing Progress Functions," *Review of Economics and Statistics* 34 (May 1952): 143–55. A less accessible, but more complete, reference to the published material is given in H. Asher, *Cost-Quantity Relationship in the Airframe Industry* (RAND Corporation, Santa Monica, Calif.), July 1956. But see P. A. Samuelson, *Economics* (New York: McGraw-Hill, 1948), p. 473, where it is mentioned but left unincorporated.

the evidence for this proposition would require a separate paper.

ON THE ADVANTAGES OF THE CAPITAL VALUE MEASURE

Use of capital values enables one to avoid misleading statements like "We are going to operate at a loss in the near future, but operations will be profitable later," "In the short run the firm may operate at a loss so long as receipts exceed variable costs," "A firm operates with long-run rather than short-run objectives." All of these statements are incorrect if liabilities or assets (other than money) are owned by the enterprise. What seems to be meant when a person talks about expecting to have losses for a while before getting profits is that cash flows will be negative for a while, but it is difficult to see how this is in any relevant sense a situation of losses. And, similarly, when a person talks about expecting losses it appears that he means he expects future events to occur which are unfavorable; and in this case the changed belief about the future is immediately reflected in current values if not in current money flows—as many a stockholder has learned. Any periods during which expectation about future events becomes more favorable are periods of increasing equity (i.e., of profits), even though the period in which the more favorable events will occur is in the future. When a firm reports that it operated during the past quarter at a loss, it means simply that the net present value of assets decreased during that period, even though the future cash receipts and outlays have not yet been realized. The profits are in the present moment—the increase in equity—as some stockholders have joyously learned. The presently anticipated increase in *future* receipts relative to future outlays means an increase in *present* equity values, profits.

Statements to the effect that a firm would willingly and knowingly operate at a loss in the short run are consistent only with an identification of costs with money flows, and are certainly inconsistent with the postulates of seeking increased wealth (or utility) as a goal or survival attribute. Such identification of costs with money flows eliminates capital theory from the theory of the firm and from much of price theory. There is no cause to pay this price since it is just as easy not to abandon capital theory, and if one retains it more useful implications will be derived.

Yet, in economic texts costs are almost always measured as *time-rates*, and only rarely as capital values. At first blush this would seem to be an irrelevant or trivial distinction, since capital values are merely the present values of *receipt* or *outlay* streams. But what about going from capital values to time rates of *cost* streams? New problems arise in this effort. Suppose that the outlay stream for some operation is used as the basis for cost calculations. If, and only if, *no* other assets or liabilities are involved can money flows be identified with costs; otherwise they represent, in part, accumulations of assets or liabilities. As soon as assets and liabilities are admitted, money flows are not synonymous with costs, and changes in values of assets or liabilities must now be included. With the break between money outlays and costs, the measure of costs becomes the change in present value of net equity consequent to some action (ignoring receipts, for present purposes).

If a firm signed a contract and committed itself to produce some quantity of output, then the cost it has incurred in signing the contract and obligating itself to produce the output is its decrease in equity, say $E_a — E_b$. At moment a, prior to the contract, the equity or net wealth of the firm is E_a. At this moment the firm considers entering into some production plan. If it does so, what will happen to its equity at the end of the plan, or how will the equity change over that interval? If, for the moment, we ignore the receipts or income from that plan, the decrease of equity by moment *b* would be the measure of cost of the output operation which it is obligated to perform. The difference, $E_a - E_b$, between the equity (E_a) at the beginning and the *present* value (E_b) of the equity (E_t) at the end of the operation, is the total cost, *C*, of the operation.

The *time rate* of costs (of change in equity) is given by dE/dt, the slope of the line from E_a to E_t, which is quite different from *C*. The former, dE/dt, is a derivative, a time rate of change. The latter, *C*, is the integral of the former. It is a finite difference, $E_a - E_t$, obtained from two different points on the *E* curve, while the former is the slope of the *E* curve and can be obtained only after an *E* curve is obtained. What is the meaning of the *E curve* in such a case? Presumably it means that, if the firm decided at any moment to stop further output, under this contract it would find itself with an equity indicated by the height of the line E_aE_t. Ignoring the contractual liability for obligation to produce according to the contract, the equity declines along the *E* line; but if one does regard the contract performance liability, the equity does not change as output is produced because there is an exactly offsetting reduction in contractual liability as output is produced. The equity of the firm stays constant over the interval if the outlays and asset values initially forecast were forecast correctly.

If the *rate* of cost, dE/dt, or if the *E* curve is plotted not against time, but against the *output rate*, we do not get a curve similar in interpretation to the usual total cost curve in standard cost curve analysis. The *rate* of cost, dE/dt can be converted to average cost per unit of rate of ouput by dividing the rate of cost, dE/dt, by the associated rate of output at that moment, and the marginal time rate of cost is obtained by asking how the slope of the equity curve dE/dt is affected by changes in x, i.e., $(d^2E/dt\,dx)$.

The difference between this curve, where dE/dt is plotted against x, and the usual time rate of cost curve analysis is that our current analysis is based on a larger set of variables, $x(t)$ and V, and hence dE/dt cannot be drawn uniquely merely against the rate of output, $x(t)$. A new curve must be drawn for each output operation contemplated; even worse, there is no assurance that such a curve of dE/dt drawn against the rate of output on the horizontal axis would have only one vertical height for each output rate. The curve might fold back on itself and be multivalued because one value of dE/dt might be associated with a particular rate of output early in the operation and another different value later in the operation, even though at both moments the output rate were the same.

The number of cost curves that could be drawn is greater by at least an extra factor, V. In fact, we have at least two families of curves, one for different values of V and one for different time profiles of $x(t)$, and it is not clear what is usually assumed about these in the standard cost curve analysis. One possibility is to assume that the length of the production run, m, or the contemplated total output, V, does not affect the rate at which equity changes for any given output rate. The difficulty with this position is not merely that it is logically wrong but that it leads to implications that are refuted by everyday events.

A kind of average or marginal cost can be defined on the basis of the approach suggested earlier. For any given contemplated operation, the change in equity implied can be computed and evaluated in present worths. If this cost is divided by the total contemplated volume of output, V, the result is present value cost per unit of product (not time rate per unit *rate* of output). If the same total output were to be produced at a higher output rate, x, and thus within a shorter time interval, m, the total cost (change in equity) would be greater, and so the cost per unit of total volume of output would be higher. As noted in the first part of this paper, the increase in total present value cost, $\partial C/x$ (not $d^2E/dt\,dx$), is the marginal cost, consequent to an increased rate of output. By varying the contemplated rates of output x for any given total output plan (V and T), one can get different total capital costs. These changes in total capital costs can be called the marginal capital costs. But it is important to note again that there are as many such marginal capital value cost functions as there are different possible total output patterns that can be contemplated, and these marginal capital costs are not time rates of costs.

CONCLUSION

Four features have been emphasized in the foregoing pages. First, the distinction between rate and quantity of output; second, changes in technology as distinct from changes in technique; third, the use of calendar time dates of output instead of technical fixity for distinguishing output operations; fourth, the use of capital value concepts instead of rates of costs.

The first and second features (and the ones that are emphasized in this paper) enable us to capture within our theory the lower costs attendant on larger quantities of output—not rates of output. Everyday experience where large rates of output are available at lower prices could be explained as a movement down the buyer's demand curve as the seller, in order to sell a larger amount, lowers price. But this seems to be incapable of explaining all such situations. Another explanation usually advanced is the economies of scale, where scale is related to *rate* of output. However, an alternative explanation suggested here is the lower cost resulting, not from higher *rates* of output per unit time, but from larger planned volume of total output quantities. An examination of the production management and engineering literature reveals much greater emphasis on batch or lot size as contrasted to the rate of output. Frequently the latter is not much of a variable in each particular firm's decision. This means that the extent to which rate of output *is* varied may be slight—not that it can't be varied or that its significance is slight. That there has been confusion between the rate of output and the batch size or quantity planned is sure. How much cannot be known.

The third feature—that of identifying each output operation with a calendar date and then postulating that the more distant the date the smaller the change in equity (the smaller the cost)—provides a way to escape the unnecessary bind imposed by the definition of short-run costs as that which results from fixed inputs. The ambiguous idea of two different costs, a short-run and a long-run cost for a given output, disappears and is replaced by one cost for each different program of output.

What must have been assumed in our present literature about the factors mentioned here? Was the rate of output profile assumed to be a constant rate extending into perpetuity? The answer could not be ascertained from an exhausting reading of the literature nor from analogically implied conditions. Certainly the standard cost curve analysis does not envisage a perpetuity output at some given rate, nor does it seem to specify the effects of shorter-length runs at any output. For example, Stigler, in his well-known paper on the effects of planning for variations in the rate of output, imagines one to be moving along a given cost curve appropriate to the case in which output varies. This desirable attempt to modify the cost curve analysis would have been more successful if the output had been further specified or identified in terms of V and T. Then the conventional curves would have disappeared, and many logical inconsistencies and ambiguities could have been removed from the standard analysis. But merely drawing the curve flatter and higher does not avoid the problems of appropriate interpretation of costs for unspecified values of the pertinent variables.

Finally, introduction of a new variable, V, complicates the equilibrium of demand and supply, for now there must be a similar element in demand which will determine the equilibrium size of V, if such there be. Suffice it to say here that even though consumers may not act or plan consciously in terms of V, their actions can be interpreted in terms of a resultant aggregative V. Producers, in contemplating the demand for their products, will be required to think of capital value or present value of income with the rate of output integrated into a V—possibly a break-even V—on the basis of which they may make production plans. A simple rate of output, price relationships, will not be sufficient. But this remains to be developed later, only if the present propositions prove valid and useful.

12

Cost

In economics, the cost of an event is the highest-valued opportunity necessarily forsaken. The usefulness of the concept of cost is a logical implication of choice among available options. Only if no alternatives were possible or if amounts of all resources were available beyond everyone's desires, so that all goods were free, would the concepts of cost and of choice be irrelevant. If choices are made on anything other than a random, purposeless basis, a criterion of choice is implied. Whatever the criterion, the chosen option will involve a loss of the highest-valued forsaken option. This implies that only if one chooses actions so as to maximize the value realized will cost be covered.

Failure to appreciate the purpose of the concept of cost can lead to confusing the concept of cost with the undesirable attributes of some event. For example, when one builds a swimming pool, the toil and trouble of digging it and the nuisance of noisy, disobedient neighborhood children and uninvited guests who use it are undesirable attributes of the pool. They are not the costs of creating and having a pool. This distinction between (*a*) undesirable attributes inherent in some event and (*b*) the highest-valued forsaken option necessary to realize that event is fundamental, for only the latter is cost as the term is used in economics.

We can illustrate. The construction and possession of the pool involve an amalgam of undesirable and desirable attributes. But if, in some sense, the desirable exceed the undesirable, it does not follow that one would choose to have the pool. One might choose something else instead, say having an extra car, and that too would involve desirable and undesirable attributes. The decision-maker must choose among events that are amalgams of "goods and bads." He cannot choose all events whose desirable features more than offset their undesirable ones, given the limited resources at his disposal. A comparison among all the *available* options (each consisting of an amalgam of good and bad) yields for each option a rank-indicating measure of value. The cost of one amalgam is the best of the forsaken amalgams. It is not necessary that for each event the good and bad attributes be separated and that there be assigned a measure of the undesirable attributes and also a measure of the desirable. Such a procedure would indicate only that many events are desirable on net, and a criterion of choice among these would still be needed.

We can illustrate with the person deciding whether or not to have a swimming pool. He determines that the "good" consequences of a pool are worth what we shall call "100 units," while the "bad" are equivalent to the loss of "70 units." The best alternative to having a pool is, let us say, to take action "*A*," with "good" attributes valued at 50 and "bads" valued at a loss of 10. The pool has a net value of 30, while event *A* is worth 40. The cost of the pool is 40 (not 70), while the cost of *A* is 30 (not 10). What is lost if the pool is selected is the 40 units of value otherwise available by opting for *A*.

The temptation to think that because events are *valued* by

comparing the good attributes with the bad, cost must be the bad attributes is encouraged by business usage. Businessmen weigh revenues (as good consequences) against expenses or costs. Considering these costs as the bad attributes overlooks the distinction between *valuation* and *costing*. The *value* of a given event is obtained by weighing its good and bad consequences against each other—if one wants to think in terms of good and bad rather than less or more desirable—but the *cost* of that event is still not revealed. The highest-valued forsaken option must still be ascertained in order to determine the cost. Even in the businessman's calculation, what his cost really measures, as shown below, is not the bad consequences of an action but the highest-valued forsaken opportunity.

It is sometimes fallaciously thought that if building a pool involved even more pain or other undesirable consequences, its costs surely must be higher. But the costs of the pool are not higher unless the best alternative is affected. More pain in building a pool may or may not affect my alternative opportunities. If an extra hour of work is involved, then my alternatives are changed because I lose another hour of other desirable uses. The definition of cost does not deny that the pain and time and trouble of producing some event are influential in the measure of cost. But it does show that these aspects enter into costs only by affecting the value of the best forsaken opportunities.

This can be seen more clearly if we consider the following situation in which the alternatives are not affected. Suppose that in building the pool, the pain to be suffered during a given time was to be more intense—but not longer-lived. In this case, the increase in intensity of pain (assuming that recovery is immediate upon the cessation of the work) does not affect the alternative opportunities. These stay the same. What this more intense pain does is *reduce the value of the pool, not raise its cost.*

Another example of an increase in undesirable attribute that does not increase costs is one that increases that attribute uniformly for *all* opportunities. In this case, the feature cannot be avoided no matter what one does. A uniform reduction in the value of all options reflects the lower level of "utility" now generally available. One could even call this effect a *decrease* in costs—since the best-valued options are now lower valued. The costs are lower because the values are lower, for that is what cost reflects.

Clarification of the logical role of the concept of cost in order to explicate clearly the distinction between the two ideas—the value of forsaken alternatives and the so-called undesirable attributes—was begun by the Austrian school of economics in the nineteenth century and was further developed by Frank Knight (1924).

MONEY COSTS IN A SOCIETY

The preceding is relatively unambiguous for choices or selections of options in a one-person world. But in a society, selection among options involves not only different options for the same person but also different options available to different people. Therefore an interpersonal value measure is necessary. A society in which choices are made in accord with a single dictator's preferences resembles the one-person world. In a pluralistic (individualist) society, an interpersonal value measure can be based on interpersonal exchange rates. Voluntary market exchanges among individuals reveal the highest values of available options and, hence, their costs in terms of values of forsaken options. These market prices, to which all people can adjust their choices, provide a common measure of the value of increments of one event relative to others.

For example, a market exchange rate of 1 Coca-Cola for 2 ounces of chocolate indicates the relative value of each. The optional event—having 1 more Coke—is compared with the option of having 2 more ounces of chocolate. In an open market—one in which all people have access to all goods—the exchange rate, or price, of Cokes must at least equal the highest-valued alternatives to 1 more Coke. If the price does not equal the highest-valued alternative, those who value a Coke at more than the market exchange price will prefer, and will be able, to enter the market and offer more for a Coke. And this will raise the exchange rate to at least the highest-valued alternative. Rather than expressing the values of alternatives to 1 Coke in terms of the amounts of chocolate, beer, or other individual goods that are as much desired as 1 Coke, convenience dictates agreement on a common measure of value. Since almost all formal contractual exchanges are conducted with the medium of money, all exchange rates typically are measured in units of money—as so many dollars or cents per Coke. The use of money prices does not mean that money is all that counts, or that people love money. It means simply that money is the medium of exchange and therefore is the convenient denominator of interpersonal exchange values of events or options.

In sum, because goods are substitutable sources of utility, and because substitution is facilitated by exchange via money, it is possible to measure the value of a forsaken option in money terms. When goods can be obtained not only by interpersonal trade but also by production, at the "cost" of other things that could have been produced, the costs incurred in production choices will be related to the market prices of interpersonal exchanges if producers have access to markets in which to offer their products.

MARKET PRICES AND COST

The preceding discussion implies that cost in an exchange economy is based on market-revealed values. If some productive resources are used in ways that yield less than their highest achievable alternative, or "opportunity," values, these uses will not cover cost. The incentive to increase one's wealth induces shifts of resources to their higher-valued use until their cost is at least matched by the value of their currently yielded product. As the output of the service now being produced at a higher rate increases, the value of additional increments will fall until there is no further shifting of resources from other uses. By drawing resources from lower-valued to higher-valued uses, the value of a producible good or service influences the allocation of resources and so the rate of output of the good or service itself.

This adjustment or reallocation of resources among various uses is often expressed less rigorously. For example: (*a*) "Lower-cost resources are shifted to their higher-valued uses." (*b*) "If costs of production are less than potential values of output, low-cost resources will be shifted to increasing the output of the higher-priced goods, thus inducing a lower price of that good, until ultimately no disparity exists between costs and values of output." Both of these formulations, while explaining the shift in resource uses, are misleading in that they refer to "lower-cost" resources. The resources are not really lower-cost; rather, they are being used in lower-valued uses. It is only the lower value of their use that makes them appear to be lower-valued or lower-cost resources. Strictly speaking, the cost of the use of any resource is never less than the highest-valued opportunity for its use; it is always equal to the amount bid by the most optimistic (highest) bidders in the market for that resource.

No matter how any particular set of resources is used, the cost of their use will be the same—only the realized value of the output, or event yielded, will be affected. If resources are used in less than their most valuable ways, their cost will not be covered, and the difference will be an economic loss. This suggests the query, Is it possible for resources to yield a value in excess of their cost? The answer is yes, in the sense that the current market values do not reflect the future value of the resources—which depends upon unforeseen events or actions. For example, if the use of a resource is changed so as to expose a preferred result to the market, the market value of the resource will be raised. This increase in value of the resource above the former market value is initially a profit. With the unforeseen revaluation, however, costs will be revised upward. In effect, profits are capitalized by the market into costs of subsequent use of the resources.

We may digress to note that we can now interpret the principles underlying the categories "demand" and "supply" as applied to factors affecting price, allocation, and value. *Demand* reflects the value of different amounts of available resources in a particular class of use, say to produce A, while *supply* represents the value of the resources in all *other* potential uses. The demand function indicates a negative relationship between the rate at which good A is made available and the value of another unit of availability of A; the supply function indicates an increasing value of all *other* opportunities of use as more and more of them are forsaken in order to increase the amount of resources devoted to the production of A. If another unit of *A* has a value greater than the highest value of other necessarily forsaken options (costs on the supply function), the output of *A* will increase, thereby lowering its unit value and increasing the "costs" (value in *other* uses only) until the two are brought to equality.

The meaning of costs in the demand for and supply of *A* refers to the value in the *second* or next best use—not in the overall best use. As long as the value of resources in other uses is lower than in the production of good *A*, more resources will be shifted to *A* until the value of another unit of *A* falls to a level that is no greater than that of its component resources in the *next* best other use. At this point the transfer of resources stops and the rate of output of *A* will not increase further. But this supply schedule reflects costs *only* in the *other* uses; it does not reflect cost of resources in the sense of *best* opportunities for use over *all* opportunities, including *A*. The demand-and-supply classification is satisfactory for investigating factors that affect the output of particular goods relative to other goods, but it is not a satisfactory analytical classification for understanding the meaning of the cost concept in its wider range of application and function.

WHEN ARE COSTS INCURRED?

Forsaken alternatives to a current choice are not necessarily composed only of present events. A decision to build a pool can involve a commitment to a sacrifice of future events. In general, a sacrifice of present consumption is valued more highly than the sacrifice of an equivalent future good is valued *now*. The relationship between the present value of two events, identical except in their time of availability, defines a rate of interest. A rate of interest of 10 percent per year means that a unit of good *A*, which would be worth $1.00 if available now, will, if it is available only a year hence, have a value *now* (referring to the time of valuation, not to the time of availability) of \$.909. It follows that if an event *A* involves the sacrifice *both* of an alternative good available and worth \$1.00 now and of a good available in one year and worth \$1.00 at *that* time (but only \$.909 now), the present-value cost of the compound event *A* is \$1.909—the sum of the *present* value of the present item (\$1.00) plus the *present* value (\$.909) of the future item. The cost of event *A* is therefore the present value of the implied chain of sacrificed options, whether they are realizable now or later.

From this it is tempting to try to draw distinctions such as the following: The present event *A* involves costs that, although incurred now, are not experienced now. That this distinction is not meaningful can be seen by carefully considering the meaning of incurring a cost. The individual incurs a cost by choosing event *A* in the sense that his choice makes unavoidable the loss of some otherwise available alternatives. Even if these alternatives were otherwise realizable only far in the future, the cost is incurred now if the present choice of the event *A* eliminates these future possibilities. The cost is incurred now in the sense that the current choice of the event has meant the irretrievable loss of certain alternatives.

Although the cost is incurred now, the consumption loss can be in the future. For example, a person who buys a car now incurs a cost, but by borrowing he can shift the reduction in consumption to the future. There is no necessity for the reduced consumption to be simultaneous with the incurring of the cost. This is especially true for an individual; borrowing from other people will permit him to transfer the consumption loss to any time he wishes within the limits of the borrowing and repayment schedules available to him.

The cost of a *decision* to perform some event is not always the same as the cost of the *event*. For example, if I decide to build a swimming pool that will cost $3,000, does my making a commitment to build a pool involve the entire cost? Not if I can change my mind tomorrow. Thus, the cost of the *contracting* for a swimming pool may be only $500, in that if subsequently I change my mind, I lose only $500. If, then, the cost of the current commitment to build a pool is $500, when are the remaining $2,500 of costs incurred? They are incurred as work progresses and the successive options are irretrievably lost. In sum, the cost of the decision *and the completion* of a swimming pool is $3,000. At any moment the whole $3,000 cost may not have been incurred, and has not been incurred to the extent that one can still avoid the loss of the subsequent options included in the $3,000 that would have been lost had the work progressed to completion. What is emphasized in this paragraph is the need to avoid ambiguity in the meaning of the *events* being costed—e.g., the decision is one event and the execution of the project may be a series of subsequent events. Exactly to what event the costs apply should be made unambiguous.

EXAMPLES OF MEASURES OF COST

Principles underlying the measurement of cost as defined above are simple and will now be illustrated, but it must be emphasized that in actual practice the measurement is very imprecise in that it involves estimates of uncertain future events. We shall consider first the cost of *purchasing* (obtaining and retaining ownership of) a care, and then the cost of *using* the car. Its purchase price is $3,000. If we retain the car until it becomes worthless (and if we incur no other costs), the cost of ownership for the indefinite future is \$3,000. Assume that we could sell the car immediately for \$2,500. At the moment of purchase, then, we have incurred a cost of \$500, the cost of acquiring ownership. If we retain the car, we will gradually incur the remaining \$2,500 of cost; however, since we can always sell the car, the cost of ownership up to any moment is not the \$2,500 but only that portion which cannot be recovered by resale. If a month later we can sell the car for \$2,300, the cost of acquiring and retaining ownership for one month is \$500 plus \$200.

TABLE 1

	Beginning of year 1	*Beginning of year 2*	*End of year 2*
Purchase price	\$3,000	\$ —	\$ —
Taxes and insurance	150	150	—
Resale value	(2,500)	(2,200)	−2,000
	\$3,150	\$ 150	−\$2,000
10% present-value factor	(1.00)	(.909)	(.826)

Present-value cost: \$1,634.35 = \$3,150.00 + \$136.35 − \$1,652.00

Suppose now we plan to keep the car for two years and then sell it (without using it in the meantime) for \$2,000. Of course, \$2,000 two years hence does not have the same value as \$2,000 now. At a 10 percent rate of interest the present value of \$2,000 deferred two years is \$1,652. The present-capital-value measure of the cost of owning a car for two years is equal to the purchase price minus the present value of the resale price two years hence: \$3,000 − \$1,652 = \$1,348. The decrease in the value of the car from the \$3,000 purchase price to the \$2,000 resale value is called *depreciation* (for expository simplicity we ignore maintenance expenditures, which are assumed to be optimal). If the reduction were greater than expected, the excess would be called *obsolescence*.

Ownership of a car usually involves more than the costs of acquisition of ownership, even though the car is never to be driven. For example, there are the costs of taxes and insurance. If these total $150 yearly, to be paid at the beginning of each year, the cost of ownership for two years is reckoned as shown in Table 1.

The cost of obtaining and retaining (insured) possession for two years is $1,634.35. By rearranging the data we can express this cost as the sum of depreciation (purchase price minus resale price, adjusted to present value) plus the other ownership costs (taxes and insurance), as in Table 2.

TABLE 2

Purchase price	$3,000	
Resale value	– 1,652	(present value of $2,000 deferred two years)
Depreciation	$1,348	
Taxes and insurance	150	(first year)
Taxes and insurance	136.35	(present value of second year's payment)
Present-value cost	$1,634.35	

Operating the car will involve more costs and a lower resale value, $1,700 rather than $2,000. Suppose outlays for gasoline, maintenance, and such amount to $500 in the first year and $400 in the second year. (Let these outlays be payable at the end of each year.) The costs of ownership and operation are now $2,667.05, compared with the cost of $1,634.35 for ownership only (see Table 3).

Events are rarely indivisible; instead, the magnitude of the

TABLE 3

	Beginning of year 1	*Beginning of year 2*	*End of year 2*
Purchase price	$3,000	$ —	$ —
Taxes and insurance	150	150	—
Gas, oil, and maintenance	—	500	400
Resale value	—	—	− 1,700
	$3,150	$650	− $1,300
10% present-value factor	(1.00)	(.909)	(.826)

Present-value cost: $2,667.05 = $3,150.00 + $590.85 − $1,073.80

event can be varied. Thus, in the automobile example, we could consider a set of alternative output programs, e.g., running the car zero miles in two years, one mile in two years, two miles in two years, etc., up to, say, 20,000 miles in two years. Suppose that for each of these we can determine the costs. The differences in costs between adjacent alternative programs in the incremental or marginal cost for the mileage increment. That is, the difference in cost between two-year programs of 19,999 miles and 20,000 miles is called the marginal cost of a mile of travel at 20,000 miles: it is the increment in cost for a 20,000-mile program over the cost for a 19,999-mile program. If we computed the cost for one mile of distance, for two miles, etc., up to 20,000 miles, we could compute a series of marginal costs at, or associated with, one mile more than no miles, one mile more than one mile, one mile more than two, etc. The sum of all these (including the cost of zero miles with two-year ownership) will total to the cost of ownership *and* 20,000 miles of travel. The concept of marginal cost is relevant for deciding among available programs because it tells by how much the cost of one program differs from that of adjacent available programs.

In the comparison of mileage programs we do not mean that one performs the program of, say, 10,000 miles of travel and then, *after* completing that program, asks how much one more mile would cost. Instead, initially one considers the cost of a proposed 10,000-mile program and the cost of a proposed 10,001-mile program. The difference in cost between the proposed programs is the marginal cost. (To run one more mile as the result of a last-minute decision may involve a higher extra cost than if one had planned for that extra mile from the beginning. In the extreme situation one might have to buy another car in which to do it.)

For any event there are two associated concepts of cost—total and marginal (the latter referring to a comparison between one particular event and another differing by one unit in some dimension of the event). For every alterable dimension there is a marginal cost of increments in that dimension. Two important dimensions in most output programs are the *rate* or speed of output and the total *volume* to be produced. We shall confine our subsequent discussion to changes in these rate and volume dimensions.

The present-capital-value measure of total (or of marginal) cost can be converted into a variety of other equivalent measures for expressing that cost. For example, the present capital value can be reexpressed as a *future* capital value with the future value measure (t units of time in the future) in the ratio $(1 + i)^t$ to the present value, where i is the rate of interest. Alternatively, the present capital value can be converted to a *rate* of costs over some interval. For example, a present-capital-value cost of $1,000 is, at 10 percent per year, equivalent to a perpetual rate of cost of $100 per year, or to a rate of $263 per year for five years.

If the event being costed consists of a group or collection of homogeneous units, e.g., the production of pianos, or the production of miles of service from a car, or the production of bushels of wheat, the cost can be prorated or expressed as an average cost per unit of each item. In the automobile example, the event consisted of owning and driving a car 20,000 miles in two years, the cost of which was \$2,667.05. This can be expressed as \$2,667.05/20,000 = 13.3 cents per mile of distance. This is the prorated amount that, if received *now* for each future mile of service, will enable the receipts to cover the cost.

Sometimes the rate at which revenues must be received in order to cover costs is measured not by dividing the capital-value measure of costs by the total volume of output, but instead by dividing an annual rate of costs by an annual rate of performance or output. For example, the present-value measure of cost in the above illustration was \$2,667 (for a two-year program of 20,000 miles of travel at the rate of 10,000 miles per year). The \$2,667 present value can be re-expressed as an equivalent-valued continuous-flow annuity for two years, at 10 percent per year compounded continuously. This steady-flow or rate measure is \$1,479 per year for two years (and since there are 8,760 hours in a year, this is equivalent to \$1,479 per year/8,760 hours per year = 16.9 cents per hour). The speed of service, at the rate of 10,000 miles per year for two years, is equivalent to 10,000 miles per year/8,760 hours per year = 1.14 miles per hour. If we divide one annual (or hourly) rate of costs by the other annual (or hourly) rate of service (i.e., \$1,479 per year/10,000 miles per year, or 16.9 cents per hour/1.14 miles per hour), we get 14.8 cents per mile. Therefore, if costs are to be covered by revenues received concurrently with the service performed, the receipts must be 14.8 cents per mile of distance. (This differs from the earlier cost measure of 13.3 cents per mile paid at the beginning of the entire two-year program because the 14.8 cents is paid later and includes interest on the *average* delay.)

Extreme care must be taken to ensure that rates are divided by rates or that present-capital-value measures are divided by volume measures of the output. Confusion will result if rate (flow) measures of output are divided into capital-value (stock) measures of cost. That would yield cost per unit of speed of output (e.g., miles per year), not per unit of output (e.g., miles). Since outputs are usually sold or priced in units of output or volume, rather than in units of speed of service, it is more useful to consider the covering of costs by receipts per unit of volume of output rather than per unit of speed or of rate of production.

FIXED AND VARIABLE COSTS

The preceding discussion distinguished among events being costed according to whether they involved (*a*) the ownership of some good, (*b*) the operation of that good to produce some service, or (*c*) a unit expansion of the event, giving a marginal cost. For some purposes a classification of costs may be useful. It may be relevant to know, for a chosen output program, what costs have been incurred even if we were, at some subsequent moment, to abandon the program. As was seen in the automobile example, at the moment of purchase we have incurred some loss of resale value, e.g., $3,000 − $2,500 = $500. That "cost" is "sunk" or "historical." Once we purchase the car, it cannot be escaped. It should play no role (except as a help in forecasting costs of similar future events) in any subsequent decision, for regardless of what we do, that historical "cost" has been incurred, and is inescapable and unaffected. For any ensuing decision only the escapable, or "variable," costs are relevant.

Having separated sunk or historical "costs" (which really are no longer costs) from future costs, we can proceed to classify future costs into invariant and variable costs. Suppose a person can choose among a *restricted* set of output programs but that associated with all those options there is a common set of activities or inputs, the cost of which is therefore common to each option in the subset. The cost of these common activities is sometimes called a "fixed" cost. Regardless of which option in the subset he chooses, he cannot avoid those "fixed" costs. But since the real range of options is greater, he really *can* escape the "fixed" cost by choosing an option outside that subset. Therefore that "fixed" cost is not a "sunk" cost. Fixed cost is a useful concept, for example, in situations in which there can be delegation of authority to choose within some subset. So long as the selection is to be made within that subset, only the costs other than the "fixed" costs are relevant. But for the larger range of options, the "fixed" costs are not "fixed" and are relevant for comparing options. To avoid the impression that "fixed" costs are fixed upon a person as an inescapable loss, it seems appropriate to use the name "invariant" rather than "fixed," but this is not yet a generally accepted terminology. (Fixed or invariant costs would be "sunk" if and only if the subset was in fact the entire set of possible options, for then regardless of what one did, one could not avoid the sacrifice of those alternatives.)

LAW OF COSTS

So far, we have classified costs according to differences in the event being costed, and also in terms of various ways of expressing the costs of a specified event or output program. The question to which we turn now is whether there are any laws or general propositions that relate the magnitude of costs to the characteristics of output programs. But first it is pertinent to identify the relevant characteristics or dimensions of an output or production program. As suggested earlier, the total volume and the rate or speed of production are two important dimensions of such a program. A third is the timing of the output. We may denote these three variables as follows: V is the volume of output, $v(t)$ is the rate of output at moment t, T_0 is the present moment, and T_m is the terminal moment. An increase in $v(t)$ will either increase V or, for fixed V, will decrease T_m (move is closer to T_0). Let C denote the capital-value measure of cost of the entire program. Several laws can now be stated in terms of these symbols.

(1) It is a well-recognized and validated law that cost is larger the larger V is (whether V is increased by increasing $v(t)$ or by increasing T_m). Simply put, a bigger output costs more than a smaller one. Symbolically this means $\partial C / \partial V$ is positive, even for fixed or unchanged $v(t)$. The expression $\partial C / \partial V$ is called the marginal cost with respect to volume.

(2) Another proposition is that $\partial C / \partial V$ is smaller (but always positive) the larger V is (again with the rate of production held constant and with the increased V being obtained by increasing T_m). In symbols, $\partial^2 C / \partial V^2$ is negative. This effect is sometimes referred to as the lower costs effect of mass or large-volume production. A larger output can always be produced by replicating the technique for a smaller output. However, sometimes a larger output can be produced at lower cost through the use of different techniques (e.g., metal dies instead of sand casting for forming metal), but this cheaper method cannot be subdivided proportionately for smaller volume. It follows that larger volume will at most involve pro-

portional increases in total cost (by replication of the cheapest methods for small volumes) and may permit utilization of lower-cost methods. Learning and improvement in methods with a larger volume of output are also predictable. Both effects, substitution of cheaper methods for larger volume and learning, contribute to the decrease in increments of total cost for increments in volume.

The two laws relating costs to volume of output imply that (3) the average cost per unit of volume of output decreases, the larger the volume—a widely recognized phenomenon. This lower unit cost with larger volume is manifested in the extensive standardization of products, in contrast with the less common individually styled, custom-built goods, which would be preferable if the costs were no higher. This lower cost with larger volume (along with the gains from specialization in production resulting from the greater heterogeneity of productive resources) is one reason why larger markets and population areas permit lower costs per unit.

(4) A law relating cost to the *rate* (not volume) of output is that the cost, C, is a positive function of $v(t)$ for any given V; that is, $\partial C / \partial v$ is positive. The more rapidly a volume of output is produced, the higher its cost.

(5) Another, possibly less general, law is that the marginal cost with respect to rate, $\partial C / \partial v$, while always positive, increases for larger v (that is, $\partial^2 C / \partial v^2$ is positive). This law is possibly less general because the evidence is contradictory for "very low" rates of output, at which it is sometimes claimed that increases in the rate might lead to decreasing increases in total cost. Nevertheless, a general and universally valid law is that for every volume of output there exists an output rate beyond which the marginal cost with respect to rate always increases. This is commonly called the law of increasing marginal costs and reflects the well-known law of diminishing

marginal returns with respect to rate of output. If expressed in terms of average costs per unit of *volume* of output, the effect of higher rates of production of *that* volume is persistently to raise the average cost—after a possible initial fall in average cost for very low output rates.

(6) Instead of increasing the rate in which some constant volume is produced, output programs can be different in that both the rate *and* the volume are proportionally larger over a specified interval of time. Joint proportional increases in both the rate and the volume (over the given interval of production) will of course raise total costs. The effect on the cost per unit of product is not predictable except for "high" rates of output. Unlike proposition (3), concerning per-unit cost, proposition (6) involves an increase in the rate of output as well as in the volume. These two work in opposite directions on the per-unit cost, with the higher rate increasing unit costs while the larger volume decreases them. The rate effect ultimately will dominate as programs with higher rates are considered. For production programs arrayed according to the rate and volume of output (both varying strictly in proportion to each other) it follows that the average cost per unit of volume of output can be decreasing for small outputs. But as larger outputs are considered, the average cost will, beyond some output rate, begin to rise persistently and with increasing rapidity until a limiting rate of production is realized—at which all the resources of the world are devoted to this one program over that given time interval.

SHORT-RUN AND LONG-RUN COSTS

We are now in position to examine another classification—short-run and long-run. Although it is common to see references to the short-run and long-run costs of some production program, there is in fact only *one* cost for any program. The short-run–long-run cost distinction rests on two concepts that are sometimes confounded with each other. A short-run cost is sometimes used to refer to a short, as contrasted with a long, program of production. At other times it is used to refer to the cost of doing something more quickly rather than less quickly. Yet in each case the shorter output and the quicker output both involve higher per-unit costs than do the longer output and the later output. Sometimes the higher per-unit short-run cost (no matter in which of the two different senses) is attributed to an alleged fixity in some of the productive units. In fact, of course, no producer is stuck with literally fixed inputs (except in the sense that momentarily it is hardly possible to increase anything). What is true is that it is more expensive to vary some inputs in any given interval than to vary others. That differential cost of adjusting various inputs is often oversimplified into an extreme bipolar classification of fixed and variable inputs.

The purpose of the long-run–short-run distinction is to note the differences in cost between *different* output programs, those achieved in the more immediate future in contrast with those undertaken later, when one can get the advantage of less expensive, less hasty adjustments. For example, if the demand for some good increases, producers will be able to respond immediately, but at a higher cost than for less hasty revisions of output. Although the "same" good is being produced (except, of course, for the important difference in the time of its availability), the cost is lower for the later output. To trace the impact of a demand change on output and prices, one will want to recognize the difference in the output and price with the passage of time. Instead of tracing out a continuous history or sequence of subsequent developments, it is convenient to divide the history arbitrarily into two episodes: the relatively immediate response (the short-run) and the limiting ultimate response (the long-run). The difference between these two "runs" indicates the path and direction of effects subsequent to the initial event.

While the long-run–short-run distinction serves as a convenient two-stage analysis of a sequence of effects, obviously there are as many "runs" as one wishes to consider. However, in analyzing total effects, three states or runs are usually considered: the "market period" (referring to that period of adjustment in prices which occurs before there is any change in output), and the afore-mentioned short-run and long-run, during both of which output is changed.

JOINT PRODUCTS AND UNALLOCABLE COSTS

Suppose that an output program yields several joint products, e.g., wool, meat, and leather from sheep; or gasoline and kerosene from crude oil; or heat and light from electrical energy; or passenger miles and freight miles from an airline. What is the cost of each of the joint products? Depending upon which one is called the residual, or by-product, a different allocation of costs can be obtained. By calling meat the "basic" product and attaching most of the costs to it, the costs of wool can be made small, and conversely. It is tempting to jump to the conclusion that something must be wrong with the concept of cost or with the economic system if such indefiniteness can result. After all, if costs cannot be uniquely allocated, how can one tell what prices are right? How can one tell on which of the joint products he is making a profit? If costs cannot be assigned, how can one tell which to produce or what prices to charge? In fact, however, the presence of cost that cannot be allocated uniquely among the joint products does not upset anything or prevent unique prices.

If we recall the purpose of the cost concept—that of enabling choices among alternatives according to some criterion of preference—we see that what is required is a way of assessing the consequences of *changes* in the output. If the airline program is revised to transport more passengers and less freight, or revised so as to transport more passengers with the same amount of freight, what happens to cost? Comparing the costs of alternative programs gives marginal costs, which with the marginal value of the revised output give a basis for a decision. There is no possibility and no necessity for allocating costs into uniquely identifiable parts for each product in order to determine what to produce and what prices to ask. The prices set will be those which allocate the amount produced among the competing claimants and yield a maximum wealth to the producer of the joint products. His power to maximize his wealth will of course depend upon competitors' access to the market. The function of inducing output does not require an assignment of portions of total cost to each of the joint outputs. What *is* necessary is a comparison of the total cost of the set of joint products with its value. If the market value of the *set* does not cover the cost, in an open market, the loss of wealth will induce reduced production (of some or all the joint outputs) and higher prices, until the value of the set of joint products covers the costs. (If joint products can be produced only in fixed combinations, then not even marginal costs of each output can be ascertained; nevertheless, everything said in the preceding two sentences is still valid and applicable.)

PRIVATE AND SOCIAL ALLOCATIONS OF COSTS

Throughout the preceding discussion the costs of a choice were assumed to be borne by the chooser; none of the forsaken options are forsaken by anyone else. If Smith builds a swimming pool, the forsaken options—the costs—are all borne by him. The options open to the rest of the community or to any of its members are in no way reduced. So we assumed. If, however, Smith builds a pool and in doing so creates a "nuisance" for his neighbor, Jones, Smith has taken away Jones's peace and quiet. If Smith's pool overflows and harmfully floods Cohen's land, Cohen has had options removed from his range of choice. Being less careful and thereby letting water run over into a neighbor's land, or having a more riotous time and disturbing the peace, is less costly for Smith if he does not incur the costs of being more careful in watching the water level or in soundproofing his play area.

The situation is similar to that of the factory owner who "dumps" smoke, waste, smells, noises, and night lights on other people's land. By doing so he keeps his land in better condition and avoids the cost of filtering his smoke, collecting and disposing of his own garbage, etc. He makes others bear some of the costs, instead of bearing them himself. His actions involve a sacrifice of alternative uses of goods, which sacrifice, instead of being borne by the decision-maker, is in part borne by or imposed on other people.

"Property rights are not private" is another way to express this situation. The use of "one's" resources is not subject solely to the owner's voluntary control, but is in fact and *de jure* controllable in part by other people. This ability to "use" other people's resources for one's benefit, and thereby remove their options, enables one to make other people bear part of the costs of one's decisions. The costs are divided between the decision-maker and outsiders. This division or separation is called a divergence between private and social costs—where social costs are treated as the whole of costs as defined in the earlier portions of this discussion, with private costs being the portion of those costs borne by the decision-maker or owner of the resources directly concerned. Social and private costs are not two different costs—they are merely classifications according to the bearer of the cost. If there is no divergence, so that all social costs are private costs, then all the costs of use are borne by the person choosing or authorizing the choice of action. The divergence between private and social costs is also characterized as the presence of "external" costs.

Parallel reasoning is relevant on the side of benefits. The *value* of a resource in *this* use may be incompletely revealed or have incomplete influence on decisions if that value is dispersed so that only a part of it accrues to the decision maker. This is a divergence between private and social value in *this* use. If the value measure assigned to any particular potential use by the chooser is less than the total value in that use, then there will be a divergence between his private valuation and the social valuation. In this case, values of some uses of resources are not as fully revealed and available as inducements to the competing resource users as are the values of other uses. As a result, the values of some uses will be understated, which encourages more of other kinds of use by leading to an underestimation of their cost. Thus the analysis of external versus private or of social versus private values or costs is an essential part of the analysis of the meaning and role of costs.

But whatever they are called, such effects are commonplace and well-nigh universal. For example, every voluntary act of exchange involves a choice of use of resources that benefits the other party as well as oneself. However, the external effect is "internalized" as an inducement on the acting agents. If you give me "that," I will do, or give you, "this"; and what you give me reflects the gains you will get from what I do. The external effects of my actions are made internal or effective by your ability to offer me a gain reflecting the value to you. The external costs of my acts are internalized or made effective in controlling my behavior by laws prohibiting my imposing any such costs on you unless I pay you an acceptable amount for the right to do so. Our laws of property and the right to engage in exchange help to make private costs also contain the social costs, and to make private gain reflect social gains. In other words, external effects are usually internalized.

In every society the extent of a divergence between private and social costs (or the presence of external effects) for some resource use depends upon the technological facts *and* upon the legal structure of property rights. The costs of defining, policing, and enforcing various types of property rights vary. Private property rights, defined as those in which external physical effects are not permissible, may be too expensive to enforce with respect to some effects. But if there is a cheap way to internalize external effects or to make the private costs equal the social costs, then the use of resources will respond more fully to the cost or values of use. If there were some cheap means of excluding other people from enjoyment of some use I may make of my resources, then I could charge them for the availability of that enjoyment and thereby make that value of use effective in my decision as to how to use resources. This is a means of internalizing external effects or of making external effects "inducive" with respect to my choices about resource uses.

Often the costs that must be borne in order to internalize

external effects exceed the value of those external effects but may nevertheless be worth incurring if they involve associated revenues and a more profitable, larger enterprise. For example, a golf course provides benefits to neighboring landowners. A golf course builder could buy enough land to build a course and to build homes on the surrounding property, thus internalizing a higher value from proximity to the golf course. Another example is that of the apartment building in which the rental includes the cost of maintenance of common gardens and recreation areas, rather than having each tenant maintain his own area. The purchase of cemetery lots includes a payment for upkeep of the whole cemetery. By such devices, neighborhood effects are made the owners' effects.

Another important means of internalizing or making external effects "inducing-effects" is the development corporation, which enables a larger venture to be undertaken so that more of the benefited resource owners can be included in the unit of ownership that provides the benefits. If all the land of a suburban shopping center is owned by one enterprise, there can be more complete response to the total value of the shopping center, which includes values external to the component units resulting from their proximity. Similarly, department stores with several departments in one building are a means of "internalizing" values or of making private and social effects converge. Signal decoders and wire transmission systems for television, fences around athletic pavilions to keep out nonpaying spectators, and walls around theaters are examples of devices (not costless) for internalizing and increasing the value of the service to those who provide it, and so are "inducive" to that resource use.

In other cases the value of complete suppression of external effects may be less than the cost. For example, automobile exhaust suppressors and smoke filters are not universally required. As a result, those who create smoke and smog thrust part of the costs of their actions on other people. An especially instructive example is provided by the problem of noisy airplanes. If an airport owner had to compensate the nearby landowners for the noise made by the airplanes using his airport, the landowners would in effect be selling rights to that particular use of their land, and the airport owner could in turn charge the airplane owners. Instead, one of the following solutions is usually adopted: (1) There is no compensation for the noise. (2) The planes are prohibited. (3) The neighboring land is bought up and people are prohibited from living there—even though many would prefer to do so, *if* they could buy the land at a low enough price to reflect the value of the lost quiet. These extreme policies are sometimes explained by an incorrect presumption that it is impossible or undesirable to buy the rights to "dump" noise on neighboring land; in fact, they are used because neighboring landowners do not have a legally recognized right to the undisturbed use of their land.

As the preceding remarks have indicated, often our *legal structure* of property rights is such that decisions are made in which only part of the costs are operative in affecting the choice. This may be a result of a deliberate attempt to attenuate the role of costs in decision-making or, because of technological features, it may be the result of the difficulty (cost) of defining, policing, and enforcing rights to resources in such a way that private and social costs do not diverge much. Laws may be what they are because those most influential in affecting them may want resources to be used with less regard to the exchange-value measure of costs. It may be thought that the values the people of the society would express in the way they would use resources are inappropriate or improper and therefore should not be so influential in affecting resource allocations. If so, choices about uses of resources should be insulated from those alternative use values (i.e., costs). This can be achieved by suppressing a marketplace in which market prices would reveal alternative use values, or it can be achieved by not sanctioning private property rights, so that no one can negotiate an exchange that would reveal alternative use values (that is, resources would not be "owned," in the sense of being salable).

Policing and enforcing of property rights is not performed exclusively by the government. In many cases other forms of control are effective. Etiquette and socially accepted codes act as determiners of rights. These institutions serve, in part, to restrict the extent to which a person can impose the costs of his choices on others. That is, they are often means of inducing behavior of a type that would occur if resources involved were "privately" owned and exchangeable. Custom and etiquette, along with property rules, affect the degree of concentration of costs on decision-makers.

EXTERNAL VALUE EFFECTS AND COSTS

Still another source of confusion is the confounding of the external *price* effects of some event with its costs. Cost has been defined as the highest-valued option necessarily sacrificed consequent to action A. Suppose that I open a restaurant near yours, and by virtue of my superior cooking talents attract customers away from you, with a consequent loss of wealth by you of, say, $50,000. So far as *you* are concerned, my effect on you is as bad as if I had burned your uninsured $50,000 building for the joy and excitement this afforded me. From an analytical point of view, the *former* loss of $50,000 of value is not a cost, whereas the destruction of the building would have been a cost. Why the difference? Simply that opening a restaurant does not necessarily involve a sacrifice to society at large, while the destruction of the building does. My superior cooking skills do not involve a sacrifice of $50,000 of alternatively valuable output, whereas my enjoying the fire would. My superior cooking may impose a *loss of wealth* on you because I outcompete you in providing services to third parties. But the $50,000 loss to you is more than matched by the gain in the value of service to the third parties who were formerly your customers but who have shifted to me, and by the increase in my own wealth. No formerly available options are forsaken by society as a whole. Everything that could be done before I opened my restaurant still can be done. That $50,000 is not a sacrificed opportunity—instead, it is a measure of a *transfer of wealth* from you to two other parties, me and the customers. The distinction between the transfer of rights to uses of resources and the costs of use of goods should be kept clear. For example, when I open a new restaurant service, and the public offers less for your goods and more for mine, they are telling you that the exchange rights formerly attached to your goods—their market value—are being transferred by them to my goods.

The transfer of rights of choice of use and the revision of exchange values consequent to changes in offers by competitors, or consequent to changes in tastes by customers, do not reduce the total set of alternative use options. The transfer changes the person authorized to control the decision as to use. When my superior culinary talents reduce the exchange value of your services (without affecting their physical attributes in any way) and so reduce your wealth, society could in principle take away some of my gains and those of my customers (who gain by accepting my offers rather than yours) and fully reimburse you, while still leaving me and the customers better off than before I entered the market. Such compensation is not possible for true costs.

The person who loses wealth either via transfer of goods or the reduction of their exchange value is suffering a real loss of wealth, but not a cost. That loss is different in principle, in kind, and in fact from a cost. From the private point of view both sources of loss of wealth are "bad" for him. Both are losses of opportunities to *him*, though only a cost is a loss to the *community as a whole*. What he loses in the pure price revaluation case, someone else gains.

There are many examples of the use of public policy to reduce such transfers. Taxes have been imposed on innovations or on new products in order to reimburse owners of resources formerly used to produce the displaced products. Sometimes laws are passed prohibiting new, cheaper devices, in order to preserve the marketable wealth of users of older, more costly methods. Sometimes general taxes are imposed to aid those whose wealth is reduced by new methods, e.g., government financing of retraining of displaced workers and low-interest loans to business firms in distressed areas. Taxes on innovations make the innovators count the taxes as part of their costs. The "costs" of innovation are thereby biased upward, with a resultant attenuation of the incentive to introduce new methods or products that would produce a larger total wealth.

Although wealth transfers via market revaluations are not costs, they may influence behavior. For example, if such market revisions of wealth are (somehow) deemed undesirable, steps can be taken to restrain people from taking actions that revise the distribution of wealth, or steps can be taken to redistribute the wealth again so as to restore the *status quo ante* wealth for each individual. Social policy (laws of property) may be evolved to insulate decisions from these effects or, conversely, to make them more sensitive. But in neither case are these market-price side effects on wealth components of costs.

We conclude by returning to the initial theme. The costs of some event are the highest-valued options necessarily forsaken. We have seen that he who is to forsake those options and he who makes the decision about the chosen option may or may not be the same person. Furthermore, the privately borne costs may be less or greater than the true costs, depending upon laws and upon the structure of property rights.

Bibliography

Böhm-Bawerk, Eugen von. *Capital and Interest*. 3 vols. South Holland, Ill.: Libertarian, 1959. First published in German. See especially vol. 2, pp. 248–56, "The Law of Costs," and vol. 3, pp. 97–115, "On the Value of Producers' Goods and the Relationship Between Value and Costs."

Clark, John Maurice. *Studies in the Economics of Overhead Costs*. Univ. of Chicago Press, 1962.

Coase, R. H. The Problem of Social Cost. *Journal of Law and Economics* 3 (1960): 1–44.

Demsetz, Harold. "The Exchange and Enforcement of Property Rights." *Journal of Law and Ecnomics* 7 (1964): 11–26.

Knight, Frank H. "Some Fallacies in the Interpretation of Social Cost." *Quarterly Journal of Economics* 38 (1924): 582–606.

Stigler, George J. *The Theory of Price*. Rev. ed. New York: Macmillan, 1960. First published (1942) as *The Theory of Competitive Price*.

Viner, Jacob. "Cost." Vol. 4, pp. 466–75 in *Encyclopaedia of the Social Sciences*. New York: Macmillan, 1931.

———. "Cost Curves and Supply Curves." Pp. 198–232 in American Economic Association, *Readings in Price Theory*. Homewood, Ill.: Irwin, 1952.

Reliability of Progress Curves in Airframe Production[1]

SUMMARY

The airframe manufacturing progress curve estimates direct labor per pound of airframe needed to manufacture the *N*th airframe, from *N*, the cumulative number of planes of a given model produced at a given facility. The relation is customarily written as a linear function between the logarithm of direct labor per pound and the logarithm of the *N*th airframe. Statistical tests of the similarity of the functions among various airframe manufacturers, on the basis of reported World War II data, have been made in this paper. An

[1] In 1948, when seeking estimates of costs of alternative weapon systems, the potentially embarrassing error of relating costs to rates of output while ignoring another relevant variable, quantity of items produced, was made obvious by access to the airframe production data analyzed in this paper. By 1949 the present paper had been completed for the RAND Corporation, but reliance on "military classified" data and sources prevented open publication at that time. Although the sources and data have been declassified for several years, it seems appropriate to publish the paper in its original form now that the phenomenon is being incorporated in formal economic theory. Any views expressed in this paper are not to be interpreted as necessarily reflecting the views of the RAND Corporation or the official opinion or policy of any of its governmental or private research sponsors. Acknowledgment is made to Charles Hitch, who encouraged and aided the study.

assessment has also been made of the reliability of predictions made with these curves.

The functions are shown to differ among the various airframe types and manufacturing facilities both in the amount and rate of change of required direct labor per pound of airframe.

Nevertheless, for practical purposes it may be appropriate to use an average of individual progress functions. One such practical purpose would be the prediction of total direct labor requirements for the first 1,000 airplanes of a particular model. The average error of prediction is shown to be about 25 percent. For the entire output of any particular airframe model produced in one facility the error of prediction is also 25 percent.

If specific curves are fitted to the past performance of a particular manufacturing facility in order to predict its future requirements, the margins of error of prediction average about 20 percent. All these margins of error, while averaging about 20 to 25 percent, represent specific errors which in .9 of the cases range between −40 and +70 percent. An illustration of the possible practical significance of such errors is given.

Finally, functions with other variables, in addition to N, are briefly considered.

GENERAL PROBLEM AND HYPOTHESES

The "progress function" or "learning curve" is one of the instruments of planning, scheduling, and forecasting used in the aircraft industry and the U.S. Air Force. It is designed to express the relation between the amount of direct labor required to produce an airframe and the number of airframes produced. It associates the number of direct man hours per pound of airframe used in the production of a specific airframe with the number of airframes of that particular type produced in a specific production facility. The relationship, in general, indicates that the required number of direct man hours decreases as more airframes are produced.

Direct labor is the number of direct man hours that, so to speak, is congealed in the Nth airframe. It is the direct[2] labor that was expended in the production and fabrication of the component parts and their assembly into that particular airframe. The N of the Nth airframe is the cumulative number of airframes accepted up to and including the Nth airframe. N is not the rate of production per unit of time.

The form of the relationship between direct labor per pound (hereafter called m) of airframe for the Nth airframe, and the Nth airframe, is usually formulated as

$$\log_{10} m = a + b \log_{10} N$$

subject to $a > 0$ and $-1 < b < 0$ where a and b are parameters of the linear form. Graphically on double log paper the equation plots as a straight line with negative slope.

A statistical study of the reliability of this function for certain types of estimates is presented in this report. It is indisputable that lower direct labor costs occur as the number of items produced increases; the evidence on this point is overwhelming. Questions can be raised, however: (1) How long does this reduction continue? (2) Can it be represented by a linear function on double log scale? (3) Does it fall at the same rate for all different airframe manufacturing facilities? (4) How reliably can one predict marginal and total labor requirements for a particular production facility from an industry average progress curve derived from the experience of all airframe

[2] Defined below on p. 339.

manufacturers? (5) How reliably can a curve fitted to the experience of all bomber (fighter) production predict labor requirements for a specific type of bomber (fighter) produced in a particular facility? (6) How reliable is a single manufacturing plant's own early experience for predicting its later requirements for producing a particular type of airframe? (7) What may be the consequences of the margins of error involved in these estimating methods?

The general order of analysis follows the sequence of the above questions. These questions are investigated on the assumption that the estimates are made for a period in which general production conditions are the same as those which prevailed during World War II.

It must be emphasized that this study is concerned with the various types of estimates and predictions that might be made from the assumed *linear* form of the relationship. No attempt is made here to evaluate other forms of relationships that might be used for certain types of predictions. Nor is there any discussion here of the reasons for the decline in labor requirements. Both of these questions may be analyzed in subsequent reports.

SOURCE OF INFORMATION

All information used was derived from the *Source Book of World War II Basic Data; Airframe Industry, Vol. I,* prepared by AAF Matériel Command, Wright Field (undated). The data reported in the *Source Book* were in turn derived from the Aeronautical Monthly Progress Reports (AMPRs). The reliability of the AMPRs has been subject to a good deal of speculation and remains a moot point. The following description of the data is based entirely on the statements contained in the *Source Book* itself. The AMPRs provided data on acceptances, direct man hours per unit and direct man-hour expenditure for the report month, subcontracting, etc. Prior to December 1942 direct man hours were obtained from letters submitted by facilities or by district offices.

The following definitions were adopted by the AMPRs:

Direct man hours per pound of airframe, m (on-site plus off-site) are obtained by dividing direct unit man hours for the *N*th airframe by its unit weight.[3]

Direct man hours for the entire airframe are the "facility's best estimate of the total number of direct hours which would be required to perform the entire airframe manufacturing operation within the reporting facility."[4] This estimate is in turn the sum of two estimates: (1) "The estimated direct man hours it would require to perform within the facility that part of the airframe . . . being produced outside the plant or plants of the reporting facility," and (2) direct man hours per unit on-site.[5]

Direct man hours per unit on-site are the "contractor's best estimate of (1) the direct unit hours expended within the reporting facility (including feeder plants) prior to acceptance on the last unit for which complete records are available in the report month, or (2) the average direct man-hours cost of the last lot produced for which complete records are available in the report month."[6] That is, the direct man hours relate either to a single unit or to an average of a lot—in either case it is the last unit or last lot for which complete records are available. Man hours per unit include all hours necessary to complete an airframe, whether these hours are spent during the month of completion (report month) or over a period of several months.

---

[3] *Source Book*, p. 37.

[4] *Ibid.*

[5] *Ibid.*

[6] *Ibid.*

"*Direct man hours charged to a model* normally are obtained from shop or work order and not from payroll records."[7] Man hours included are hours expended on the airframe manufacturing process, which includes machining, processing, fabricating, assembling, and installing all integral parts of the airplane structure, flight operations (but not test piloting), and reworking prior to acceptance.[8] Not included are hours expended in the production of raw stock, equipment items, spare parts, and reworking after acceptance.[9] Direct man hours are not the same as *productive man hours*. The latter include also hours expended in mold loft, in jig fixture and tool production, in inspection, shipping, receiving, and warehousing.[10]

It is important to note that the observations are the contractor's best estimates of the direct labor used. The methods of making these estimates varied considerably among the manufacturing facilities. It is believed that in some cases very crude estimates were presented. This does not affect the validity of the present study, which is designed to test the predictive utility of progress curves based on reported data. If the progress curves had been derived from exact data, their reliability might be either higher or lower. As long as present and future methods of obtaining data are basically similar to those used in the past, it makes no difference how they were obtained.

Cumulative plane number, N. Through April 1944 these are total *acceptances* for each model from a given manufacturing facility as reported to the Air Matériel Command Statistical Division in a "Special Historical Report of Airframe Weight," or in letters submitted by the facilities. Beginning

[7] *Ibid.*

[8] *Ibid.*

[9] *Ibid.*, p. 23.

[10] *Ibid.*, p. 1.

with May 1944 the source of these data is the AMPR, #2, or the corrections thereto submitted by the facility or the district office.[11]

All model-facility combinations in the *Source Book* that satisfied the following criteria were used in the analysis:

1. More than 1,000 airframes of a given model were produced in the facility.
2. Data for airframes with *N* of less than 100 were available for the facility.
3. More than 60 percent of direct labor in any given month was on-site production in the facility provided the cumulative *N* had reached 100.

The model-facility combinations that satisfied these criteria were:

1. B-29 Boeing, Wichita
2. B-18 Boeing, Seattle
3. B-24 Ford, Willow Run
4. B-24 Con-Vult., Ft. Worth
5. B-25 N. American, Inglewood
6. B-26 Martin, Baltimore
7. A-20 (DB-7) Douglas, Santa Monica
8. A-30 Martin, Baltimore
9. A-26 Douglas, Long Beach
10. TBM Eastern, Trenton
11. P-40 Curtiss, Buffalo
12. P-39 Bell, Buffalo
13. P-51 (A-36) N. American, Inglewood
14. P-51 N. American, Dallas
15. RP-63 A & C Bell, Buffalo
16. FM1 Eastern, Linden
17. F6F Grumman, Bethpage

---

[11] *Ibid.*, p. 37.

18. PT-13-17 (N2S) Boeing, Wichita
19. C-46 Curtiss, Buffalo
20. C-47 Douglas, Oklahoma City
21. AT-6 (SNJ) N. American, Dallas
22. AT-10 Beech, Wichita

The above facilities were classified into four groups: bombers, fighters, trainers, and transports.

STATISTICAL ANALYSIS

Question 1: *How long does the decline continue?* In every case there was no evidence of any cessation of a decline. This conclusion is based on visual examination of the graphs presented in the *Source Book*. No elaborate statistical analysis appears to be needed to answer this question, given the available data. Whether or not the decline would cease for substantially larger *N* could not, of course, be determined.

Question 2: *Does the progress curve correspond fundamentally to a linear function on double-log scale?* The purpose of this study is to evaluate the reliability of the learning curve as commonly used in its linear form. Furthermore, a test for linearity would require specification of some alternative nonlinear functional forms for comparison. Since it appeared that the observations would not be sufficient to give a very powerful test of the linear hypothesis with respect to some acceptable alternative, it was believed best to postpone such possible tests until more adequate observations were available. For the rest of this study linearity is simply postulated.

The appropriateness of the linear function as a descriptive device for the accumulated data is indicated by the coefficients of correlation. These exceeded .90 in 16 of the model-facility combinations and exceeded .80 in the six other cases.

Question 3: *Is the progress curve slope or height the same for all the model-facility combinations?* For the first three categories of airframe the following hypotheses were tested for *each category separately:* H_1—The k samples from the bombers ($k = 9$), fighters ($k = 8$), and trainers ($k = 3$) are samples from populations with constant height, a_0 (unspecified). H_2—The k samples are from populations with slope b_0 (unspecified). Transports were not tested since there were only two acceptable model-facility combinations (hereafter called MFCs).

TABLE 1
Analysis of Variance Test of H_1
H_1: The samples from each category (bombers, fighters, trainers) are from populations with equal intercepts; A_0 (unspecified)

Category	*Source of variation*	*Sum of squares (a)*	*Degrees of freedom (b)*	*Mean square (a/b)*	*F*
Bombers	(1) among MFC	26.24	8	3.28	
	(2) within MFC	1.3400	300	.00447	
					733
Fighters	(1) among MFC	22.1007	7	3.157	
	(2) within MFC	.88806	248	.00358	
					882
Trainers	(1) among MFC	46.042	2	23.021	
	(2) within MFC	.2757	122	.00226	
					11.371

Note: $F_{.01}$ exceeded in all cases.

One difficulty in applying standard statistical tests to these hypotheses is that the residuals around the progress function are serially correlated. This reduces the number of degrees of freedom and almost always understates the size of the internally estimated error. Crude allowance can be made for this effect by assuming that the degrees of freedom are equal to a fraction of the number of observations. In this study the fraction is one fourth, which is believed to err on the side of making it more difficult to deny the two hypotheses.

Table 1 presents the analysis of variance of H_1 for each of the three categories. Table 2 summarizes the analysis of covariance for H_2 for each of the three categories.

Because of the qualifications expressed above about the available degrees of freedom, the critical F ratios for .05 and .01 probability are degrees of freedom estimated at one fourth of the number of observations.

In every case the hypotheses H_1 and H_2 are very clearly denied. This means that question 3 has a negative answer. One may conclude that if a linear relationship between log m and log N exists, it exists only uniquely for each particular MFC. The relationships differ in slope and height even among the various facilities producing the same general type of airframe (bombers, fighters, or trainers). The denial of H_1 and H_2 also constitutes a denial of homogeneity of the a_i and b_i where the MFCs are not classified according to bomber, fighter, and trainer types.

This means that it is wrong to regard all the individual MFCs as having the same progress function. It is wrong in the sense that if there are linear functional relationships between log m and log N within individual MFCs, they do not have the same heights or slopes. But just as we do not require that everything be equal before considering them fundamentally alike for practical purposes, so one may talk of an average of the curves. Whether the use of the average as typical is appropriate or adequate can be judged only in terms of the margins of error resulting when one uses this averaging technique. It is these margins of error which will now be evaluated.

TABLE 2

Analysis of Variance Test of H_2

H_2: The samples from each category (bombers, trainers, fighters) are from populations with equal slopes, β (unspecified)

Category	*Source of variation*	*Sum of squares (a)*	*Degrees of freedom (b)*	*Mean square (a/b)*	*F*
Bombers	(1) among individual regression coefficients	1.57685	8	.19711	
	(2) within sample individual regression coefficient residuals	2.09592	300	.00698	
					28.2
Fighters	(1) among individual regression coefficients	1.2467	7	.17811	
	(2) within sample individual regression coefficient residuals	1.11903	248	.00451	
					39.49
Trainers	(1) among individual regression coefficients	1.24	2	.62008	
	(2) within sample individual regression coefficient residuals	.4847	122	.00397	
					156.2

Note: $F_{.01}$ exceeded in all cases.

MARGINS OF ERROR

The margin of error depends upon what is being predicted. One may predict the direct labor per pound of a given type of airframe or the cumulated direct labor requirements for the production of a given number of airframes of a particular type. The latter was selected for study as more important. The margins of error will be relatively smaller for cumulative requirements than for marginal requirements, since variations in marginal requirements will offset each other and tend to cancel out when cumulated into a sum of direct labor requirements. It might be added that if one were to seek a method of estimating cumulated direct labor requirements, he would ordinarily obtain a prediction equation directly between cumulated direct labor and N, rather than between marginal direct labor, m, and N. This particular study, however, was directed toward an examination of the progress curve concept as postulated in the *Source Book*.

The margin of error also depends on the type of progress curve used, of which there are at least three: (1) An industrywide average progress curve is one in which the a coefficient and b coefficient are obtained by combining all the data into one heterogeneous set. (2) The airframes can be classified on some basis, such as type of airframe (bomber, fighter, trainer), and for each class the a and b coefficients can be computed by pooling the data for that set. (3) The various MFCs can be kept separate and a and b can be derived for each from the early buildup part of its operations (to an approximate peak rate—usually occurring 1 to 1½ years after the tenth frame was produced). Questions 4, 5, and 6 deal with predictions made from each of these three progress curve types, respectively.

It is essential to note that because H_1 and H_2 were denied, which means that progress curves type (1) and (2) are really averages of heterogeneous concepts, there is no readily available method of deriving from the internal error variance the margin of error of any of the estimates that might be made with these two types of curve. Therefore an alternative procedure was used for estimating the margin of error. For each facility predictions of direct labor requirements were made by means of the progress curves and compared with realizations as given in Table 3 of the *Source Book*.

Question 4: *How reliable are the predictions derived from an industrywide average progress curve?* An industrywide average progress curve was obtained by combining all the observations from the 20 selected MFCs (excluding transports) into one large sample. The resulting progress curve was integrated from zero to 1,000 to obtain an estimate of the cumulated direct labor requirements for the first 1,000 airframes in any MFC. Since these requirements are on a per-pound basis and since weights of airframes differ from type to type, the cumulated direct labor requirements per pound were multiplied by the weights of the airframes. Adjustments were made for changes in the weights of airframes due to modifications in design. Thus for each MFC an estimate was obtained of the required cumulated direct man hours for the first 1,000 airframes.[12] The prediction of direct labor requirements was confined to 1,000 airframes because it was presumed that by the time 1,000 airframes had been made the particular MFC could use its own experience for further prediction. Table 3 presents the resulting predictions and realiza-

[12] In the cases of a few models the estimate had to be made for a range starting a little beyond the first plane and extending to the 1,000th airframe. This was necessitated by the lack of check data for early production.

TABLE 3

Predictions of Direct Labor Requirements for First 1,000 Planes (Less N_0) by Industry Progress Curve and by Airframe-Type Progress Curve

			Man hours (Millions)			$\frac{P_r - A_c}{A_c}$ *(Percent)*	
j	*Model-Facility combination*	N_0	*Predicted by*				
			Industry curve	*Airframe type curve*	*Actual reported*	*Industry curve*	*Airframe type curve*
	Bombers:						
1	B29 Boeing, Wichita	0	107	99	76	+41	+30
2	B17 Boeing, Seattle	45	48	40	52	− 8	−23
3	B24 Ford, Willow Run	0	52	48	35	+49	+37
4	B24 Con. Vult., Ft. Worth	79	43	37	25	+72	+48
5	B25 N. Amer., Inglewood	0	28	26	18	+56	+44
6	B26 Martin, Baltimore	0	34	31	30	+13	+03
7	A20 (DB7) Douglas, Santa Monica	0	21	19	21	0	−10
8	A30 Martin, Baltimore	0	20	19	19	+ 5	0
9	A26 Douglas, Long Beach	0	32	30	28	+14	+07
	Error per bomber facility					29	22
	Weighted average* per bomber facility					29	24
	Fighters:						
10	TBM Eastern, Trenton	7	15	17	17	−12	0
11	P40 Curtiss, Buffalo	9	7	8	7	+ 9	+22

12	P39 Bell, Buffalo	0	8	9	9	− 7	+ 4
13	P51 (A36) N. Amer., Inglewood	0	10	11	7	+41	+57
14	P51 N. American, Dallas	0	10	11	7	+37	+52
15	RP63 A & C Bell, Buffalo	—	—	—	—	—	—
16	FM1 Eastern, Linden	23	7	8	13	−41	−34
17	F6F Grumman, Bethpage	22	12	13	12	− 3	+ 9
	Error per fighter facility					21	25
	Weighted average* per fighter facility					20	21
	Trainers:						
18	AT6 N. American, Dallas	0	6	7	3	+73	+87
19	AT10 Beech, Wichita	19	7	8	4	+58	+71
20	PT13-17 Boeing, Wichita	20	3	3	5	−45	−40
	Error per trainer facility					59	66
	Weighted average* per trainer facility					56	62
	Transports:						
21	C46 Curtiss, Buffalo	0	53	—	55	−04	—
22	C47 Douglas, Oklahoma City	0	28	—	23	+22	—
	Weighted average* per transport facility					09	—
All Facilities:							
	Error per facility (nonalgebraic average)					28	29
	Weighted* error per facility (nonalgebraic)					25	25

*Weighted by actual man hours.
—Means not computed.

tions. It will be seen that the absolute differences between predicted and actual values[13] average 25 percent of the actual.

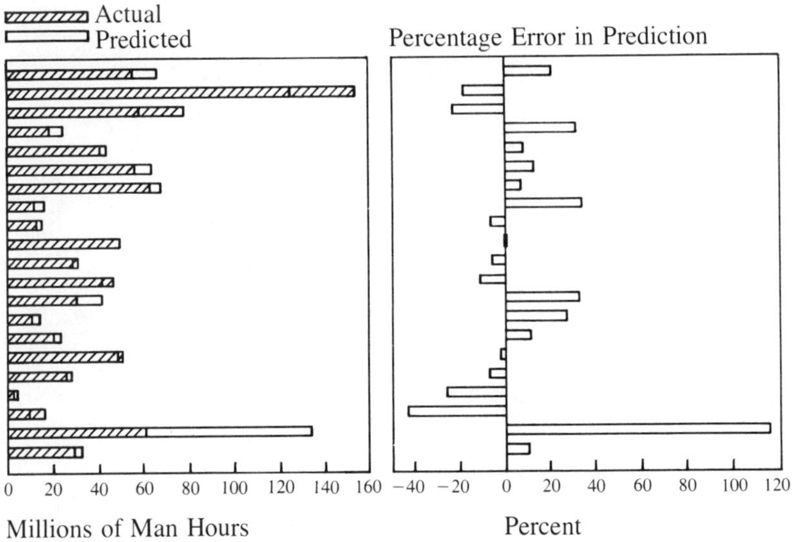

Figure 1. Predicted and actual direct labor requirements (after production buildup); predictions by each model-facility combination's progress curve during buildup period.

Question 5: *How reliable are the predictions derived from a general airframe-type progress curve?* With the airframe-type curve (bomber, fighter, trainer) predictions for each MFC were made for both zero to 1,000 airframes and for the entire run of airframes produced by the various MFCs. The bomber-type curve was obtained by combining the observations from the nine bomber MFCs into one large sample. That is, the observations were pooled but not the sample covariances. The fighter-type coefficients were obtained by similarly combining observations on the eight fighter types, and the trainer

[13] Weighted by actual man hours.

coefficients were obtained from the three trainer types. For each MFC prediction the corresponding type curve was integrated over the appropriate range. This integral, when multiplied by the weight of the plane, is the predicted cumulated direct labor requirement.

Predictions and realizations are given in Table 3 for the first 1,000 airframes. The percentage of error is defined as the ratio of the difference between predicted and actual values to the actual. The weighted average of these errors (nonalgebraic) is 25 percent. This failure to obtain a smaller margin of error by using type curves rather than the industry average curve suggests that there is no significant difference between the average *a*'s and *b*'s by airframe types. Table 4 contains the results for the complete run for each MFC. In this latter set of predictions the error again averages 26 percent.

Question 6: *How reliable is a single MFC's own early buildup progress curve for predicting its subsequent direct labor requirements?* For each particular MFC a progress curve was estimated from the buildup portion (usually lasting about one year) of its own production experience. With this equation predictions were made of the direct labor requirements for the rest of the production run. Predictions were obtained by integrating the progress curve and multiplying by airframe weight. These predictions were then compared with realizations. Coefficients of the "buildup" progress curves are presented in Table 5. The results of the predictions are presented in Table 6. The average margin of error (ratio of absolute error to actual requirements) is about 22 percent. Inspection of the results does not indicate any correlation of the relative size of the error or prediction with either the number of airframes for which direct labor is predicted, or the type of the airframe. Figure 1 is a graphic summary of the results.

TABLE 4

Predicted and Actual Direct Labor Requirements for Total Production
Based on Airframe-Type Progress Curves

j	*Model-facility combination*	N_o	N_z	*Direct man hours* — *Predicted based on type curve*	*Direct man hours* — *Reported actual*	$\frac{P_r - A_c}{A_c}$
				(Millions)		(Percent)
	Bombers:					
1	B29 Boeing, Wichita	0	1606	132	94	+40
2	B17 Boeing, Seattle	45	6949	151	179	−21
3	B24 Ford, Willow Run	0	8238	169	108	+56
4	B24 Con. Vult., Ft. Worth	79	1927	60	37	−62
5	B25 N. Amer., Inglewood	0	3180	52	47	+11
6	B26 Martin, Baltimore	0	3677	71	71	0
7	A20 (DB-7) Douglas, Santa Monica	0	5685	58	81	−20
8	A30 Martin, Baltimore	0	1566	25	25	0
9	A26 Douglas, Long Beach	0	1107	31	29	+07
	Error per bomber facility					24
	Weighted error* per bomber facility					27

	Fighters:					
10	TBM Eastern, Trenton	7	7190	73	72	+01
11	P40 Curtiss, Buffalo	9	13686	63	87	−28
12	P39 Bell, Buffalo	0	9407	46	56	−18
13	P51 (A-36) N. Amer., Inglewood	0	9872	60	38	+58
14	P51 N. Amer., Dallas	0	4650	35	19	+84
15	RP63 A & C Bell, Buffalo	—	—	—	—	—
16	FM1 Eastern, Linden	23	5715	30	35	−14
17	F6F Grumman, Bethpage	22	12211	86	71	+21
	Error per fighter facility					32
	Weighted error* per fighter facility					25
	Trainers:					
18	AT6 N. Amer., Dallas	0	12811	41	35	+17
19	AT10 Beech, Wichita	19	1700	11	7	+64
20	PT13-17 Boeing, Wichita	20	8419	14	20	−30
	Error per fighter facility					37
	Weighted error* per trainer facility					27
Total — all facilities:						
	Error per facility					29
	Weighted error* per facility					26

*Weighted by actual man hours.
—Means not computed.

TABLE 5
First and Second Portion Progress Curves — Individual Model-Facility Combinations

j	*Model-facility combination (MFC)*	*Range of product 1st portion*	*Progress curve for 1st portion intercept*	*slope*	*Progress curve for 2nd portion intercept*	*slope*	*Range of production for 2nd portion*
1	B29 Boeing, Wichita	0— 267	1.41	.48	2.21	.78	268— 1606
2	B17 Boeing, Seattle	45— 385	1.87	.58	1.45	.43	386— 6949
3	B24 Ford, Willow Run	0— 769	1.69	.61	1.62	.55	770— 8238
4	B24 Con. Vult., Ft. Worth	79— 711	1.25	.43	1.94	.68	712— 1927
5	B25 N. Amer., Inglewood	0— 242	.64	.19	1.14	.35	243— 3180
6	B26 Martin, Baltimore	0— 409	1.17	.35	1.54	.47	410— 3677
7	A20m Douglas, Santa Monica	0— 623	1.14	.30	—	—	624— 5685
8	A30 Martin, Baltimore	0— 651	.88	.21	—	—	652— 1566
9	A26 Douglas, Long Beach	0— 402	1.24	.38	1.20	.35	403— 1107
10	TBM Eastern, Trenton	7—1335	1.23	.32	1.86	.49	1336— 7190
11	P40 Curtiss, Buffalo	9—8494	.81	.16	.13	.08	8495—13686
12	D30 Bell, Buffalo	0—1073	1.05	.26	.99	.22	1074— 9407
13	P51 N. Amer., Inglewood	0— 910	.77	.21	—	—	911— 9872
14	P51 N. Amer., Dallas	0—1248	1.04	.32	3.19	.97	1249— 4650
15	RP63 Bell, Buffalo	—	—	—	—	—	—
16	FM1 Eastern, Linden	23—1215	1.65	.42	2.14	.57	1216— 5715
17	F6F Grumman, Bethpage	22—2097	1.27	.35	1.43	.39	2098—12211
18	AT6 N. Amer., Dallas	0—2089	.52	.15	.97	.26	2090—12811
19	AT10 Beech, Wichita	19— 560	1.11	.39	—	—	561— 1700
20	PT13-17 Boeing, Wichita	20— 720	2.19	.63	1.37	.33	721— 8419
21	C46 Curtiss, Buffalo	450	.63	.06	—	—	451— 2526
22	C47 Douglas, Oklahoma City	1384	1.50	.48	.90	.31	1385— 5190

—Means not computed

Question 7: What are some possible consequences of these errors of estimate? The consequences of the errors of estimate in predicting cumulated direct labor requirements can be determined only in the context of some specific problem. As an illustration the following example is presented. If 1,000 airframes have been produced and if a total of 5,000 is to be produced, one may estimate the required amount of labor for the next 4,000 airframes. Suppose that the slope of the progress curve had been computed to be $-.32$.[14] Now suppose it is discovered that the predicted amount of direct labor required was 20 percent less than that actually required. How many planes would have been produced by the time the predicted amount of direct labor had been used? Only 3,100, or 22 percent less than the extra 4,000 required. If instead the prediction had overstated the required amount, then utilization of the predicted amount would have resulted in 5,030 airframes or 27 percent too many.[15] A review of the figures given in the earlier part of this report will indicate that the above example is not an unusual one. In general, an error in estimating direct labor requirements implies a greater discrepancy between actual and expected airframe production.

ALTERNATIVE PROGRESS FUNCTIONS

Alternative relationships between direct labor per pound of airframe, cumulative N, time and rate of production have been suggested and investigated with the present data. The results cast doubts on any of the alternatives being better fits than the usual progress curve. The principal reason that little improvement would be expected is the presence of very high correla-

---

[14] This is equivalent to an 80 percent progress curve.

[15] See Appendix for mathematical derivation.

TABLE 6

Predicted and Actual Direct Labor Requirements for 2nd Portion of Production Based on Individual Model-Facility Combination Progress Curves (1st Portion)

j	*Model-facility combination*	*Second portion range of cumulative production*	*Predicted direct labor man hours based on MFC curve of first portion*	*Reported actual*	$\frac{P_r - mA_c}{A_c}$
			(Millions)	(Millions)	
1	B-29 Boeing, Wichita	268— 1606	67	56	+.20
2	B-17 Boeing, Seattle	386— 6949	125	154	−.19
3	B-24 Ford, Willow Run	770— 8238	59	78	−.24
4	B-24 Con. Vult., Ft. Worth	712— 1927	25	19	+.31
5	B-25 N. Amer., Inglewood	243— 3180	44	41	+.07
6	B-26 Martin, Baltimore	410— 3677	64	57	+.12
7	A-20 (DB-7) Douglas, Santa Monica	624— 5685	68	64	+.06
8	A-30 Martin, Baltimore	652— 1566	16	12	+.31
9	A-26 Douglas, Long Beach	403— 1107	14	15	−.07
10	TBM Eastern, Trenton	1336— 7190	50	50	.00
11	P-40 Curtiss, Buffalo	8495—13686	29	31	−.06
12	P-39 Bell, Buffalo	1074— 9407	42	47	−.11
13	P-51 (A-36) N. Amer., Inglewood	911— 9872	41	31	+.32
14	P-51 N. Amer., Dallas	1249— 4650	14	11	+.26
15	RP-63 A & C Bell, Buffalo	*	*	*	*

j	*Model-facility combination*	*Second portion range of cumulative production*	*Predicted direct labor man hours based on MFC curve of first portion*	*Reported actual*	$\frac{P_r - mA_c}{A_c}$
16	FM1 Eastern, Linden	1216— 5715	23	21	+.10
17	F6F Grumman, Bethpage	2098—12211	50	51	−.02
18	AT-6 (SNJ) N. Amer., Dallas	2090—12811	26	28	−.07
19	AT-10 Beech, Wichita	560— 1700	3	4	−.27
20	PT-13-17 (N2S) Boeing, Wichita	721— 8419	9	16	−.44
21	C-46 Curtiss, Buffalo	451— 2526	134	62	+1.16
22	C-47 Douglas, Oklahoma City	1385— 5190	32	29	+.10
	Error per facility				.21
	Weighted error per facility				.22

*Not computed.

tion among time, N, and ΔN. The various other relationships considered for each particular MFC were:

a. $\log m = a_2 + b_2 T$, where T is time.

b. $\log m = a_3 + b_3 T + b_4 \Delta N$, where ΔN *is rate of production* per month.

c. $\log m = a_4 + b_5 \log T + b_6 \log \Delta N$.

d. $\log m = a_5 + b_7 T + b_8 \log \Delta N$.

e. $\log m = a_6 + b_9 T + b_{10} \log N$.

f. $\log m = a_7 + b_{11} \log N + b_{12} \log \Delta N$.

CONCLUSION

The preceding analysis has been concerned with the margin of error to be expected when estimating direct labor requirements and cumulative airframe production by the linear progress curve if the basic assumption of historical similarity of production conditions is fulfilled. The virtual certainty of nonfulfillment of some part of the basic assumption would increase the magnitude and seriousness of error. In each case there should be an investigation of the range of uncertainty in prediction (e.g., acceleration curves and program feasibilities, which are in part derived from and based on "progress curves") before making decisions. This follows from the fact that reliable decisions can be made only among those alternative programs that are disparate beyond the range of uncertainty of error of estimate of the predictive method.

Appendix [16]

The basis for the calculations on page 355 is as follows.

Labor expended in the production of the first n_0 items is A_0. Total labor, A_e, required for the production of a total required number, n_r, is estimated by the formula

[16] This mathematical derivation was made by H. Germond.

$$A_e = A_0 \left(\frac{n_r}{n_0}\right)^{1-m}.$$

The total labor actually required for the production of n_r is some quantity $A_r = A_e$.

Assuming the formula is correct, but that the estimation of the value of m is in error, what would have been the actual production, n_a, had the estimated labor, A_e, been expended? This is given by

$$\log n_a/n_r = \frac{-(\log n_r/n_0)\ (\log A_r/A_e)}{(1 - m)\ (\log n_r/n_0) + \log A_r/A_e}$$

where the logarithms are taken to any convenient base.

In terms of the additional labor estimated, B_e, and the additional labor required, B_r, to build the additional $n_r - n_0$ items,

$$\frac{A_r}{A_e}\ \frac{A_0 + B_r}{A_0 + B_e} = 1 + \left[1 - \left(\frac{n_0}{n_r}\right)^{1-m}\right] \frac{B_r - B_e}{B_e}.$$

In terms of P, the "slope of the progress curve,"

$$m = \frac{-\log P}{\log 2}.$$

The ratio of the difference between actual and required output to the required additional output is

$$\frac{n_a - n_r}{n_r - n_0} = \sum_4 \left(\frac{n_a}{n_r} - 1\right).$$

Example: Suppose $n_r = 5\, n_0$, and P is erroneously estimated to be 80 percent. Then

$$m = \frac{-\log 0.80}{\log 2} = 0.321928,$$

$$\frac{A_r}{A_e} = 1 + \left[1 - (0.2)^{0.678072}\right] \frac{B_r - B_e}{B_e}$$

$$= 1 + 0.664225 \frac{B_r - B_e}{B_e},$$

$$\log_{10} n_a/n_r = \frac{-0.69897 \log_{10} A_r/A_e}{0.47395 + \log_{10} A_r/A_e},$$

and

$$\frac{n_a - n_r}{n_r - n_0} = \frac{5}{4}\left(\frac{n_a}{n_r} - 1\right).$$

Suppose, now, the estimated labor for the production of the $n_r - n_0$ additional units is found to be error by 20 percent, depending upon (1) $B_e = 1.2\, B_r$, or (2) $B_e = 0.8\, B_r$. Carrying out the computation yields the results given in the text.

IV

Inflation: Impact and Measurement

14

Effects of Inflation

The object of this paper is to derive the implications of inflation, defined as rising prices. The ensuing analysis attempts to discern the consequences or implications of inflation itself—whatever may have caused it. Therefore little attention will be paid to the other effects of the events that may be regarded as causes of inflation, such as increases in the quantity of money, velocity changes, reductions in physical stocks, droughts, plagues, unemployment, wars, or other events that have produced inflation.

Inflations may be usefully classified as (*a*) anticipated or (*b*) unanticipated. Anticipated inflation is characterized by market phenomena implied by the postulate that prices are expected to rise. Unanticipated inflation is characterized by market phenomena implied by the alternative postulate that the contemporaneous level of prices is expected to persist.[1] Inflation,

This article was coauthored by Reuben A. Kessel and is part of a larger study of inflation financed by the Merrill Foundation for the Advancement of Financial Knowledge. An earlier version of this paper was presented at the Money Workshop of the University of Chicago. The authors also benefited from the comments of Professor Karl Brunner, University of California, Los Angeles.

[1] Widespread expectation that current prices will remain unchanged, when they are in fact rising, is not a necessary condition for the existence of unanticipated infla-

of either type and regardless of cause, is defined as a rise in the general level of prices.[2]

This paper discusses the demand for money, the economics of unanticipated inflation, the transitional or intermediate stage between unanticipated and anticipated inflation, fully anticipated inflation, and deflation.

I. THE DEMAND FOR MONEY

Inflation and the demand to hold money are intimately related. Therefore it is relevant to inquire: how is the effectiveness with which money performs its functions affected by inflation? To answer this question, it is convenient to classify the spectrum of assets into two categories, monetary and real (or nonmonetary). Monetary assets are claims to fixed numbers of dollars, currency, bank deposits, bonds, notes. In contrast, real assets refer to assets whose nominal yields are affected by price-level changes. Examples are equities, real property, inventories.[3] For business firms and individuals money is an asset and in equilibrium the marginal net productivity of a dollar of money is equal to that of a dollar's worth of any other assets—bonds, inventories, houses.

---

tion. Some may expect prices to rise, others may expect them to fall. On balance, the anticipations of the market can be different from the anticipations of every individual in the market.

[2] Problems of defining a measure of the general price level, although present, are ignored on the grounds that general agreement among observers as to when the general level of prices has or has not risen is sufficiently common to permit unambiguous identification of periods of inflation.

[3] Resort to the credit market is of course another alternative to the holding of cash balances and constitutes a substitute for money. Since repayment of debt is never certain, credit costs must reflect the existence of this risk. Therefore, for some fraction of an individual's wealth, it is cheaper to hold some cash balances than it is to hold no cash at all and utilize credit markets. This is especially true when ''assets'' are in human as against nonhuman form.

Money, like any asset, is a store of value. Yet money appears, superficially, to be at a disadvantage because real assets yield an income stream whereas money yields "nothing." This raises the questions: What properties of money enable it to compete successfully with assets that yield an explicit income stream? What are the services that money provides that offset the absence of an explicit yield?

Two interdependent properties are relevant. First, money can be used to hedge against changes in both relative prices and interest rates. Factors that affect relative prices have comparatively little impact on the general level of prices and conversely. As a result, the purchasing power of money is unaffected by relative price changes. In a world in which future price changes cannot be foreseen, money provides a hedge, and if prices are stable or falling, a cheap hedge, against this uncertainty.

The second distinctive attribute of money in modern societies is the zero, or near zero, transactions cost associated with the exchange of money for other resources. Money is the most liquid of assets, if liquidity is measured by the difference between buying and selling prices at any instant of time. Because of these zero transaction costs, virtually everyone finds it optimal to hold some money. In principle, the rate of savings on transactions costs resulting from holding money equals the rate of interest. For any given rate of interest, the proportions of wealth held in money, money substitutes, and other assets will depend at any moment upon the probability of converting various amounts of wealth into other economic resources in ensuing moments. In other words, the degree to which receipts and expenditures are synchronized influences the fraction of wealth that one chooses to hold in the form of money. For example, the portion of a farmer's wealth held in the form of money will often be larger than that proportion for a civil service worker or *rentier*.

For performing the functions of money there exists substitutes. A portfolio of real assets could be selected so as to provide a hedge against most relative price changes. Only interest-rate changes could not be hedged thereby. Securities with low transactions costs and short maturities, such as Treasury bills, can also function as a money substitute.

An asset's substitutability for money depends upon its value as a hedge against relative price changes and its transactions costs. Government fiat or debt money is better than private debt money (demand deposits), because private money can be affected by the particular fortunes of individual banking enterprises, as has been demonstrated by the banking crises in American economic history (particularly during the Great Depression); and it often can be negotiated more cheaply. Insofar as a government insures bank deposits, savings and loan shares, or mortgages, it reduces the vulnerability of private debt to the risks of private enterprise. The value of bank deposits is affected less by imprudent lending policies of banks, embezzlements, and so on. Hence such insurance improves the substitutability of private debts for government money. This analysis also implies that short-term securities are a better substitute for money than comparable long-term obligations, and government securities are better than privately issued securities.[4] Human resources in the form of effort and ingenuity devoted to achieving a more perfect synchronization between receipts and expenditures are also substitutes for money. This suggests that the use of money in modern societies is a result

[4] For a more detailed statement of the ideas presented here see J. C. Gilbert, "The Demand for Money: The Development of an Economic Concept," *Journal of Political Economy* 61 (April 1953): 144–59.

of cost advantages, and that the ratio of money to other assets held, particularly money substitutes, will change with these costs.

Some of these costs are specific to money and would not necessarily be incurred if assets other than money are held; examples are charges for checking accounts and depreciation through inflation (appreciation in the value of money through deflation can be regarded as a negative cost).[5] As with any asset, the relevant cost and income streams are those expected or anticipated. At the margin, the difference between the capitalized value of the expenditure and receipt streams associated with holding a dollar must of course be equal to a dollar. Similarly at the margin, the difference in the yield between an interest-bearing security and money represents an equalizing difference that measures the difference in the money services of the two assets. A change in this difference attributable to changes in the yield of physical capital implies a change in the demand for money.

The demand for money, like the demand for any resource, is a real demand. People want to hold command in the form of money over some volume of real resources, and not just over a certain number of pieces of paper. This demand can be expressed in either nominal or real terms. To convert from one to the other, an index number of general prices is necessary. The stock of nominal balances in existence at any moment of time is independent of the real value of that stock. Price-level changes, changes in output and employment, and interest-rate

[5] Economists have become accustomed to viewing the interest rate as the opportunity cost of holding money. This is correct in only a world of interest-bearing securities and money; it is not correct in a world that contains assets such as Van Gogh paintings, houses, and automobiles, for holding these assets also involves that interest cost.

changes can bring into equality desires to hold real balances with any specified stock of nominal balances in existence.

Inflation, whether or not it is anticipated, increases the cost of holding money. However, inflation will reduce the real balances a community is willing to hold only if it is anticipated. The fact that the costs of holding money have increased in the past as a consequence of unanticipated inflation has implications for the future costs of holding real balances only insofar as past inflation influences expectations about the future. It is only with respect to the future that one has alternatives with respect to the size of cash balances held; present and past costs are "sunk" costs. The same is true for deflation: unless a decrease in the cost of holding money is anticipated because falling prices are expected, the real demand for money will not be influenced.

For these reasons the state or expectations about inflation are crucial for predicting the effects of inflation. If inflation is unanticipated, that is, if the holders of cash balances on the average expect the contemporaneous level of prices to persist, then one set of implications is generated. These are the economics of unanticipated inflation. But, if the holders of cash balances taken as a group expect the general level of prices to rise, then a second and quite different set of implications follow. These constitute the economics of anticipated inflation.

II. ECONOMICS OF UNANTICIPATED INFLATION

A. Inaccurate Foresight and Wealth Transfers

The defining characteristic of unanticipated inflation is the expectation that the current price level will persist when prices are in fact rising. Estimates of future price-level changes are biased downward, that is, below realized price-level changes.[6] Consequently, the impact of realized but unanticipated inflation upon the actual costs of holding money fails to affect the quantity of real balances held. Yet prices, the nominal stock of wealth, and the demand for nominal money all increase.

The expectation that the current price level will persist implies that the equilibrium money rates of interest observed in capital markets are unaffected by unanticipated inflation. No changes in the relative demand and supply of bonds are implied by the observed depreciation in the purchasing power of money.[7] Consequently, interest rates fail to rise enough (real yields on bonds fall below that required) to maintain preinflation economic relations between debtors and creditors. The nominal rate of interest fails to reflect rising prices because estimates of the course of future prices are biased, not because of market imperfections. As a result there are transfers of wealth from net monetary creditors to debtors.[8] What is true of debtors and creditors linked by indebtedness in the form of bonds is equally true of all debtors and creditors regardless of the specific security creating this relationship, which may be bonds, mortgages, notes, bills, acceptances, or contingent sales contracts; relationships between debtors and creditors are

[6] Expectations about the future course of prices need not be uniform. They may vary yet be so balanced that rising prices do not affect holdings of real balances.

[7] There is an absolute increase in the demand for bonds because the proportion of debt to wealth has decreased. If both demand and supply increase to the same extent, there will be no change in either bond prices or interest rates.

[8] This difference between the yield required to maintain pre-unanticipated inflation debtor-creditor relations and the yield realized corresponds to what I. Fisher termed the difference between the money and the real rate of interest (*The Theory of Interest* [New York: Macmillan, 1930], pp. 43–44).

systematically affected.[9] No income effects, other than those flowing from the wealth transfer, are implied.

This wealth transfer can be detected in the stock market. Prices of common stocks of net debtor companies (whose monetary liabilities exceed their monetary assets) rise relative to those of net creditor companies (whose monetary liabilities are less than their monetary assets). Similarly, individuals whose monetary liabilities exceed their monetary assets realize gains. These gains are the losses of those whose monetary assets exceed their monetary liabilities. Unanticipated inflation transfers wealth from net monetary creditors to net monetary debtors, regardless of whether the creditors and debtors are corporations, governments, widows, orphans, schoolteachers.

Taking all debts into account, public and private, the largest debtor in an economy is usually a governmental unit. Holders of government debt lose directly to the government. This gain can be used to reduce taxes or increase governmental expenditures without increasing taxes. Creditors, who lose wealth, typically react by reducing their consumption (and possibly saving). They have lost wealth because of rising prices and this loss is the wealth gain of net monetary debtors.[10]

---

[9] The rate of interest will temporarily fall in response to an increase in the nominal stock of money; with an increased stock of money (sprinkled, say, from the sky), people will increase their demand for other assets, among them bonds. Presumably this increased demand for bonds will lead to a rise in interest rates followed by an increase in the volume of bonds outstanding. The willingness to issue bonds increases as a result of the increase in wealth.

[10] Conversely, private debtors increase their consumption. No one is forced to reduced consumption or engage in "forced savings" in order for inflation to transfer wealth. An entire community can, in principle, maintain its consumption standards in the face of wealth losses attributable to rising prices. The maintenance of consumption standards is not inconsistent with the use of inflation to acquire resources. What is crucial for taxation through inflation, as shall be developed, is the willingness of the community to exchange real resources for money in the face of rising prices.

B. The Inflation Tax on Money

Inflation can be deliberately utilized as a tax. A government can acquire resources by creating and spending new fiat money. This policy can cause prices to rise, and it is this rise in prices that reveals the transfer of wealth to the government from money-holders and reduces the wealth position of all (including government) creditors.[11] Thus it is not merely the creation of fiat money, it is the inflation that "taxes" money-holders and creditors. The gain in wealth by the government or creator of fiat money is revealed to the community when rising prices reduce the value of a nominal unit of money.[12]

This distinction may be illustrated by an analogy. If a thief steals your car (and his wealth increases), does your wealth decrease when you go out to use your car and discover it is gone, or does it decrease at the instant it is stolen, even though you don't know about it? The temptation to say it is decreased at the moment the car is stolen is strong, yet it must be remembered that behavior and expenditure patterns are unaffected until the theft of the car is discovered! For purposes of deriving implications about reactions to a reduction in wealth, it is the discovery of the theft that is crucial. For other purposes, it may be the moment that the theft occurred.

---

[11] For an exposition of how a government obtains resources through inflation, see A. Alchian and R. Kessel, "How the Government Gains from Inflation," *Proceedings of the 30th Annual Meeting of the Western Economic Association* (Stanford, Calif.: Stanford University Press, 1955), pp. 13–16; also M. Friedman, *Essays in Positive Economics* (Chicago: University of Chicago Press, 1953), p. 253.

[12] In a full-employment economy, an increase in the nominal monetary stock implies a tax upon creditors whether or not prices rise. The creation of fiat money implies a higher level of prices than would otherwise exist. Consequently, the welfare of creditors is adversely affected. For example, a policy designed to maintain stable prices in a progressive society characterized by an income-elastic demand for money implies a tax upon creditors. H. Simons proposed discharging governmental interest-bearing obligations by such a policy (*Economic Policy for a Free Society* [Chicago: University of Chicago Press, 1948], p. 234).

Only if the new fiat money were initially given to individuals (instead of spent by the government) in proportion to the money already held could there be no wealth transfers from fiat money-holders. The reduced value of a unit of fiat money could be offset by the new money acquired. Other interpersonal transfers would remain, because other assets and liabilities are fixed in terms of money. With respect to interest-bearing government obligations, the rise in the price level (inflation) implies a relatively lower return (or a lower "real" return) to the holders of these securities and a correspondingly lower cost of servicing this debt.

Virtually analogous reasoning applies to government-sponsored creation of money by banks for the purpose of monetizing governmental debt. When the yield on that debt is kept so low that a government cannot successfully compete for savings in the capital markets, it sells its obligations to the banking system in exchange for newly created private debt money (demand deposits). The expenditure of these demand deposits increases the price level, and thus reduces the wealth of the holders of governmental debt. Whether unanticipated inflation is caused by the issuance of fiat money or the expansion of bank deposits in order to monetize governmental debt, it constitutes an alternative to formal taxation.

Insofar as governments employ taxation through unanticipated inflation as an alternative to formal taxation, governmental creditors replace conventional taxpayers. The losses of holders of government interest-bearing obligations (the declines in the real values of the income streams accruing to owners of these securities) constitute a reduction in the costs to taxpayers of servicing governmental obligations. The beneficiaries of taxation through inflation are those whose total taxes, conventional and inflation, are lower than they otherwise would be.[13]

Unanticipated inflation can also be used as a means of private finance. When unanticipated inflation is caused by an expansion of bank credit at the instigation of private parties, banks exchange bank demand credit (money) for the obligations of their customers. These newly created deposits are spent for real resources in commodity markets, thereby driving up prices. This produces a gain in wealth for net monetary debtors at the expense of net monetary creditors. The initiating private individuals who exchanged their debt for bank money gain when prices rise only insofar as they are *net* monetary debtors.[14] The act of borrowing increases both the monetary assets and the liabilities of bank customers. Hence the act of borrowing does not per se imply gains during inflation. Bank borrowers typically become debtors by converting their newly acquired deposits into real resources. Hence they gain through inflation as debtors and not as initiators of inflation.[15]

---

[13] The transfer of wealth within the private sector of an economy as a result of the existence of private debt can be regarded as a negative or a positive "tax," as the case may be, for the purpose of evaluating the impact upon an economic unit of taxation through inflation as compared with alternative forms of taxation.

[14] This refers only to direct effects. Indirectly, neutrals (neutrals are defined as economic units whose monetary assets just equal their monetary liabilities) and possibly some creditors gain. This indirect gain is a result of a decrease in the real costs of servicing interest-bearing governmental liabilities.

[15] The losses of the holders of non-interest-bearing governmental obligations are not offset. There is, of course, a loss to the holders of cash and monetary assets generally as a result of the creation of new money regardless of what happens to prices. If the marginal effect of the creation of new money upon prices is positive, then losses are implied.

Considering only wealth effects constitutes an incomplete analysis of the forces operating to reconcile the demands for resources with the volume of resources available for acquisition. To illustrate: consider an inflationary expansion of bank credit in an economy that uses nongovernmental money exclusively. The ensuing

All of the foregoing has been an analysis of the effects of unanticipated inflation produced by an increase in the absolute stock of money. What if inflation results from a decrease in the physical stock of nonmoney resources? Suppose a community finds that its ratio of wealth in the form of money to wealth in nonmonetary forms is greater than it desires. It succeeds in reducing this ratio by increasing prices. This inflation results in transfers of wealth from net monetary creditors to net monetary debtors. Insofar as the government is a debtor, it gains even though it had no intention of acquiring resources through inflation. Whether or not there is a transfer of resources from creditors to debtors, there is a net loss of liquidity in the community.[16] This may be seen by considering the implications of the same event, a decrease in the stock of physical wealth, in an economy whose only money is fiat money and where there are no private or public debts. The real value of the money stock declines, total liquidity in the economy falls, and there are no transfers of wealth. Inflation still taxes the holders of money, but it produces no tax receipts.[17]

---

price increase does not reduce wealth; it does reduce the real value of liquid assets. Hence the stock of money and liquid assets falls relative to other assets and liabilities until that stock becomes an equilibrium stock. Then this inflation is brought to a halt. The effect of the expansion of bank credit is to reshuffle real resources and claims against these real resources with no decrease in the wealth position of the community as a whole.

[16] An interesting question can be posed. Suppose a community has only private debt money and every person, for the sake of analysis, has a private bank debt exactly equal to his demand deposit. In this event a decrease in real resources will produce an inflation, but will the inflation (not the reduction in real resources) also change anyone's real wealth if his monetary assets just equal his monetary liabilities? No. The real value of bank money and obligations to the banks will decrease by the same amount. Hence the fall in the real value of the monetary stock will not be associated with the redistribution of wealth.

[17] Objections to the use of inflation as a means of taxation have rested on equity grounds. Pesek has compared inflation, sales taxes, and income taxes and concludes, given the 1950 distribution of assets and incomes, that inflation is relatively

Employment and output effects are implied by inflation if the supply of labor is a function of money wage rates and if unemployment exists. For these circumstances inflation implies falling real wage rates. Hence inflation implies increases in the quantity of labor demanded and increases in output and employment.

C. Unanticipated Deflation

Formally, the analysis of unanticipated deflation is symmetrical to the analysis of unanticipated inflation. Wealth is redistributed from debtors to creditors. Falling prices produced a subsidy to the holders of governmental debt and a redistribution of wealth from debtors to creditors within the private sector of an economy. A subsidy to the holders of governmental debt through deflation is an alternative to other governmental expenditures just as taxation through inflation is an alternative to other taxes.

---

regressive. Hence he infers that lower income groups have an economic interest in the use of sales and income taxes, particularly income taxes, as an alternative to taxation through inflation. His conclusion follows only if a change from one tax to another affects the overall progressivity of a tax system, that is, of all taxes taken together. It is possible to hold constant both the progressivity of a tax system and tax receipts while varying the fraction of tax receipts attributable to a specific type of tax.

Pesek also maintains that we are continuously threatened by inflation. The evidence of the last hundred years indicates that the bulk of the inflation that has occurred in the United States is associated with wars when efficiency considerations are assigned more weight and equity considerations less weight than during peacetime.

A major difficulty with taxation through inflation as a long-run alternative is that it will become anticipated. Therefore it will have efficiency costs for an economy. For peacetime inflations that are not explained by desires to obtain resources for governmental purposes, but to achieve full employment, the appropriate opportunity costs of inflation are the loss in output resulting from unemployed resources (see B. Pesek, "A Comparison of the Distributional Effects of Inflation and Taxation," *American Economic Review* 50 [March 1960]: 147).

III. ECONOMICS OF TRANSITION FROM UNANTICIPATED TO ANTICIPATED INFLATION

The effects of the transition from unanticipated to anticipated inflation are, by definition, results of changes in beliefs about the course of future prices.[18] When the current price level is no longer expected to persist and this expectation is supplanted by the anticipation of rising prices, certain adjustments that uniquely characterize this transition state are implied. These adjustments are a consequence of the expectation that the cost of holding money will increase.

The expectation that the cost of holding monetary assets will increase relative to that of real assets implies that the stock of money and other monetary assets is in excess of the desired stocks. Alternatively, the market value of the monetary assets of a community is in excess of the new present worth of the net income stream that these assets are now expected to generate. For real assets the converse is the case. Therefore, there is a communitywide attempt to shift from monetary to real assets. This attempt to substitute real for monetary assets produces, through a complex chain of substitutions, a rise in real asset prices, a rise in the money rate of interest, a fall in the real rate, and a decrease in bond prices.[19] The rise in prices and the

---

[18] The sequence in which this analysis is developed, in particular presenting the economics of unanticipated inflation before that of anticipatory inflation, corresponds to the temporal sequence of economic events during an inflation. In this light, the inflations of the United States during the last century failed to reach the anticipated stage whereas the German inflation following World War I went through all three stages.

[19] On this point, see C. Kennedy, ''Inflation and the Bond Rate,'' *Oxford Economic Papers*, N.S. 12 (October 1960): 269–73.

decline in real rates of interest equilibrates desires to hold wealth in the form of money with the nominal balances available to be held, desires to hold wealth in the form of real assets with the real assets available to be held, and desires to hold wealth in the form of monetary assets with the monetary assets available to be held.

For any given expectation of the future course of prices, there exists some current level of prices and interest rates that reconciles the desires of a community to hold wealth in various forms with what is available to be held. (In the limiting case, this price level can be infinity and the stocks of money balances zero.) At this equilibrium price level and new rate of interest, the marginal yield derived from holding money equals the higher marginal yield on other assets, both monetary and real.

A decline in the real value of nominal balances attributable to the expectation of rising prices is implied by the recognition of a tax on money. Similar effects are produced by a tax on physical assets. For example, a tax on houses will lead to a decrease in the long-run equilibrium value of a housing stock. The key difference between the effects of these two taxes is in the time required to adjust stocks of housing and money to long-run equilibrium conditions. For a noncommodity money, short-run equilibrium conditions are nonexistent. The stock of real balances adjusts, once a tax on money is recognized, to long-run equilibrium conditions. Hence current holders of money must bear all of the tax on money.

In contrast, several years may elapse after a tax is imposed on housing before a housing stock reaches long-run equilibrium. From the imposition of a housing tax to the moment the housing stock reaches long-run equilibrium, current users do not bear the full tax. Only after long-run equilibrium conditions are satisfied is a tax on housing borne completely by current users.

The effects of changes in expectations concerning the future course of prices are capitalized in the capital market. The prices of all debt securities fall until the gap between money and real yields reflects the current state of beliefs about the future course of prices. All assets whose explicit money yields are independent of the rate of change of prices are revaluated and converted into assets whose effective money yields are a function of the rate of change of prices. Therefore, holders of debt securities (creditors) incur capital losses. These losses represent the present worth of the future value decreases that the owners of these securities expect to bear as a result of inflation. The longer the maturity of a debt security the greater the capital loss. Corresponding to the capital losses of creditors are the capital gains of debtors. These gains are the present worth of the future reductions in real interest and principal obligations expected to result from higher prices. The process of recognizing and compounding the capital gains and losses associated with monetary securities (other than non-interest-bearing money) converts these securities into purchasing power obligations. The extent to which the new capital values reflect the present values of losses that will in fact be realized depends upon the correctness of the expectations held. The change in expectations from stable to rising prices, if it is accompanied by uncertainty about the magnitude of the expected rise, usually induces the business community to incorporate price-revising procedures in its contracts. This is particularly important for long-term commitments such as mortgages and bonds. Inability to predict correctly the magnitude of an expected rise in prices may be expected to lead to a greater utilization of escalator clauses.

The revaluation of monetary assets and liabilities of enterprises causes changes in the prices of equities. In general, the prices of shares of firms whose monetary liabilities exceed their monetary assets rise relative to the price level. Conversely, the relative prices of shares of firms whose monetary assets exceed their monetary liabilities fall, and neutral firms' share prices move with the price level.[20]

Governments, almost invariably the largest debtors in an economy, gain in wealth at the expense of the owners of their interest-bearing obligations. These gains of wealth are the capitalized values of the expected reductions in the real tax liabilities of taxpayers (governments). If the subsequent inflation is correctly anticipated during the transition, then the holders of governmental obligations (creditors) will, after the loss of wealth during the transition, incur no further losses of wealth as a result of the now correctly anticipated inflation. Only the holders of non-interest-bearing money, either government or private, will continue to incur losses attributable to inflation after the transition. The real value of fiat money balances will decrease during the transition without any counterpart gains elsewhere in an economy.

The impact on current prices of changes in expectations about future prices is shown in Figure 1. *AB* represents price level stability; *BC* denotes a period of unanticipated inflation. During both periods current prices are expected to persist, although the realized cost of holding cash balances rises during

[20] To determine whether or not capital gains exceed capital losses as a consequence of changes in expectations from stable to rising prices, both the relative magnitudes and average durations of monetary assets and monetary liabilities are relevant. To the extent that monetary assets are of shorter term than monetary liabilities, which appears to be the case for many if not most business firms, the foregoing conclusions would have to be modified.

the second period. There is no change (attributable to inflation) in the quantity of real cash balances demanded. *CD* represents an adjustment from unanticipated to anticipated inflation. The rise in prices indicated by *CD* is purely the result of a change in expectations and is consistent with there being no change in the nominal monetary stock. This rise in prices is associated

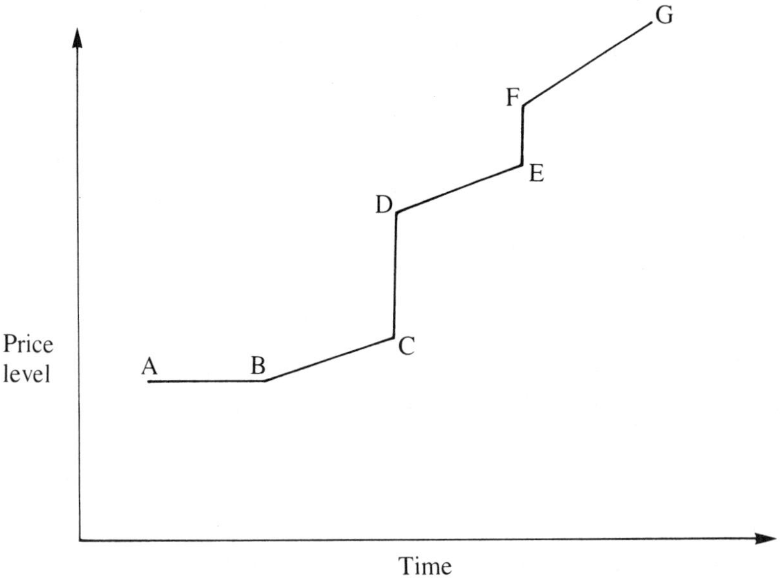

Figure 1. The effect of changes in expectations upon the absolute level of prices.

with a rise in velocity and a fall in the real value of the nominal monetary stock of a community. It is caused by a change in the long-run equilibrium conditions for the stock of money. *DE* represents price rises during an inflation that was anticipated and is consistent with no further change in the real value of money holdings. If the rate of change of prices experienced during the *DE* time interval is the expected rate, then the transition adjustments during *CD* were complete. However, if the actual rate of change of prices continues to be greater than the expected rate, another adjustment may occur. Again, real balances fall and velocity rises because of a change in long-run equilibrium conditions for the stock of money. This second round of adjustments is represented by *EF* and the subsequent rate of change of prices by *FG*. The actual realized costs of holding money are the same for both *DE* and *FG*. The jump in prices denoted by *CD* and *EF* does not reflect an increase in the actual cost of holding money. It reflects an increased awareness of the true costs.

After the transition from nonanticipated to accurately anticipated inflation (which could occur instantaneously or over a period of time), the ensuing rate of change of prices is an "equilibrium" rate of change. This rate of change of prices will not accelerate in the absence of exogenous forces. It is of course conceivable that expectations can be formed in such a manner that price-level increases per se will generate expectations that will lead to an acceleration of the rate of change of prices. Assuming expectations of this character, one can conceive of inflations that feed upon themselves in the absence of exogenous forces, such as those resulting from increases in the stock of nominal balances or decreases in the stock of physical wealth. Available evidence produced by the inflations the Western world has experienced, as well as existing knowledge of how expectations are formed, fails to support the belief that inflations feed upon themselves, purely by expectations feeding upon expectations.[21]

[21] The seven hyperinflations studied by Cagan did not feed upon themselves (P. Cagan, "The Monetary Dynamics of Hyperinflation," in M. Friedman, ed., *Studies in the Quantity Theory of Money* [Chicago: University of Chicago Press, 1956], p. 74).

IV. ECONOMICS OF ANTICIPATED INFLATION

The previous section concentrated primarily, but not exclusively, on those economic effects that distinguished the transition stage. Here the implications of a fully anticipated inflation, and not just the transition adjustments resulting from changes in price expectations, are of paramount concern. The greater the inflation and the greater the extent to which inflation is expected, the more significant will be these effects.

A. Tax on Money and Reduced Real Balances

Changes in expectations from stable to rising prices imply higher costs of holding money. Therefore the real value of money balances falls; this is a symptom of efforts to economize on the use of a resource expected to become dearer. Taxation of money through (partial or complete) anticipated inflation implies reductions in the real value of money balances.[22] Suppose the money in a community is inconvertible, non-interest-bearing, fiat money issued by a government. Suppose also that this government announces its intention of doubling the nominal monetary stock each year through the issuance of new money in exchange for resources. The issuance of this new money is an alternative to conventional taxes. Because of the announcement, a transition occurs during which prices rise sharply; this is followed by a steady-state rate of increase. This transition stage is a result of individuals' decisions to reduce their money holding in view of the higher costs of holding money. The more elastic the cost elasticity of demand for money the higher the transition increase in prices. Assume that the fraction of income (wealth) held in the form

[22] This is consistent with a fully and accurately anticipated inflation, if the cost of holding money is not driven so high that its use is abandoned entirely.

of money immediately drops by one-half to, say, 15 percent. This decline occurs by means of an immediate doubling of prices and of income velocity. If this immediate doubling of prices is followed by an annual 100 percent rate of change, then the holders of money would lose, every year thereafter, 7.5 percent of their wealth, which would represent the proceeds of the inflation tax.[23]

It is incorrect to infer from this example that higher rates of inflation will necessarily produce larger tax receipts for a government. A higher rate of anticipated inflation will produce larger tax proceeds per unit of real value of money balances held by a community, but it also reduces stocks of money balances in real terms. What is relevant for calculating the proceeds of an inflation tax is the elasticity of demand for money in real terms with respect to the rate of change of prices. The principles of optimal pricing for monopolists are relevant for determining the rate of anticipated inflation that maximizes the proceeds of an inflation tax for a government.[24]

B. Money Substitution

Given the expectation of an increase in the costs of holding money, the preexisting marginal rate of substitution of money for real resources becomes nonoptimal. At first blush, this suggests that fewer resources will go into the production of money and more into the production of all other output than

---

[23] This calculation is implicitly based on the assumption that there are no welfare or efficiency costs associated with this tax, so that postinflation and preinflation real incomes are equal. This assumption does not change the analysis in any essential way. The use of a more appropriate assumption would reduce the estimated tax receipts.

[24] An application of these principles to an inflation tax may be found in M. Bailey, "The Welfare Cost of Inflationary Finance," *Journal of Political Economy* 64 (April 1956): 105.

would be true under a regime of stable prices. However, in a fiat or noncommodity money economy, only a negligible volume of resources goes into the production of money. Therefore, virtually no resources are released if less money, in real terms, is used as a result of inflation. An increase in the cost of holding money induces a community to divert some resources to the production of money substitutes. Consequently, a good that is nearly costless to society is in part supplanted by goods that have greater costs. These costs constitute the efficiency losses, or the welfare effects, of anticipated inflation.[25] Both the duration of an inflation and the rate of change of prices affect the costs of holding money. Hence both play a role in determining the volume of resources that goes into economizing on cash balances. The expectation of rising prices leads to a revaluation of securities, both debt and equity, so that their effective yields are consistent with the real rate of interest.

Since assets differ in their capacities as money substitutes, the anticipation of rising prices produces relative price changes among assets. In general, this implies that long-lived assets, such as land, and purchasing-power securities will rise in value relative to wealth in human form. The use of money substitutes that are infinitely elastic in supply in the short run, such as foreign currencies, increases very rapidly.[26] For assets whose supply is less elastic in the short run, and which are

[25] Bailey (*ibid.*, p. 95) has estimated the welfare costs of anticipated inflation to be a function of the size of the reduction in the real value of the nominal monetary stock. For comparing inflation with other tax alternatives, a relevant criterion is the relative size of these efficiency losses.

[26] A country whose currency is relatively stable in purchasing power has a comparative advantage in producing money, and as a result its money is held by foreign nationals. Therefore, in a world of currencies whose purchasing power is unstable, a stable currency can be a valuable national asset.

good money substitutes, the revaluation produces rents and quasi-rents for their owners, with subsequent effects on production. This increased demand is spread out generally over the entire range of highly marketable assets. In the long run, the pattern of output in an inflationary economy changes toward the production of more money substitutes. Human capital is a poorer money substitute than nonhuman capital. Therefore the output of capital in nonhuman form rises, and the output of capital in human form falls, relative to what it would be in the absence of inflation.[27]

The substitution of real resources for money, and the corresponding welfare loss caused by any given rate of change of prices, is greater in the long run than in the short run. In the long run, by definition, the supply conditions of money substitutes are more elastic. Hence more resources will flow into the production of money substitutes in the long than in the short run. The more a community shifts from money to money substitutes the greater the welfare loss and the smaller the real tax receipts attributable to any given rate of change of prices.[28] The difference between the income yielded by the allocation of resources under a regime of stable prices and the income

[27] This assumes that inflation replaces an income or generalized sales tax as a source of governmental revenues. Taxes on other classes of nonhuman wealth or an explicit excise tax on money of the type that was proposed in the 1930s as an antidepression measure could produce effects similar to those of inflation. These taxes are capable of producing the relative price effects of anticipated inflation with stable prices.

[28] Insofar as the supply of money substitutes is completely inelastic, there can be no reallocation of resources to the production of them. Hence there can be no change in the way a society uses its resources and no welfare losses resulting from inflation. The more elastic the supply of money substitutes, the smaller the stock of real balances a community will want to maintain for any given rate of change of prices. Therefore, the tax potential of inflation is inversely related to its effect on efficiency.

yielded during inflation, both measured using the relative prices that exist during price-level stability, constitutes a measure of the cost to a community of using real resources as money substitutes.[29]

A recognized increase in the cost of holding cash balances can lead to decreases in the currency-deposit ratio. Rising prices imply, in the absence of controls, that interest rates on demand deposits will rise. Hence the advantage of holding non-interest-bearing currency relative to demand deposits changes in favor of deposits, and the currency-deposit ratio decreases.

Barter increases during anticipated inflation. No economy, even during stable prices, negotiates all of its output through its market sector; every economy contains a barter sector. Anticipated inflation raises the costs of using money in exchanges as compared with "do-it-yourself" activities or barter. Therefore, some of the economic values that are normally created through money exchange will, in the presence of anticipated inflation, pass from the market to the barter sector. The greater the expected rate of change of prices, the greater will be the relative advantage of barter vis-à-vis using money exchange markets and the greater will be the bias in the usual measurements of national income. At some rate of change of prices, the costs of holding money become so high that barter replaces money exchange entirely.

Money economizing, somewhat related to barter, is achieved through vertical integration, so that transactions for-

[29] This measure, as well as that used by Bailey, should not be interpreted as an answer to the question: how much larger would income be if inflation did not occur? If inflation did not occur, then governmental tax receipts would be smaller. What is being measured is the welfare costs of inflation, holding constant the volume of real resources going to the government, and assuming inflation is replaced by a tax completely free of efficiency losses!

merly involving the use of money can be consummated without it. The internal bookkeeping and transfer pricing arrangements of a firm, which may be thought of as a form of private money, replace higher-cost money during anticipated inflation. Consequently anticipatory inflation implies the existence of incentives to form more highly integrated firms.[30]

C. Product Shifting

The relative profitability, in the short run, of producing particular products is affected by an increase in the costs of holding money. Since money, like inventory, plant and equipment, and labor, is an agent of production, a rise in the costs of using money is a change in the relative prices of inputs. Just as production techniques vary in their mixes of capital and labor, so also do they differ in the extent to which they use money. For industries that employ relatively money-intensive methods of production, anticipated inflation implies that their product costs rise and their profitability falls relative to industry generally. In the long run, this difference in profitability implies a reallocation of resources toward less money-intensive products and techniques.

A money-intensive production process employs a large volume of money services relative to the services of other human and nonhuman capital. This suggests that the ratio of average cash balances to sales represents a criterion by which the money

[30] Shortening of pay periods, which appears to be a uniform feature of hyperinflations, represents a substitution of bookkeeping services for money. During the height of the post–World War I German inflation, some workers were paid as often as three times a day. This made it possible to reduce the volume of real balances held.

Similarly banks find it profitable to expand their banking services to include deposits of stable foreign currencies. During the height of the German inflation, a large fraction of the deposits of German banks consisted of foreign currencies.

intensiveness of a production process can be evaluated.[31] The long-run impact of an inflation tax upon the relative prices of products is greater the greater the dispersion of the cash to sales ratio.[32] The short-run effects on profits are a function of the size of cash balances relative to the investment of equity holders. The larger this ratio the greater the adverse effects on profits, and presumably stock prices, of a tax on money.[33]

In general, holdings of money are related to the future outlay and receipt streams of an enterprise. The greater the outlays and receipts per dollar of share capital the higher the ratio of money to equity. Firms with relatively low outlays and receipts per dollar of share capital usually employ capital-intensive methods of production that involve the use of long-lived capital. At the other extreme, firms with relatively high outlays and receipts per dollar of share capital are usually labor-intensive enterprises such as retailing and service trades. Consequently, an increase in the cost of holding money implies increased output and employment in the long run, and profits in the short run, for capital-intensive economic activities; conversely for labor-intensive activities.

If the use of long-lived assets economizes on money bal-

---

[31] The market price of a product represents a fuller accounting of its economic costs of production than do accounting costs. Since the ratio of costs to sales varies from product to product, the former is a better criterion. The size of a cash balance is by definition perfectly correlated with the size of the service stream rendered by that cash balance. Consequently, no useful purpose is served by computing the service stream of a stock of money. The ratio of cash balances to total assets of an enterprise would be an indicator of the money intensiveness of its products if all of the resources employed were the property of that enterprise.

[32] The substitutability of other resources for money by business firms and their demand elasticities are both assumed to be randomly and independently distributed with respect to this ratio.

[33] This abstracts from differences in the length of the short run for various enterprises.

ances through the reduction in the size of receipt and expenditure streams during anticipated inflation, a community is induced to use longer-lived assets than it otherwise would. To illustrate, consider a firm that is indifferent between investing in two wooden buildings or one steel building during price-level stability. Either alternative involves the same capital costs and the same present worth of the difference between the expected cost and income streams. The steel building, however, has a lower annual rate of receipts and outlays per dollar of invested capital. Consequently, smaller cash balances are held on the average as a result of investing in the steel building. Therefore, a rise in the cost of holding money, aside from any interest-rate changes, increases the relative value of the more durable asset.

D. Factor Price Effects

In factor markets, anticipated inflation leads to a fall in wages and other factor prices relative to consumer prices. This fall is not a manifestation of market imperfections. It results from an increase in business costs produced by a tax on money. Such an increase in business costs implies a decline in the returns to the cooperating agents of production relative to prices. The effects of anticipated inflation are similar to the effects of excise taxes upon wage-price relationships. A decline in wage and other costs relative to final prices is a result of the imposition of any form of indirect taxes that affects business costs and is not specific to money.[34] The fall in real

[34] For a discussion of the effects of indirect taxes on wage-price relationships, see R. Kessel, "The Measurement and Economic Implications of the Inclusion of Indirect Taxes in the Consumers' Price Index," in G. Stigler, ed., *The Price Statistics of the Federal Government* (New York: National Bureau of Economic Research, 1961), p. 517. Per dollar of tax receipts, indirect taxes produce a greater

wage rates attributable to an increase in business costs reinforces the other, already mentioned, effect on real wages. This is the decline in the profitability of labor-intensive business enterprises.[35] The withdrawal of labor from the market into barter partially mitigates these forces. With respect to capital, the rise in the profitability of capital-intensive enterprises constitutes a force operating to counter the effects of an inflation tax on the return to capital. Consequently, rents rise relative to wages.

Anticipated inflation affects the real rate of interest. An increase in the demand for money substitutes implies the replacement of money with physical assets as a means of holding wealth. Hence an increase in the savings function is implied. The improvement in the profitability of enterprises producing goods with capital-intensive production techniques implies the substitution of capital for labor-intensive methods of production. Hence the investment function increases. The increases in the investment and savings functions produce higher rates of capital formation and conflicting forces acting upon the real rate of interest.[36]

---

fall in measured real wages than an inflation tax. Wage-price relationships are affected by an inflation tax only insofar as the money-holdings of enterprises, but not of private individuals, are taxed. In contrast, all excises are business taxes and therefore affect wage-price ratios. At the other extreme are personal income taxes which are not business taxes and do not affect wage-price ratios.

[35] This does not necessarily imply that all wage rates will decline. Anticipated inflation probably leads to an increase in the real demand for accountants, bookkeepers, and brokers; hence their wages will rise relative to wages generally.

[36] This argument is capable of explaining the observation of Bresciani-Turroni: "Germany offered the grotesque, and at the same time the tragic spectacle of a people which, rather than produce food, clothes, shoes and milk for its own babies, was exhausting its energies in the manufacture of machines or the building of factories" (as quoted by D. Robertson, *Essays in Monetary Theory* [London: P. S. King, 1940], p. 183).

V. DEFLATION

For deflation, many of the foregoing conclusions are reversed. During the transition, real money balances are increased. Associated with a rise in the equilibrium size of real money balances is a fall in the quantity of real assets demanded. Hence interest rates rise, and the prices of real assets fall.

During anticipated deflation, the output of nonhuman capital falls and that of human capital rises. This is caused by the replacement of capital-intensive by labor-intensive methods of production and the substitution of money for physical assets as a means of holding wealth.[37] Hence the fraction of national income devoted to capital formation falls, and both investment and savings functions decrease. What happens to the real rate of interest depends upon the relative strength of these conflicting forces.

The economic costs of holding non-interest-bearing money when prices are not falling are less than the private costs. Additional real balances can be obtained, if prices are stable, only by surrendering the income from other assets. If prices are rising, there are of course additional costs. Because falling prices imply an appreciation in the value of money, it is possible to lower the cost of holding real balances relative to the cost of holding other forms of wealth. In principle, there exists a negative rate of change of prices that will make the private and economic costs of holding money equal; this rate of fall

[37] If a policy of falling prices is an alternative to one of stable or rising prices, then alternative monetary-fiscal policies are also being compared. To achieve falling prices, either higher interest rates, or greater budgetary surpluses, or some combination of the two is required. In any case, the holders of money are subsidized by taxpayers.

will make the marginal costs of holding real balances zero. This rate of change of prices will satisfy the Pareto optimality condition that the marginal rate of substitution of money in consumption and production be equal, and will induce a community to hold what can be regarded as an optimal stock of real balances.

Insofar as a society moves in the direction of Pareto optimality with respect to its money-holdings, resources are liberated from activities associated with the use of money for other economic activities.[38] The specific activities from which these resources are liberated depend upon whether a community is holding too much or too little money. In the case of too little money, which is the usual situation, resources are devoted to the production of assets because of their money substitute properties. Resources in the form of bookkeeping and clearing services are taken from other activities. For the case of too much money, which is rare in nature, resources are devoted to safeguarding and maintaining cash balances that have a negative marginal social product.

A deliberate policy of anticipated deflation to achieve "optimal" utilization of society's cost-free ability to create money involves two problems. One is an equity problem. An anticipated deflation produced by reducing the absolute money stock constitutes a subsidy to money-holders from taxpayers, and in the absence of compensating changes in the tax structure, will affect the tax system. To offset such changes may involve the creation of new inefficiencies. If anticipated deflation is achieved with a stable nominal monetary stock through in-

[38] See W. Vickrey, "Stability through Inflation," in K. Kurihara, ed., *Post-Keynesian Economics* (New Brunswick, N.J.: Rutgers University Press, 1954), pp. 89 ff.; and G. Tolley, "Providing for Growth of the Money Supply," *Journal of Political Economy* 65 (December 1957): 477.

creases in desired real cash balances resulting from growth in real per capita income, then an explicit subsidy from taxpayers is not required.

The other problem is the historical association of deflation and unemployment. This association has been explained by ad hoc assumptions about the supply conditions of labor. These assumptions are ad hoc because supply conditions usually are specified in real terms independently of the absolute level of prices. When the price level is relevant for specifying the supply conditions of labor, then it is the current, not any, price level that is pertinent. For such supply conditions, it can be demonstrated that deflation causes unemployment. Since this is a widely accepted explanation of unemployment, it must be regarded as a strong indictment of anticipated deflation as a means for achieving optimal real balances.[39]

VI. CONCLUSIONS

Inflations, or types of inflations, should be distinguished according to prevailing anticipations about the future course of prices, a distinction essential for analyzing the economic consequences of rising prices. They should also be regarded as a tax on money and hence an alternative to conventional explicit

[39] Often it is asserted that the distribution of productivity gains is affected by the course of prices. If price-level changes are anticipated, and the supply of labor is a function of real wage rates, then the distribution of productivity gains is determined by real forces and is independent of both the absolute level of prices and the rate of change of prices. If price-level changes are not anticipated, then debtor-creditor relationships affect the personal but not the functional distribution of income. There seems to be virtually no evidence that real wages, interpreted as either functional or personal income, are affected (see R. Kessel and A. Alchian, "The Meaning and Validity of the Inflation-Induced Lag of Wages Behind Prices," *American Economic Review* 50 [March 1960]: 43).

taxes. When rising prices are not anticipated, but nevertheless occur:

1. Net monetary debtors gain at the expense of net monetary creditors.
2. Governments, that is, taxpayers, gain at the expense of the holders of governmental obligations, both interest-bearing and non-interest-bearing.

During the transition to a correctly anticipated inflation:

1. The quantity of real balances demanded decreases, the real value of the nominal stock of money falls, and prices rise. The rise in prices, unlike the rise in prices during unanticipated inflation, represents an adjustment by money-holders to the increased costs of holding money. This implies a decrease in the efficiency with which a community utilizes its resources and of course a loss to money-holders.
2. All existing interest-bearing securities are revalued so that their yields will reflect an unbiased estimate of the future course of prices. Consequently, the holders of all debt, both governmental and private, incur capital losses.

And during a correctly anticipated inflation:

1. Prices can rise at a constant rate.
2. The continuing depreciation in the purchasing power of a unit of money induces a series of substitutions for money. In particular, real assets are substituted for money as a means of holding wealth, except for interest-bearing money.
3. The tax on money bears most onerously upon economic

activities that are relatively labor-intensive. Converse implications hold for economic activities characterized by low cash-to-equity ratios. Consequently, the demand for labor falls and real wages decline. The demand for capital rises, and rents rise relative to wages. The fraction of national income devoted to capital formation increases.

Redistribution of Wealth Through Inflation

Economists have long speculated about the effects of inflation upon the economic welfare of the owners of business enterprises. This speculation has almost invariably led to the conclusion that business firms gain through inflation. This conclusion has been reached through two independent arguments. One, enunciated by both J. M. Keynes and I. Fisher, is that inflation enables business firms to discharge their debts with depreciated money, the creditors' losses being the debtors' gains.[1] Strictly speaking, the validity of this conclusion depends upon two propositions: (i) that business firms are debtors, and (ii) that interest rates reflect biased estimates of the future course of prices when prices are rising. The other argument, advanced by E. J. Hamilton and W. C. Mitchell, is that inflation causes prices to rise faster than wage rates.[2] Consequently workers are systematically underpaid during

---

This article was coauthored by Reuben A. Kessel.

[1] J. M. Keynes, *Tract on Monetary Reform* (London, 1923), p. 18; I. Fisher, *The Purchasing Power of Money* (New York, 1920), pp. 58–73, 190–91.

[2] E. J. Hamilton, *J. Econ. Hist.* 12 (1952):325; W. C. Mitchell, *A History of the Greenbacks* (Chicago, 1903), pp. 347–48; ———, *Gold, Prices, and Wages Under the Greenback Standard* (Berkeley, 1908), pp. 275–76.

inflation, this loss by the working class being a gain for the entrepreneurs.[3] This explanation rests upon special assumptions about the character of labor markets that are generally regarded as invalid in other markets.

Practical men of affairs, in particular investment advisers, have been much less confident than professional economists that the owners of business enterprises gain through inflation. They have generally concluded that investors can maintain their capital intact during inflation by investing in common stocks, such an investment being roughly equivalent to an investment in inventories. (Common stocks are ownership or equity shares in a corporation, while bonds represent debt obligations of the corporation.) In other words, an investor in common stock could expect neither to increase nor to decrease his wealth, whereas an investor in bonds and other cash-type investments would suffer a real loss.

This cautiousness of investment counselors is traceable to the experience of investors in equities during the great inflations that have occurred in countries with organized stock markets. It was found during the German runaway inflation following World War I, during the Austrian and French inflations of the 1920s, and more recently during the inflation in Chile that the owners of business firms did not obtain the gains that might have been expected on the basis of the hypotheses set forth by Keynes and Fisher, on the one hand, and Hamilton and Mitchell on the other. These observations are also consistent with the behavior of stock price indexes in the United

[3] Some economists and noneconomists also contend that anyone who holds inventories gains through inflation. Since the price of inventories rises above their cost, this difference is regarded as a real gain in economic welfare. But holders of inventories cannot acquire with their inventories any more of the world's goods and services than they could in the absence of inflation.

States during the inflations associated with World Wars I and II.

What was especially puzzling was the fate of the owners of banks. Banks are typically enormous debtors, larger debtors, in fact, than most business firms by an order of magnitude. Furthermore, banks employ relatively more labor per dollar of invested capital than is characteristic of business firms generally. Consequently, it is an implication of both hypotheses that banks ought to be enormous gainers through inflation. Yet the available evidence suggests that one of the regular results of inflation is that the owners of bank shares suffer. The experience of the owners of bank shares in the United States, Germany, Austria, Chile, and France suggests that the real value of bank shares declines during inflation. (Real value is simply price divided by an index number reflecting changes in the price level. Consequently, if the price of an asset rises more than the price level, then its real value has increased, and conversely.)

RECONCILING HYPOTHESES WITH EXPERIENCE

How can this evidence be reconciled with either of these hypotheses? A step toward reconciling the Keynes-Fisher reasoning with the lessons of experience as revealed by the stock market was taken by Kessel when he showed that, despite the enormous debts owned by banks to depositors, there exist offsetting credits that are even larger than these debts.[4] These credits are bank assets which are almost entirely (with the exception of bank buildings and business machines) either

[4] R. A. Kessel, *Am. Econ. Rev.* 46 (1956): 130.

money or money-type assets such as notes and other obligations payable to banks by either private customers or the government. The existence of these credits led Kessel to argue that one should do more than merely look at the credit that business firms have extended to their customers. What business firms gain from bondholders may be lost to those to whom these firms have extended credit and may never redound to the interests of the owners.

From his analysis emerged a classification for determining whether or not a business firm is, on *net* balance, a debtor or creditor. Kessel classified assets and liabilities into categories, monetary and real. A monetary asset was defined as an asset whose market value is independent of changes in the price level. These would include money, accounts and notes receivable, government and corporate bonds, life insurance, prepaid taxes, and so on. A monetary liability was defined as a liability whose amount is independent of changes in the price level; these would include accounts payable, notes payable, mortgages, bonds, preferred stock, and so on. Preferred stock, although called a stock, is typically corporate debt rather than equity. A net monetary debtor was then defined as a firm whose monetary liabilities exceeded its monetary assets; and conversely for a net monetary creditor. The net monetary status would indicate the magnitude of the gain or loss a firm would incur from a given amount of inflation. However, firms with the same amount of indebtedness but of unequal size, where size is measured by the aggregate value of the equity of the owners, would have unequal movements in absolute stock prices. Therefore, in order to compare corporations of unequal size, the ratio of net monetary debt to equity, as measured by the market price of shares times the number of shares outstanding, is used as the measure of net monetary debtor or creditor status.[5] The effects of stock dividends, stock splits, and rights offerings were held constant and did not affect measurements of changes in stock prices. "Stock dividends" and "splits" increase the number of shares of common stock without changing the total investment, whereas "rights" entitle existing stockholders to increase the investment in the corporation by purchasing new shares at a price below existing market prices, thereby also involving some dilution in per-share value. And it was assumed that dividends were continuously reinvested in the shares of the companies that issued them, because this would eliminate variations caused by differences in the extent to which profits were reinvested.

For the United States, Kessel found in his preliminary study that banks were typically net monetary creditors, and that the real value of their shares actually did decline during the World War II inflation, in accordance with the Keynes-Fisher hypothesis. Furthermore, the real value of bank shares seems to have gone down during inflation for every country for which data are available.

Kessel also examined the balance sheets of a small random sample of industrial firms whose stock is traded on the New York Stock Exchange. (Railroads, utilities, and investment companies were omitted. Railroads and utilities were not included because it was supposed that their very close regulation might conceal the effects of inflation upon their stock prices. Investment companies were omitted because of the magnitude of the problems encountered in evaluating the debtor-creditor status of their assets.) In 1939, about 40 percent of the ob-

[5] This is one of the respects in which the present study is an advance over Kessel's early work. While his concept of net debtor or net creditor was correct, his criterion of *intensity* of debtor or creditor status was wrong, and consequently the measurements based upon his criterion were also wrong.

served firms were creditors and could be expected to lose through inflation, according to the Keynes-Fisher reasoning. After the firms had been divided into the two categories, debtor and creditor, and after the changes in share prices between 1939 and 1946 had been examined, a significant difference was detected between the rise of share prices in the two categories. The share prices of net monetary debtor firms rose significantly more than the prices of net monetary creditor firms. For a period of deflation, 1929–33, the reverse was found to be true. The share prices of net monetary creditors fell significantly less than the share prices of net monetary debtors.

The behavior of the stock prices of bank shares during the inflation associated with World War II was indistinguishable from the behavior of the shares of equivalent industrial creditors. Other evidence indicates that banks were characterized by large amounts of labor per dollar of invested capital as compared with enterprises generally. This evidence casts doubt upon the validity of the Hamilton-Mitchell reasoning, that inflation causes real wages to fall. If the wage lag had been operative, the value of bank shares would have risen more than the value of the shares of equivalent industrial creditors.

This evidence validated the proposition that during inflation interest rates are systematically lower than they ought to be if inflation is not to transfer wealth from creditors to debtors, but it also challenged the assumption that business firms are, in large part, debtors. The mechanism for redistribution that Keynes and Fisher envisaged was correct, but their assumption that business firms were generally debtors was wrong, and it was this that led them to the erroneous conclusion that business firms gain through inflation. This evidence also explains the behavior of stock-price indexes during inflation. If a substantial fraction of all business firms were net monetary creditors, then an index number of stock prices that was composed of both net monetary debtors and net monetary creditors would not necessarily rise in real value during inflation. Indeed, if the debtors just balance out the creditors, one would expect stock prices generally to keep pace pretty closely with the general price level. These results led to a much larger-scale investigation, designed both to provide stronger evidence of the validity of the mechanism for redistribution envisaged by Keynes and Fisher and to enlarge our empirical knowledge of stock prices.[6]

NEW EVIDENCE FOR MECHANISM OF REDISTRIBUTION

The population of firms investigated includes all of the industrials whose common stock was traded on the New York Stock Exchange at any time between 1914 and 1952. For 1933–52, the American Stock Exchange was also included. Furthermore, four separate industries were studied for the period 1940–52—chemicals, steels, retailing, and textiles—in order to hold constant any industry differences. The period of the study, 1915–52, includes two inflations (World Wars I and II), two deflations (1921–22 and 1928–33), and two periods of relative price stability (1923–30 and 1933–40). The number of firms observed in a year ranged from a minimum of 71 to a maximum of 885. In all, nearly 14,000 firm-years of data were observed and analyzed.

[6] This study was undertaken with the aid of a research grant from the Merrill Foundation for the Advancement of Financial Knowledge. The article, from this point on, constitutes the first statement of some of the results of this study.

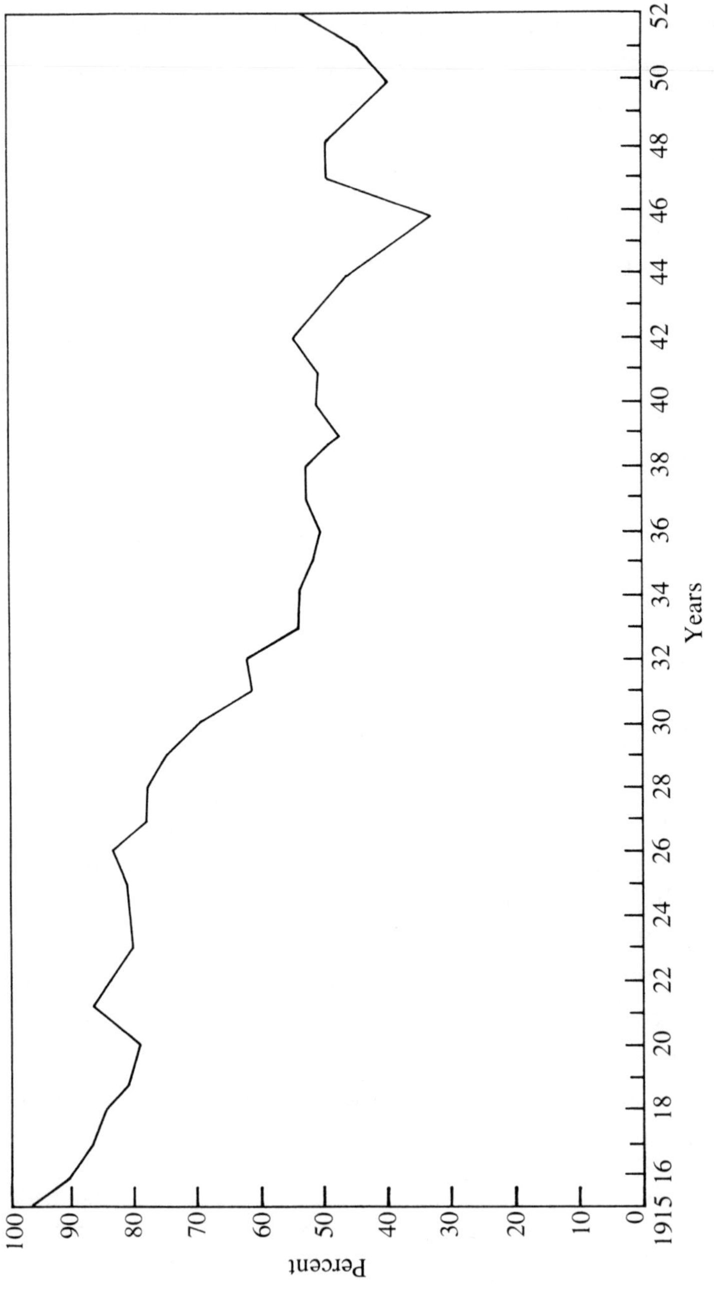

Figure 1. Net monitary debtor firms as percentage of all firms. [Based on New York Stock Exchange data for 1915 to 1952 and on American Stock Exchange and "over-the-counter" data for 1940 to 1952]

What do these data show? The distribution of firms by net monetary debtor and net monetary creditor status has changed spectacularly since 1914. The percentage of firms in each category is shown in Figure 1. These data are based on the New York and the American Stock Exchange samples. The shift from predominantly net monetary debtor status, around the time of World War I, to a ratio of approximately 50:50 in 1952 may explain why Keynes and Fisher made the assumption they did about business firms being debtors.

Apparently individual firms usually did not shift their net monetary status frequently. A firm that was a net monetary debtor in one year was very likely to be one in the next year, despite a gradual shift of the population as a whole. A classification of firms during the 1915–20 inflation according to net monetary status shows that 78 of the firms were net monetary creditors during at least four years of the six-year span, while 22 were net monetary debtors during at least four of the six years. A few did not retain their status for as long as four years. According to Keynes and Fisher the net monetary debtors should have had an increase in the values of their stocks relative to the net monetary creditors. The observed data show that $1.00 of equity of the net monetary debtors increased to $2.66, while the net monetary creditors' dollar increased to only $1.60; the superiority is 57 percent and one which would have less than one chance in 1,000 of occurring by an unusually favorable random selection of firms if there really were no transfers of wealth from creditors to debtors.

Table 1 contains more details, as well as the results for the inflation of 1940–52, for each of the populations of firms studied. In every instance the net monetary debtors did better. In Figure 2 these results are given in the form of a graph. The probability sampling levels are sufficiently small to make it

TABLE 1

Observed stock prices values (with reinvested dividends) for episodes of inflations, deflations, and stable prices, by exchanges and industries. [From *Moody's Industrials* (1914–53); *Commercial and Financial Chronicles* (1921–53); *Bank and Quotation Journals* (1928–53); and New York *Times* (1915–53)]

Population sampled	*Kind and no. of firms**		*Mean resulting equity value † ($)*	*Mean of debtor minus creditor‡ ($)*	*t§*	*p¶*
		Inflations				
1915–1920:						
New York Stock Exchange	Debtors	78	2.66	+ 1.06	3.27	.001
New York Stock Exchange	Creditors	22	1.60			
1940–1952:						
New York Stock Exchange	Debtors	29	5.93	+ 1.47	1.80	.05
New York Stock Exchange	Creditors	35	4.46			
American Stock Exchange	Debtors	57	11.30	+ 3.25	1.65	.05
American Stock Exchange	Creditors	70	8.05			
Over-the-counter	Debtors	22	9.38	+ 2.93	1.19	.12
Over-the-counter	Creditors	45	6.45			
Steel industry	Debtors	29	6.92	+ 0.25	.15	.44
Steel industry	Creditors	27	6.67			
Chemical industry	Debtors	19	7.17	+ 2.53	1.24	.12
Chemical industry	Creditors	19	4.54			
Textile industry	Debtors	29	16.33	+ 6.67	1.45	.07
Textile industry	Creditors	22	9.66			
Department stores	Debtors	29	8.96	+ 4.81	2.64	.007
Department stores	Creditors	22	4.15			
New York Stock Exchange wage firms	Debtors	50	7.85	+ 2.07	1.76	.04

New York Stock Exchange wage firms	Creditors	32	5.78			
		Deflations				
1921–1922:						
New York Stock Exchange	Debtors	118	1.48	− 0.30	− 1.73	.045
New York Stock Exchange	Creditors	24	1.78			
1928–1933:						
New York Stock Exchange	Debtors	63	.49	− 0.60	− 3.17	.001
New York Stock Exchange	Creditors	35	1.09			
		Stable prices				
1923–1930:						
New York Stock Exchange	Debtors	50	2.78	+ 0.45	1.08	.14
New York Stock Exchange	Creditors	15	2.33			
1933–1940:						
New York Stock Exchange	Debtors	56	4.31	− 0.80	− .89	.81
New York Stock Exchange	Creditors	54	5.11			
American Stock Exchange (curb)	Debtors	17	6.44	+ 1.72	+ .71	.52
American Stock Exchange (curb)	Creditors	20	4.72			

* Number of firms that maintained debtor (or creditor) monetary status during at least ⅔ of the episode.

† Mean price plus reinvested dividends at the end of the episode, per dollar of 1940 stock prices.

‡ Mean equity value for net monetary debtors minus mean value for net monetary creditors.

§ Student's t test coefficient:

$$t = d \Big/ \left(\frac{s_1^2}{N_1} + \frac{s_2^2}{N_2} \right)^{1/2}$$

¶ Sampling probability of t (one-tailed) based on Welch approximation. [B. L. Welch, "The generalization of student's problem when several different population variances are involved," *Biometrika* 34 (1947):28. Two-tailed test is used for periods of price stability] extraordinarily difficult to attribute such results to random sampling. And when the probability levels are combined by the Fisher chi-square method, the sampling probability falls to below one chance in 10,000.

To test whether the results are attributable to inflation rather than to a hidden factor which makes the better firms become net monetary debtors, the deflationary episodes were also considered. In the two deflations of 1921–22 and 1928–33, the firms were again classified according to whether they were persistently net monetary debtors or creditors. In the short deflation of 1921–22, each firm in the sample maintained its monetary status during the entire period. In the 1928–33 episode, one deviation was permitted. In both deflations the net monetary creditors did better than the net monetary debtors—just the opposite of the finding for inflations and in conformance with the predictions of the Keynes-Fisher model. The sampling probability levels are small, being less than five percent for the shorter deflation of 1920–22 and less than 0.1 percent for 1929–32. The combined sampling probability is less than 0.01. Finally, for the periods of price stability of 1923–30 and 1933–40, a similar classification of firms revealed no difference in performance between the net monetary creditors and the net monetary debtors, again in conformance with the Keynes-Fisher hypothesis as modified here. These results are also given in Table 1.

But what about the Mitchell-Hamilton wage-lag hypothesis and its implications for business profits? Possibly labor intensiveness is correlated with net monetary status. Under these circumstances, the wage lag, while unrevealed, might yet be operative. To explore this possibility as well as the possibility that growth might be correlated with debtor-creditor status, a sample of 113 firms listed on the New York Stock Exchange

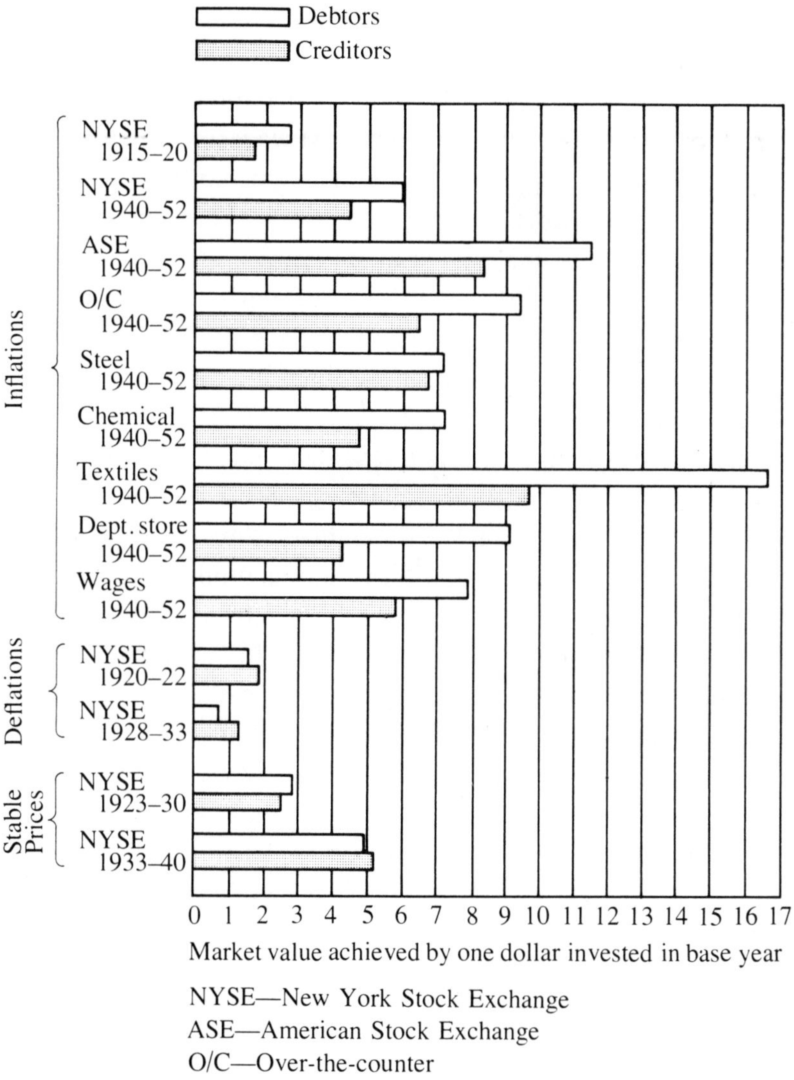

Figure 2. Market value of equity for debtors as compared to that for creditors (per dollar of base-year common stock value).

was obtained. These firms were the entire population of industrials that reported wage bills some time during the interval 1940 to 1952. Three variables—(i) net monetary debtor or creditor status per dollar of equity, (ii) wages paid per year per dollar of equity, and (iii) yearly sales per dollar of equity—were evaluated for potential predictive content by means of partial correlation analysis. (Equity values were determined by the market price of shares.) And in order to avoid violating assumptions underlying probability tests of significance for correlation analysis, ranks for the three independent variables were used.

The results of this analysis revealed that *only* net monetary status was correlated with relative stock price changes, and that this correlation was in the predicted direction. Moreover, the chance that this observation would be produced by random sampling from a population characterized by an absence of this correlation is less than one in 1,000. This evidence is completely consistent with the hypothesis that the wage lag is inoperative—that is, that the imperfection of the labor market postulated by the wage-lag theorists is nonexistent. Consequently, these results must be regarded as evidence against the hypothesis that a wage lag increases business profits during inflation. However, one must not lose sight of the fact that this is only partial evidence, from a nonrandom sample consisting of 113 firms.

CONCLUSION

These results, reported here for the first time, while constituting overwhelming evidence in support of the Keynes-Fisher reasoning about the bias in interest rates during inflation, fail to support their conclusion that business firms gain through inflation. The frequency of debtors in the business population is not great enough to justify Keynes and Fisher's sweeping statements about the gains of business enterprise through inflation. This evidence also suggests that the Keynes-Fisher theorizing about the effects of inflation is not specific to business enterprises; it is a general theory of wealth transfers caused by inflation and is equally applicable to individuals. What count are monetary asset and monetary liability positions and not the type of economic activity in which one engages.

Especially pertinent to much of the current discussion of the consequences of inflation is that the present evidence, by validating the wealth-transfer effect from monetary creditors to monetary debtors (and rejecting the wage-lag hypothesis), verifies the implication that inflation is basically a "tax" on creditors in favor of debtors. Inflation constitutes a tax on the wealth of individuals to the extent that they are holders of money-type assets rather than savers, wage earners, businessmen, widows, orphans, or retired schoolteachers.

These results have implications for the adjustment of personal investment and wealth portfolios (including not only stocks, but bonds, life insurance, mortgages, charge accounts, cash holdings, and so on) in order to hedge against inflation or to profit if inflation comes. Similar reasoning applies to the management of investment, pension, and trust funds.

16

The Meaning and Validity of the Inflation-Induced Lag of Wages Behind Prices

Many economists write as if the proposition that inflation causes prices to rise faster than wages were well established. From this proposition at least two important classes of inferences have been derived.

1. A lag of wages behind prices as a result of inflation produces extraordinarily large business profits. These swollen profits generate a high rate of capital formation. In this role, the wage-lag axiom constitutes the foundation of a theory of industrial development.

2. The lag of wages behind prices caused by inflation accentuates oscillations in the general level of economic activity. The failure of wages to keep pace with prices reinforces disequilibrating movements in the general level of economic activity. In this capacity, the wage-lag axiom functions as an

This paper is coauthored by R. A. Kessel and is one of a series reporting the results of a study of inflation made possible by a grant from the Merrill Foundation for the Advancement of Financial Knowledge. The authors are indebted to Karl Brunner, Gregg Lewis, William Meckling, Albert Rees, and William Taylor for improvement in analysis and exposition.

The first numeral in each citation refers to the corresponding reference at the end of this chapter.

integral part of both overinvestment and underconsumption business cycle theories [14, pp. 137 ff].

The contention that inflation causes real wages to fall appears frequently in the literature of economics. Those who make this contention argue in effect that inflation produces a negative correlation between real wages on the one hand and money wages and prices on the other. As a practical matter, it is extremely difficult to employ this idea as a tool of analysis for understanding observed movements of time series of wages and prices. This difficulty stems from the fact that, as almost everyone would agree, the level of real wages can be affected by such real forces as the relative supplies of labor and capital, the quality of the labor force, the pattern of final demands in the economy, and the state of the arts. Furthermore, increases in the general price level can be produced by changes in the real stock of goods, e.g., by droughts, plagues, wars, etc., even with a fixed money stock. For any time series of real wages, there exists a fantastically difficult problem of imputing changes in the level of real wages to one or the other of two classes of variables, i.e., real or monetary forces. Only if one is able to abstract from the effects of real forces can one determine the effect of inflation upon an observed time series of real wages.

To illustrate this problem, consider the data showing real wages, money wages, and prices in the United States since 1889 [39, pp. 15–16]. These data indicate a high positive correlation between real wages on the one hand and money wages and prices on the other. Are these positive correlations to be interpreted as evidence against the proposition that inflation causes real wages to fall? Surely not. Real wages rose during this time, according to most observers, because of the per capita increase in capital, improvements in technology, and improvements in the skills of the labor force. Those who believe that inflation causes real wages to fall would not deny this. Their position would be that real wages rose despite inflation and that if the effects of real forces upon real wages were properly abstracted, one could observe a fall in real wages attributable to inflation.[1]

I. SOME ALTERNATIVE WAGE-LAG HYPOTHESES

What, then, is the wage-lag hypothesis? To answer this question, we have turned to the works of those economists who have used this idea. The most important "explanation," importance being measured by either the extent to which it has been used or its deviation from the way economists explain behavior in nonlabor markets, is the belief that wages have more "inertia" or "sluggishness" than other prices because of custom, weak bargaining power of labor, or lack of foresight of workers. For example, Hamilton states: "The chief factor in the failure of wages to keep pace with soaring prices in the second half of the eighteenth century was the 'natural' inertia of wage movements in both directions. History records few instances of wage movements in unison with rapidly changing commodity prices" [18, p. 259]. And:

> There have been no such offsets to the strong tendency during most of the last four hundred years for wages to lag behind prices whenever they were rising. This lag has benefited capitalists as a class at the expense of laborers as a class and awarded gains that dwarf into

---

[1] Or for a less recent inflation, consider the Black Death period. During this time prices rose and real wages rose. Clearly what explains this phenomenon is the decrease in the stock of labor which also produced a fall in rents. See Lipson [30, pp. 93 *ff*.].

> insignificance the profits from inventory appreciation and from declines in the real value of debts. A tendency for wages to lag behind falling prices has inflicted losses on businessmen, discouraged saving and investment, and aggravated commercial crises [20, p. 327].

Mitchell also contended that an imperfection exists in the labor market. He wrote:

> In the 60's and, though in somewhat less degree, in the 70's, the labor market of the United States was one in which individual bargaining prevailed. Now the individual laborer is a poor bargainer. He is ignorant of the possibilities of his situation, exposed to the competition of others with the same disabilities, more anxious to sell than the employer to buy. Moreover, custom in the form of rooted ideas about what is a "fair wage" has a peculiarly tenacious hold upon the minds of both parties in the labor market, weakening the wage-earner's aggression and strengthening the employer's resistance [35, pp. 275–76].

In his study of the Civil War, Mitchell concluded: "All of the statistical evidence that has been presented in the preceding pages supports unequivocally the common theory that persons whose incomes are derived from wages suffer seriously from a depreciation of the currency" [34, p. 347]. Basically, the rationale for this position is that there exists a flaw in the labor market which, during times of inflation, lowers the wage rate below the marginal product of workers. In effect Mitchell and Hamilton are saying that the same principles economists use in explaining what happens in other markets are invalid for explaining what happens in labor markets during inflation.[2]

Bresciani-Turroni enunciated, in his famous study of German inflation, a hypothesis that could explain declines in real wages during inflation and be consistent with a perfectly func-

[2] Explanations of this type may be found in [31, pp. 7 *ff.*] [41, p. 213] [6, p. 380] [29, p. 222] and [32, p. 88].

tioning labor market.[3] This hypothesis rests on the postulate that employees, as a condition of employment, are almost invariably creditors of their employers. And as creditors, employees lose to their employers for the same reason that creditors generally lose to debtors as a result of inflation. Therefore, even if wage rates correctly represented the marginal product of workers, the fact that wages accrue, i.e., that wages are paid after they are earned, implies that workers extend credit to their employers and incur a loss on this account.

There exists strong prima facie evidence for accepting the wage-accrual hypothesis of Bresciani-Turroni. This explanation rests upon a debtor-creditor relationship that is essentially similar to debtor-creditor relationships between, say, department stores and their charge customers, finance companies and the credit purchasers of automobiles and other appliances, corporations and their bondholders, etc. Since there already exists evidence that supports the belief that interest rates are biased downward during inflation, because of the public's lack of knowledge of the course of future prices, there appears to be a reasonable basis for accepting the proposition that wealth is transferred from employees to employers when inflation occurs.[4]

[3] "In fact, wages were fixed on the basis of an index number of prices which, at the time of payment, no longer represented actual conditions" [7, p. 310]. It failed to represent actual conditions because of the bias in interest rates. Also he argued that wage earners lost because they held cash during inflation [7, p. 302]. Both of these are of course special cases of the proposition that creditors lose during inflation.

[4] This of course does not imply that business firms gain through inflation. Such a statement would be correct only if an examination of all of their debtor-creditor relations, of which relations with employees are only a part, revealed that business firms are on balance debtors. On this point, as well as for evidence that interest rates are biased during inflation, see Kessel [23, p. 128]. Nor does the "bias" of

As a practical matter, it does not appear that this relationship between employees and employers, at least in modern times, has the potential for transferring a great deal of wealth from employee to employer. Consider a case that is most favorable for sustaining the proposition that accrued wages constitute an important source of business profits during inflation. Assume that cash is acquired for wage payments at the very instant these payments are made by a business firm. Therefore this firm may be regarded as a consistent net debtor with respect to its employees.

What can be said about the magnitude of such profits under these assumptions? Of all industrial firms listed on the New York Stock Exchange in 1952, approximately 200 reported the size of their aggregate wage bills, or more properly the size of their aggregate wage and salary bills, for at least one year between 1939 and 1952. Among these 200 firms, the ratio of total annual wages to equity (equity being measured by the market value of outstanding shares) ranged from a low of .1 to a high of about 4, depending upon firm and industry. If it is assumed that wages are paid biweekly, then the average amount of wages and salaries accrued is 1/52 of the annual wage bill. Consequently it follows that accrued wages range from a low of about .2 percent to 8 percent of equity. This analysis implies that if the price level doubled in any given year, the real value of stock prices would rise from a minimum of .1 percent to a maximum of 4 percent.[5]

---

interest rates imply any defect in the capital market; instead it reflects people's inability to predict future prices.

[5] The Bresciani-Turroni hypothesis also appears in Meyer [33, p. 17]. "Creditors lost in inflation. Wage-earners and salary-earners normally work before they are paid. They lend their labour until pay day; their work is work given on credit." Meyer also asserts that wages lag because of contractual arrangements between employers and employees.

Using this same debtor-creditor relationship, Fisher had earlier set forth still another explanation of why real wages would fall during inflation. Like the Bresciani-Turroni explanation, Fisher's was consistent with a perfectly functioning labor market. Fisher contended that relations between employer and employee can be viewed as being contractual, just as are economic relations between, say, bondholders and those who incur bonded debt [10, pp. 185*ff*.]. The same lack of foresight that would lead to too low an interest rate to permit debtor-creditor relations to be unaffected by inflation would lead to an effective wage below the marginal product of labor when prices are rising. Only at the time wage contracts are signed would wages be equal to the marginal product of labor. Between contract negotiations, real wages would fall as a result of rising prices.

Prima facie evidence does not support this hypothesis. Wage contracts are typically nonenforceable when broken by employees. Consequently, the legal reasons for arguing that contracts between employers and employees are on a par with contracts between creditors and debtors are of dubious validity. As far as employees are concerned, wage contracts have generally been continuously renegotiable, at least until relatively modern times. Employees can almost always leave their current jobs in favor of alternative employment possibilities in complete freedom from legal sanction by employers. Consequently, in the absence of other evidence there is very little basis for accepting Fisher's hypothesis.

However, there is more to a substantive hypothesis than its logical structure. In its broader aspects, the Fisher hypothesis implies that during inflation there exists a differential in the movements of wage rates of workers under contract as compared with workers employed without contract. It also implies that the longer the life of a contract, the greater the differential in the movements of real wages during inflation. No evidence is contained in this paper for evaluating these two implications.

If one abandons a legalistic frame of reference and argues, as Fisher has, that custom plays a great role independent of contractual arrangements, then this hypothesis becomes indistinguishable from the argument of Hamilton and Mitchell, namely, that a flaw exists in the labor market which manifests itself during times of inflation by a fall in real wages.

The use of inflation as a means of taxation appears to have created a belief that inflation causes real wages to fall. Inflation is a means of taxation, and has been used by those who control the stock of money as an alternative to explicit forms of taxation, such as income taxes, excises, tariffs, etc. Using their power to create money, governments have exchanged money for real resources. Such an exchange reduces the volume of real resources available to the private sector of the economy. The mere existence of an exchange of this character has led many observers to conclude that a fall in real wages is necessarily implied [e.g. 25, pp. 171–74]. Yet it can and has been shown that taxation through inflation is consistent with no reduction in real wage rates.[6]

Inflation constitutes a tax upon monetary wealth and not upon wages or other factor incomes. This tax affects the real functional returns of the cooperating agents of production if inflation is anticipated, i.e., when the increased cost of holding money caused by rising prices is recognized and enters into

---

[6] A discussion of the mechanism by which the government acquires resources from the rest of the community through inflation has been presented in [1]. For the first published analysis of this mechanism that the authors have encountered, see the revised portion of Friedman [11, p. 263]. See also Cagan [8].

the calculations of the community. Under these circumstances, both velocity and the nominal or money rate of interest rise. These higher costs of using money are ultimately reflected in a rise in product prices relative to the sum of the returns to the cooperating agents production. Whether or not real wages fall depends upon the cross elasticity between the price or cost of holding money and the quantity of labor demanded. If one is prepared to argue that capital is a better substitute for money than labor, and to assume that the alternative to inflation as a means of taxation is no tax or a wealth or income tax, then the argument that anticipatory inflation can cause real wages to fall can be sustained.

However if inflation is not anticipated, then the losses of the money holders are on a par with an *ex post facto* penalty or Knightian profits and do not affect resource allocation. In general, it appears that the inflations associated with our Civil War in the North and our two world wars were unanticipated. If excise taxes or turnover taxes are regarded as the alternative to taxation through an unanticipated inflation, then inflation implies a higher level of real wages than would otherwise be true.

II. THE EMPIRICAL EVIDENCE

The remainder of this paper falls into two parts: (1) a review of the statistical evidence that has been used to support the Mitchell-Hamilton hypothesis and (2) a new test of this hypothesis based on differences in the labor intensiveness of business firms and the performances of their stock prices during inflation.[7]

[7] The field of income and employment theory contains still another hypothesis that implies the existence of a lag of wages behind prices when prices are rising. It stems from the observation that less than full employment, where full employment

What is the empirical evidence used to support the hypothesis that inflation, independently of real forces, causes real wages to fall when prices are rising? Major data used to support this hypothesis have been collected for six inflationary episodes: (1) the period from 1350 to 1800 in Spain, (2) the early days of the industrial revolution in England, (3) the U.S. Civil War in the North, (4) the U.S. Civil War in the South, (5) the German inflation following World War I, and (6) the inflation in the United States associated with World War I.

A. Spanish Data

E. J. Hamilton probably has contributed more to the acceptance of the hypothesis that inflation causes real wages to fall than has any other single economist.[8] His evidence consists

---

is defined as a labor market in which everyone who wants a job at the prevailing wage rate can find one, implies nonprice rationing of employment opportunities. This is consistent with an infinitely elastic supply function of labor that relates the quantity of labor offered with money wages if rising prices will restore full employment. Under these assumptions, increases in prices at times of less than full employment imply a fall in real wages.

This hypothesis is clearly relevant to the present discussion, if it is relevant at all, only for inflations or portions of inflations associated with less than full employment. Since the authors cited believe that inflation causes wages to lag behind prices independently of whether full or less-than-full employment exists, this is not a hypothesis they considered extensively although it appears in the work of Mitchell and Bresciani-Turroni.

This model leads to difficult questions. One is: Shouldn't the wages of unemployed workers be considered in the wage index? If they are included in the wage index, then it is not clear that real wages decline under these circumstances. Another difficulty is that we do not know enough about how an economy returns to full employment to impute to inflation a fall in real wages of those continuously employed. Possibly real supply conditions have not changed but demand conditions have changed. Real aggregate demand could increase, through an increase in the nominal monetary stock, and with an infinitely elastic aggregate supply function, full employment would be restored with no fall in real wages.

[8] This view runs through most of his works. See particularly [18, p. 256] [20, pp. 335–36].

almost entirely of time series of wages and prices. In order to use such data as evidence of a wage lag, the impact of real forces must be distinguished from that of inflation. Hamilton is not unaware of this difficult problem of imputation. Throughout his monumental three-volume work on Spanish wages and prices, which covers the interval from 1350 to 1800, are references to real forces and their impact upon the price level and real income [17, pp. 100–104]. Yet, as far as we can discover, he consistently forgets about real forces when using his time series to test the hypothesis; any fall in real wages when prices are rising he interprets as evidence supporting the wage-lag hypothesis.

Yet even with this implicit assumption that real forces are constant during inflation and consequently any change in real wages is attributable to inflation, Hamilton's data in his study of Spanish wages and prices fail in large part to support his thesis.[9] Of the three areas studied in the first episode from 1350 to 1500, Valencia, Aragon, and Navarre, only Navarre incurred inflation during this time. He concludes: "The greatest anomaly disclosed by the present study is the complete failure of wages to lag behind prices in any of the kingdoms during a single period of upheaval. In fact, Navarrese wages advanced much faster than prices in the last decade of the fourteenth century" [17, p. 203].

For the second period, 1501 to 1650, he concludes: "With few interruptions, the trend [in real wages] was downward from 1520 to 1600" [16, p. 280]. And, "The calamitous depreciation of the inflated Castilian vellon and debased Valencian silver coinage in 1623–1650 impaired the economic welfare of

[9] In the ensuing examination of his statistical results, the reported data will be taken at face value. However, the statistical procedures employed merit more extended critical examination than is possible here.

workers no less catastrophically than had the influx of American gold and silver in the last eight decades of the sixteenth century'' [16, p. 282]. However again, and once more holding real forces constant, Hamilton's conclusion is not supported by his data. While it is strictly true that real wages as reported by Hamilton were lower in 1600 than they were in 1520, the trend he reports is absent from his data. The reason he gets the results that he does is that 1520 is a year when real wages were exceptionally high when compared with the years immediately preceding and succeeding 1520. On the other hand, 1600 appears to be a year when real wages were exceptionally low when compared with the years immediately preceding and succeeding 1600. If real wages in 1522 are compared with real wages in 1602, then one can conclude that real wages rose. The results Hamilton obtained can be obtained from random series. There is no downward trend in real wages nor any coincidence of wages lagging with inflation.[10] Hamilton's data for the episode are reproduced in Table 1.

In his third volume, Hamilton covers the time interval from 1651 to 1800 and he finds that real wages declined in the urban areas, Madrid and Valencia, in the second half of the eighteenth century. What happened to real wages for the country as a whole is unclear since real wages rose in some rural areas and presumably the country as a whole was predominantly rural [19, p. 210]. The second half of the eighteenth century was characterized by rising prices. However it was also a time when the Spanish population was increasing sharply; it doubled during this century, and was associated with migration

[10] Alternatively one might say that the base year for Hamilton's observations had a strong plus random factor and the final year a strong minus random factor, and what he attributes to inflation can be attributed very easily to sampling error. In statistical jargon, he commits the regression fallacy.

TABLE 1

Composite Index of Real Wages* Base 1571–1580, Period 1501–1650

Year		Year		Year		Year		Year		Year	
1501	112.78	1526	105.66	1551	100.27	1576	103.47	1601	100.88	1626	101.15
1502	115.55	1527	102.26	1552	98.64	1577	106.52	1602	108.68	1627	97.82
1503	118.96	1528	106.62	1553	102.76	1578	102.95	1603	112.80	1628	102.44
1504	111.56	1529	100.15	1554	108.40	1579	97.81	1604	111.94	1629	104.22
1505	108.62	1530	91.35	1555	110.41	1580	102.86	1605	112.10	1630	109.31
1506	92.47	1531	94.39	1556	109.60	1581	104.43	1606	116.80	1631	110.89
1507	99.68	1532	99.40	1557	100.66	1582	101.12	1607	119.60	1632	107.79
1508	102.75	1533	106.25	1558	101.75	1583	100.09	1608	121.35	1633	111.11
1509	117.06	1534	102.43	1559	111.05	1584	102.48	1609	127.83	1634	113.47
1510	127.84	1535	114.03	1560	110.75	1585	102.22	1610	125.49	1635	114.60
1511	120.80	1536	104.49	1561	102.02	1586	106.01	1611	130.56	1636	111.63
1512	126.85	1537	108.19	1562	96.50	1587	103.14	1612	127.96	1637	105.83
1513	125.48	1538	99.82	1563	100.96	1588	111.63	1613	128.09	1638	105.86
1514	122.04	1539	104.06	1564	102.12	1589	107.31	1614	122.85	1639	110.81
1515	118.56	1540	102.30	1565	101.27	1590	105.85	1615	126.57	1640	111.59
1516	120.62	1541	103.73	1566	99.22	1591	107.70	1616	121.45	1641	106.13
1517	123.87	1542	98.23	1567	103.37	1592	104.12	1617	119.81	1642	98.07
1518	118.36	1543	97.24	1568	105.80	1593	107.07	1618	122.90	1643	101.30
1519	119.77	1544	101.45	1569	108.14	1594	106.47	1619	127.08	1644	102.45
1520	125.56	1545	105.14	1570	105.56	1595	106.29	1620	121.61	1645	105.91
1521	112.61	1546	98.36	1571	99.58	1596	103.84	1621	122.11	1646	102.07
1522	104.81	1547	99.28	1572	100.02	1597	99.00	1622	121.85	1647	103.10
1523	109.89	1548	95.54	1573	97.40	1598	93.02	1623	120.16	1648	98.20
1524	109.36	1549	93.61	1574	100.11	1599	91.40	1624	114.64	1649	97.53
1525	106.87	1550	97.61	1575	94.18	1600	91.31	1625	113.82	1650	93.30

Reproduced from Hamilton [16, p. 278], with permission of Harvard University Press.

from rural to urban areas [19, p. 216]. Consequently one would expect, in the absence of any imperfections in the labor market, that such a population increase would lower real wages. Yet Hamilton did not disentangle the effects of this population increase from the effects of inflation upon real wages, and he concluded in the final sentence of his last volume:

> By involuntarily sacrificing real income through the price-wage squeeze, the laboring class bore the burden that implemented material progress, just as laborers and peasants in Soviet Russia, sacrificing through governmental directives, have largely financed the mechanization of industry that was instrumental in the recent expulsion of German invaders [19, p. 225].

B. English and French Data

Hamilton buttresses his conclusions about the effect of inflation upon industrial development by citing similar effects for England and France during inflations that occurred in these countries. Specifically, in his third volume he says:

> The concurrence of profit inflation and of rapid economic development in England and France tends to confirm the thesis that the lag of wages behind prices was an important factor in the great material progress in Spain during the second half of the eighteenth century [19, p. 224].

Again, even if the potential impact of real forces upon wage-price relationships is ignored, can it be said that wages fell during the inflation in England?

Hamilton's study of the movement of prices and wages in London between 1729 and 1800 indicates that real wages fell.[11] Mrs. Gilboy, however, who also studied prices and

[11] [18, p. 259]. One of the relevant problems for analyzing Hamilton's data, which he fails to discuss, is the fact that he has more observations, typically, in his price

wages in England at this time, supports Hamilton's findings of fact but not his conclusions. She found that real wages fell in London and rose in the north of England [12, pp. 191–215]. Therefore she concluded: "Generalizations as to what happened to English wages as a whole must at present meet no little skepticism." [12] Her findings were particularly damaging to Hamilton's interpretation of the implications of a fall in real wages during inflation. Capital formation in the north of England was especially high, whereas Hamilton's hypothesis implies that capital formation ought to have been particularly low in this area.[13]

Hamilton has also examined data for an earlier period of English history, 1500 to 1702 [15, p. 351, Chart 1]. Will these data support the hypothesis that inflation causes wages to lag behind prices if one abstracts from the effects of real forces? (See Table 2.) Taking the period as a whole, Hamilton is right. Real wages declined. However, virtually all of the decline occurred during the first 50 years of this period, and it is unclear whether this shorter time interval ought to be regarded as being on net balance inflationary or deflationary. Prices were about 17 percent lower at the end of these 50 years than they were for the base observation. The first 40 years were

---

than in his wage index. Consequently, if the price and wage observations change with the same degree of frequency, say once a year, it will appear, falsely, as if wages were lagging behind prices. This error accounts for much of the intuitive appeal of the wage-lag hypothesis. If during inflation one sees prices moving up day by day whereas one's own wage rate changes once a year, the conclusion that wages lag behind prices during inflation is difficult to resist.

[12] [12, p. 227]. In a paper dealing with this same issue, Mrs. Gilboy puts the case even more forcefully. "Sufficient data are not at present available to make any statements concerning the movement of real wages in England as a whole for this period" [13, p. 141].

[13] For a partially overlapping time period, 1790–1830, Ashton does not believe that real wages declined [4, p. 158].

TABLE 2
Index Numbers of Prices and Wages in England, 1500–1702*
(Index for 1451–1500 = 100)

Period	*Prices*	*Wages*
1501–1510	95	95
1511–1520	101	93
1521–1530	113	93
1531–1540	105	90
1541–1550	79	57
1551–1560	132	88
1561–1570	155	109
1571–1582	171	113
1583–1592	198	125
1593–1602	243	124
1603–1612	251	124.5
1613–1622	257	134
1623–1632	282	138.5
1633–1642	291	152.5
1643–1652	331	175
1653–1662	308	187
1663–1672	324	190
1673–1682	348	205.5
1683–1692	319	216
1693–1702	339	233

* Reproduced from Hamilton [15, p. 352], with permission of London School of Economics and the author.

inflationary, and real wages fell. However, the next 10 were deflationary, and real wages fell even more. Again these data will not support even this very simple conception of the wage-lag hypothesis.[14]

[14] Using time series of wages and prices as Hamilton does involves the vexing question of how to choose one's starting point or base observation. Presumably one wants to start observations when prices start to rise. But the trough of a price series is usually determined by random components. This produces a transitory peak in the real wage series; the subsequent decrease, if interpreted as a lag, provides an

Tucker studied real wages in London during the latter half of the eighteenth century but has no data for the country as a whole [40]. In view of Gilboy's findings, his data are not of great relevance for England as a whole. Tucker, for reasons

TABLE 3
Index Numbers of Prices and Wages in France, 1500–1700*
(Index for 1451–1500 = 100)

Period	*Prices*	*Wages*
1501–1525	113	92
1526–1550	136	104
1551–1575	174	103
1576–1600	248	113
1601–1625	189	113
1626–1650	243	127
1651–1675	227	127
1676–1700	229	125

* Reproduced from Hamilton [15, p. 353], with permission of London School of Economics and the author.

quite different from Hamilton's, was interested in testing the hypothesis that real wages fall as a result of rising prices. However, every time he observes a fall in real wages, he is able to explain this fall by real factors such as poor crops, resources consumed by wars, etc. [40, p. 82, for example]. Yet he ignores these explanations when drawing his conclusions.

example of the regression fallacy. Only by averaging out transitory or random variations about some turning point can one avoid part of this problem.

Only after acceptance of this paper for publication did we discover the following corroboratory conclusion, "It follows that Keynes was misled when he argued in the *Treatise* that the general rise in prices had stimulated industrial growth by widening profit margins," in E. H. Phelps Brown and S. V. Hopkins, "Wage-rates and Prices: Evidence for Population Pressure in the Sixteenth Century," *Economica*, N.S. 24 (November 1957): 299.

For France, Hamilton does have data that unambiguously show that real wages fell [15, p. 353]. (See Table 3.) However his explanation of why they fell is not supported by related evidence. His hypothesis implies that the larger the fall in real wages, the greater the rate of industrial development. Differences in the rates of capital formation between England and France ought, therefore, to be related to differences in either the observed fall in real wages or the rates of change of prices. Nef was unable to explain differences between the rates of capital formation in France and England with Hamilton's hypothesis.[15] Similarly, the failure to find "correlation between inflation, or its absence, and variations in the rate of economic growth" has led another student of industrial development, Felix, to reject Hamilton's theory of development.[16]

C. The Civil War in the North

Mitchell's basic time series of wages and prices for the North during the Civil War [34] are substantially better than the data for the early days of the industrial revolution. And there is little doubt that real wages truly fell during the Civil War; most of Mitchell's results cannot be rationalized as an artifact resulting from the choice of the time period said to be inflationary. Moreover, these data [34, p. 343] indicate that a substantial fall in real wages occurred.

One might quarrel with Mitchell's use of a wholesale price index as a deflator of real wages. This index was in large part composed of commodities like opium, mercury, zinc, soda ash, tin plate, blue vitriol, etc. A mere count of such items

[15] J. Nef has collected evidence that fails to show a relationship between the magnitude of the lag and the rate of industrial development. He also has evidence that Hamilton's data exaggerate the magnitude of the fall in real wages [37].

[16] See also Felix's discussion, "Hamilton's *Tour d' Horizon*" [9, pp. 457–59].

indicates that an unweighted index overrepresents their effect on the cost-of-living index. Rent, as is typically the case for wholesale price indexes, was absent. But it is easy to make too much of this point. Mitchell also computed a cost-of-living index for this period, and when either this index or one computed by Ethel Hoover, who used the same source material, is used as a deflator, the results still indicate a substantial fall in real wages, although smaller than when wholesale prices are used.[17] (These data are reproduced in [24, p. 102]).

These results led Mitchell to conclude that: "All of the statistical evidence that has been presented in the preceding pages supports unequivocally the common theory that persons whose incomes are derived from wages suffer seriously from a depreciation of the currency" [34, p. 347]. They also led Mitchell to embrace the hypothesis that the labor market in the 1860s and 1870s was imperfect and that this imperfection was of a kind that virtually no serious student of industrial organization asserts exists in any other factor or product market [35, p. 276]. However, there is an alternative explanation of the fall in real wages in the North during the Civil War that is consistent with the way economists explain changes in price relationships in markets other than labor and it explains more of the relative price movements that occurred. Indeed, this explanation is consistent with the postulate that the labor market was operating perfectly during the inflation associated with the Civil War. Because it has none of the ad hoc character of the explanation employed by Mitchell and Hamilton, it is to be preferred.[18]

---

[17] Ethel Hoover's index [22, p. 40, Table 1] is better than Mitchell's CPI because it uses more of the available data and better techniques for accounting for gaps in the data.

[18] The analysis which follows is more fully developed in a paper which appears elsewhere. See [24].

The outbreak of the Civil War substantially destroyed a triangular trading relationship among the North, the South, and England. The South earned foreign exchange through its exports of cotton, which accounted for roughly two thirds of all U.S. exports. It, in effect, traded these foreign exchange earnings for Northern goods and services, and the North in turn used this foreign exchange to purchase imports. The outbreak of hostilities, in addition to destroying a mutually profitable trading relationship between the North and the South, presented the North with what would be regarded today as an extremely difficult balance-of-payments problem. This problem was aggravated by a capital flight of foreign investments during the early years of the war.

That this important problem confronting the North has been largely unrecognized is in large part to be explained by the fact that it was solved unobtrusively and successfully by a measure designed for a largely unrelated function. During the war, the North engaged in the printing of greenbacks; and the resulting inflation and the maintenance of convertibility at the prewar exchange rate were incompatible. In consequence, the North abandoned the gold standard in favor of an inconvertible paper standard and a freely fluctuating exchange rate which inadvertently solved the balance-of-payments problem.

The rise in the prices of imports relative to the rise in domestic prices and wages inevitably produced a fall in real factor incomes of all types. In so far as money wages are deflated by a price index that includes international goods, particularly imports, real wages decline. Since Mitchell's wholesale price index was more heavily weighted by imports than his consumer price index, the use of the former as a deflator produces a greater fall in real wages than does the latter. And of course if imports are excluded from his consumer price index and what remains is used as a deflator of money wages, a still smaller fall in real wages is measured.

However, this is only part of the explanation of the fall in real wages that Mitchell observed. The North, in addition to taxing through inflation, also employed turnover taxes and tariffs as means of war finance. The severity of these taxes increased during the course of the war. These taxes produced a divergence between the sum of the payments to agents of production and final product prices, because unlike retail sales taxes today, they became a part of final product prices. One would also expect for this reason to find that real wages, as measured by Mitchell, declined during the course of the Civil War.

Both the balance-of-payments problem and the turnover taxes would have produced a fall in real wages whether or not inflation had occurred. If the government's increased expenditures had not been financed by inflationary methods, some other means of taxation would have been required. Had tariffs or turnover taxes in any part replaced the inflation tax, an even greater fall in real wages would have occurred. The inflation tax implies that real wages were higher than they otherwise would have been.

D. The Civil War in the South

In a number of respects, Eugene Lerner's study of the Confederacy [27] [28] is parallel to Mitchell's work. In particular, both found that real wages declined. In neither case can most of the decline be attributed to the special characteristics of the base or terminal years for the time period defined as inflationary. Like Mitchell, Lerner attributes the fall in real wages to the lag of wages behind prices and accepts the extraordinary profitability implication of the wage-lag argument. "Prices rose much faster than wages in the Confederacy, and southern businessmen made large profits'' [28, p. 31]. His paper contains virtually no evidence on profits.

The acceptance by Lerner of the wage-lag explanation of the fall in real wages is inconsistent with another interpretation of the events of the time that may be found in his own papers. He indicates that much of Southern capital was highly specialized to the production of cotton for an international market and that the Northern blockade sharply reduced the productivity of this capital. Lerner also reports that excises, either in the form of taxes or payments in kind, constituted an important means of war finance. In fact, Lerner implicitly presents a hypothesis that explains the fall in real wages by nonmonetary

TABLE 4
Hansen's Series of Money Wages, Cost of Living and Real Wages*
(1913 = 100)

Year	*Index of Money Wages*	*Index of Cost-of-Living*	*Index of Real Wages*
1910	94	94	100
1911	95	92	103
1912	98	96	102
1913	100	100	100
1914	102	102	100
1915	104	104	100
1916	118	111	106
1917	134	131	102
1918	168	159	106
1919	193	183	105
1920	232	208	112
1921	207	182	114
1922	201	168	120
1923	220	171	129

* Reproduced from Hansen [21, p. 32].

phenomena, but he explicitly accepts the thesis that the fall in real wages is attributable to inflation.

E. World War I

Hansen's study is concerned with real wages and price changes in the United States from 1820 to 1923 and thus includes the inflation associated with World War I. His position is much like that of Mitchell and Hamilton. "Rising prices cause a gap between the marginal productivity of the various factors employed by the entrepreneur and the return that each receives. Indeed in such periods it is literally true that 'labor does not receive the full value of its product'" [21, p. 40].

However, even if real forces are assumed to be constant, as Hansen presumably assumed, the data do not support the wage-lag hypothesis. Indeed, they can be just as easily construed as undermining the hypothesis. Only if one chooses the year 1916 as a base and compares it with 1919 or 1917, can one show that real wages fell.[19] (See Table 4.) If one uses 1913 as a base, and every succeeding year through 1920 as a terminal point, there is nothing to indicate a fall in real wages. In fact, Hansen's data show that real wages were almost 10 percent greater in 1920 than in 1917.

These data of Hansen's contain an unfortunate bias in favor of the wage-lag hypothesis for the entire time interval with which he was concerned. Starting with 1890, Hansen uses weekly earnings rather than hourly earnings. If leisure is a superior good, and if real hourly earnings per capita rise, then

[19] Hamilton in a parenthetical remark [15, p. 355] selects 1916 as a base year and observes that ". . . American profiteers reaped [income] from a similar divergence between prices and wages from 1916 to 1919." Hansen's data, reproduced as Table 5, show a less than one percent fall in real wages for this period.

weekly earnings understate real wages because of the substitution of leisure for income from work. Consequently, evidence collected to reveal a fall in real wages can be explained, at least in part, by the hypothesis that they were in fact rising. This bias is particularly unfortunate in a study of secular inflations because the longer the time period considered, the greater the error it introduces into the calculations.

F. The German Inflation

Bresciani-Turroni contends that real wages declined as a *result* of the inflation in Germany following World War I [7].[20] For the entire inflationary episode, he concluded: "But it may be said that on the whole the inflation generally favored the entrepreneurs and the owners of material means of production, especially strengthening the positions of industrial capitalists; that it caused a lowering of the real wages of workmen . . ." [7, p. 286]. However, leaving aside questions of the impact of real forces upon real wages, Bresciani-Turroni's wage data, which consist almost exclusively of miners' wages, show that real wages sometimes declined and sometimes rose during the course of the inflation. Over the period as a whole, real wages did not fall [7, pp. 307, 309].

During the later stages of the inflation when the real value of the nominal stock of money declined sharply, or during the time that velocity increased at a rate more rapid than the rate of increase of the monetary stock, Bresciani-Turroni found that real wages fell. This rise in velocity was attributable to the recognition by the community of the increased cost of holding

[20] "The increase in nominal wage rates was slower than the increase in prices caused by monetary inflation. In other words, real wages fell" [7, p. 305; also pp. 186–88]. This fall in real wages, according to Bresciani-Turroni, continued until the summer of 1922.

cash balances caused by rising prices. In this respect the German hyperinflation was unlike the inflations examined by Mitchell, Hansen, Hamilton, Gilboy, and Tucker, and it led to a marked reduction in the effective stock of capital in money form. Under these circumstances, the higher marginal cost of using money is an additional cost of doing business, and this implies that the share of the final output of the economy going to the other cooperating agents of production has decreased. Consequently, a fall in real wages during an inflation that is generally anticipated is consistent with a perfectly functioning labor market and does not imply an increase in business profits. In fact this analysis is consistent with Bresciani-Turroni's data on share prices, which do not support the thesis that business firms are extraordinarily profitable as a consequence of inflation [7, p. 253].

In general, it appears that a highly selective sampling from the population of all inflations has produced two important unambiguous cases of a fall in real wages for individual economies, those of the North and the South during the Civil War. For these cases, the wage-lag hypothesis has to compete with price theory. For the one case that has been studied in great detail, that of the North during the Civil War, price theory offers a more satisfactory explanation.

Whether or not available data indicate that real wages fell during inflation for some particular economy does not in itself establish or disprove the existence of an inflation-induced wage lag unless one assumes real forces to be inoperative. A time series of wages and prices can be made relevant evidence for testing the wage-lag hypothesis only after the effects of real forces are controlled. Unfortunately, the wage-lag theorists have generally ignored real forces. In the case of the North during the Civil War, the real forces ignored are substantial in magnitude and capable of producing the effects upon real wages imputed to the wage-lag hypothesis. When one considers the implications of this hypothesis, as the wage-lag theorists have not, the differences between industrial development in the North and South of England during the early days of the industrial revolutions, along with the Nef findings, must be regarded as still more evidence against this hypothesis.

III. NEW EVIDENCE

In an effort to bring some new evidence to bear on the validity of wage-lag hypothesis, the annual wage bills for 56 industrial corporations listed on the New York Stock Exchange during the time interval 1940 to 1952 have been collected. These were all the industrial firms listed that reported their wage bills during this entire period.

The proposition tested was that the firms with large annual wage bills would experience an increase in profits (and wealth) relative to firms with smaller annual wage bills. That is, for any given rise in prices, sales and costs other than wages rise by the same proportion, whereas total wages [W] rise by less, e.g., by only some fraction, α, of the general price rise. Thus, $W(1 - \alpha)$ constitutes the size of the gain in profits for any firm. The relative magnitude of the gain is a function of the size of a firm's wage bill relative to its equity, as measured by its market value. In other words, the ratio of wages to equity is an indicator of the relative rise in stock prices attributable to a lag of wages behind prices.[21]

[21] Hamilton evidently regards the ratio of wages to total costs as the correct indicator of the size of the gain attributable to the lag of wages behind prices [18, p. 262]. However, two firms with identical equity values and identical ratios of wages to total costs might have different markups and consequently different aggregate

The ratio of wages to equity was obtained for each of the years from 1940 to 1952 through the use of the annual wage bill and the market value of stock outstanding at the end of the year. Unfortunately, testing for a relationship between the relative change in market value and the wage-to-equity ratio produces a bias in favor of finding a positive correlation because ratios with the same denominator are being correlated. To reduce this bias, the annual wage-to-equity ratios, one for each year in the 1940 to 1952 period, were averaged for each corporation and then used as a predictor of relative changes in equity values.[22]

The use of this average seemed reasonable because the differences between firms with respect to this average were significantly greater than the variations of any given year from the average for any firm. (The wage-to-equity ratios exhibited no trend over time.) The standard deviation of the ratio of wages to equity for any given year was about 20 percent of the average for any firm. On the other hand, the average ratio varied, from firm to firm, from a low of 1 to a high of 7.[23] And because the interfirm variation was so much greater than the intrafirm variation, it seemed sensible to enlarge the size of the sample by using data for firms that reported annual wage bills for as little as two years of the time-span studied. This brought the sample to 113 firms. (A listing of the firms and other

---

wage bills. (For example, consider a jewelry store and a supermarket grocery.) What is relevant is the size of the wage bill. And for interfirm comparisons, the relationship of the wage bill to total equity is the appropriate one.

[22] This also buys some insurance against committing the regression fallacy. If the wage-to-equity ratio at the beginning of the time period were used, firms with large wage-to-equity ratios might be those with transitorily small equity valuations and conversely.

[23] This ratio is affected by the financial structure. A firm with large debts and small equity financing will have a high wage-to-equity ratio and conversely.

relevant data may be obtained through personal communication with the authors. Unfortunately, space constraints do not permit us to publish them here.)

By trying to detect a correlation between wage-to-equity ratios and changes in stock prices, the effects of a lag of wages behind prices caused by inflation can be disentangled from the effects of real forces upon real wages. After all, if one believes that real and monetary forces can operate independently and concurrently, the wage lag should be operative regardless of whether time series of wages and prices during inflation show that real wages fell, rose, or were constant. Given independence between real forces and the wage-to-equity ratio of a firm, this test ought to reveal the presence of the effects of inflation upon real wages.

According to the wage-lag hypothesis, the greater the wage-to-equity ratio, the larger should be the rise in equity values as a result of inflation.[24] To test whether or not this implication is in fact correct, firms were ranked according to their average ratio of wages to equity. The percentage increase in equity for firms with an average ratio of annual wages to equity below .5 were compared with those above 1. The results of this comparison are presented in summary form in Table 5. The average equity rise was greater the lower the wages-to-equity ratio. Such a difference in the wrong direction clearly does not support the wage-lag hypothesis. Dividing the sample into two equal parts, one consisting of firms with the larger wage-to-equity ratios and the other of firms with the smaller wage-to-equity ratios, yields similar results.

[24] For example, if a firm's stock sold for $4 at the end of 1939 and $40 at the end of 1952, the equity increase is shown as a ratio, 10. Dividends paid are assumed to be reinvested into more shares of the same firm, and thus their growth was compounded. In this way, differences in dividend payout policy were held constant.

In any attempt to impute the absence of causality to the absence of correlation between two variables, there always exists the danger that still another variable is so correlated with what is regarded as the independent variable that the effects of the independent variable upon the dependent variable are con-

TABLE 5
Mean Equity Increases of Firms Classified by Wage-to-Equity Ratio*

Ratio of Wages-to-Equity	*Average Increase in Equity (1939–52)*	*Number of Firms*	*Variance*
Under .5	8.41	34	48.4
.5 to .99	7.40	30	39.1
1. and over	6.19	49	26.5
"t" for 8.41 − 6.19 = + 1.58			
P(t ≥ 1.26) = .12			

* *Sources*: Moody's *Industrials* [36], *Annual Reports* [3], and *New York Times* [38].

cealed. Relevant to this problem is the fact that a relationship is known to exist between the net monetary status of a firm and the relative change in its stock prices during inflation [23, p. 128]. The increase in the equity of the 43 firms in the sample that were net monetary debtors at least two thirds of the time from 1940 to 1952 was greater than that experienced by the 29 firms in the sample that were net monetary creditors at least two thirds of the time.[25] These results are consistent with known effects of debtor-creditor status upon stock price

[25] There were 43 debtor and 29 creditor firms. The mean rise for the debtor firms was 8.25 with a variance of 39.67; for the creditor firms, the mean was 5.94 and the variance 19.20. $\bar{x}_d - \bar{x}_0 = 2.31$, $t = 1.82$, $P\ (t \geq + 1.82) \approx .04$ Sources: [3] [36] [38].

TABLE 6

Matrix of Simple and Rank Correlation Coefficients Among Equity Rise, Wage-to-Equity Ratio, Net Monetary Status, and Sales-to-Equity Ratio*

		(1)	*(2)*	*(3)*	*(4)*
Equity Rise, 1952/1939	(1)	1.	.04 (− .09)	.01 (.24)	.10 (.02)
Ratio of Wages-to-Equity	(2)		1.	.33 (.15)	.51 (.83)
Net Monetary Status	(3)			1.	.10 (.36)
Ratio of Sales-to-Equity	(4)				1.
Partial Correlation Coefficients	$r_{12.34}=$		− .09 (− .11)		
	$r_{13.24}=$		.04 (.36)		
	$r_{14.23}=$		.16 (.08)		

* The rank correlation coefficients are in parentheses. For the ranks, the one-tailed 5 percent probability value is .16, the two-tailed probability value is .22, $P\ (r > .36) < .001$.

changes during inflation.[26] Consequently, if firms that were large net debtors were also firms that had large wage-to-equity ratios, debtor status would counteract the effect of the wage lag upon stock prices, and the consequences of inflation-induced lags of wages behind prices would go undetected.

In order to determine whether or not debtor-creditor effects were masking the effects of inflation upon business profits, the relationships among (1) changes in equity values, (2) annual wage-to-equity ratios, (3) debtor-creditor status, and (4) annual sales-to-equity ratio (for those who think that sales are correlated with wage-to-equity ratios) were explored by means of a multiple correlation analysis. As a measure of a firm's net monetary creditor or debtor status over the interval 1940 to 1952, the average of debtor-creditor status in each year was weighted by the price rise for the year as measured by the change in the consumer price index of the Bureau of Labor Statistics.[27] For each of 113 firms there are observations with respect to four variables. The simple correlation coefficients among these four variables are presented in Table 6 along with the partial correlation coefficients of each predictive variable with the other two predictive variables held statistically con-

[26] Possibly this is too strong a statement. Bach and Ando [5] report that they were unable to detect the debtor-creditor effect. There seem to be two reasons for the apparent difference between the outcome of Kessel's early work and the results reported here on the one hand, and the results reported by Bach and Ando on the other. Bach and Ando used several different criteria for determining whether or not the debtor-creditor effect existed. Only one of these criteria was implied by the hypothesis being tested. On that one pertinent criterion their results do verify the debtor-creditor wealth transfer. But they relied on the rule of the majority rather than the rule of a decisive test. This error was compounded by their erroneous use of a "two-tailed" probability calculation instead of a one-tailed calculation. For additional evidence, published subsequent to the Bach and Ando paper, see [2, p. 537].

[27] Subsequent examination indicates that an unweighted average, which is cheaper to compute, would have given essentially similar, but not quite as effective, results.

stant. Results of this partial correlation analysis do not support the wage lag.[28] However, these correlation coefficients are difficult to interpret because the necessary conditions for computing their sampling distribution are not satisfied. In particular, the predicted or dependent variable is not normally distributed.[29] Therefore, no reliable probability tests of significance can be applied.

To obtain a probability test, the values associated with each of the variables were converted to ranks, and rank correlation coefficients were computed. These are reported in Table 6. These calculations indicate a positive partial correlation between net monetary status and increases in equity values. And there is only once chance in 1,000 that such a result could be obtained by randomly sampling from a population characterized by an absence of this relationship. The negative partial correlation of wage-to-equity ratios and changes in stock prices still persists; however, this correlation can be easily rationalized as the result of random sampling from a population characterized by an absence of this relationship. Again the wage-lag hypothesis is not supported after the potential masking effects of two variables are specifically eliminated. The absence of a relationship between sales and changes in equity values is probably the result of using the level of sales rather than the rate of change of sales as an independent variable.

If neither a regression phenomenon nor a masking effect

---

[28] Since these are the same data used in the previous test, these results cannot be construed as new independent evidence against the wage-lag hypothesis.

[29] One objection to this procedure that does not seem warranted is the objection that correlations among ratios, such as these are, must be invalid because they are subject to biases. But it is the ratios themselves that are interesting in an economic sense. Secondly, even if one thinks in absolute terms, the weighting of observations by the inverse of their standard deviation eliminates the bias. Moreover, the bias of ratios, if present, would work in favor of the wage-lag hypothesis, not against it.

from monetary status is operating, can the results obtained be attributed to a correlation among specific industries? Relative price changes have possibly favored industries consisting of low wage-to-equity firms. Eight of the 34 firms in the low wage-to-equity class are oil firms. The removal of these firms from the sample failed to alter significantly the results obtained. The average equity rise, with the oil firms removed, of the low wage-to-equity firms was still greater than for the other class by a 6.76 to 6.19 margin. Needless to say, there exists an indefinitely large number of variables that might be so correlated with wage-to-equity ratios that the effects of the wage lag upon changes in equity values would be concealed. All any investigator can do is to eliminate only the most promising candidates in the light of his knowledge of the economics of the problem.

IV. CONCLUSIONS

One of the important advances in economic analysis in the postwar period has been the formal incorporation into theory of the effects of wealth upon consumption expenditures. Previously it seemed reasonable to argue that wages must lag behind prices during inflation if the government acquired resources through inflation. The logic of this argument has been shown to be false.

Another independent line of argument for the proposition that inflation causes real wages to fall is based on sluggishness or flaws in the labor market whereby wage earners receive less than their marginal product when prices are rising. But much of the data which investigators have collected to show a fall in real wages during the course of selected inflations simply fail to support the hypothesis. By one selection of beginning and terminal points for an inflation it can be shown real wages fell; by another selection it can be shown that real wages rose. The fall in real wages reported by these observers is a product of the arbitrary way the time period during which inflation occurred was defined.

However, data do exist, particularly in Mitchell's work, that unambiguously indicate a fall in real wages. But before such data can be seriously considered as supporting the wage-lag hypothesis, one must first show that even after price theory has done all it can to explain the altered price-wage relationship, there is still something left to explain. The advocates or investigators of the wage-lag hypothesis have never shown this. As for the time period studied by Mitchell, it appears that known and measurable real forces can and do explain the fall in real wages that he has observed.

Efforts to detect the existence of the wage lag during inflation through the examination of stock prices of firms that differed with respect to the volume of labor hired per dollar of invested capital by owners have also failed. This evidence contradicts the wage-lag hypothesis. Still, it is easy to make too much of this evidence since it was based on a nonrandom sample and was obtained for only one inflation.

In general, it appears that unwarranted validity has been assigned to the wage-lag hypothesis, given the character of the evidence that has been used to support it. A rereading of this evidence suggests that the wage-lag hypothesis ought to be regarded as essentially untested.

References

1. A. Alchian, and R. Kessel. "How the Government Gains from Inflation," *Proceedings of the Thirtieth Annual*

Conference of the Western Economics Association (1955), Salt Lake City, 1956, pp. 13–16.

2. ———. "Redistribution of Wealth through Inflation," *Science* 130 (September 4, 1959): 535–39.
3. *Corporation Annual Reports*, Godfrey Memorial Library (New Haven, Yale University), 1939 to 1952.
4. T. S. Ashton. "The Standard of Life of the Workers in England, 1790–1830," in *Capitalism and the Historians*, ed. F. A. Hayek, Chicago, 1954, pp. 127–59.
5. G. L. Bach, and A. Ando. "The Redistributional Effects of Inflation," *Rev. Econ and Stat.* 39 (February 1957): 1–13.
6. E. M. Bernstein, and I. G. Patel. "Inflation in Relation to Economic Development," *Internat. Mon. Fund Staff Papers* 2 (November 1952): 363–98.
7. C. Bresciani-Turroni. *The Economics of Inflation*. London, 1937.
8. P. Cagan. "The Monetary Dynamics of Hyperinflation," in *Studies in the Quantity Theory of Money*, ed. M. Friedman, Chicago, 1956, pp. 25–117.
9. D. Felix. "Profit Inflation and Industrial Growth: The Historic Record and Contemporary Analogies," *Quart. Jour. Econ.* 70 (August 1956): 441–63.
10. I. Fisher. *The Purchasing Power of Money*. Rev. ed. New York, 1926.
11. M. Friedman. "Discussion of the Inflationary Gap," *Essays in Positive Economics*, Chicago, 1953, pp. 251–62.
12. E. Gilboy. *Wages in Eighteenth Century England*. Cambridge, Mass., 1934.
13. ———. "The Cost of Living and Real Wages in Eighteenth Century England," *Rev. Econ. Stat.* 18 (1936): 134–43.

14. G. Haberler. *Prosperity and Depression*. 3d ed. New York, United Nations, 1946, pp. 137–41, 481.
15. E. J. Hamilton. "American Treasure and the Rise of Capitalism (1500–1700)" *Economica* 9 (November 1929): 338–57.
16. ———. *American Treasure and the Price Revolution in Spain, 1501–1650*. Cambridge, Mass., 1934.
17. ———. *Money, Prices, and Wages in Valencia, Aragon, and Navarre, 1351–1500*. Cambridge, Mass., 1936.
18. ———. "Profit Inflation and the Industrial Revolution, 1751–1800," *Quart. Jour. Econ.* 56 (February 1942): 256–73; reprinted [26, pp. 322–36].
19. ———. *War and Prices in Spain, 1651–1800*. Cambridge, Mass., 1947.
20. ———. "Prices as a Factor in Business Growth," *Jour. Econ. Hist.* 12 (Fall 1952): 325–49.
21. A. H. Hansen. "Factors Affecting Trend of Real Wages," *Am. Econ. Rev.* 15 (1925): 40–53.
22. E. D. Hoover. *Prices in the United States in the 19th Century*. (Mimeographed and unpublished manuscript presented at a National Bureau Conference on Research in Income and Wealth, September 4–5, 1957.)
23. R. A. Kessel. "Inflation-Caused Wealth Redistribution: A Test of a Hypothesis," *Am. Econ. Rev.* 46 (March 1956): 128–41.
24. R. A. Kessel, and A. A. Alchian. "Real Wages in the North During the Civil War: Mitchell's Data Reinterpreted," *Jour. Law and Econ.* 2 (October 1959): 95–113.
25. J. M. Keynes. *A Treatise on Money*. Vol. 2. New York, 1930.
26. F. C. Lane, and J. C. Riemersma, eds., *Enterprise and Secular Change*. Homewood, Ill., 1953.

27. E. M. Lerner. "The Monetary and Fiscal Programs of the Confederate Government, 1861–65," *Jour. Pol. Econ.* 62 (December 1954): 506–22.
28. ———. "Money, Prices, and Wages in the Confederacy, 1861–65," *Jour. Pol. Econ.* 63 (February 1955): 20–40.
29. W. A. Lewis. *The Theory of Economic Growth*. Homewood, Ill., 1955.
30. E. Lipson, *The Economic History of England*. Vol. 1, 4th ed. London, 1926.
31. A. Marshall. "Answers to Questions on the Subject of Currency and Prices Circulated by Royal Commission on the Depression of Trade and Industry (1886)," *Official Papers by Alfred Marshall*, London, 1926, pp. 3–16.
32. G. M. Meier, and R. Baldwin. *Economic Development: Theory, History, Policy*. New York, 1957.
33. F. V. Meyer. *Inflation and Capital*. Cambridge, Eng., 1954.
34. W. C. Mitchell. *A History of the Greenbacks*. Chicago, 1903.
35. ———. *Gold Prices, and Wages under the Greenback Standard*, Berkeley, 1908.
36. *Moody's Manual of Investments, American and Foreign, Industrial Securities*. Moody's Investor's Service, New York. Annually from 1939 through 1953.
37. J. Nef. "Prices and Industrial Capitalism in France and England, 1540–1640," *Econ. Hist. Rev.* 7 (May 1937): 155–85, reprinted in [26, pp. 292–321].
38. *New York Times*, daily ed., 1939–1952.
39. A. Rees. "Patterns of Wages, Prices and Productivity," in *Wages, Prices, Profits and Productivity*, Fifteenth American Assembly, New York, 1959, pp. 11–59.

40. R. S. Tucker. "Real Wages of Artisans in London, 1729–1935," *Jour. Am. Stat. Assoc.* 31 (1936): 73–84.
41. H. P. Willis, and J. M. Chapman. *The Economics of Inflation*, New York, 1935.

Real Wages in the North During the Civil War: Mitchell's Data Reinterpreted

The hypothesis that inflation causes real wages to decline has won wide acceptance among economists.[1] Probably the strongest piece of empirical evidence that has been mustered in its support is the data on wages and prices contained in Mitchell's famous study of inflation in the North during the Civil War. It is the thesis of this essay that there exists an alternative explanation that Mitchell failed to consider which constitutes a more satisfactory explanation of the phenomena he observed. The purpose of this essay is to present this alternative explanation.

In his study of inflation in the North during the Civil War, Mitchell, after examining the evidence for the period, concluded:

This article was coauthored by Reuben A. Kessel. The authors benefited from the comments of Professor Cagan of Brown University, Professors Hamilton, Lewis, Rees, and Stigler of the University of Chicago, and Professor Evans of the Massachusetts Institute of Technology.

[1] This is the subject of another paper entitled: "The Meaning and Validity of the Inflation-Induced Lag of Wages Behind Prices," which appeared in *Am. Econ. Rev.* 50 (March 1960). Both of these papers are part of a larger study of the redistributive effects of inflation sponsored by the Merrill Foundation for the Advancement of Financial Knowledge.

> All of the statistical evidence that has been presented in the preceding pages supports unequivocally the common theory that persons whose incomes are derived from wages suffer seriously from a depreciation of the currency. The confirmation seems particularly striking when the conditions other than monetary affecting the labor market are taken into consideration. American workingmen are intelligent and keenly alive to their interests.[2]

The evidence that led Mitchell to this conclusion consists primarily of the time series of real wages shown in Table 1.[3]

TABLE 1
Average Change in Real Wages of Over 5,000 Wage Earners

Date	*Index of Real Wages*	*Date*	*Index of Real Wages*
Jan. 1860	100	Jan. 1863	89
July 1860	100	July 1863	86
Jan. 1861	102	Jan. 1864	81
July 1861	104	July 1864	71
Jan. 1862	102	Jan. 1865	67
July 1862	101	July 1865	97

Mitchell also arrived at the conclusion that "real profits were unusually large during the Civil War, therefore, but large because real wages, rent and interest were low," with virtually no direct evidence on real returns to profit receivers.[4] In reaching this conclusion that real profits increased because real wages and real returns to rent and interest receivers declined, Mitchell postulated, and this is not explicit, that the rate of

[2] W. C. Mitchell, *A History of the Greenbacks* (1903), pp. 347–48.

[3] *Ibid.*, p. 342. This is one half of Table 46. It is the half computed with variable weights for the wage index. Since Mitchell regarded variable weights as better than constant weights, the index with variable weights will be used as Mitchell's wage index throughout this paper.

[4] *Ibid.*, p. 382.

return to all agents of production taken jointly was constant between 1860 and 1865.[5]

The price index for Mitchell's real wage calculations is based on the median observation of ninety wholesale prices using 1860 as a base. Observations (January, April, July, and October) were recorded for every year studied. The observations for the wage index are weighted. Mitchell, in his chapter on prices, argues that a wholesale price index ought to be satisfactory for detecting the effect of the issuance of greenbacks upon prices, but he revealed some reservations about the suitability of this index for cost-of living calculations.[6] Despite these reservations, Mitchell used this wholesale-price index for measuring real wages.

The representativeness of the ninety commodities in Mitchell's wholesale-price index of wage goods (or, for that matter, prices generally) is highly questionable. His index, like most wholesale-price indexes, contains no rent component. Internationally traded goods are strongly represented, and this, as will be developed, gives the index a strong upward bias for most of the time period with which Mitchell was concerned. (Almost two thirds of the commodities that could be unambiguously classified as either domestic or international were found to be international [see the Appendix].) Furthermore, many of the commodities in the index—opium, copper, linseed oil, soda ash, quinine, oxide of zinc, sulfuric acid, turpentine, rubber, copperas, lead, tin plate, and alum—should be regarded as of little direct significance for measuring prices of wage goods.

---

[5] *Ibid.*, chaps. 6, 7 (Part II), which contain direct evidence on the real returns to interest and rent receivers. Almost no evidence on profits appears in this volume.

[6] *Ibid.*, p. 244. Even for this limited purpose of detecting the effect upon prices, it appears that this index overstated the extent of inflation, particularly from 1860 through 1864.

Yet it is easy to make too much of the fact that Mitchell employed a wholesale-price index as a deflator. In his subsequent work on the Civil War, Mitchell computed a consumers' price index for this same period with an independent set of data.[7] These data (reproduced as part of Table 2)[8] also reveal a

TABLE 2
Consumers' Prices, Money Wages, and Real Wages

Year	*Prices*	*Wages*	*Real Wages*
1860	100	100	100
1861	104	99	95
1862	117	104	89
1863	140	119	85
1864	170	142	83
1865	179	155	87

substantial fall in real wages, although neither as large a fall as observed when the wholesale-price index is used nor as sharp a recovery in 1865. They buttress Mitchell's conclusion that real wages fell during the Civil War. Incidentally, this later study seems to have shaken Mitchell's earlier confidence in the alertness of American workmen to their interests; and he observes in this later work:

[7] W. C. Mitchell, *Gold, Prices, and Wages Under the Greenback Standard* (1908). This is the data contained in the so-called Weeks report. They were collected in 1890 by questionnaires sent to businessmen. The data used for Mitchell's wholesale-price index are contained in the Aldrich report, also collected in 1890 but by government agents from actual records rather than from questionnaires. Consequently, it appears that Mitchell chose the wholesale-price index because it contained what most observers would regard as "better data."

[8] The semiannual wage data are reported for January and July of each year. The July observations are used on the grounds that they are a better match for the annual price data than either the January figures or an average of January and July. See *ibid.*, p. 91, Table 30, for the price data. The wage data are from Mitchell, *A History of the Greenbacks*, p. 310, Table 30.

> In the 60's and, though in somewhat less degree, in the 70's, the labor market of the United States was one in which individual bargaining prevailed. Now the individual laborer is a poor bargainer. He is ignorant of the possibilities of his situation, exposed to the competition of others with the same disabilities, more anxious to sell than the employer to buy. Moreover, custom in the form of rooted ideas about what is a "fair wage" has a peculiarly tenacious hold upon the minds of both parties in the labor market, weakening the wage earner's aggression and strengthening the employer's resistance.[9]

Mitchell readily accepted the hypothesis that inflation accounted for the observed fall in real wages, with substantially no consideration of conditions other than monetary despite his protestation to the contrary.[10] Because of his failure to consider conditions other than monetary (i.e., "real forces"), Mitchell accepted an explanation of his observations that is inconsistent with the way economists explain changes in price ratios in markets other than labor. He rejected a standard explanation with a wide range of applicability in favor of an ad hoc explanation, without first showing the inapplicability of the standard explanation. It is the thesis of this paper that, if Mitchell had considered nonmonetary conditions more extensively, he would not have regarded his observations as unequivocally supporting the hypothesis that the observed fall was attributable to inflation. Indeed, there are grounds for inferring that the inflation resulting from the issuance of greenbacks led to a higher level of real wages than Mitchell would have observed in the absence of inflation.

Mitchell's real wage data and the observed fall in real rates

---

[9] Mitchell, *Gold, Prices, and Wages Under the Greenback Standard*, pp. 275–76.

[10] The factors other than monetary that Mitchell considered are: (1) the withdrawal of one-seventh of the labor force for war services; (2) more fully employed workers during the war than before the war started; and (3) a decline in the average quality of the labor force. Mitchell, *A History of the Greenbacks*, pp. 348, 350, 383, respectively.

of return to other agents of production can be explained as a consequence of three nonmonetary phenomena. These phenomena can be regarded as "real" forces, in the sense that the implications of their existence for real wages can be analyzed by the theory of relative prices as distinguished from monetary theory. These three forces are (1) the outbreak of warfare between the North and the South, which curtailed, if it did not eliminate, previous trading relationships; (2) the special economic characteristics of the base year, 1860; and (3) the tax system used to divert resources from the community to the government. All three of these phenomena operated jointly and independently of inflation to drive up the prices of goods and services relative to wages and other factor incomes generally during the Civil War. The remainder of this paper is concerned with the economic implications of these events.

I. THE OUTBREAK OF WARFARE

The outbreak of the Civil War almost completely destroyed the triangular trade relationship between the North, the South, and England. Before the war the North had an export surplus on current account in its trade with the South and a deficit with England, while the South had a surplus with England. Hostilities and the ensuing blockade forced all three parties into what must be presumed inferior trade relations with a consequent loss in real income for all. In particular, the North was left with inferior markets for its exports and inferior sources for many commodities such as cotton and turpentine formerly imported from the South. Similarly, the South had to find new markets for its cotton and new sources for the manufactured goods and foodstuffs previously obtained from the North.

An examination of the relevant trade statistics leads to the conclusion that the outbreak of hostilities presented the North with what would be regarded, by modern standards, as an incredibly difficult balance-of-payments problem. Before the war, roughly two thirds of all exports of goods and services for the entire country consisted of cotton.[11] This source of foreign exchange was, for all practical purposes, completely lost to the South and hence to the North. Moreover, Southern sources of cotton were in part replaced by imports of cotton from abroad. This implies that not only did the North lose much of its power to earn foreign exchange at the prewar exchange rate but also that its foreign-exchange "requirements" increased because foreign cotton in part replaced Southern cotton.

During the early years of the war the loss of foreign-exchange earnings resulting from decreased cotton exports was partly offset by extraordinarily large Northern wheat crops at a time when crops were short elsewhere in the world. Consequently, exports of wheat, particularly to England, increased sharply.[12] Wheat exports, as compared with prewar, increased by a factor of between four and five during the fiscal years 1861, 1862, and 1863.[13] Nevertheless, total wheat exports in each year represented less than one fourth of the decline in the yearly value of cotton exports caused by the Northern blockade. Consequently, one would expect enor-

[11] U.S. Dept. of Commerce, *Historical Statistics of the United States, 1789–1945*, p. 247, series M56-67 (1949); and Secretary of the Treasury, *Commerce and Navigation of the U.S.* (1859), and (1860).

[12] C. W. Wright, *Economic History of the United States* (1941), p. 530; and Mitchell, *A History of the Greenbacks*, p. 530. Fite says: "The largest increase in demand came from foreign countries, for in the three years 1860, 1861 and 1862 the harvests of Great Britain were a failure, and in one of the years those of all Europe" (E. D. Fite, *Social and Industrial Conditions in the North During the Civil War* [1930], pp. 17 et seq.).

[13] *Historical Statistics, op. cit.*, p. 247. These are fiscal years ending on the last day of June.

mous deficits on current account for this reason and large exports of gold as a result.

The difficulties of the North with respect to its trade balance on current account were aggravated by capital flights during the early part of the war. Before the war the United States was normally a net importer of capital. This source of foreign exchange was lost during the early years of the war, and, in addition, many foreign investors converted their American securities into gold.[14] Net interest payments to foreigners declined by one third between 1860 and the wartime low point (1863).[15] In part, these capital movements out of the country were offset by the sale of American-owned ships abroad.[16] Nevertheless, for the early years of the war, international capital movements intensified the North's balance-of-payments problems.

The problem of reconciling the reduction in the North's ability to pay for imports with its desires for imports was resolved by a measure undertaken to achieve quite another purpose. The suspension of specie payments was the consequence of the incompatibility between the issuance of greenbacks and the maintenance of convertibility of notes into gold at prewar exchange rates. As a result, the North abandoned the gold standard at the end of 1861.[17] Gold became a commodity

---

[14] D. R. Dewey, *Financial History of the United States* (12th ed., 1934), pp. 294–95.

[15] Graham, "International Trade Under Depreciated Paper: The United States, 1862–79" *Q. J. Econ.* 36 (1922): 220, 231.

[16] *Ibid.*

[17] The departure from gold was precipitated by the so-called Trent affair. However, the run on the banks would not have been as severe as it was if notes had not been created as a means of war finance. And, in any case, suspension was inevitable if greenbacks were to be issued as they in fact were. See Mitchell, *A History of the Greenbacks*, pp. 37 et seq.

that was freely bought and sold without the government's taking a position in the gold market. Consequently, gold was released from some of its monetary functions, and the hoarding which had begun as a result of gold's undervaluation at the old exchange rate was reversed.

Abandonment of the gold standard, while the major trading countries of the world remained on this standard, made the price of foreign exchange a function of the price of gold, or, to use the language of the times, the premium on gold. Inconvertible fiat money, referred to popularly as "greenbacks" and officially as "United States notes," was issued as a means of war finance and became the currency of the times (except in California and Oregon). As a result, the price of gold as measured in greenbacks determined the cost of foreign exchange. The free exchange rate eliminated the development of foreign-exchange "shortages," and the magnitude of the foreign-exchange problem of the North was largely unrecognized both then and now.

After the abandonment of the gold standard, the price of gold rose relative to prices generally. This change in the real cost of gold (i.e., the increase in the cost of gold as measured by the exchange value of gold for goods and services generally) is crucial for sustaining two related propositions: (1) that Mitchell's wholesale-price index overstated the rise in prices because of the strong representation of internationally traded goods in the index, and (2) that nonmonetary forces played a role in reducing real wages as measured by Mitchell.

A rise in the price of gold relative to prices generally implies that the real costs of imports rose. Or, to put the matter another way, the amount of a typical export the North exchanged for a pound of pepper increased. This is equivalent to saying that the terms of trade turned against the North. However, inflation should not cause the terms of trade to change. Inflation, according to purchasing-power-parity theory, causes the money cost of foreign exchange to rise as the price level of domestic goods and services within a county rises relative to comparable price levels abroad. Consequently, the domestic prices of imports should increase *pari passu* with the general price level as a result of inflation.[18] Any increase in the domestic price of imports beyond what is implied by purchasing-power-parity theory reflects the operation of nonmonetary forces. Changes in the prices of domestic goods vis-à-vis corresponding foreign price levels reflect the increase in the greenback cost of gold attributable to inflation. The rise in the price of gold beyond that attributable to the inflation is to be ascribed to nonmonetary or "real" forces.

As a practical matter, foreign price levels can in this instance be represented by English prices, since most of American foreign trade was with England. Therefore, the ratio of United States to English domestic prices can be used as an indicator of how much the exchange rate (i.e., the price of gold) should have risen as a result of the issuance of greenbacks. And the difference between the rise in the price of gold predicted by purchasing-power parity and the actual price of gold is imputable to noninflationary forces.

Fortunately, at that time English prices and price ratios were relatively stable. Therefore it is of little consequence whether a wholesale or a consumers' price index is used. This is borne out by calculations of purchasing-power parity based on the

[18] During an inflation that was generally anticipated, i.e., one in which the real value of the nominal stock of money fell and velocity rose, and the interest rate reflected the future course of prices, there are reasons for expecting the exchange rate to increase more than the price level. The evidence presented by Mitchell on the behavior of interest rates during the Civil War suggests this inflation was largely unanticipated. See Mitchell, *A History of the Greenbacks*, pp. 367–68.

Wood (consumers') and Sauerbeck (wholesale) price index.[19] If there had been less stability, then the Wood index would be better. It is strongly weighted by rents and includes marketing costs in bringing goods from the wholesale to the retail level. Both classes of services are unambiguously noninternational. The results of these calculations are summarized in Table 3. For the United States the consumer's price index computed by Ethel Hoover with the Weeks data is used in preference to Mitchell's consumers' price index.[20] It is decomposed to show the relative price movements of imports, international goods, and domestic goods. (See Figure 1.)

The greatest discrepancy between purchasing-power-parity exchange rates and actual exchange rates occurred in 1864 when real wages were at their lowest (see Table 3). And this was the time when grumbling about the cost of living was loudest:

[19] Cotton and wheat prices are exceptions and did change substantially. Wheat was relatively expensive around 1860 and 1861, and cotton rose dramatically in price during the latter years of the war. In large part the differences in weighting of these commodities account for the differences in the movements of the two indexes. This leads one to suspect that the Wood index overstates the fall in English domestic prices and that the Sauerbeck index overstates the rise in prices and that, on the whole, English domestic prices were stable. See Wood, "Real Wages and the Standard of Comfort since 1850," *J. Royal Stat. Soc.* 72 (1909): 91; and Sauerbeck, "Prices of Commodities and the Precious Metals," *J. Royal Stat. Soc.* 49 (1886): 581.

	Sauerbeck	*Wood*		*Sauerbeck*	*Wood*
1857	105	119	1863	103	107
1858	91	109	1864	105	106
1859	94	107	1865	101	107
1860	99	111	1866	102	114
1861	98	114	1867	100	121
1862	101	111			

[20] A mimeographed and unpublished manuscript by E. D. Hoover, "Prices in the United States in the 19th Century," Conference on Research in Income and Wealth, National Bureau for Economic Research, Sept. 4, 5, 1957, is the source of this index. In principle it is better than Mitchell's CPI because it uses more of the

TABLE 3
Exchange Rates Implied by Purchasing-Power Parity Compared with Actual Exchange Rates and Real Wages

Year	(1) Actual Exchange[a]	(2) Real Wages[b]	(3) England Consumers Price Index (Wood)[c]	(4) England Wholesale Prices Sauerbeck Index[d]	(5) U.S. Consumers Price Index (Hoover)[e]	(6) (5)÷(3)	(7) (5)÷(4)	(8) (5)÷(3)[f]	(9) (5)÷(3)[g]	(10) (5)÷(4[h])
1860 . .	Parity	100	100	100	100	100	100	100	100	100
1861 . .	Parity	98	103	99	101	98	102	98	97	99
1862 . .	113	91	100	102	114	114	112	107	107	104
1863 . .	145	85	96	104	140	146	135	128	126	119
1864 . .	203	80	96	106	177	184	167	163	152	142
1865 . .	157	88	96	102	176	183	172	167	157	153

[a] Mitchell, *Gold, Prices, and Wages Under the Greenback Standard*, p. 4.

[b] These are the July wage data taken from variable weight column of Mitchell, *A History of the Greenbacks*, p. 310, Table 30, and the Hoover price data, Hoover, *op. cit.*

[c] Wood, *op. cit.*, p. 91.

[d] Sauerbeck, *op. cit.* p. 581.

[e] Hoover, note 20, *infra*.

[f] Imports are excluded from the Hoover index.

[g] Internationally traded goods are excluded from the Hoover index.

[h] Internationally traded goods are excluded from the Hoover index.

> There was indeed much grumbling over high prices, especially toward the end of the period, which must not be mistaken for direct dissatisfaction with government exactions. The spirit was most pronounced when the premium on gold was highest, in the summer of 1864, and when, consequently, the war was coming home to the people every day through high prices.[21]

Similarly, the second largest discrepancy occurred in 1863, when the fall in real wages ranked second in severity. And, of

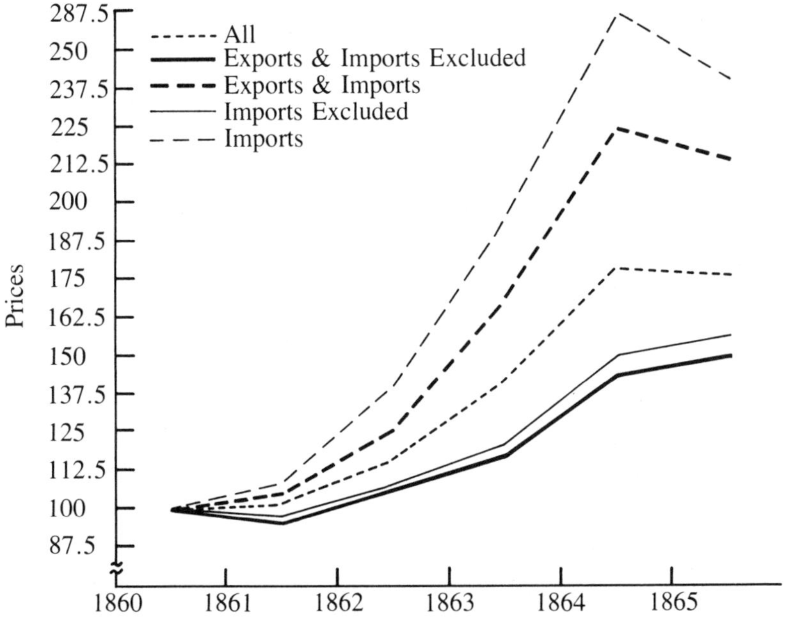

Figure 1. Hoover's consumer price index decomposed into imports, imports plus exports, all except imports, and all except imports and exports.

available data and better techniques for accounting for lapses in the data. Actually there is very little difference in the final result:

	Mitchell	*Hoover*		*Mitchell*	*Hoover*
1860	100	100	1863	140	140
1861	104	101	1864	170	177
1862	117	114	1865	179	176

[21] Fite, *op. cit.*, p. 136.

course, the differences between purchasing-power parity and actual exchange rates are in the right direction. The exclusions of internationally traded goods from the Hoover index suggest that a rise in the prices of internationally traded goods, imports

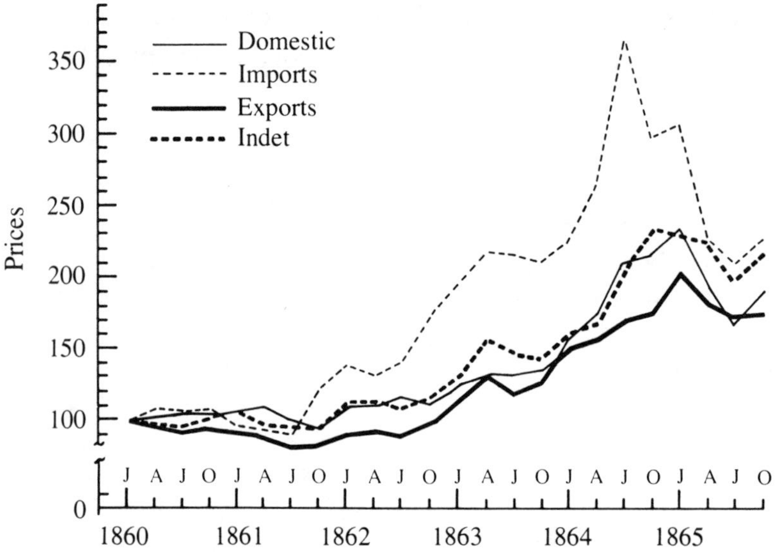

Figure 2. Components of Mitchell's wholesale-price index: mean values of prices of imports, exports, and domestic and indeterminate goods.

in particular, which was not compensated for by a decline in other prices accounted for most of the observed fall in real wages during these two years. This is precisely what would be expected if one argued that adverse movements in trade terms lowered real incomes.

The change in the relative prices of internationally traded goods may be seen more clearly by examining the relative movements of the import and domestic goods components of Mitchell's wholesale price index (see Figures 2 and 3). Imports at wholesale are "purer" international goods than the same commodities at retail because of differences in domestic marketing costs. Consequently, these relative price movements are more pronounced if wholesale rather than retail

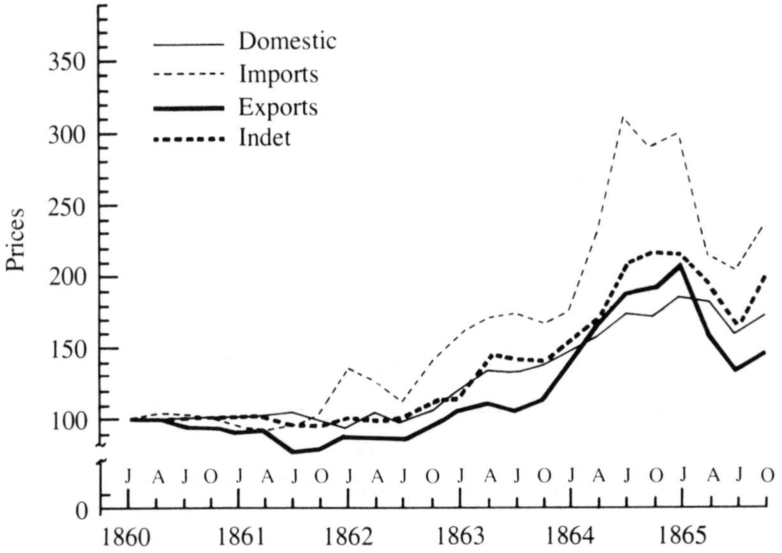

Figure 3. Components of Mitchell's wholesale-price index: median values of prices of imports, exports, and domestic and indeterminate goods.

prices are observed. If Mitchell's wholesale-price index is divided into four categories—exports, imports, domestic goods, and unclassified goods—it is very clear that the prices of internationally traded goods rose relative to domestic goods when the gap between the purchasing-power-parity exchange rate and the actual exchange rate was widening. Conversely, when the gap between the two exchange rates narrowed, the spread between domestic and import prices narrowed.

Mitchell's observations, however, are far from fully explained. In 1865 real wages were lower than they were in 1860, although, with the given premium on gold, purchasing-power-parity theory implies that they should have been roughly identical. Similarly, the prices of imports should have been lower in 1865 in order to reflect the absence of a discrepancy between purchasing-power parity and actual exchange rates. The answer to these problems turns on two independent phenomena, the special characteristics of the base year, 1860, and the tax system used for financing the war.

II. THE BASE YEAR FOR MITCHELL'S CALCULATIONS

The fiscal year that started in July 1860 was a very remarkable one in many respects. It was the only such year between 1850 and 1877 that the United States was a net importer of gold. Mitchell observed that sterling was selling at a discount in New York during part of this year, which is what one would expect if gold were being imported.[22] An inflow of gold, for a country on a gold standard, can be rationalized as the result of a fall in internal prices relative to the rest of the world. This implies an increase in exports and a fall in imports. An alternative to this explanation was used by Mitchell. He argued that the inflow of gold was a consequence of a depression at home which reduced the flow of imports with little effect on exports.[23] Part of Mitchell's explanation of this depression was the failure of Southerners to pay Northern creditors, which caused some business failures and a worsening in general business conditions.[24]

[22] Mitchell, *A History of the Greenbacks*, p. 22.

[23] *Ibid.*, pp. 21–22.

[24] Mitchell seems to have overestimated the importance of the recession in explaining the inflow of gold and underestimated the role of the special conditions in the

Neither of these interpretations of events can be justified by the movements of the well-known price indexes of the time or by data reflecting the international trade of the time.[25] The deficit on current account for fiscal 1860–61 increased by a factor of three over the previous year.[26] Moreover, the widening of the trade gap on current account is primarily, although not wholly, attributable to a decline in reported exports. Clearly, part of the reason these gold imports are not explained by either of these hypotheses is that the trade data are internally consistent only if one assumes that there was an extraordinarily large inflow of capital during this year. Simon and Graham both estimate international capital movements from the balance-of-payment statistics for the time. For fiscal 1860–61 Graham simply has an unexplained excess of debits over credits of about $90 million, which represents about one third of total credits.[27] Simon obtained capital flows as a residual after estimating gold flows and trade of all kinds on current account. His estimate of a $100 million capital inflow for the year exceeds the inflow for the peacetime years of 1865 and 1866.[28]

However, it is difficult to accept such estimates for the year in which the Civil War began. This year can be characterized as one in which it was widely recognized that the country was at the brink of war. This circumstance would hardly appeal to

wheat market. According to Thorp, business conditions were much worse in 1858, and yet there was a substantial gold outflow that year. See W. L. Thorp, *Business Annals* (1926): 127.

[25] *Historical Statistics, op. cit.*, pp. 232, 234–35.

[26] *Ibid.*, p. 244.

[27] Graham, *op. cit.*, p. 231.

[28] M. Simon, ''Statistical Estimates of the Balance of International Payments and the International Capital Movements of the United States, 1861–1900,'' Conference on Research in Income and Wealth, 1957, p. 116, Table 27.

English and Continental investors. A rereading of the available evidence suggests, if anything, that there was a net outflow of capital during this year. Fiscal 1861 ended about two and a half months after the firing on Fort Sumter. The blockade of Southern ports was proclaimed on April 19, 1861. Southern states were seceding from the Union during the preceding winter. With the secession of these states, in particular Louisiana, reports of what was going into and coming out of Southern ports were no longer reported to Washington. As a result, Southern exports, which for all practical purposes may be regarded as cotton, were grossly understated in the Commerce and Navigation publications issued by the government in Washington. These official trade statistics report exports of about $40 million of cotton.[29] Yet available evidence suggests that about $190 million of cotton were in fact exported. Since cotton is harvested in the fall, there was plenty of time to ship the cotton crop of 1860 before the blockade of 1861. Hunt reported that cotton exports in physical terms for 1861 had declined only 20 percent from the previous year.[30] When price differences are taken into account, there was almost no fall in value. This interpretation is supported by data reflecting imports and stocks of cotton in England, which at the time was receiving over 80 percent of her cotton from the United States.[31] These cotton exports, combined with an increase in

[29] Secretary of the Treasury, *Commerce and Navigation of the U.S.* (1863): 6.

[30] *Merchant's Magazine & Comm. Rev.* (Hunt's) 45 (1861): 498. See also J. L. Watkins, *Production and Price of Cotton for One Hundred Years*, United States Department of Agriculture (1895), p. 11.

[31] *Merchant's Magazine & Comm. Rev.* 45 (1861): 10, reports that stocks in Liverpool were about 10 percent smaller in April 1861 than in April of the preceding year. The preceding year's crop was the largest pre–Civil War cotton crop on record. This report is confirmed by English sources. Arnold wrote: "There was a larger supply of cotton in England, than there had been for years previous to this

the exports of grain of about $40 million, resulting from our abundant crops and unusually small crops abroad, explain the bulk of the gold inflow. It is true that imports into Northern ports decreased somewhat during this fiscal year, but this decrease may have been more than offset by unreported increases in imports into Southern ports. Some imports that normally were shipped into the North were instead shipped directly to the South. And the South probably imported larger quantities than usual in anticipation of hostilities and the blockade.

The calendar year 1860 is labeled by Thorp as "Prosperity; Recession," with the "slackening" coming late in the year. This recession continued into the fall of the following year and gave way to a rapid revival of business activity.[32] The recession in 1861 was associated with a large number of business failures resulting from the unwillingness of Southerners to remit to Northern creditors.[33] Thorp also characterizes 1860 as

---

time. The increasing probability of hostilities in America had induced the shippers of the Southern states to bring forward the crop of 1860 with unusual haste; and before the end of May 1861 the imports from America for the five months of the year amounted to 1,650,000 bales—a supply largely exceeding the total importation from the same source during the whole year of 1857." R. A. Arnold, *The History of the Cotton Famine* (1864), p. 43.

[32] Thorp, *op. cit.*, p. 127.

[33] See Mitchell, *A History of the Greenbacks*, p. 21, especially note 5. The evidence on this point is not unambiguous. McCulloch, who was president of the Bank of Indiana and subsequently Secretary of the Treasury, reports: ". . . I cannot forbear to refer to the action of the New Orleans banks towards their Northern correspondents at the outbreak of the civil war. The Southern branches had large dealings with men who were engaged in the Southern (Mississippi) trade, and when measures were being instituted for the secession of Louisiana from the Union, and, indeed, after the ordinance of secession had been adopted, these branches had large cash balances and large amounts of commercial paper in the New Orleans banks. Against the remonstrances of the secession leaders, and in disregard of threatened violence, these cash balances and the proceeds of the commercial paper as it matured were remitted for according to directions—not a dollar was withheld." H. McCulloch, *Men and Measures of Half a Century* (1888), pp. 138–39.

a foreign-trade boom year. Given the high world prices for wheat that prevailed at this time, this evidence, considered in conjunction with the extraordinary gold inflows, implies that 1860 was a year when the terms of trade were relatively favorable for the country.[34] This favorable development is by and large attributable to the extraordinary output and prices of wheat that occurred and should not normally be expected to recur. Consequently, real wages as measured by Mitchell, particularly with respect to imports, were abnormally high during this year. These considerations suggest that the real wage level measured by Mitchell in 1860 was higher than the level that normally could be sustained.[35]

III. THE TAX SYSTEM USED TO FINANCE THE CIVIL WAR

Three means of war finance, important because of their implications for real wages during the Civil War, are the use of excises, import duties, and the tax on money imposed by inflation. Excises and import duties grew in importance during the war years with extension of coverage and increases in rates. In 1861 the Morrill tariff (under consideration in the House of Representatives before the war) was enacted. This tariff increased the cost of many imports, particularly iron and

[34] For the prices of wheat in England, see Fite, *op. cit.*, p. 18; and Wood, *op. cit.*, p. 91.

[35] This suggests that time series of real wages from 1858 or 1859 ought to be rising at an abnormal rate. This can or cannot be shown, depending upon which time series one chooses to employ. For a time series favorable to this interpretation, see Hansen, "Factors Affecting the Trend of Real Wages," *Am. Econ. Rev.* 15 (1925): 27, 32. The Federal Reserve Bank of New York and the Burgess cost-of-living indexes (*Historical Statistics, op. cit.*, p. 235, series L36-39) will also support such an interpretation. On the other hand, the Hoover index will not.

wool.[36] While this tariff was announced as a revenue measure, the heaviest duties were imposed on commodities produced in the United States, and revenue was in part sacrificed for protection.[37]

In 1862 a comprehensive system of excise taxation was enacted. Specific taxes were imposed on the production of iron, steel, coal oil, paper, leather, and several other goods. A general ad valorem tax was imposed on manufacturing output. Import duties were also increased.[38] In 1864 all these taxes were once more increased and enlarged in scope.

> Every ton of pig-iron produced was charged two dollars; every ton of railroad iron three dollars; sugar paid two cents a pound; salt, six cents a hundred weight. The general tax on all manufactures was five percent. But this tax was repeated on almost every article in different stages of production. Raw cotton, for instance, was taxed two cents a pound; as cloth it again paid five cents.[39]

Wells observed that, under the impact of these turnover taxes, "the government actually levied and collected from eight to fifteen and in some instances as much as twenty percent on every finished product."[40] The average rate on dutiable com-

---

[36] F. W. Taussig, *The Tariff History of the United States* (1923), p. 160.

[37] Mitchell, *A History of the Greenbacks*, p. 9.

[38] Taussig, *op. cit.*, p. 163.

[39] *Ibid.*, p. 164. Taussig argues that increases in internal taxes were used to justify prohibitive tariffs. As a consequence, tariffs increased more than excises on internally produced goods.

[40] D. A. Wells, *The Recent Financial, Industrial, and Commercial Experiences of the United States* (2d ed., 1872), p. 18. Another source reports: "Every product of the mill or factory was taxed at each turn of its manufacture, so that not infrequently an article bore a duty imposed twice, thrice, and even four times, before it reached the market. The system operated like a series of barriers, across which passage could be secured only by the payment of toll, which was re-enacted at every phase of the process of manufacture" (F. C. Howe, *Taxation and Taxes in the United States Under the Internal Revenue System, 1791–1865* [1896], pp. 155–56).

modities, which had been 37 percent under the act of 1862, became 47 percent under that of 1864.[41] Indeed, import duties became so high in 1864 that collections from this source decreased relative to the preceding year as a result of smuggling.[42] The five percent tax on manufacturing imposed in 1864 was increased to six percent in 1865.[43] Needless to say, as a result of the imposition of these taxes, revenues from customs and internal revenue increased enormously over their prewar level (see Table 4).[44]

It is evident that these excises and import duties diverted resources from consumers to the government and raised the prices of all goods and services relative to factor incomes. These excises were to a great extent turnover taxes and as such became imbedded in the prices observed by Mitchell in the latter years of the war. As a consequence, taxation operated to

---

[41] Taussig, *op. cit.*, p. 167.

[42] Mitchell, *A History of the Greenbacks*, p. 130.

[43] *Ibid.*, p. 268. By 1865, the tax system had broadened considerably. Gross receipts taxes of 2½ percent were imposed upon railroads, steamboats, canals, ships, barges, stage coaches, and canal boats. Ferryboats, toll bridges and roads, advertisements, telegraph, and express companies paid 3 percent. Insurance companies paid 1½ and lotteries 5 percent. The deposits and capital of banks were taxed. Federal stamps were required for a wide variety of transactions involving legal instruments and the sale of proprietary articles. Sales of goods at auctions and sales of stocks and bonds and foreign exchange were taxed. Licenses were required to enter many trades and professions as well as certain types of business enterprises. For a description of these taxes and a statement of the receipts derived from each tax category, see H. E. Smith, *The United States Federal Internal Tax History from 1861 to 1871* (1914), especially his tables in the appendix.

[44] Mitchell, *A History of the Greenbacks*, p. 129. Total receipts include the issuance of greenbacks. It must be remembered that not all internal revenue came from excises. A general income tax was imposed in 1862 and was raised in 1864 to 5 percent on moderate incomes and 10 percent on incomes of more than $10,000. See Taussig, *op. cit.*, p. 164. About 20 percent of all internal revenue receipts were from income taxes in 1864 and about 15 percent in 1865. See E. Young, *Special Report on the Customs-Tariff Legislation of the United States* (1874), p. 136.

widen whatever divergence existed between the value of final output and the sum of the payments to the cooperating agents of production. This means that some of the fall in real wages Mitchell observed resulted from custom duties and excises and would have taken place whether or not inflation occurred during the Civil War.

TABLE 4
Receipts from Custom Duties and Internal Revenue
(In Millions of Dollars and as a Percentage of All Receipts)

	1861	*1862*	*1863*	*1864*	*1865*
Customs					
	$39.6	$49.1	$69.1	$102.3	$ 84.9
	(61.4%)	(10.1%)	(9.8%)	(10.9%)	(7.1%)
Internal Revenue					
	0	0	$37.6	$109.7	$209.5
			(5.3%)	(11.7%)	(17.5%)

As a result of the extensive use of turnover taxes, real wages as measured by Mitchell ought to have fallen, even if the foreign-exchange rate were equal to the rate implied by purchasing-power parity. Consequently, the level of real wages observed in 1865 ought to be below that of 1860, by an amount greater than the differential attributable to the abnormally high real wages in 1860. This comprehensive system of excise taxation taxed imports much more heavily than it taxed goods produced in the United States, and imports as a class were therefore forced up in price relative to domestically produced goods and services. The fall in real wages attributable to taxation should be concentrated upon internationally traded goods, and this appears to be the case. Or this is why, at the end of the war, the prices of imports were high relative to domestic goods, despite equality between the exchange rate implied by purchasing-power parity and the actual rate.

The inflation associated with the Civil War in the North was caused by a government-imposed tax on cash balances. Through the exchange of greenbacks for real resources, the government progressively reduced the real value of a unit of currency, and the rising prices that resulted imposed economic losses upon money holders. But if inflation had not occurred, and if real expenditures by the government had not been reduced, then alternative taxes would have had to be employed. If the inflation tax on cash balances were replaced by a tax on income or wealth, then Mitchell's real wage measurements would be unaffected. On the other hand, if the alternative tax were higher tariffs or turnover taxes, then a greater fall than Mitchell measured is implied.[45] If turnover taxes or higher tariffs are regarded as the alternatives to taxing through inflation, the Civil War inflation kept the real wages measured by Mitchell from falling more than they in fact did. Therefore, a rationale exists for a conclusion that is the converse of Mitchell's—were it not for the inflation, he would have found that real wages would have fallen more than they did.

The analysis contained in this paper constitutes an alternative explanation that is better than Mitchell's interpretation of these data in at least two senses: (1) It explains why the fall in real wages was greater with respect to internationally traded goods than it was with respect to domestic goods. The wage-lag hypothesis implies that there ought to be no difference between the fall in real wages with respect to the two classes of

---

[45] This analysis is based on the premise that the inflation associated with the Civil War was largely unanticipated. This seems to have been the case, judging by the behavior of interest rates. Consequently, the losses of the money holders were negative profits in the Knightian sense and never became part of the cost of doing business during this time. In the case of an inflation such as the one following World War I in Germany, these costs do become anticipated, and both excises and taxing through inflation will lower Mitchell-type measurements of real wages.

goods. Consequently, the interpretation of events presented here constitutes, at least in this respect, a fuller explanation of Mitchell's observations. (2) The interpretation presented in this paper is consistent with the analysis used by economists to explain similar changes in price relationships in markets other than labor. And, in general, the hypothesis which explains a wider range of phenomena is to be preferred.

However, a word of caution is in order. It is possible that the destruction of prewar trading relationships, the rise in the premium on gold relative to prices, and the excises and import duties could have so affected factor incomes that the returns to labor did not decrease *pari passu* with the fall in the sum of all factor incomes.[46] All the preceding analysis has assumed that what happened to real factor incomes also happened to real wages. The analysis presented here has not included the effects of the change in the composition of the final output of the economy on the real demand for labor. Nor have we considered the impact of the mobilization of manpower for the armed forces, the influx of new migrants into the United States during the concluding years of the war, or the damage to Northern resources imposed by Southern armed forces, upon the supply of labor.[47] A more complete analysis might still find that there

[46] The principles affecting the real returns to labor as a result of changes in import duties may be found in Stolper and Samuelson, "Protection and Real Wages," *Rev. of Econ. Studies* 9 (1941): 58.

[47] Migration into the United States seems to have been at a low ebb during the early years of the war and increased toward its end. In this respect, the movements of human and nonhuman capital seem to be alike. In *Historical Statistics, op. cit.*, p. 34, immigration, by fiscal year, is shown as:

Year	*Immigrants*	*Year*	*Immigrants*
1859	121,282	1863	176,282
1860	153,640	1864	193,418
1861	91,918	1865	248,120
1862	91,985	1866	318,568

was some lag of wages behind prices to be explained by monetary forces. Alternatively, it might reinforce the argument presented here, or indicate that both explanations have a role to play in interpreting Mitchell's data. However, in the absence of such a demonstration, and in view of the preceding evidence, it appears that Mitchell's conclusion—that "all of the statistical evidence that has been presented in the preceding pages supports unequivocally the common theory that persons whose incomes are derived from wages suffer seriously from a depreciation of the currency"[48]—cannot be sustained.

In summary, the fall in real wages observed by Mitchell can be explained by the kind of analysis appropriate to the analysis of changing price relationships in other markets. An ad hoc theory is unnecessary. This fall in real wages can be rationalized as a consequence of the extraordinary level of real wages in the base year, 1860, the rise in the price of foreign exchange relative to domestic prices and wages, and the tax system used to finance the war.[49] Most of the fall in 1865 relative to 1860 is attributable to the tax policy used to finance the war. The extraordinary characteristics of the 1860 base ought to be assigned minor responsibility. In the year 1864 the fall in real wages was greatest, and so, too, was the discrepancy between purchasing-power-parity exchange rates and the actual

[48] Mitchell, *A History of the Greenbacks*, p. 347.

[49] The recognition of the implications of excise taxes for the relationship of wages and other factor incomes to prices is of some contemporary interest. Our present consumers' price index reflects state sales taxes, import duties, manufacturers' excises, and property taxes upon dwellings. Insofar as these taxes rise in real terms. as a result of our desire to allocate more resources to governmental activities, real wages, as measured by the ratio of wages to the consumers' price index, will fall. If instead income taxes are increased and these taxes correspondingly decreased, real wages will rise.

rate. This analysis suggests that at least half of the fall in that year was attributable to the relative rise in the foreign exchange rate and that taxes and the properties of the 1860 base account for the remainder.

APPENDIX

The practical problem of determining which of the 90 commodities in Mitchell's wholesale-price index ought to be regarded as internationally traded involved a number of arbitrary decisions. Graham, working with a series composed of 92 commodities taken from Mitchell's *Gold, Prices, and Wages Under the Greenback Standard* and in large part the same as the series used for Mitchell's real wage computations, classified 14 of the 92 as import, 18 as export, 42 as purely domestic, and 18 as indeterminate.[50] Graham, incidentally, was also concerned with the movements in the prices of internationally traded goods relative to all prices. The time period of concern to Graham began in 1866. The series used in *A History of the Greenbacks* contained several commodities which did not enter into Graham's series and conversely.

Using the information provided by Graham, who unfortunately failed to list specifically the commodities in each of his categories, and (1) allowing for the differences between the series used in *A History of the Greenbacks* and by Graham, (2) taking account of the differences in time periods which would change the classification of some commodities such as cotton and turpentine, (3) using whatever clues provided by Graham as to his classification procedure, and (4) employing the Commerce and Navigation reports of the time, the classifica-

[50] Graham, *op. cit.*, p. 250.

TABLE A

Export	*Import*	*Domestic*	*Indeterminate*
1. Wheat	1. Coffee	1. Beef	1. Flaxseed
2. Tobacco	2. Nutmeg	2. Mutton	2. Rye flour
3. Ship biscuit	3. Pepper	3. Pork	3. Salt
4. Alcohol	4. Cotton	4. Eggs	4. Bichrom of potash
5. Dried apples	5. Jute	5. Bread	5. Brimstone
6. Butter	6. Quinine	6. Cement	6. Blue vitriol
7. Lard	7. Silk	7. Chestnut lumber	7. Castor oil
8. Glass	8. Zinc—spelter	8. Hemlock	8. Linseed oil
9. Tables	9. Opium	9. Pine lumber and boards	9. Muriatic acid
10. Cheese	10. Sugar	10. Starch	10. Oxide of zinc
11. Corn	11. Turpentine	11. Brick	11. Sugar of lead
12. Mercury—quick-silver	12. Currants	12. Corn starch	12. Sulfuric acid
13. Rye	13. Tinplate	13. Codfish	13. Coal: anthracite
14. Barley	14. Raisins	14. Vegetables	14. Coal: bituminous
15. Oats	15. Rubber	15. Pails	15. Matches
16. Chairs	16. Lead	16. Tubs	16. Lime
17. Corn meal	17. Alum	17. Harness leather	17. Spruce
18. Tallow	18. Soda ash	18. Timothy seed	18. Butts
19. Candles	19. Copperas	19. Hides	19. Copper
	20. Carpets	20. Putty	20. Iron wire
	21. Molasses	21. Rifle powder	21. Shovels
		22. Beans	22. Wood screws
		23. Clover seed	23. Rope
		24. Soap	

tion of export, import, domestic, and indeterminate shown in Table A was obtained.[51]

Mitchell, to obtain his 90 commodity series, started out with a list of 135 and winnowed them down to 90 by averaging closely related commodities in order to avoid duplication. These 90 were not specifically listed as such. By following Mitchell's directions, this same base of 135 was reduced to 87 here.[52]

In Hoover's consumers' price index, the commodities classified as import were rice, tea, coffee, sugar, molasses, and all cotton and wool materials. These constituted 22.6 percent by weight of all commodities in the index. The exports were wheat flour, rye flour, corn meal, butter, cheese, and lard and constituted, again by weight, 16.6 percent.

---

[51] Graham regarded cotton, textiles, furniture, glass, metals, paper, pottery, tanneries, and wool textiles as export industries. Lumber and hides, fish, flesh, and fowl were in the indeterminate category. *Ibid.*, pp. 249–50, 268.

[52] For Mitchell's directions for winnowing, see *A History of the Greenbacks*, pp. 248–57. The difference between these results and Mitchell's, and this is only a guess, is attributable to two series for beef and one each for zinc—spelter, mercury, and quicksilver. These six are represented by three commodities in the series presented here.

On a Correct Measure of Inflation

Two commonly cited and newsworthy price indices are the Bureau of Labor Statistic's Consumer Price Index and the Commerce Department's GNP deflator. These indices have become an important part of our economic intelligence and are frequently considered to be the operational counterparts of what economists call "the price level." They, therefore, often are used as measures of inflation and often are targets or indicators of monetary and fiscal policy. Nevertheless, these price indices, which represent measures of current consumption service prices and current output prices, are theoretically inappropriate for the purpose to which they are generally put. The analysis in this paper bases a price index on

Reprinted by permission. Armen A. Alchian and Benjamin Klein, "On a Correct Measure of Inflation," *Journal of Money, Credit, and Banking* 5, no. 1 (Part 1, February 1973): 173-81.

The authors are indebted to Michael DePrano, Michael Hamburger, Joseph Ostroy, Earl Thompson, Jai Hoon Yang, and participants at seminars at the University of Washington, Carleton University, and the National Bureau of Economic Research for helpful comments and to Irene Abramson for able research assistance. Financial assistance was provided by the National Bureau of Economic Research and by the Lilly Foundation, Inc. grant to UCLA for the study of property rights. This work has not undergone the full critical review accorded National Bureau Studies and is not a National Bureau publication.

the Fisherian tradition of a proper definition of intertemporal consumption and leads to the conclusion that a price index used to measure inflation must include asset prices. A correct measure of changes in the nominal money cost of a given utility level is a price index for wealth. If monetary impulses are transmitted to the real sector of the economy by producing transient changes in the relative prices of service flows and assets (i.e., by producing short-run changes in "the" real rate of interest), then the commonly used, incomplete, current flow price indices provide biased short-run measures of changes in "the purchasing power of money." The inappropriate indices that dominate popular and professional literature and analyses are thereby shown to result in significant errors in monetary research, theory, and policy.

I. AN ISO-UTILITY PRICE INDEX WITH INTERTEMPORAL CONSUMPTION

A well recognized principle is that the appropriateness of a price index depends on the question to which an answer is sought.[1] For many situations we are interested in measuring

[1] See, for example, Frisch [15, p. 10], Mitchell [28, p. 23], Keynes [23, book II], and Ulmer [37, ch. 2]. Fisher, on the other hand, considered the problem of constructing a price index independent of purpose and concluded that "from a practical standpoint, it is quite unnecessary to discuss the fanciful arguments for using 'one formula for one purpose and another for another' in view of the great practical fact that all methods (if free of freakishness and bias) *agree*!" [11, p. 231, his italics]. However, Fisher [10, ch. 10] earlier stated that the correctness of an index depended on its purpose and he emphasized the theoretical importance of not basing an index of purchasing power to be used in long-term loan contracts solely on consumer service prices. Using an analysis similar to our own, he argued that

> Borrowers and lenders, in other words, may be more interested in purchasing factories, railroads, land, durable houses, etc., which yield services during a long future, than in purchasing more or better food, shelter and entertainments, which yield immediate

the *money* cost of a fixed welfare or constant utility vector of goods as money prices change. This iso-utility price index, often called a cost-of-living or fixed welfare index, was first discussed formally by Könus [24]. However, as early as 1906 Irving Fisher [9] (and others earlier, we conjecture) pointed out that an iso-utility vector included claims to future consumption. And more recently, Samuelson [31] elegantly restated the significance of wealthlike measures (instead of current income) in comparisons of welfare. We, therefore, regard the utility or preference ordering of any situation as a function of a vector of claims to present and future consumption,[2]

$$U = U([q(i, t)]) \tag{1}$$

where the $q(i, t)$ element represents the quantity of the ith consumption service flow at time t.

Assume, initially, that markets exist for every consumption service flow to be delivered at every moment of time. At any moment an individual is assumed to be constrained by a scalar

satisfactions. To base our index number for time contracts solely on services and immediately consumable goods would therefore be illogical.

Although he asserts that the practical differences may be inconsequential, the broad-based index which he concludes that it is, on the whole, it is best to use the *P* in his equation of exchange, which is similar to our index in terms of its inclusiveness.

[2] Samuelson notes that Pigou [29, p. 37] explicitly recognized that economic welfare depends upon "total consumption" and not solely "immediate consumption." See any recent mathematical price theory textbook, e.g., Henderson and Quandt [19, pp. 229–40], for a formal statement of this commonly accepted proposition.

While we consider present and future consumption as the sole elements in the utility function and emphasize wealth as claims to future consumption, we do not deny the possibility that individuals are willing to hold wealth in, and of, itself. See, for example, Dewey [8] for an analysis where consumption is not the sole end of economic activity. This alternative view is not inconsistent with the analysis of this paper.

W (wealth), which he allocates over claims to present and future consumption flows at present prices quoted on these markets. If at each (current and future) moment there are n consumption services, then

$$W_A \equiv \int_0^{\infty} \left[\sum_{i=1}^{n} q_A(i, t) p_A(i, t) \right] dt; \qquad (2)$$

where W_A is the individual's current nominal wealth, $p_A(i, t)$ is the current rental price of the ith consumption service for moment t (i.e., present prices include prices of present claims to future consumption) and $q_A(i, t)$ is the magnitude of the ith consumption service flow at moment t which at the current price vector and wealth level maximizes the individual's intertemporal utility. All of these values are described as given under condition A.[3]

Let present flow prices, including present prices of future consumption services, change and describe this new state as condition B. The question we are asking is whether prices, measured by a constant-utility index, have risen or fallen. We can, in principle, compute at the new set of present prices, $[p_B(i, t)]$, the cost of an iso-utility consumption service vector, $[q_B(i, t)]$. If, for example, the new cost under price condition B, W_B, is greater than under the initial price condition A, we can

[3] This model, like the standard microeconomic model under which the usual price indices are derived, assumes the absence of all information or transaction costs and therefore lacks a theoretical justification for the value of a price index. (Introduction of uncertainty by the use of costlessly made contingency contracts—e.g., Arrow [4]—where all transactors know the true state of the world when it occurs, is also economically equivalent to a world of perfect information with no rationale for a price index.) We will here ignore this fundamental question and concentrate solely on defining what is commonly considered to be a fixed welfare price index, recognizing that the usefulness of this or any other index depends crucially on the particular information and transaction costs assumed.

say that the money cost of an iso-utility vector of goods has risen.[4] The iso-utility price index implicit in this can be represented by

$$P_{AB} \equiv \frac{W_B}{W_A} \equiv \frac{\int_0^{\infty} \left[\sum_{i=1}^{n} q_B (i, t)\, p_B (i, t) \right] dt}{\int_0^{\infty} \left[\sum_{i=1}^{n} q_A (i, t)\, p_A (i, t) \right] dt} \tag{3}$$

where $q_B (i, t)$ represents the (i, t) element in the minimum cost consumption vector that yields the same condition A utility at the new condition B price vector. If P_{AB} is greater than one, the nominal money cost of condition A utility has increased; an inflation has occurred.

To emphasize the intertemporal nature of this price index and the fact that it does not refer solely to the cost of the current moment's consumption it could less misleadingly be called the current "cost-of-life" index. Current instantaneous prices of current consumption flows enter this index, but insignificantly.

II. FUTURES AND ASSET PRICES

Current cash prices (to be paid now) for future consumption services are here called futures prices.[5] Any price index that

---

[4] But we cannot, with a fixed quantity weighted index, say it has risen. The analysis is exactly parallel, indeed is identical, to the standard price index theory where q is interpreted as current services. See Allen [2, pp. 197–203].

[5] The current futures price of the ith consumption service at moment t, $p\ (i, r)$, is related to the future (or forward) price currently anticipated at moment t, $f\,(i, t)$, by an implicit market rate of interest, $r\ (i, t)$; $p\ (i, t) = f\,(i, t)\, e^{-r(i,\, t)}$. If interest rates

fails to include these current futures prices is deficient in not including the cost of all relevant elements of the utility function. Its incompleteness can result in a severe (negative or positive) bias of indicated change in the money price level of "life." Prices of current services may rise while futures prices (present money prices of claims to future services) fall more than enough to lower the money cost—or the opposite may happen.

The major difficulty in making our index operational is that separate futures markets or contracts do not exist for all future consumption services.[6] As a result, some futures prices required for a complete iso-utility price index will not be directly observable in explicit market prices. But since assets are sources of future services, asset prices provide clues to prices of present claims on future consumption. Current wealth can

---

are assumed not to vary over different consumption service flows, equation (2) restated in terms of forward, rather than futures, prices is therefore:

$$W_A \equiv \int_0^{\infty} \left[\sum_{i=1}^{n} q_A(i, t) f_A(i, t) \right] e^{-\int_0^{\infty} r_A(t)\, dt} dt \qquad (2)$$

Our terminology here may be somewhat confusing since "futures" conventionally refers to the price paid later but agreed to now in a futures contract on a commodity exchange, while "forward" price is also often used to refer to a price to be paid in the future upon future delivery but agreed to now. With apologies to our readers, and on the assumption that forewarned is forearmed, we use the word "futures" to denote a price agreed to now, "payable now" for services to be received in the future.

[6] Houthakker [21] theoretically examines why futures markets exist only for a rather small number of commodities. The answer to this important question must be based on the transaction costs of purchasing and selling particular commodities. These costs are determined, in part, by the costs of obtaining information about "characteristics" of assets and the distribution of such information among transactors in society (where "characteristics" is an economic and not a physical concept) and have implications for the essential properties of money (cf. Brunner and Meltzer [5, pp. 258–61]).

be represented by the sum of all asset values, or, equivalently, interpreted as the sum of all present valued claims to all consumption service flows over time. Symbolically, if there are m assets, wealth is denotable by:

$$W_A \equiv \sum_{j=1}^{m} P_A\,(j)\,Q_A\,(j) \equiv \int_0^{\infty} \left[\sum_{i=1}^{n} q_A\,(i,\,t)\,p_A\,(i,\,t) \right] dt \quad (4)$$

where W_A is the individual's current nominal wealth and $[Q_A\,(j)]$ is the current vector of asset quantities that would yield his intertemporal utility maximizing consumption service stream $[q_A\,(i,\,t)]$. If assets are standardized in terms of their present and future service flows, the current vector of asset prices $[P_A\,(j)]$ can therefore be used as a proxy for current futures prices, $p_A\,(i,\,t)$.

When relative prices change, one can, in principle, determine the vector of assets $[Q_B\,(j)]$, which will yield the minimum cost iso-utility consumption service stream $[q_B\,(i,\,t)]$ at the new set of asset prices $[P_B\,(j)]$ and implicit futures prices $p_B\,(i,\,t)$. Current asset prices can therefore be used to construct our constant welfare price index

$$P_{AB} \equiv \frac{W_B}{W_A} \equiv \frac{\sum_{j=1}^{m} P_B\,(j)\,Q_B\,(j)}{\sum_{j=1}^{m} P_A\,(j)\,Q_A\,(j)} \quad (5)$$

where W_B is the nominal cost of the vector of assets that will yield a flow of present and future consumption services equal in utility to the initial condition A consumption service stream.

It is crucial to emphasize that the vectors $[Q_A\,(j)]$ and $[Q_B\,(j)]$ must include all assets—consumer and producer, durable and nondurable, tangible and intangible, financial and nonfinancial, human and nonhuman. All sources of present and future consumption services must be considered. The vectors do not represent the actual assets held by the representative individual, but the asset combination that would yield the individual's desired consumption service flows. An individual may hold some assets that yield the exact pattern of consumption service flows that he demands over time, e.g., a house that yields his present and future desired housing service flow. But, more generally, due to transaction costs individuals will hold some assets not because they yield services that coincide with their consumption plans, but because they are an efficient form in which to hold wealth. The services from these assets or the assets themselves are later sold and exchanged for desired consumption services. Human capital is the most obvious example.

Since our asset price index is not constructed on the basis of assets actually owned by an individual we are therefore not measuring whether the individual is better or worse off after a change in prices, only whether he requires more or less money to reach the same utility level. We must distinguish between actual shifts in the budget constraint with corresponding welfare changes and changes in our measure of inflation. W_B is compared to W_A to determine the change in the individual's money cost of a constant utility level. The individual's actual nominal wealth under condition B must be compared to W_B to determine if he is better or worse off under the new set of prices. An individual, for example, may own a coal mine not because he consumes the coal yielded by the mine over time, but because the coal mine is an efficient form in which to hold his wealth. He sells most of the coal for income to purchase other consumption flows, and he intends to sell the mine and retire to an Hawaiian resort in a few years. If under condition

B the only change is an increase in the price of coal, the individual's current wealth will rise more than W_B; he is better off while he experiences an inflation. Alternatively, if the price of Hawaiian land increases under condition B, the individual's nominal wealth remains unchanged (if he did not own any of the land) while W_B increases; he is worse off and experiences an inflation. Any combination of inflation or deflation and better off or worse off is possible.

III. THE SYSTEMATIC BIAS OF CURRENT SERVICE FLOW PRICE INDICES

A money price index based on considerations we have outlined is fundamentally different from the CPI, which is constructed on the basis of prices of *current* consumption services. The CPI considers the prices of only a part of the utility function and is therefore inadequate in principle as a constant utility money price measure. The CPI attempts to measure changes in the cost of only the iso-utility current consumption flows and therefore supplies an answer to a question distinct from whether the present money cost of consumer utility has changed.[7]

Current service flow prices are related to asset prices by implicit real rates of interest and therefore our iso-utility price index is logically equivalent to an index based on current

[7] It is interesting to note that a major gap between a theoretically correct constant utility price index and the actual CPI is often said to be the improper inclusion of some consumer durable prices, such as new and used automobiles and houses, in the index. The proper price for these durables is said to be the current rental price or current cost of using the services from the asset and not the purchase price of the asset itself (cf., for example, Steiner [34]). We would claim, on the other hand, that the CPI is inappropriate because of the emphasis on current prices and the insufficient weight given to asset prices.

service flow prices and a broadly defined interest rate vector. If our representative individual moved to a new society where current service flow prices are identical but where real interest rates are higher, our iso-utility price index would fall. The individual would substitute future consumption for present consumption and his money cost of life would decrease.[8]

If we assume that society's equilibrium rate of time preference and real productivity of investment remains constant, is there any reason to suppose that use of a current service flow price index provides a deceptive measure of inflation? If real interest rates remain constant and the prices of current services and the prices of current assets move together then, as a practical matter, a current service price index can be used as a perfect proxy for the theoretically correct wealth price index. There is, however, reason to expect a major systematic discrepancy in the transitory movement of a current service flow price index and a current asset price index. And it is this discrepancy which makes a current service flow price index an especially poor short-run indicator and target of monetary policy.

Changes in the quantity of money cause a "nonadiabatic" adjustment process in the money market which is terminated when all prices have changed proportionately. The initial price changes will depend upon how the monetary change is accomplished; but, ignoring distribution effects among individuals which may cause permanent changes in relative prices, the initial changes will "*diffuse* themselves equally after a certain time through all price levels alike" [23, p. 90]. But all prices

---

[8] On the contrary, *nominal* interest rates (current mortgage rates) enter the CPI positively. An increase in nominal interest rates due to an increase in anticipated future (or forward) prices which leaves real rates and current futures prices unchanged will not alter our price of wealth index.

may not change at the same rate. Keynes [23, ch. 7] emphasized the possibility that price levels might not be rapidly "diffused" and that the failure of different price levels to move in the same way was a crucial element in the explanation of short-period fluctuations. Differential adjustment speeds among prices, of consumption goods and capital goods (or of service flows and durable assets) in particular, formed a cornerstone of his theory of the trade cycle.[9]

The behavior of current service flow prices relative to asset prices as a crucial element in the transmission process between monetary stock changes and economic fluctuations has also been emphasized by Friedman and Schwartz [14, pp. 229–31]. They maintain that monetary changes temporarily affect real income by producing transient changes in the interest-rate structure, defined by the ratio of current rental prices of services to the price of current assets as sources of the services, i.e., by changing wealth relative to income. A decrease in the supply of nominal money, for example, decreases the demand for and prices of financial and nonfinancial assets as individuals adjust their portfolios by attempting to add to their depleted cash holdings. This causes asset prices to fall relative to service flow prices and relative to the cost of producing new assets. (The general fall in the asset price level is a rise in "the" real interest rate; wealth falls relative to income.) In turn, the reduced profitability of producing new assets decreases their production (i.e., leads to a fall in the rate of "investment"), and the higher interest rate implicit in the current rental asset price ratio stimulates asset purchases rela-

[9] Leijonhufvud's recent interpretation of Keynes emphasizes the importance Keynes placed on an "inappropriately" low relative price of assets (or high interest rate) as a "cause of unemployment" [26, pp. 335–38].

tive to rentals (i.e., leads to a rise in the rate of "saving"—in the sense that consumption of current services is reduced).[10]

If such an "interest-rate" mechanism actually operates, then short-run effects on "the purchasing power of money" of a change in the rate of growth of money will be underestimated by a current service flow price index compared to an index that also includes asset prices. But, unfortunately, we have not been able to verify the existence of such a mechanism. Very little reliable information exists on transaction prices of used assets and almost none on a quarterly or monthly basis.[11] Given the assumed importance of asset prices in the transmission of monetary changes, this deficiency in the data and lack

---

[10] In addition to asset prices generally adjusting more rapidly than current flow prices, prices of "liquid" (low transaction costs) assets will adjust more rapidly than prices of "illiquid" assets.

Even if relative prices are not affected by the monetary change, real income will be affected if anticipations about market clearing prices lag behind changing reality—which is costly to detect and adjust to instantly. Cf., Alchian [1].

[11] Goldsmith and Lipsey [16] have constructed an annual wealth price index in the context of estimating a national and sectoral balance sheet. The components of their index, however, are not based on transaction prices but on owner estimates of the market value of their property (for farm real estate and for most of the single-family house data) and on construction costs (for commercial, industrial, and residential structures and for producer and consumer durables). Reliance on cost data limits our indices solely to measures of new asset prices. Over long periods this procedure may not yield biased price estimates of all existing assets but will most certainly yield misleading current asset price measures in a short-run cyclical context when reproduction costs are considerably more rigid than market prices. Grebler, Blank, and Winnick [17, Appendix C], for example, compare the market "prices" (i.e., owner estimates) of houses with the construction costs for the 1890–1934 period and conclude that, although there is close conformity between the two series over decade-long periods, market prices fluctuate more widely than construction costs and there are significant divergencies between the series over shorter periods of several years.

Market transaction price data for used assets are available in trade publications and dealer catalogues for cars, trucks, and farm equipment; and less complete price data possibly may be collected by other trade associations.

of any previous systematic empirical analysis of the behavior of asset relative to flow price is truly shocking. Some suggestive evidence on the existence of this cyclical relative price process can be obtained, however, by examining recent movements in common stock price indices relative to flow price indices and by examining movements in estimates of "the" real rate of interest. Although there are significant problems in the interpretation of the movement of stock prices (see section VI), they should be included in our iso-utility price index since they implicitly measure current prices of capital assets owned by corporations and represent the only readily available data on current market prices of assets. And changes in the real rate of interest can be considered an indirect measure of changes in the relative prices of service flows to capital stocks.[12]

The sharp decrease in the growth rate of money during 1969 provides a classic example of the bias involved in measuring inflation by considering only, for example, movements in the CPI. Narrowly defined money, which had grown at a 7.6 percent annual rate over the two previous years, grew at only a 2.9 percent annual rate from January 1969 to February 1970. (Most of this restraint, as recorded in the figures revised for the unusually large volume of Eurodollar borrowing in early 1969, came in the second half of 1969.) Although real magnitudes were clearly affected, this policy was generally considered to have been a failure in curbing the rate of inflation. The CPI, which rose at a 5.8 percent annual rate during the second half

[12] It should be noted that although our discussion emphasizes that movements in asset and service prices differ largely because of differing rates of adjustment to cyclical monetary disturbances there may also be a significant secular bias due to changing equilibrium real asset yields. (The apparent increase in real rates of interest over the years is ignored in our discussion.)

of 1969 showed no sign of decelerating and rose at a 6.0 percent annual rate during the first half of 1970. Absence of any perceived response of prices in the face of rising unemployment led to the total abandonment of monetary restraint during 1970 and early 1971 and ultimately to the imposition of wage and price controls. But there is some evidence that asset prices responded almost immediately and quite dramatically to the change in policy.

Standard and Poor's Composite (500) Common Stock Price Index started to decline in early 1969, and by June 1970 had fallen nearly 30 percent to the level of early 1964. In addition, the real rate of interest as measured by the Federal Reserve Bank of St. Louis (the nominal corporate Aaa bond yield minus the average annual rate of change of the GNP deflator over the previous 24 months) rose about one percentage point during the last half of 1969 and the first half of 1970—from 2.3 percent in June 1969 to 3.3 percent in June 1970.[13] This evidence suggests that asset prices declined relative to flow

[13] The Federal Reserve Bank of St. Louis discontinued publishing their real rate series shortly after this episode. Although their measured real rate showed remarkable stability over the 1960s, this unique precipitous rise should have been expected as part of the normal relative price reaction to monetary disturbances. What might have been misleading is that the previous tight money episode of 1966, although similar in magnitude to 1969, did not produce such severe relative price changes. (The money stock showed no change from April 1966 to January 1967 after rising at about a six percent annual rate over the previous year. This produced a clear deceleration of the rate of increases in the CPI, which rose at a 4.5 percent annual rate from January to August of 1966 and only a 1.6 percent annual rate over the following six months; while stock prices, which fell more than 13 percent from January to August 1966, quickly recovered and rose more than eight percent over the next six months; the St. Louis real rate remained essentially unchanged over the period, rising less than ten basis points from April to August 1966 and then quickly falling back to and then below its original level.) This dramatic difference in the relative price movement between the two most recent contractionary episodes may explain why the downturn in economic activity was much milder in 1966–67 than in 1969–70, but the surprising flexibility of flow prices in 1966 remains unexplained.

prices over the period and that movements in the CPI severely underestimated the deflationary effects of the tight money policy.

IV. CURRENT OUTPUT FLOW PRICES, STOCK PRICES AND THE DEMAND FOR MONEY

Another commonly employed index of inflation is the GNP deflator, which measures the price of current output flows. This price index includes the prices of newly produced assets but does not include the prices of previously existing items of wealth and therefore is conceptually distinct from our iso-utility wealth price index. Therefore, although it is useful for other purposes, a current output price index also provides a biased estimate of changes in the money cost of consumer utility. The theoretical considerations outlined above with regard to the bias in the movement of the CPI compared to a wealth price index also suggest a similar systematic bias in the movement of the GNP deflator relative to a wealth price index. Prices of already produced assets will, we conjecture, generally be more flexible than prices of currently produced goods, which are based on current costs that are often made less flexible by long-term contracts. And given the rigidity of current production costs relative to asset prices, a fall in the rate of growth of money decreases the profitability (and therefore the rate) of new asset production. Concern during 1969–70 about the rigidity in the rate of rise of current output flow prices should therefore be based on the evidence this gave us on the extent of the recession, not on the extent of the inflation.[14]

[14] In a crude "monetarist" model such as Anderson and Carlson's [3] changes in money imply changes in nominal income; and the movement of current output

The GNP deflator is incorrectly used not only as a measure of inflation, but also almost universally used as the deflator of nominal money balances in demand for money studies. If, however, money is considered to be a capital asset and the demand for money treated as an application of the general theory of wealth constrained intertemporal portfolio choice, the purchasing power of money is more meaningfully measured in terms of our price of wealth index.[15]

Final choice of the proper price deflator in the demand for money, however, is conditional upon the particular structural specification from which the demand for money is derived. An explicit theory of the demand for money is necessary before we can determine the price index that should be used. If money is alternatively considered, for example, solely as a medium of exchange and the demand for money derived on the basis of an inventory-transactions-type model, the use of the GNP deflator as the relevant price variable in the demand for money function remains theoretically unjustified. Money is used to purchase assets of varying durability and age. The demand for money therefore cannot be dependent solely on the prices of current output flows which represent only a part of

---

prices, which depends on past output price changes, determines the division of the nominal income change between real income and prices. Therefore, the flexibility of current output flow prices is an important determinant of cyclical economic activity.

[15] One of the major developments in monetary theory in the postwar period has been the integration of monetary theory with capital theory and the recognition of money as an asset in an optimum wealth portfolio (cf., e.g., Friedman [12] and Tobin [36]). Friedman's empirical work explicitly takes account of the fact that money holders ''judge the 'real' amount of cash balances in terms of the quantity of goods and services to which the balances are equivalent, not at any given moment of time, but over a sizable and indefinite period'' [13, p. 121] by deflating nominal balances by ''permanent'' or ''expected'' prices. But this price variable is merely a weighted average of current and past GNP deflators and does not properly consider anticipated future prices as embodied in current asset prices.

what money can buy. Hence, within the context of a transactions demand framework or a wealth portfolio choice framework, the GNP deflator is incomplete and the purchasing power of money could be more meaningfully measured in terms of our more inclusive price of wealth index.[16]

If nominal money balances are deflated by our asset price index, then the connection between income (not wealth) velocity of money and the demand for real cash balances is no longer as direct as once thought. The ratio of our asset price index to the current output price index that is used to deflate nominal income now enters as an additional variable, i.e., both asset prices and current output prices enter the velocity function. Since asset prices are generally more flexible than output prices, if "real" balances are (incorrectly) defined in terms of a current output price index (and asset prices ignored), a decrease in the nominal stock of money leads to an overestimate of the initial resultant decline in real cash balances and hence to an "unexplained" increase in velocity. Movements in the relative prices of assets to flows may explain the initial offsetting changes of velocity in response to monetary changes without invoking a presumption of a short-run disequilibrium (i.e., slow adjustment). The introduction of a vector of interest rates (to reflect relative prices of current services and wealth) in an incorrectly specified demand for

---

[16] Keynes [23, ch. 6] defines two price indexes, a cash-transactions index and a cash-balances index, that may be superior deflators of nominal balances within these theoretical frameworks. Both of these indexes, like our iso-utility wealth price index, include all objects of possible expenditure, but the weights applied to the objects are significantly different. The cash-transactions index weights objects in proportion to the amount of money transactions to which they give rise per-unit time, and the cash-balances index weights objects in proportion to the demand for money they occasion, representing the *P* in the Fisher and Cambridge quantity equations respectively.

"real" money may then serve as a proxy for the more complete price of wealth deflator. This implies that use of the incomplete current output price index as the price deflator in the demand for money induces, to some extent, the observed existence of a significant interest rate effect on the demand for "real" cash balances. If a wealth price index were employed instead, interest rates would then implicitly enter in a more general way, while "the" observed interest rate effect would be reduced and possibly eliminated.[17]

The question is essentially an empirical one of whether the commonly used interest rates on financial assets are sufficient to pick up this short-run "liquidity" effect of changes in money on the relative prices of existing stocks and flows. The significance of the dividend yield in the demand for money (cf., e.g., Hamburger [18]) may, in fact, be reflecting the inability of the prices of financial assets to completely pick up this relative price movement. The dividend yield is statistically significant in a quarterly demand for money regression over the 1951–71 period.[18]

---

[17] This factor is taken account of most fully in Brunner and Meltzer's empirical work (e.g. [5] and [27]). They, however, use a price index for nonhuman wealth not as a measure of the purchasing power of money, but as a deflator of the wealth constraint. They assume the relevant deflator of nominal balances is the GNP deflator and it is therefore entered as an additional variable in the demand for money.

[18] M_1 equals currency plus demand deposits, P is the GNP deflator, Y is nominal GNP, r_s is the four-to-six month commercial paper rate, r_D equals Standard and Poor's dividend yield of corporate stock, log refers to natural logarithm, $\overline{R}^2$ is the coefficient of determination adjusted for degrees of freedom, DW is the Durbin-Watson statistic and SE is the standard error of estimate. The values in parentheses are the t-values of the estimated regression coefficient. The regression is reported in first difference form since r_D enters a level regression highly positively with a DW less than .2, indicating that clearly a variable is missing. Even in the first difference form the autocorrelation of the residuals remains disturbingly high.

$$\Delta \log (M_1/P) = -\ .0011$$

$$+\ \underset{(4.66)}{.3096}\ \Delta \log (Y/P) - \underset{(0.78)}{.0044}\ \Delta \log r_s - \underset{(2.87)}{.0359}\ \Delta \log r_D$$

$$\bar{R}^2 = .295$$
$$DW = 1.06$$
$$SE = .0058 \qquad (1.1)$$

But the significance can be attributed solely to the variability of real stock prices and not to the variability of real dividends. If we substitute stock prices deflated by the GNP deflator for the dividend yield in the above regression (where S refers to Standard and Poors 500 Common Stock price index), we observe that stock prices actually enter slightly more significantly than the dividend yield. This implies that, if anything,

$$\Delta \log (M_1/P) = -\ .0011 + \underset{(4.29)}{.2914}\ \Delta \log (Y/P) - \underset{(0.95)}{.0053}\ \Delta \log r_s$$

$$+\ \underset{(2.91)}{.0369}\ \Delta \log (S/P) \qquad \bar{R}^2 = .297$$
$$DW = 1.03$$
$$SE = .0058 \qquad (2.1)$$

changes in dividend payments go in the "wrong direction." Further, stock prices become insignificant when the same regression is run over the same period using annually averaged data.[19] Both of these pieces of evidence suggest that the divi-

[19] Our hypothesis implies that cycle average data would reduce the statistical significance even further. The annually averaged regression for the dividend yield indicates slightly better results.

$$\Delta \log (M_1/P) = -.0129 + \underset{(3.57)}{.5757}\ \Delta \log (Y/P)$$

$$-\ \underset{(1.36)}{.0217}\ \Delta \log r_s - \underset{(1.42)}{.0420}\ \Delta \log r_D \quad \bar{R}^2 = .463$$
$$DW = .871$$
$$SE = .0134 \qquad (1.1)$$

$$\Delta \log (M_1/P) = -\ .0127 + \underset{(3.36)}{.5767}\ \Delta \log (Y/P) - \underset{(1.68)}{.0266}\ \Delta \log r_s$$

$$+\ \underset{(0.98)}{.0282}\ \Delta \log (S/P) \qquad \begin{aligned} \bar{R}^2 &= .429 \\ DW &= 1.01 \\ SE &= .0138 \end{aligned} \qquad (2.1)$$

dend yield enters the demand for money function not as a measure of the direct cost of holding money but as a proxy for the short-run movement of asset prices relative to the GNP deflator.[20] In addition, the significance of stock prices in a short-run but not in a long-run demand for money regression also provides evidence against the hypothesis that stock prices enter as a wealth variable as, for example, Thompson and Pierce [35] maintain.[21]

---

[20] Similarly, changes in the quantity of money can be expected to influence stock prices in the short run not, as commonly believed, because stocks are close substitutes for cash balances or because the short-run liquidity effect influences the rate at which future earnings are discounted but because of the differential flexibility of stock prices to the monetary change. Fisher [10, ch. 9] outlined a similar mechanism in the context of the transactions version of the quantity theory. He emphasized that many prices are rigid and are likely to change less than in proportion to monetary fluctuations in the short run and, therefore, other prices must change more than in proportion in the short run for the quantity equation to hold; and he noted that stock prices are likely to be the most "supersensitive" of these other prices to changes in the quantity of money. Since the quantity equation is now generally stated in income form where "the" price level that is determined does not include existing items of wealth, this mechanism cannot be recognized.

[21] Thompson and Pierce [35] use a total public wealth variable based on Goldsmith and Lipsey's work in a monthly demand for money study. But month-to-month changes in their variable are dominated by stock price changes. In addition, Thompson and Pierce fail to distinguish between nominal and real values of wealth and money and assume (as most macro models do) that the money market can only be cleared by movements in a small subset of interest rates on financial assets, ignoring the possible short-run adjustment of a broader spectrum of asset prices.

V. POLICY IMPLICATIONS

Nearly fifty years ago Keynes emphasized the fundamental policy mistakes risked by the use of an inappropriate price index. He claimed [22, pp. 249–50] Churchill returned England to the gold standard in 1925 at the prewar parity primarily because Churchill was "gravely misled by his experts" who, by using the inappropriate but commonly employed wholesale-price index, significantly underestimated the extent of the necessary deflation.

An analogous situation may exist today. Presently employed price indices are improper measures of the change in the money cost of an iso-utility consumption package. Reliance on these biased numbers as an indicator or target of monetary policy makes it difficult for the monetary authorities to know what they are doing, let alone what they should be doing. And action on the basis of these numbers can lead to inappropriate decisions; policy changes will often come too late and move too far. Recent monetary policy provides an instructive example. The authorities' preoccupation with the movement of inappropriate flow prices indices to the almost complete exclusion of asset prices was partially responsible for a monetary policy that was too easy for too long a period (1967–68) and then a policy that was too tight for too long a period (1969) followed by a policy that was once again too easy (1970–early 1971). A crude modification of the CPI, with say, an index of stock prices would have provided a much more useful indicator and target for price level stability.[22]

---

[22] Simons [32, p. 349], in discussing the feasibility of a monetary policy designed to stabilize a price index, notes that the particular price index chosen "must be highly sensitive; otherwise, the administrative authority would be compelled to postpone its actions unduly after significant disturbances."

Realization of our ignorance about movements of the appropriate iso-utility price

Our discussion also helps explain the general reluctance of contracting parties to adopt escalator clauses. If long-term contracts were set in "real" terms, i.e., tied to "the price level," economic uncertainty would seem to be decreased.[23] But "the price level" must be made operational by a particular, arbitrary and incomplete, price index. And the fact that price indices are not generally used in long-term contracts (or a tabular standard not adopted) provides some evidence that the indices are poor measures of "the price level." Only if the variance of future anticipated price change is high will the use of, for example, a CPI price escalator clause decrease the anticipated variance of the real pay off. This may explain the more frequent use of price escalators in foreign countries that have experienced great price variability and the recent trend towards increased use of price escalators in the U.S. (see [7]).

Strictly speaking there is no such thing as a "correct" price index. As we stated initially, the appropriateness of an index can be judged only by the answer it supplies to a particular decision problem. Our price index answers the standard

---

index does not necessarily imply that we should adopt a monetary rule. Discretionary monetary policy can still be based on income and employment statistics, and, of course, the inappropriate flow price indices could be used if we knew and took cognizance of the differing lags of adjustment of prices to monetary disturbances. In this context, our discussion may supply some support for those that believe that "money market conditions" (i.e., the behavior of interest rates) are a relevant short-run indicator of monetary policy. If the acceleration of the money supply is not considered, the inclusion of short-run interest rate movements with price movements may provide a much less misleading monetary indicator than price movements alone since price anticipations are probably relatively rigid over the short term and therefore short-run changes in market interest rates will be related to short-run changes in real rates and short-run changes in the relative prices of assets and current flows.

[23] And a rationale for administrative wage-price "jawboning," that it is necessary to convince negotiating parties that the government intends to reduce the future rate of inflation, would be eliminated.

textbook question of whether an individual needs more or less money to remain at the same level of satisfaction. An individual in attempting to determine how much money wealth he now needs for a particular level of present and future consumption would use our index.

But why, then, isn't there a demand for a price index that includes asset prices and why do movements in the CPI appear to be politically important?[24] Within the context of our model it is difficult to find a rationale for the fact that rising consumer service flow prices are generally unpopular while falling asset prices are generally unpopular. The relevance of our intertemporal iso-utility index appears to be seriously questioned by common attitudes. One possible explanation may be that individuals fail to recognize that price changes of assets they do not own may significantly affect their money cost of life and their welfare. While individuals that, for example, own houses are aware of the decrease in their wealth when prices of houses fall, individuals that do not own houses do not appear to recognize that such a price change also affects them by lowering future housing service prices. Individuals are more fully aware of changes in their nominal wealth than of changes in the nominal cost of future consumption, possibly because an intertemporal consumption index is not now published. Alternatively, the CPI may be a politically relevant index because many individuals have utility functions that only contain current consumption service flows. Old individuals who do not have the real quantity of wealth they can leave their heirs as an important argument in their utility function and housewives

[24] However, Kramer [25] found that movements in the CPI, holding real income and some other variables constant, had no significant effect on the division of the national vote for the U.S. House of Representatives over the 1896–1964 period.

who do not make any capital transactions or budgeting decisions within the family, for example, will both be myopic in terms of the time horizon of consumption services prices they are concerned with. This is the major unanswered question we are left with. Is the focus that is presently placed on the CPI as a measure of inflation merely an historical "accident," or are individuals narrowly concerned only about movements in prices of a small subset of the goods in their utility function?[25]

Would a redefinition of our concepts and the replacement of what is now commonly called "inflation" by "current consumer service flow price inflation" alter any of the recent discussion of many journalists, politicians and economists of the extreme rigidity of the rate of price change and the need for some form of wage-price controls?[26] We will be able to answer these questions more satisfactorily after a price of wealth index is constructed and employed.

VI. CAN THE ISO-UTILITY PRICE INDEX BE MEASURED?

Our imprecise statements indicate what we think should ideally be (1) the modification in present measurements of the impact of monetary polity on the rate of inflation using an asset and service price index and (2) how they would influence monetary theory and policy. Although the direction of effect seems obvious to us, our conjecture that presently employed numbers yield misleading conclusions can be verified only by

[25] Historically, the original price indices were narrowly based on internationally traded commodities (e.g., spices and grains).

[26] It is particularly interesting to note that many of the important prices in our wealth price index, e.g., land and security prices, are not covered under the recent wage-price controls.

the construction of a superior index number (i.e., it takes a number to beat a number).

The desired constant utility price index, however, is difficult (expensive) to make operational. As we have already noted, without future contracts in all commodities, the explicit futures prices and quantities needed for construction of a wealth price index are unavailable. Current prices of assets of different life lengths provide a theoretical substitute since they embody present prices of expected future service flows. But both the asset prices and asset quantities necessary for this index are extremely expensive to determine. We must have prices of a very broad spectrum of assets on which we presently have very little information. Our data must include prices of generally nonmarketable assets, such as human capital, and of assets of varying durability, so that we are able to produce the exact optimum current and future consumption service flows by adjusting the asset mix. We may not be able to determine all these prices with any reasonable expenditure of resources, but surprisingly little reliable information exists on current prices of assets and given the assumed importance of these prices in the transmission of monetary impulses, some effort in this direction would seem to be clearly economic. Collection of transaction price data on land, commercial and residential structures, producer and consumer durables and other tangible and financial assets and the construction of a crude quarterly wealth price index would probably be worthwhile.[27]

[27] Stigler's price statistics committee [38, Part 1, App. C., pp. 95–99] makes a similar proposal. Considering the resources expended on the collection of price data on, for example, current food prices, which are such a small element in the relevantly defined utility vector, a reallocation of funds would seem to have a payoff in terms of providing a relevant answer to the question of determining price-level-induced changes in consumer welfare. Carl Snyder's [33] attempt to measure "the

Determination of the asset quantity vectors is also extremely difficult. As we have already noted, the assets actually held by an individual cannot be used as an index of the individual's desired future consumption. Some way of determining the composition of the individual's desired intertemporal consumption services, i.e., of specifying his utility function or fixing particular constant asset weights must therefore be devised. In addition, a more complete specification of the constraints on the individual's intertemporal transactions is also necessary to determine the relevant asset weights. An individual may, for example, demand a particular time stream of housing services under conditions of costless perfect futures or asset markets, but due to transactions costs actually buy and sell houses over time and consume a housing service flow that does not coincide with this "ideal" service flow.

And finally, even if asset prices and quantities were available, we would have significant problems in the interpretation of asset price changes. A change in the market value of an asset may reflect (i) a change in the price of an unchanged future service flow from the asset, (ii) a shift in preferences for this assets service relative to other assets, (iii) a shift in preferences for present consumption relative to future consumption, or (iv) a change in the anticipated magnitude of service flow from the asset. Any or all of these changes are likely to be occurring simultaneously and therefore the cause of a change in a particular asset price is difficult to determine. Changes (ii) and (iii) represent a shift in tastes while (iv) represents a change in asset quality; however, they are not conceptually

general price level" (defined essentially as the P in the equation of exchange) included realty values, security prices, and equipment and machinery prices in addition to the standard cost-of-living items was a movement in the correct direction.

different from the problems encountered in constructing the presently used indices. Changes in the preference or utility maps are ruled out in the presently used consumption service cost-of-living indices.[28] And the quality change problem whereby a change in the price of a given service flow must be distinguished from changes in the service flow, is also present in current indices and has already been handled in an innovative way for transactions prices of used cars (cf. Cagan [6]).

For example, consider changes in common stock prices. The prices of common stock are included in our index because whether an asset such as a house is owned by a single proprietor or owned by him as a corporation should have no effect on the price of the house as manifest in the price of the stock. If the corporation represented not just the house but, as is typically the case, the services of a manager who rented and maintained the house, then the stock price would reflect also the manager's specific talents. Changes in the price of common stock would reflect changing prices of two things: the house services and the manager's talents specific to this activity. So much the better, for we have included human and nonhuman assets; the physical service flow being priced now has a second dimension, the flow of human services, and that may change just as a house may deteriorate. Stock prices contain no more conceptual problems than do the prices of any assets—or for that matter of current service flows in which one has to separate quantity changes and quality changes from price changes.

[28] This is not to say that there is in principle no computable index, for there is. One needs to know the equivalent utility vectors under the shifted preference map. But the base weighted indices (and all other for that matter) no longer can be interpreted as they are now. The difficulty posed by shifting preferences is no greater than for the present incomplete indices.

Although some of the conceptual problems in constructing a wealth price index are similar to those encountered in presently used flow price indexes, the practical problems in the interpretation of asset price movements are more difficult. What would one do, for example, with the drop in common stock prices of 1969–70? Did it reflect claims to reduced real future services (a decrease in quality), or lower prices of unchanged flows of future services (a deflation), or a shift in demand towards more present consumption relative to future consumption due to higher real rates of interest (brought about by "tight" monetary policy or by increased uncertainty leading to an increase in the rate of time preference), or perhaps a combination of all of these forces? For business corporation stocks, the price decrease reflects, at least in part, reduced or deferred outputs of future services. Fewer future cars will be produced or more will be deferred. The stockholder may think of anticipated future money earnings; they have fallen not necessarily because future, i.e. forward, prices (not futures) are expected to fall but possibly because of reduced anticipated profitability—much as if a tree would be expected to yield fewer apples as less fertilizer is applied in the coming years with lower demand expected for apples. If, however, all prices were expected to be lower in the future, the reduced earnings reflected in lower present stock prices would be truly a reduced price level of unchanged real claims. We conjecture both factors were present in the stock price fall—a reduction in present prices of given future services and a reduction in the future anticipated output and earnings relative to what it was before.[29] In other words, real future services are reduced and also

[29] These two factors are related. Since the prices of primary factors (especially labor) purchased by a firm are generally the most rigid, an unexpected decrease in the prices of future services sold by the firm will reduce future anticipated earnings.

the present price of a unit of future service has decreased. It is the latter we want to measure.

We can attempt to approximate the division of an asset price change into these two components by estimating changes in real rates of interest. A rise in the real rate would indicate a fall in future prices relative to current service prices. But we observe only nominal interest rates, which reflect the anticipated future rate of inflation. Market estimates of changes in the currently expected rate of change of future prices can be obtained by examining the ratio of stock prices of net monetary neutral firms to bond prices.[30] Alternatively, we could examine the movement of money interest rates relative to forward price spreads, quoted on commodity exchanges. The usefulness of these suggestions for obtaining market measures of anticipated inflation can only be determined by further empirical work.

The empirical problems involved are enormous. But whatever efforts may be made in this direction and whatever the results, we believe it is an error to assign all of the change in common stock and other asset prices to changes in anticipated future service flows with no change in present prices of such future flows . . . which is what is implicitly done now in commonly used price indices that ignore asset prices.

It may be cheaper to make empirical judgments about quality and quantity changes of current than for future service flows. But what has been added is essentially a significantly larger number of items that should be priced; and weights for

---

[30] Movements in the stock price to bond price ratio will not, however, represent solely a changing price anticipations effect. If the change in the anticipated rate of change of prices alters the demand for and quantity of real cash balances and hence the savings function, real interest rates will change. Stock prices of net monetary neutral firms will therefore not remain unchanged, but move in the same direction as the anticipated rate of price change movement.

assets in the "typical" man's portfolio of possession of claims must be ascertained. This is not a new theoretical problem—it is an enlargement of an existing task. And we believe that the marginal cost of improving a price index along these lines is less than the marginal gains of improved monetary and fiscal policy consequent to less misleading indicators of inflation.

References

1. A. A. Alchian. "Information Costs, Pricing, and Resource Unemployment," *Western Economic Journal* 7 (June 1969): 109–28 Reprinted in E. Phelps, ed., *Microeconomic Foundations of Employment and Inflation Theory*. New York: Norton, 1970. Pp. 27–52.
2. R. G. D. Allen. "The Economic Theory of Index Numbers," *Economica* 16 (August 1949): 197–203.
3. L. C. Anderson, and K. M. Carlson. "A Monetarist Model for Economic Stabilization," Federal Reserve Bank of St. Louis, *Review* 52 (April 1970): 7–25.
4. K. J. Arrow. "The Role of Securities in the Optimal Allocation of Risk Bearing," *Review of Economic Studies* 31 (1964): 91–96.
5. K. Brunner, and A. H. Meltzer. "Some Further Investigations of Demand and Supply Functions for Money," *Journal of Finance* (May 1964): 240–83.
6. P. Cagan. "Measuring Quality Changes and the Purchasing Power of Money: An Exploratory Study of Automobiles," *National Banking Review* 3 (December 1965): 217–36.
7. J. V. Conti. "Price Escalators Gain in Popularity as Means to Pass on Cost Hikes," *Wall Street Journal* (June 3, 1971).
8. D. Dewey. *Modern Capital Theory*. New York, 1965.

9. I. Fisher. *Nature of Capital and Income*. New York, 1906.
10. ———. *The Purchasing Power of Money*. New York, 1911.
11. ———. *The Making of Index Numbers: A Study of Their Varieties, Tests and Reliability*. 3rd ed., Boston, 1927.
12. M. Friedman. "The Quantity Theory of Money: A Restatement" (1956), in M. Friedman. *The Optimum Quantity of Money and Other Essays*. Chicago: University of Chicago Press, 1969. Pp. 51–67.
13. ———. "The Demand for Money: Some Theoretical and Empirical Results" (1959), in *The Optimum Quantity of Money and Other Essays*. Pp. 111–39.
14. ———, and A. J. Schwartz. "Money and Business Cycles" (1963), in *The Optimum Quantity of Money and Other Essays*. Pp. 189–235.
15. R. Frisch. "Annual Survey of General Economic Theory: The Problem of Index Numbers," *Econometrica* 4 (January 1936): 1–38.
16. R. W. Goldsmith, and R. E. Lipsey. *Studies in the National Balance Sheet of the United States*. Vol. I. Princeton: Princeton University Press, for NBER, 1963.
17. L. Grebler, D. M. Blank, and L. Winnick. *Capital Formation in Residential Real Estate*. Princeton: Princeton University Press, for NBER, 1956.
18. M. J. Hamburger. "The Demand for Money by Households, Money Substitutes, and Monetary Policy," *Journal of Political Economy* 74 (December 1966): 600–623.
19. J. M. Henderson, and R. Quandt. *Microeconomic Theory*. New York: 1958.
20. E. D. Hoover. "Index Numbers: Practical Applications," *International Encyclopedia of the Social Sciences* 7 (1968): 159–63.

21. H. S. Houthakker. "The Scope and Limits of Futures Trading," in Abramovitz, et al. *The Allocation of Economic Resources*. Stanford: Stanford University Press, 1959. Pp. 134–59.

22. J. M. Keynes. "The Economic Consequences of Mr. Churchill" (1925), in *Essays in Persuasion*. New York: Norton, 1963. Pp. 244–70.

23. ———. *A Treatise on Money*. Vol. I. London: Macmillan, 1930 (1938 reprint).

24. A. A. Könus. "The Problem of the True Index of the Cost of Living," *Econometrica* 7 (January 1939): 10–29 (first published in Russian in 1924).

25. G. H. Kramer. "Short-Term Fluctuations in U.S. Voting Behavior, 1896–1964," *American Political Science Review* (March 1971): 131–43.

26. A. Leijonhufvud. *On Keynesian Economics and the Economics of Keynes: A Study in Monetary Theory*. New York: Oxford University Press, 1968.

27. A. H. Meltzer. "The Demand for Money: The Evidence from the Time Series," *Journal of Political Economy* (June 1963): 219–46.

28. W. C. Mitchell. *The Making and Using of Index Numbers*. 3rd ed. Washington: U.S. Bureau of Labor Statistics, Bulletin no. 656, 1938.

29. A. C. Pigou. *The Economics of Welfare*. 4th ed. (1932), London, 1960.

30. E. Ruist. "Index Numbers: Theoretical Aspects," *International Encyclopedia of the Social Sciences* 7, New York (1968): 154–59.

31. P. A. Samuelson. "The Evaluation of 'Social Income': Capital Formation and Wealth," in F. A. Lutz and D. C. Hague, eds., *The Theory of Capital*, London, 1961. Pp. 32–57.

32. H. C. Simons. "Rules Versus Authorities in Monetary Policy," in F. A. Lutz and L. W. Mints, *Readings in Monetary Theory*. Homewood, Ill., 1951. Pp. 337–68.
33. C. Snyder. "The Measure of the General Price Level," *Review of Economic Statistics* (February 1928), 40–52.
34. P. O. Steiner. "Consumer Durables in an Index of Consumer Prices," in U.S. Congress, Joint Economic Committee, *Government Price Statistics*, Part 1, *The Price Statistics of the Federal Government: Review, Appraisal and Recommendations*: 305–35.
35. T. D. Thompson, and J. R. Pierce. "A Monthly Model of the Financial Sector," presented at the Konstanzer Seminar on Monetary Theory and Policy, Konstanz, West Germany, June 1971.
36. J. Tobin. "Money, Capital, and Other Stores of Value," *American Economic Review* (May 1961): 26–37.
37. M. J. Ulmer. *The Economic Theory of Cost of Living Numbers*. New York, 1949.
38. U. S. Congress Joint Economic Committee, *Government Price Statistics*, 2 parts. Washington, 1961.

Index

A NOTE ABOUT THE AUTHOR

Armen Albert Alchian is a native of California, and received his undergraduate and doctoral degrees from Stanford University. During World War II he served as an instructor and statistician with the U.S. Army Air Forces. He joined the faculty of the University of California in 1946, and has been Professor of Economics at UCLA since 1958. He also served as a consultant to the RAND Corporation from 1946 to 1964, and was 1974-75 president of the Western Economic Association. Professor Alchian has contributed to numerous professional and scholarly journals, and is coauthor with William R. Allen of the textbook *University Economics*, now in its third edition.

Liberty*Press* is a publishing imprint of Liberty Fund, Inc., a foundation established to encourage study of the ideal of a society of free and responsible individuals.

The cuneiform inscription that serves as the design motif for our endpapers is the earliest known written appearance of the word "freedom" (*ama-gi*), or liberty. It is taken from a clay document written about 2300 B.C. in the Sumerian city-state of Lagash.

This book was photo set in the Times Roman series of type. The face was designed to be used in the news columns of the *London Times*. The *Times* was seeking a type face that would be condensed enough to accommodate a substantial number of words per column without sacrificing readability and still have an attractive, contemporary appearance. This design was an immediate success. It is used in many periodicals throughout the world and is one of the most popular text faces presently in use for book work.

Book design by Design Center, Inc., Indianapolis, Indiana
Typography and printing by North Central Publishing Co., St. Paul, Minnesota